A History of India

Peter Robb

palgrave

First published 2002 by
PALGRAVE
Houndmills, Basingstoke, Hampshire RG21 6XS and
175 Fifth Avenue, New York, N. Y. 10010
Companies and representatives throughout the world

PALGRAVE is the new global academic imprint of
St. Martin's Press LLC Scholarly and Reference Division and
Palgrave Publishers Ltd (formerly Macmillan Press Ltd).

ISBN 0–333–69128–8 hardcover
ISBN 0–333–69129–6 paperback

This book is printed on paper suitable for recycling and made from fully managed and sustained forest sources.

A catalogue record for this book is available from the British Library.

Library of Congress Cataloging-in-Publication Data

Robb, Peter (Peter G.)
    A history of India / Peter Robb.
        p.   cm.—(Palgrave essential histories)
    Includes bibliographical references and index.
    ISBN 0–333–69128–8
    1. India—History.   I. Title.   II. Series.

DS436 .R63 2002
954—dc21

                                                            2001058772

10   9   8   7   6   5   4   3   2   1
11   10   09   08   07   06   05   04   03   02

Printed by Creative Print & Design Ltd (Wales) Ebbw Vale

For Lizzie, and Ben and Tom

Contents

Maps

Boxes and Tables

Preface and Acknowledgments

The immensity of India makes most national histories seem parochial. Many popular books portray India's past; India's worldwide significance, and vast records, have attracted historians internationally; and a remarkable range of subject-matter is now explored. Yet huge subjects still await their first study. Moreover, Western writers in other fields have often not given India an appropriate importance. Material or intellectual connections have long made India of interest in Britain and parts of Europe, but India has also frequently been ignored, even in its external influence, by Eurocentric researchers or, in the Americas, because of the prominence of East Asian studies. Also the Indian archive is relatively inaccessible, hidden by time, language, bureaucracy and climate – especially from the vantage point of some of the world's more comfortable academic billets.

For these and other reasons, it has been notoriously hard to recommend short introductions to Indian history that encompass recent findings and interests, are accessible to general readers and students, and offer a starting point and overview for scholars in other fields. Some recent works have introduced India to general scholarship mainly at the level of theory. Whatever their merits, works of that kind are pointless as an introduction *to India*. They often make hard subjects unapproachable.

By contrast, I have tried to keep this book simple. It is directed first at readers who are unfamiliar with its subject. It is meant to be read as a general introduction rather than searched for basic information, as a compendium of 'facts' or comprehensive narrative. Though not aimed at readers in any one place, it was written in England and thus draws a few comparisons with Europe (where they are appropriate historically, and not out of any sense that Europe can or should be a yardstick for India). Because of its emphasis, the book might well have had the subtitle 'modern India and earlier'.

I have deliberately eschewed detailed historiographical discussion, believing that too much attention to scholarly debates is more likely to confuse than enlighten those new to the subject. There is another reason too. The passionate divisions and disputes of historians have been diverting but often counterproductive. They tend to treat subjects and evidence as pawns in some greater scheme, a diversion from the study of elements of India's history in their own right. For example, the broad brush of Edward Said's *Orientalism* (1978), an exercise in rhetoric rather than history, reinforced Indianists' awareness of the perils of Eurocentrism, but also tended to encourage too sharp a division of time and ideas along arbitrary racial-cultural lines. Secondly, a prevalent approach to modern economic history has regarded the most important questions, for two hundred years after 1780, as the wrongs committed by colonialism and capitalism. Plausible though this is, it may forestall systematic analysis of the various features of the economy. Thirdly, in political history, we find nationalists in one corner tending towards hagiography and celebration, and in the other corner certain studies (of the 1970s and 1980s) that have been called 'neocolonialist' or 'conservative imperialist'. The 'imperialism' apparently consists in an association with Cambridge University, and a focus on political networks, factions and interests rather than the anti-imperialist struggle. It is right to debate the emphasis accorded to ideology or inherited patriotism; but it seems unwise to rule out the commonplaces of political study, for India alone, and by slogan rather than argument. Fourthly, there is the important contribution made to 'histories from below' by the 'Subaltern' group, from the 1980s. Perhaps it has been hindered rather than helped by a rather combative doctrine about the peculiar autonomy and similarity of widely divergent subordinate groups. In this *History* I intend to avoid predetermined judgements, as far as possible, by not attending to the shouting which has engulfed some debates.

No doubt all experts will find something to object to in this book, as 'not quite right' or even (I regret) mistaken. However, as said, too much detail or nuance would have defeated the main object. This is not to say that I am not in great debt to more sophisticated efforts. This book rests almost wholly on the writing of others. It is only because there is now so much more being published on the Indian subcontinent that this book could be contemplated, and that another generation of general histories is now appearing. It is for the same reason, of course, that new surveys are needed by students and general readers.

I have not tried to record the tangled web of my borrowings and adaptations in footnotes or references (apart from direct quotations). But to all the scholars whose work has been used I offer my heartfelt thanks. I had thought to single out here those who, in print and mostly also in person, helped with information or to form the ideas that run through the book; but my first list ran to over sixty names, all of them indispensable. I trust, therefore, that scholars will recognize their own contributions. General readers may track them down in the References and Readings section at the end of the book.

Possibly less obvious to others but vitally important to me are the large contributions that several generations of my research students have made to my education; again it would be invidious to name names, but they will see the marks they have left.

I benefited from comments made on versions of a few paragraphs at the end of Chapter 1, and on revenue settlements in Chapter 5, when they were presented to the World History Association conference at Victoria, Vancouver Island, in June 1999; that paper will be included in conference proceedings edited by Gregory Blue, Martin Bunton and Ralph Crozier.

I am very grateful to several colleagues who have helped directly with improving the text: Daud Ali and Avril Powell in their own specialist areas; David Anderson and Ian Brown with the agrarian sections of Chapter 9. My wife, Elizabeth, bears considerable responsibility as usual, not least for urging me to bring the project to an end. She has *my* thanks, at least.

PETER ROBB
SOAS, London

Indian Words and Names

The bewildering range of Indian names and places, with their varying spellings and mutations, is a major hurdle even for the initiated. Many such words have been included here, for future reference as it were. Most place names that have been mentioned are included in one of the maps, but readers will find it helpful to have access to an atlas, preferably an historical one.

Where a South Asian word appears in English dictionaries I have usually followed its spelling there, even if the transliteration is now thought incorrect, with the exception of a few modernizations such as 'zamindar' for 'zemindar' and 'raiyat' for 'ryot'. Elsewhere (except in quotations, which retain the original spelling) I have used the spelling which is most common in recent scholarly English, unless it is particularly unhelpful for showing pronunciation; for example I have preferred 'Shudra' to 'Sudra', and 'Kshatriya' to 'Ksatriya'. Consistency has not been completely achieved.

No diacritical marks are included, but the letters *hamza* (') and *'ain* (') are, if they appear in a medial position – between long vowels *hamza* indicates a pause in Indo-Persian pronunciation (for example *fara'izi*), and *'ain* adds a short 'e' or 'ye' sound to the following vowel, as Shi'a. Neither is shown at the start or end of words when they are often more or less voiceless. With a few exceptions (e.g. *ulama*), plurals have been made using English '-s'. The adjectival '-i' is used occasionally, as in 'zamindari' (also an adjectival noun: 'the institution of zamindari').

I

Introduction: Region and Civilization

INDIA AND ITS HISTORY

Nationalism supplies and feeds on continuous histories of discrete peoples and cultures. But the nation-state is a phenomenon of the modern era and long-term national histories are therefore more or less bogus. Peoples have linear inheritances, but also they experience discontinuities and external influences. How then can there be a history of 'India'?

A history of India must justify itself firstly through its focus on place. To some extent this too is arbitrary, for the territory of present-day India has not always had a clear regional identity. At different periods, parts of it were clearly excluded from the cultural and political mainstream. Apart from many political subdivisions, environments could be divisive, as in other parts of the world: uplands were often distinct from lowlands, and dry from irrigated tracts, and west–east linkages mostly proved easier and more integrating than north–south ones. Often too parts of the subcontinent seemed to belong more closely to wider regions than with each other, as was seen in the connections between southern India and south-east Asia around the end of the first millennium CE (Common Era), or in north India's involvement with a Turko-Persian world from the sixteenth to eighteenth centuries, or even, adding a class divide, in the economic and intellectual engagement of some elites with the West during the British colonial era. These links, and local destinies, define regions *within* India. A major theme of this book is the interplay between such regions and empires of rule, custom and belief.

India is *now* a recognizable (if contested) unit, for all its internal variety. Most of the subcontinent does not now comprise a congeries of small nations, but rather the modern all-Indian state. It is possible to describe how it was established, both as a matter of recent history and over the longer term. It is a newly demarcated people and territory, but also rests upon very long experience of imperial governments, and also, from even earlier and more consistently, upon a unifying 'civilization' – not some unchanging essence, but persistent ways of thinking and doing. This book will argue that, despite the frequent, originally colonial, emphasis on India's essential diversity, its unity has probably been its most important feature – unlike Europe, and not unlike China.

The continuities of a civilization are like a storehouse in which things decay or are lost, to which things are added, and from which things are selected. Civilizations differ because these inheritances do, because of different experiences, preferences and possibilities. Civilizations may draw together and even merge, or they may draw apart, but their being civilizations means that they have developed with some degree of separation, and within some limits of similarity – physical, economic and ideological. For example, across greater India some features we now call 'Hindu' have been very persistent. To say this is not to endorse the recent equation of 'Indian' with 'Hindu', which has encouraged religio-political schisms in the sub-continent, helped separate off Pakistan and Bangladesh, and led certain factions to contest the Indianness both of India's many millions of Muslims, and of certain colonial legacies (including secular government, even the rule of law).

The story of India's partition and 'Hindu-ization' are among those to be told in this book, but there are many others, for India has not been defined by 'Hindu' civilization alone, nor are its features identical in different regions or classes. It has always contained a great variety of traditions. It has also been influenced by exports from other civilizations – for example those of other parts of the prehistorical and ancient world, of West Asian Islam, of European Christianity, or of Western modernity. A second task of this book is to identify and explain these varieties and influences, which also contribute greatly to the unfolding of Indian civilization.

Because civilizational boundaries exist, and yet are porous, diverse influences have added to the storehouse of 'Indian' civilization within a greater 'India'. Sometimes the imports were modified, and sometimes they became accepted as 'Indian', indigenized but more or less unchanged, just in the way that languages may forget the foreign origin of loan-words. Though India may now be more 'Hindu' than it once was, by new processes of selection and reinvention, that 'Hindutva' (or Hindu-ness) is always a new amalgam. No amount of effort will remove India's historical eclecticism, nor (one suspects) resist the blandishments of new technology and the messages carried by modern communications – which in their turn will be made 'Indian' too, until or unless the civilizational differences themselves fade away.

These issues invite a number of interrelated discussions. Firstly, we need to explore the exercise of political power and political assent or resistance, and the nature and limits of legal, administrative and civic institutions. Secondly, we need to examine the ways society operated – the main social categories (gender, households, kin groups, clans, castes and classes); the distribution of rights, benefits and influence; the enforcement of norms and co-operation; and the religious and philosophical ideas that underwrote the ways in which people lived. Thirdly, we need to consider how people related to the physical environment and met their material needs – including land use, processing and manufacture, technologies and other resources, the means of organizing production, and matters of work, food and health, and demographic trends.

This book cannot be comprehensive in its geographical, chronological or thematic coverage, especially if it hopes to give due weight to the experience of different regions and to subordinate as well as dominant levels of society. Rather, it will examine some aspects of its three main subject areas successively over four different periods. It will make repeated use of headings relating to rule and protest; customs and belief; and material culture, production and trade. The periods are (1) early (prehistorical, from, say, 7500 BCE (before the Common Era), ancient, and early mediaeval); (2) mediaeval (roughly 1000–1560 CE); (3) early modern (roughly 1560–1860); and (4) modern (the 'high colonial' years, 1860–1920, plus decolonization and early independence to about 1970).

The periods are mainly a convenience. There is no very strong logic about them, and each has characteristics that overlap with others. The terms used to describe them are basically chronological, and the dividing dates more or less arbitrary. Yet attempts *will* be made to show how different times developed different characters. In particular, 'modern' is taken to mean 'fairly recent', but also 'new-fashioned' in regard to forms of knowledge, state bureaucracy,

systematic law, social relations, and economy. The assumption is
not that India could be modern in exactly the same way as Europe,
but rather that both shared in some of the experiences characteristic
of the last 150 years or so, common features of (for example) commodities and markets, official policies, public institutions, print and
transportation, and generalized social, religious or national identities.
This fourth, modern, period will receive the fullest attention. An
epilogue will outline the start of what is arguably a new era in
India's history, since the 1970s.

This first chapter will now introduce some general aspects of the
book's main themes: continuity, plurality and trends in political
economy. Because this is a history of 'India', continuities will tend
to be emphasized over localism and heterodoxy, both here and in
later chapters. Each time, a case will be made to justify such generalization. Because that inevitably involves distortion, however, this
book has to be only 'a' history among many potential histories of
India. As said, however, unifying tendencies are emphasized also
because of their importance for defining the history of these lands
and peoples.

RULE

It is implicit in most discussions that different periods of history
may be characterized by different kinds of state (usually in combination with different kinds of economy). Changes may be attributed
to the stimulation of competition – such as when warfare developed
technologies, fiscal capabilities and national identities. Unfamiliar
situations also demand responses, and so conquest and colonialism
also helped spawn bureaucracies and new laws. India's systems of
government have included some very early city cultures, nomadic
military regimes, settled farming communities, family dynasties,
commercial and foreign-imperial powers, and modern constitutional
systems. Political changes have not been even or irreversible. But,
as elsewhere, the long-term trend has been towards consolidation
and expansion, towards centralized, bureaucratic, information-rich
states controlling relatively integrated economies and intervening
in social life. In India such states emerged from time to time over
the millennia, and have persisted more or less continuously since the
Mughals in the sixteenth century. Though the Mughals succumbed
to internal and external challenges in the early eighteenth century,

they were succeeded by centralized regional states, which were overtaken by British colonial rule, which in turn was followed by the would-be hegemonic states of independent South Asia.

On the other hand, though state policy and capacity have plainly evolved, the Indian state's geographical, ethnic and ideological boundaries have continued to be contested – in recent times by Sikhs, Tamils, Kashmiris and many others. Despite central planning, unified law and nationwide communications, India has not achieved a fully integrated economy or society, either regionally or socially. As already suggested, Hindu nationalists now seek to deny India's religious and ethnic plurality, but India does not and arguably cannot have that popular sense of unitary nationhood which elsewhere has justified highly centralized democracies. These paradoxes were also important to India's political development.

The first evidence of organized communities in South Asia is provided by palaeolithic implements dating back more than 400 000 years. The first recognized cultures, based on agriculture, domestic animals, and the production and exchange of pottery and other artefacts, date from around 7500 BCE. The earliest literate city-states, implying sophisticated political and economic systems, can be traced to about 3000 BCE. The Harappan or Indus valley civilization, as the best-known of these is called, lasted between about 2500 and 1750 BCE. Over the next two thousand years, settled cultivation expanded considerably across the north Indian plains, probably aided by the progressive migration of formerly pastoral peoples and by the development of Sanskrit-speaking elites (neither to be crudely imagined as an 'Aryan invasion'). Classes of rulers and priests were defined, and recorded in the earliest of the surviving texts of Indian philosophy and law. The learned commentaries and philosophical texts (discussed below), which were composed between the seventh and fourth centuries BCE, suggest a mature civilization: cities, social divisions, and stable law and structures of power. In the third century BCE, the first of the great Indian empires developed, under Chandragupta Maurya and Ashoka, centred upon north-eastern India, in what is now Bihar. These rulers had theories of government, the ability to extract tribute or taxation, and the administrative capacity to promote codes of behaviour over wide regions. Under these 'ancient' or 'classical' regimes, some of the continuing features of Indian society were established.

Later, doctrines of law and kingship were further defined and developed, but few subsequent early rulers matched the Mauryans' centralizing ability, not even the Gupta empire of the fourth and fifth centuries CE. Instead, especially after about the sixth century, successive regional polities emerged, often in the wake of invasions or military immigration which had become an important influence a little before the start of the Common Era. From around 1000 CE, notable among these regional powers were various Rajput dynasties in the west and north, the Cholas who emerged to replace the Pallavas in the south, and Islamic rulers intruding from the north-west. This rise and fall of local kingdoms and the lack of sustained central authority led to later assertions that, in India, kingly and political power was subordinated to social, religious and local authority. These arguments will be discussed later. It will suffice for now to note that they rest on false dichotomies.

The later mediaeval period in north India began with the estab-lishment in Delhi of the Turkic Delhi sultanate, holding power over almost all of north India by 1236, and the dominance of Hindu kingdoms in the south, particularly, from about 1340 to 1565, one centred upon Vijayanagara (City of Victory) in present-day Karnataka. These regimes began to introduce distinctive forms of government based upon military coercion and alliances. The Delhi sultans reached their height in the fourteenth century (under the Khaljis and early Tughlaqs) when they had created systems of administration incorporating indigenous elites. The Vijayanagara empire developed paid village officials, and military and bureaucratic relations with subordinate lords in order to extract tributary pay-ments in money; but it also had to accommodate these territorial chiefs and other local or community rights, and depended on the sponsorship of temples and on Brahman military commanders. The importance of family and personal relations, and the still indirect control over the localities, make these empires transitional but still 'mediaeval'.

The Mughal empire eventually ousted its rivals, and claimed control over almost all of the subcontinent from the mid-sixteenth to the late seventeenth centuries. It was continually reinforced from outside India, especially from Iran. It saw a flowering of Islamic scholarship, supported Muslim religious endowments, and was influenced to varying degrees by the *ulama* (scholars of Islam). It also continually used military force, and even emperors (notably Akbar, who ruled (r.) 1556–1605, and Aurangzib, r. 1658–1707) took to the field of battle in person. But, unlike the Ottomans and other Islamic empires of the day, the Mughals depended neither on a slave bureaucracy nor on an elite wholly centred on court and harem. Mughal generals and administrators were appointed competitively, and increasingly positions of power were awarded and recorded through written documentation. The Mughals depended upon complex networks of patronage and personal allegiance, from *mansabdars* (honorific rank-holders who were high military and civil officials) to local *zamindars* (rural revenue-collecting elites and chiefs).

The local chiefs and also many hereditary local officials could not be dislodged, but they were largely incorporated into new systems of administration. The Mughal state drew upon the support of non-Muslim gentry, merchants and literati, forging alliances mainly through policies of religious tolerance and conciliation devised by Akbar. Such collaboration was vital outside the garrison towns and north Indian heartlands of the Mughals, and important even within those centres. The state's growing roles were necessary (and possible) because its wealth derived from a high taxation of the vast and expanding production of the land, and also from the encouragement of trade, including that with Europe, and from an economy that was highly monetized in its upper levels.

There was always a danger that local elites would become entrenched as regional factions, as happened during the eighteenth century. But the Mughals may be termed 'early modern' because they added a panoply of general concepts and procedures, and indeed of manners and culture, much of which was adopted in the eighteenth century by the successor regional powers, including the British East India Company. Perhaps, like the British, they were forced to develop bureaucratic and presentational strengths because they were a small and not particularly united ruling elite in an alien land.

The British rose to supreme power in India between about 1740 and 1860. Their government rested on existing practices, imported ideologies and pragmatic responses to unfamiliar situations. To a much greater extent than the Mughals, however, they developed regular forms and means of governance, standardizations of law and policy, and maximizing and even developmental economic strategies. The twentieth century saw the culmination of a long change in emphasis in the resourcing of states, as tributes from agrarian producers developed into the taxation of commercial activity and trade. It also saw the culmination of a nineteenth-century burgeoning of public institutions which enabled Indians to develop and express their ideas of regional, class, community and caste identity, and which led to organized struggles for social, political and economic rights, and for national independence. Much of this framework of rule was inherited and developed by the successor government of India after 1947, at least until the 1970s.

The establishment of modern nation-states eventually divided up the subcontinent into India, Pakistan, Bangladesh, Nepal and Bhutan. These states reflected different (though also sometimes shared) historical experiences. They both contained and divided earlier regional consolidations – linguistic and cultural units – many of which are still clearly evident. Particularly violent and painful were the partitions of India and Pakistan in 1947, and of West Pakistan and Bangladesh in 1971; but other regional divisions have often threatened or succeeded – of various 'marginal' peoples such as Nagas or Santhals from the regional states which enveloped them; of Sikhs from Hindus in the Punjab; of Gujaratis and Maharashtrians in western India; of southern Tamil- or Telegu-speakers from the Hindi-dominated north.

REGION AND UNITY

There is a strong (and often justified) temptation to see the Indian case as particular; but its political history is a familiar one in outline. In most parts of Europe and Asia, local polities and economies frequently predominated in ancient and mediaeval times, but there were also 'imperial' systems of varying form: large empires of rule, thought, language and practice that produced a degree of cultural and social unity among elites, at the expense of commonality across classes in each given place. These 'empires' suppressed or diffused competition between localities. In western Europe, for example, one had Latin and Christianity; in India, Sanskrit and Buddhism or Brahmanism. Then, in early modern and modern Europe, narrower polities and economies developed that sought to unite all the people within given regional territories or nations. They managed, in Durkheimian terms, to extend and merge the solidarities of similarity and proximity, to mobilize whole communities and places, under unified rule.

Dominant, multi-purpose national languages were an important indicator of these solidarities. In many parts of Europe, though effective linguistic unity came quite late, the forms of modern language that were developed were demotic, regional and relatively uniform, serving all the functions and peoples of the nation. This indicates a particularly Indian problem. The mirror image of, say, classical Sumerian used by the elites for writing in ancient Mesopotamia – 'The Sumerian monitor said, "You spoke in Akkadian!" and he beat me' (*The Epic of Gilgamesh*, tr. Andrew George) – is multifunctional French being forced on nineteenth-century Breton schoolboys, or the less successful efforts of the Hindi movement in twentieth-century India. But even Hindi/Urdu did not develop as a dominant standard language in India in the sense that French did within France. The regional Indian languages, including Hindi, did so develop within their regions, but their role was generally qualified by different 'national/imperial' – here meaning specialist or elite – languages. Persian and English filled these roles, as Sanskrit had. So too, once they had emerged, Indian regional identities achieved political expression to different degrees, being most evident in the mediaeval period, in the eighteenth century, and in recent Indian politics; but they were more generally subordinated to larger polities.

What has made India distinct, therefore, is not the vitality of its regional states (many at least the size of European nations) but the trajectory of greater consolidation that we have just traced, intermittently, from ancient to early modern times. As explained at the outset, evidence of overlap, separation and subdivision qualifies the story of state expansion in India. But it does not refute it. The present-day nation-states do mark a triumph for unitary sovereignty, centralized administration and firm boundaries. They contend with, but ultimately subsume, other modes of political power, including those which had existed among marginal peoples and territories. Moreover, the rivals of such 'modern' regimes mostly use modern means and ideologies to frame their political demands and identities. Thus the present states of the Indian subcontinent may be said to mark a stage in time, in the project of political consolidation and incorporation that began with Chandragupta Maurya and Ashoka, and ebbed and flowed until it produced its current definition and borders, under Mughal and then British rulers.

The Mughal empire overlaid regional or national conflicts, and encouraged a generalization of elite culture; fertile rivalries were reduced. From the late seventeenth century, regional powers began, in competition, to generate economic and political change. But then British rule intervened: it quashed regional conflicts, and re-adopted imperial forms. Moreover, it perpetuated or reinvented the elite–popular cultural divide. The British, like the Mughals, tried to install a superior government, but it connected only loosely to existing local institutions and deployed organizations in parallel with them. Independent India too has often depended more on national elites than on all-India solidarities.

The nineteenth century provided improved means to sustain these elites, including new laws, bureaucracy, market rationales and modern communications. Many of the innovations were readily adapted and adopted by Indians, but others were foreign to Indian experience. They were applied as an artificial imperium rather than as a reflection of territorial and social particularities. This resulted in some disparities of development. Like England, but unlike (say) Poland or Hungary, India developed a powerful bureaucracy before it had local or national assemblies. This drew the state's attention to the reform and regulation of common or central institutions, and meant that there were no organized special interests strong enough to thwart the state. Arguably 'India' was anyway the wrong size for such an effort.

Moreover, unlike England, colonial India had no participatory local self-government linked to the centralizing state. The early colonial regime had tended to ignore or damage such links as existed – it often overrode local power-brokers, marginalized religious leaders and sometimes abolished village officials. Later efforts were made to rebuild such institutions, through the reinvention of a supposedly indigenous village community, through quasi-feudal fantasies of prince and landlord, or by transplanting English local or representative government. The inconsistency and relative weakness of these efforts meant that local interests had difficulty not just in impeding the state, but also in influencing or sharing in it. One result was the persistence of social and political arenas – intermixed (socio-political) black economies – outside the formal purview of the state and its laws, but inside the broad 'civilizational' fields of Indian culture.

The all-India nationalist movements followed the colonial lead and attempted to mobilize all the peoples within 'India' in rivalry with the colonial state. Like that state, they tried to incorporate local and sectional concerns. These concerns were vital and growing (as recent scholarship on low-class protest and 'subaltern' movements has richly demonstrated), and yet (as that scholarship is not so ready to admit) they were still only patchily articulated and mobilized.

Kinship and interest groups were evolving into communities – that is, groups whose identity and moral codes shaped their responses over broad spheres – in the way that the 'interest' of religious orthodoxy expanded so as to define positions on most other political and social issues for a whole organized 'community' of adherents. In India these communities could not be confined within the one nation. The 1947 partition and the post-independence political adjustments were, in part, attempts to unravel the confusions of such uncompleted evolution. This helps explain why the Indian state is in many respects strong and 'modern', but the identity of 'India' remains problematic. This point leads us from politics towards society.

BELIEF

India has been enormously influential in the world through its systems of belief. 'Hindu-*ism*', however, is something of a misnomer, in that it is a religion without a unitary doctrine, revelation or textual authority. Its most noticeable attributes are its mythological richness, which can be traced back to the Vedic religion or before, and the variety of its sects and doctrines, also to be seen from the earliest times, but not least in the last 150 years or so. Thus, paradoxically, among the wide range of Indic beliefs, stories, ideas and customs, there are some recurring tenets which hold something of the same significance as notions of sacrifice and salvation in the Judeo-Christian tradition, or the omnipotence of Allah and his Word, the Qur'an, for Islam. Some of these oft-repeated features of 'Hinduism' can be briefly introduced through a discussion of the region's early religious ideas. Later, the developments will be placed in their political and economic contexts.

The earliest important text is the *Rig Veda* ('veda' meaning 'knowledge'), written around 1000 BCE and based on earlier oral traditions. It is the earliest of four texts or *samhitas*, the others being *Yajur Veda*, *Sama Veda* and *Atharva Veda*. It contains rich celebrations of nature, and sophisticated reflections upon creation, life and death. Its ten books comprise about one thousand hymns (*mantras*), mostly descriptions or invocations of gods, some of which are similar to those in Greek mythology. The Vedic deities, like the Greek, are allocated characteristics, a metaphysical significance, and roles in the creation and sustenance of the physical world. Together they provide an ethical, mythological and material explanation of a unified cosmic order. They were used in, and are explained by, the great sacrifices and ceremonies which lay at the heart of the Vedic rites – typically the gods provided boons when gratified by large-scale animal sacrifice.

Box 1 Some Vedic gods (devas)

Indra	the fierce warrior-god of rain, thunder and lightning
Varuna	the god of the heavens, sea and the moral order
Agni	the god of fire and sacrifice (and of priests, the Brahmans)
Surya and **Savitar**	the sun, sun-god
Pushan	another sun-god, guardian of flocks and journeys
Vishnu	also a sun-god and a god of the sacrifice
Soma	a god of vision, joy and immortality (from an intoxicating plant taken during rituals)
Rudra	god of healing, disease and disaster
Aryaman	god of marriage
Mitra	god of vows, attendant on Varuna

Most noticed of the gods is Indra, 'He of whom all this world is but the copy, who shakes things moveless' (*Rig Veda* II. 12); 'the bull, the thunderer', who dug the channels of the waters (VII. 49). Some of the hymns also lay down rules of human conduct, for example exhortations to charity, since 'The riches of the liberal never waste away, while he who will not give finds none to comfort him' (X. 117). One hymn, which has gained special attention, celebrates the cosmic sacrifice of Purusha, the anthropomorphic spirit of the universe, from which the texts and their truths derived, and from whom all living creatures were formed (X. 90):

The Brahman was his mouth, of both his arms was the Rajanya
    [Kshatriya] made,
His thighs became the Vaisya, from his feet the Sudra was
    produced.

Here supposedly established are the four *varna* – priests (*brahmana*), warriors (*kshatriya*), merchants (*vaishya*) and menial or physical labourers (*shudra*) – which provide the great divisions of Indic society. Here too, as elsewhere in *Rig Veda*, one finds the first indications of those perpetual passions of Indian thought, classification and enumeration.

The importance of the sacrifice suggests that the texts were ritualistic and not revelatory in origin. It also implies a society that was highly violent, each successive social level being sustained at the expense of those below it – the 'law of the fishes' (*matsyanyaya*), whereby the big ate the little. This may be relevant to another of the most important of India's recurrent ideas which does not appear in the Vedas, namely that life is a cycle of rebirths, from which there can ultimately be an escape (*moksha*), dependent upon the performance in each lifetime of the proper duties (*dharma*) of one's calling, and on the transcending of material goals (*artha*) and human desires (*kama*). Some elements of this idea are already apparent in *Rig Veda*. The later emphasis on *kama* is foreshadowed, for example, and linked to the creation of the cosmic order out of darkness and chaos:

Then was not non-existent nor existent: there was no realm of
    air, no sky beyond it.
What covered in, and where? and what gave shelter? Was
    water there, unfathomed depth of water?
Death was not then, nor was there aught immortal: no sign was
    there, the day's and night's divider.
That one thing, breathless, breathed by its own nature: apart
    from it was nothing whatsoever....
Thereafter rose desire in the beginning, Desire, the primal
    seed and germ of spirit.
Sages who searched with their heart's thought discovered the
    existent's kinship in the non-existent (X. 129).

As they evolved, the Vedic ideas divided into or were superseded by two main streams – coming, that is, from origins within *and* beyond the Vedic priesthoods. One (the yogic way) emphasized the importance of desire, and hence the need for renunciation. Another emphasized the unity of creation and hence the proper performance of earthly duties. By such means, both developments transformed the 'law of the fishes' from a metaphor of order into one of chaos. The yogic impulse is well represented by Jainism and Buddhism. Jainism is an atheistic religion and the first known attempt to create a single doctrine from the rich Indic traditions. It includes the idea that life (*jiva*), as opposed to inanimate matter and to all worldly actions, is caught in an endless cycle of reincarnation. Through complete self-abnegation and profound contemplation, man can be liberated into an eternal, uncreated infinity beyond the cosmos. Jainism was associated with great teachers, especially Vadhamana, known as Mahavira (great hero), who probably lived in the sixth century BCE, and organized and instructed disciples so that his teachings survived. He, like his much earlier predecessor, Parshva, was said to have practised great austerities, renounced the world, gained true omniscience, and hence immortality.

Buddhism is a subtle and elaborate version of similar ideas of rebirth and austerity. It was developed by Siddhartha Gautama, the Buddha (enlightened one), also born in the sixth century BCE. Buddhism spawned a truly vast literature, starting with canonical texts, the *Tripitaka* (Three Baskets), that contain rules, narratives and commentaries. At the heart of their doctrine is the Noble Eightfold Path: including right thinking and goals, moral conduct, and a proper degree of renunciation and self-discipline (a Middle Way between extremes of abnegation and indulgence). The Buddha gained enlightenment through intense meditation, a contemplation without form, an utter but conscious emptying of the mind – ultimately breaking the cycle of rebirth by transcending the individual, becoming non-self (*anatta*), and perceiving *nirvana*, a state without creation or death.

Though convinced of the transitory nature of things, the followers of the Buddha nevertheless developed orders of nuns and monks (the *Sangha*), proselytized for their beliefs (on the Buddha's instructions), and built monasteries and *stupas*, with their characteristic rounded shape, containing Buddhist relics. The monks in these institutions were dependent upon the alms and bequests of lay followers. Then, as these lay people also sought to approach a higher state of exist-ence, there arose cults of personal devotion (*bhakti*) to the Buddha and his successors (the Buddhas-to-be or Boddhisattvas) – one answer perhaps to the Vedic refrain 'What god shall we adore with our oblation?' (*Rig Veda* X. 121). Lay involvement gave rise in turn to the wider, 'compassionate' or Mahayana Buddhism (Greater Vehicle) as opposed to the stricter, monastic Hinayana Buddhism (Lesser Vehicle). This divide was also marked by doctrinal and philosophical differences. The second emphasis, upon ritual sacrifice and *dharma* rather than renunciation and contemplation, was found in the developments of the Brahmanist religion which coexisted and competed with the growth of Buddhism.

In response to such challenges, Vedic ideas were expanded into vast commentaries. The *Brahmanas* elaborate and explain myths and rituals. The *Aranyakas* or forest books, possibly so-called because they were produced by hermits, reflect on the rituals and their symbolic meanings. Finally, the *Upanishads* contain both philosophical exposition and teachings in the form of dialogues and parables, offering a variety of explanations of creation, and rules of conduct and of contemplation. Over some five hundred years before the Common Era, the Vedic texts thus became a religious canon, a distinction being made between their authority (*shruti*) and their exposition or explanation (*smriti*). Actual sacrifice became more or less obsolete. The aid sometimes provided by the Vedic gods became a power sustaining all, an intercession to be evoked. The sacrifice of Purusha, the 'kinship' of existent and non-existent, the idea of *brahman* (sacred power), and the practice of ritual, were refashioned into domestic cults, incorporating many current yogic and ethical ideas.

Together they evolved as a notion of *advaita* (non-dualism) – that is, of the essential unity of *Brahma* with the eternal in each individual (*atman*): the self being at one with, of the same essence as, the whole universe, though inhabiting a mortal body. The immanent self or *Brahma*, according to the *Brindaranyaka Upanishad*:

> cannot be seen, for, in part only, when breathing, he is breath by name; when speaking, speech by name; when seeing, eye by name; when hearing, ear by name; when thinking, mind by name. All these are but the names of his acts.[1]

Alternatively this is translated:

> You could not see the seer of seeing. You could not hear the hearer of hearing. You could not think the thinker of thinking. You could not understand the understander of understanding. He is your soul, which is in all things.[2]

This implied, as well, new emphasis on the individual self, in both Buddhist and Brahmanical traditions.

Classical Hinduism may be regarded as yet another fusion of the devotional (*bhakti*) and Upanishadic tendencies, one in which the gods took on a new and vital significance, as in the great Hindu epic, the *Mahabharata*, and especially that part known as the *Bhagavad Gita*, or Song of the Lord. These developments built upon the so-called *smarta* religion of the reforming Vedic priesthoods, originally a minority, to create a theistic (effectively, a monotheistic) religion – the God being Vishnu in these early texts. It emphasized not sacrifice but worship and devotion (*puja* and *bhakti*). Subsequently the traditions continued to evolve as a religion based around the worship of deities. It was adopted by courts and households, focused in temples, and repeatedly caught in popular imagination through buildings, pilgrimages, rituals, recitals, dance and drama. Local cults and deities were repeatedly assimilated into this religion, as different peoples and areas were incorporated into political systems, and thus into the realms of Vishnu and Shiva.

From the nineteenth century the traditions were popularized through printed words and images; in the twentieth century by film and television. By this time they had begun to contest with Christianity as well as Islam, and with modern science. As the early texts were more recently re-examined, three points were repeatedly made that had long been implied in some form. Firstly, there were accusations (mostly but not only from Westerners) about Brahmanical dominance and the sapping effect of religions so deeply concerned with renunciation and contemplation. Secondly, there were contrary claims (mostly but not only from Indians) that such a long religious and intellectual tradition marked the superiority of Indian morality and spirituality. Thirdly, there were pseudo-historical arguments linking features of current Indian society with this ancient past, as in claims about 'Aryan' or 'non-Aryan' traditions and characteristics, and above all in the new vigour with which caste-status was contested. All of these issues will be considered in their place; but we will turn now to the last of them, the problem of caste.

CUSTOMS: THE PROBLEM OF CASTE

Commonly Indian civilization is identified by distinctive forms of social organization, in particular by 'castes': separate, closed and ranked groups each with defined social behaviours. Caste-like arrangements were once thought to have existed, essentially unchanged, from time immemorial. The famous study of Henri Dumont was entitled *Homo Hierarchicus* (1966), as if Indians, or at least 'Hindus', constituted a particular kind of humanity. In India, it was supposed, people were ranked permanently, acquiring an unchangeable status through birth and traditional occupation, and particularly in accordance with ideas of purity and pollution (according to work, conduct and inheritance). Caste was said to be India's most distinctive institution in the sense that it *determined* social behaviour – marriage, diet, meal-sharing, death-rituals, occupation, and so on. It *explained* economic and political alliances and the range of social control or dependence.

Not only defining the Hindus, caste also seemed dominant in the region. Though it never applied fully to all the peoples of South Asia, it was important even among non-Hindus, among 'outcastes' and outsiders (or *mleccha*). Indian Muslims or Christians might be divided into castes or treated as castes, though caste contradicted their egalitarian religious doctrines. For European missionaries the right attitude to caste observances became a matter of prolonged argument. Alternatively, through economic, political and environmental change, 'tribal' groups could be assimilated into the mainstream, as low-caste Hindus or 'Untouchables'. By some accounts, the caste system itself was attributed to an ancient reaction to South Asian indigenes by 'Aryans'; and the Untouchable, the most 'impure', was the necessary antithesis of the Brahman, the most 'pure'.

Given this pre-eminence, caste has also been variously characterized. The fact that caste status could persist independently of actual occupation and wealth or power led some to believe that it was a solely ritual or ideal system. Others noted that it could adapt itself to changing economic and political standing, leading to the suggestion that it was after all ultimately pragmatic and material, and that there was no unchanging hierarchy of castes. More recently, it has become increasingly common among scholars to deny the very existence, before the nineteenth century, of caste as defined by Dumont.

One problem is that the terms are treacherous. 'Caste' was a word of Portuguese origin (from *casta*, meaning type or birth), and reflected European attempts to understand what they observed and what was 'explained' to them. The informants were mostly Brahmans and Brahmanical texts. Particular accounts and treatises therefore came to be regarded as describing general and consistent conditions. These normative descriptions then paved the way (along with geographical and demographic measurements) for the introduction of the generic terms 'Hindu' and 'Hinduism', supposing a single 'race' and 'religion'. But 'caste' did not equate neatly with indigenous terms, such as *varna* (roughly meaning occupational and status-band, order or category) or *jati* (endogamous, notionally occupational group or birth-type). And those terms themselves have not had consistent meanings or applications.

In the *Rig Veda*, as we have seen, the four *varna* are briefly related to parts of the body of the Purusha or cosmic man. The term may be translated as 'colour' (and each *varna* was given a colour in the *Mahabharata*), but it must have originally meant something like 'type' or 'kind', and one should not assume that skin colour had anything to do it. Nor is the hierarchy unambiguous. In subsequent social, religious and legal documents the four *varna* reappear with differing emphasis and meaning, arguably as an ideal rather than as practice. In the *Upanishads*, *varna* is elaborated into a formal code and explained by doctrines of reincarnation, *karma* and *dharma* (roughly fate and duty). *Manusmriti*, the laws of Manu (around 100 BCE), describe each *varna* as having a different function.

The term *jati* continues to be understood variously, but seems most usefully described as meaning a group of similar origin and type (from its etymology, thought to refer to birth, as does the related Latin word 'genus'). A *jati* is whatever unit is defined in practice by the actual contacts of marriage, interdining and so on. To the everyday importance of this term must be added the fact that the boundaries and *varna* ranking of different *jati* often could not be fixed or readily agreed – both were open to contestation and negotiation.

This implies that 'Hindu' society was not necessarily as rigid or as priest-ridden as suggested by the textual rules, which were largely produced by and for Brahmans. In practice, it was common to find dominant caste groups (often but not always Kshatriya) who lorded it over others, but Brahmans were not always regarded as either the highest caste or the arbiters of caste-status. Nor were the occupational associations uniformly meaningful: for example, Brahmans were mostly *not* priests, professionally, and many who acted as priests were not Brahmans.

This explains why it is sometimes argued that a rigid sense of caste, in which *jati* were definitively ranked in relation to *varna*, was not common until quite recently. In some senses this must be true, because modern means of labelling, enumerating, organizing and communicating were not available in India until the nineteenth century. But we should not take this too far. The European observers invented the term 'caste' and undoubtedly affected Indian practice and understanding; but they did not imagine caste *ab initio*. They applied a misleading term, compounding at least two different concepts, but they did so to describe social behaviour which they had generally encountered.

Thus, over the millennia, social and political authority and behaviour have been influenced by recurrent 'caste-like' ideas. The 'civilizational' character of caste lies in the persistence of *varna* and *jati* over time and space within the Indian region. No one aspect defines their importance – not restrictions on marriage or occupation, not even ideas of pollution – for these may be found in many civilizations. Their role obviously is also much more than the mere existence of hierarchy. 'Caste' matters not because it is unchanging or in outline unique, but simply because of its persistence. India had long shared philosophical traditions, and had long been a literate society – not having mass literacy, but (as in mediaeval Europe) having widespread understanding of the power of writing and the authority of texts. The texts were selectively and differently interpreted at different times. They nevertheless enabled the generalization of certain codes in each period, and some perpetuation of particular traditions over time.

We will discuss the evolution of these ideas in later chapters, but it is worth adding now that we do need to distinguish caste's different meanings and practices over time. In the warring but vigorous eighteenth century, for example, warrior virtues were emphasized, not only among 'warrior' castes, but among 'priests' and 'cultivators'. The Brahmans who largely ruled western and central India were soldiers and administrators, rather than priests, in their values and daily life, though they retained their priestly label. In the succeeding colonial era, more pacific and 'private' virtues became useful. British orientalist scholars defined fixed caste and communal categories which the rulers endorsed; and the advent of print transformed the availability and influence of certain 'orthodox' religious texts. As many Brahmans became men of (Western) learning and modern professionals, they were more likely to be defined by the ritual 'purity' of their private lives (by ceremonies, exclusivity, vegetarianism and so on). Also, during the great economic transformations of the nineteenth and twentieth centuries, Banias and other merchant castes found many of these same elements of 'purity' congenial and important. The Bania and lawyer, M. K. Gandhi, made his own selection among 'pure' attributes to shape his very public private life and his struggle against colonial rule.

By the twentieth century, in spite (or in some ways because) of the alien government, a sizeable minority of Indians enjoyed richer resources, of technology and information, than their forebears had in the eighteenth. These could be used in a variety of ways. For example, some women gained independence, awareness and education, and the law began to identify rights and offer protection for 'women' as a category and as individuals – over *sati* (immolation of widows), in factory work, for the age of sexual consent, and so on. At the same time there was wider support for certain Brahmanical (which, perhaps crucially, were also to an extent 'Victorian') norms, such as the *pativrata* (perfect wife), that also marginalized women and their work. As individual property rights gained importance, Western law lumped women together with infants and incompetents. Similarly 'Hindu-ization' sought to isolate Hindus from non-Hindus, through the ideas of space, community and history that were propagated by Indian elites. So rich peasants often secluded their women when they could afford the housing and the loss of field labour, and prospering Brahmans and merchants tried to enforce a 'Hindu' morality and exceptionalism on law, literature, festivals and everyday life (even co-opting colonial rulers and missionaries as allies). Those they sought to include in their 'community' they also wished to exclude from power. Solidarities were promoted by fear of disapproval and fear of others.

ISLAM AND INDIAN PLURALITY

Many of the parts of South Asia which are now included in Pakistan were broadly associated with an 'Islamic world' as early as the eighth century, starting with Arab conquests in Sind, and developing further with the advent of the Turks from the eleventh century. Later, Islam was spread by other Muslim rulers, who, however, as we saw with the Mughals, were mostly also Indian in the sense of being based locally and having to accommodate local mores and interests. Islam was also spread through trade – for example, from very early times, by Arabs on the western seaboard; by Arab missionaries of the Shi'i Ismaili sect from the ninth century; and later by mystic Sufis, especially in Bengal from about the thirteenth century.

Indian Muslims, as might be suggested by these various origins, ranged from rulers to merchants to artisans to farmers, from the rich and mighty to the poor and oppressed. They were widely and unevenly dispersed. By the nineteenth century, when their distribution became transparent through censuses, they constituted large majorities in Sind and what is now Bangladesh, about half of the population in undivided Punjab, an often influential tenth in north India, and much smaller minorities elsewhere.

Nowadays, as indeed in the past, Islam is seen as a culture and an identity as well as a religion, and often in opposition to other cultures, especially of the West but also of 'Hindu' India. Such views rest on an essentializing of the cultures which are being compared: for example, regarding everything in the West as rational and materialist, and everything in the East, including Islam, as irrational and religious. Cultural ethnicities were encouraged during the nineteenth and twentieth centuries not only by Christian colonialists who denigrated the 'pasts' which they supposed replaced by their superior 'modernity', but also because similar ideas were taken up by some who were trying to defend Islam or 'Hinduism'.

Indian Islam, however, was also both particular and various, taking forms related to but also often different from the sects which divided Muslims, including the main Sunni–Shi'a split. (Differing also over descent from the Prophet, the Sunni held that scholars had the right only to interpret divine law by studying what was recorded in the *hadith* or tradition, and the Shi'a that divine law may also be revealed by the chosen *imam* or descendent from the Prophet's son-in-law Ali, whom they hold to be the first legitimate successor as caliph. Shi'i influence was greatest in India in Sind and Gujarat before the nineteenth century, among immigrants from Iran and in the Deccani sultanates from the sixteenth century, and in Awadh under the eighteenth-century nawabs (rulers).) Most of all, Indian Islam reflected not only the expected orthodoxies, but also political accommodations with Hindu elites, as well as doctrinal and ritual overlaps with devotional Hinduism, and ignorance of the *shari'a* (Islamic law) in some regional and rural customs or worship. On the other hand, India was not a mere outpost: at times it contained some of the most important and vital centres of Islam, for example in the Sunni revival led in Delhi by Shah Wali-Allah (1703–62). The history of Islam in India made its adherents there well placed to

suggest responses to the crisis which beset all Muslims with the rise
of European colonialism and Western science.

The range of reactions will be discussed in appropriate chapters.
What may be noticed here is the extent to which they were religious
in character. Muslim leaders naturally often traced their declining
political fortunes to failures of religious orthodoxy. Modern means
made it easier to communicate those rules and norms. They
included newspapers, pamphlets and books; new societies and
organizations; formal or 'professional' training of the *ulama*; new
schools and universities with 'modern' but acceptable curricula;
and large-scale travel by train and steamer to participate in the *hajj*
(pilgrimage to Mecca). The outcome was a more unified Indian
Islam and renewed pan-Islamic connections, as if in fulfilment of
Allah's command that there should be a universal social and political
community of believers. But also, paradoxically, the outcome was
an Islam divided between nations. Within India, Islam became
another unifying or 'imperial' force, alongside Hinduism, rather
than an element of regional or class identities. Significantly, the
political separatism of Muslims was generally weaker in Muslim
majority than in Muslim minority areas.

ENVIRONMENT, TECHNOLOGY AND SOCIO-ECONOMIC
CHANGE

Two images are sometimes juxtaposed in regard to the economic
history of India. One shows a long stagnation and a more recent
chaos interrupted by capitalist investment, pax Britannica and the
supposedly new penetration of trade. The second (to be considered
in later chapters) portrays a long-term economic development that
had been well advanced but was thwarted by colonial rule and
European dominance.

The first view has several parts, including interpretations of
immediately pre-colonial conditions. Here we will consider mainly
the assertion that India stagnated, and indeed was resistant to
profit, science and technology, at least until after the end of Mughal
rule. This is a very misleading idea. In common with the rest of the
Euro-Asian land mass, India had very long experience of movements of peoples and technologies, which generated different kinds
of polity and economy. As we have seen, a series of migrations and
invasions linked the Indian plains with Iran and west and central

Asia, from the earliest times. In the south, contacts with western Asia probably began before the Megalithic period (around 500 BCE). Thus trade has always been important, from the extensive exchanges of prehistory to the nineteenth-century revolution and the evolving world economies.

Technologies provided similar if less cyclical evolutions. The first to leave a lasting impact in India (developing over a very long period) were those related to domesticated animals, artificial irrigation, the plough and writing, all of which were familiar at least 5000 years ago. The wheel probably became important some two millennia later, when it was associated with the renewed expansion of the agricultural frontiers under the Aryans. The use of copper and possibly iron, and the Sanskrit language, were also all important at this time. The *noria* or *arghatta*, a wheel lined with buckets for raising water, was vital for irrigation, possibly as early as the start of the first millennium CE (though it is not unequivocally described in the sources), while its geared version, the Persian wheel, turned by bullock-power, was certainly taken up in mediaeval times under Islamic influence. Though technological innovation did not proceed at an even pace, there was little resistance to it. Empirical chemistry, mathematics, astronomy and medicine were all familiar to Indians. Military technologies too, from cavalry to cannon, were readily developed and adopted. Financial and accounting procedures were also refined from early times.

Adaptations and technical innovation resulted from both foreign contacts and indigenous effort. Some specifically 'Indian' features may be traced to environmental conditions. The landscape itself is mobile. It derives from vast tectonic movements that are building up the Himalayas by driving the subcontinental land mass against and under the main Asian plate. At the same time, great alluvial plains are still growing between the northern mountains and the old rocks of eastward-sloping peninsular India, which is itself punctuated by great river valleys. All these rivers are subject to silting and flooding and dramatic changes in their course. A mutating landscape has provided challenges for land management and reclamation. Another environmental reason for technological (and political) responsiveness is the periodicity and unreliability of India's rainfall. The predominant climatic force is the moist south-westerly monsoon, which prevails for three to five months in most years. It brings immensely heavy rainfall to the south-west and north-east, but progressively less towards the dry north-west.

On the other hand, the facts that north Indian civilizations were land-rich and generally well-watered played an important part in determining their stable agrarian character, allowing similarities to extend over time and space. Across the vast featureless plains, the culture was borne on sacred rivers and through the repetition of texts in word and stone. Gradually it spread from ancient landscapes into outlying regions, including the southern river valleys where water-management chiefly determined the social and political organization. In rocky and inaccessible places, by contrast, more isolated, heterodox traditions pertained. The landscape has also been shaped and reshaped by man over the millennia, though with more rapid change over the previous two or three centuries. Each generation has been influenced by its successors, even when they appeared very different from one another. Today archaeologists and historians agree that there was more continuity than used to be thought between the urban Harappan and the pastoralist Aryan civilizations, as indeed there was between all those that followed, to the present day.

Environmental homogeneity (unlike isolation) need not imply stagnation. Unified and commercial peoples arose repeatedly, and gave way to vigorous migrants or military groups, which in turn became sedentary and urban. An overall trajectory can be discerned, despite physical transience, technological adaptability, and political and economic variety. The predominant (though not steady) trend was firstly towards the expansion of agriculture, and then from dispersed and artisanal production to centralized and mechanized industries. India has participated, in its own ways, in a universal movement from pastoral and peripatetic production to a settled agriculture. Thus, ancient India was defined by the beginnings of long processes of centralization whereby lands and people (so-called 'tribals') were incorporated into a civilizational mainstream, to which they also contributed distinctive elements. The mediaeval period, once seen as a period of dislocation and decline, seems rather to have extended these inexorable regularizations, as illustrated by the distribution and chronology of the very many surviving inscriptions that celebrate and record gifts of land to temples and so on. The continual expansions and elaborations of political and social regimes, and of agriculture and production, were building 'Hindu' and 'Muslim' societies, and allowing the development of states, cities, markets and shrines.

Of course, the frontiers of settled agriculture have contracted as well as expanded, and generally throughout India's history only certain regions have been fertile, wealthy and peaceful at any one time. At the end of the eighteenth century too, many still could and did live peripatetic lives: there were swidden (slash-and-burn) culti-vators and pastoralists; horse and cattle raisers and dealers; tinkers, merchants and moneylenders; farm-workers and professional diggers or builders; soldiers, cavalry and military suppliers; *sadhus* (holy men) and warrior-monks; genealogists, minstrels, players and storytellers; and so on. As a consequence, there was *repeatedly* room for more people to become settled on the land. Many 'traditional' land tenures were designed specifically to bring new lands under the plough.

But, to repeat the point, this was not just a cyclical pattern. Even in the dry Tamil lands of the south, settled cultivation has been spreading for almost a thousand years. In the north and where artificial irrigation was possible, it has been doing so even longer. Subsistence, specialist and commercial cropping have been extended, through the establishment of both wet- and dry-farming regimes, and through great deforestations (though some forest still remains) or reclamations, for example in reaction to the eastward movement of the river systems in Bengal from the sixteenth century. Cultiva-tion spread, sometimes into more marginal areas, and total output increased, until the so-called green revolution of the 1970s and beyond.

As already implied, closer and regular means were needed for the control of land and labour, wherever the agricultural frontier advanced. This brings us almost back to the political outline which began this chapter. Over hundreds of years from the point when groups first began to settle on land, appropriate political institutions and commercial production also began to evolve, and some people were subordinated as an agricultural labour force. Settled agricul-ture was linked to profit, land control, culture and mythology. The very early development of cities implied the existence of surplus extraction and probably market exchanges. The social hierarchy reflected this need to bring and keep land under the plough, to amass and protect capital, and to manage labour. Hindu texts, and for that matter Mughal manuals, provided theory and practical advice.

Especially in fertile, irrigated and densely populated regions, land had acquired value at an early date. Land control was justified by various tales of origin – rights of clearance, inheritance, gift or conquest. Rules tended to define land and restrict access, in the form of many closely defined or overlapping rights. In practice it was possessed (and exchanged) by kings, temples, villages, castes, families and individuals as a core of specific rights embedded in networks of shared or contiguous interests, in the way that empires or settlements dominated their central and valuable territory, but held a more ambiguous suzerainty or 'common' rights over outlying areas or waste. These different principles of land use and land definition long coexisted.

However, the trend was towards subsuming them under state rule. All governments of India, as they sought to expand revenue, tried with greater or lesser success to develop independent central records, and to bypass or co-opt local intermediaries, and overcome local resistance. They imposed overarching supralocal structures and principles, at least within the heartlands of their empires. Over the last 150 years, increasing production for sale and export has similarly required and facilitated the expansion of capitalist management and modern forms of government. These did not wholly remove overlapping rights but tended to standardize all land into a few general types, governed by scientific measurement or a legal definition which overrode differences of use or ownership: not only distributing what had been common among separate owners or to the state, but also attributing the same legal incidents to a temple or a corporation's estate as to the land of an individual. Going further than most of their predecessors, the British also clamped down on 'vagrants', using military campaigns, legal and economic force, and ethnographical typing. Paradoxically they also encouraged mobility – through improved communications; protection for pilgrims, travellers and merchants; some education; and the recruitment of seamen, soldiers, and migrant or emigrant labour. They favoured movement, however, only within the norms and laws of a settled society.

On land, as on most other aspects of life, many prevailing accounts of modern India are narratives of loss. We are used to regarding the divisions of land and society in India – including religious communalism, casteism and poverty – as a decline from social and ecological harmony and from a self-sufficient localism, under the malign influence of capitalism and an exploitative, categorizing and divisive state. The long history of India invites the question: had that harmony ever really existed?

2

. . . .

Early India

CULTURES AND PEOPLES

In early times, the Harappan or Indus valley civilization (from around 3000 to 1700 BCE) developed agriculture, trade and civic life. Sites such as those at Harappa, Mohenjodara and elsewhere in present-day Pakistan and north-western India give evidence of literacy and political organization, and of a productive surplus, sufficient to provide for city dwellers and religious rites, the latter based around auspicious sites and signs, sacred animals, and both female and male fertility symbols. This city culture eventually declined, possibly due to climatic changes, but left elements inherited by later civilizations, most notably that of the Aryans. Among other successors was a less developed culture in eastern India from around 1100–500 BCE; it was based on agriculture, bred cattle and horses, used iron and copper, and produced pottery, the Painted Grey Ware after which it is named. There is also evidence at a somewhat later date of Megalithic societies in southern India that depended on artificially irrigated agriculture, and may have had some contact with similar cultures in west Asia.

In the transition from this prehistory, three broad stages may be discerned in Indian society and polity, paralleling the evolutions of religious belief outlined in Chapter 1. The first, so-called Aryan, stage was characterized by pastoralism, warrior clans, sacrifice and violence. In the second, the spread of settled cultivation was accompanied by the rise of city-states and empires, and equally of households and private property as units of production. A corresponding focus on domesticity in place of sacrifice, and on the individual self (*atman*), was expressed in (for example) devotional practices and a

---

Box 2   Texts and dates

c.1500–900 BCE	Rig Veda (oral and written)
c.900–500 BCE	Later Vedas
c.600–300 BCE	Brahmanas, Aranyakas, Upanishads
c.380–230 BCE (?)	Buddhist canon (Tripitaka)
c.300 BCE	Earliest ideas later recorded in Artha Shastra
	Megasthenes
	Ramayana of Valmiki (of Tulsi Das, c.1600 CE)
c.300 BCE–500 CE	Jaina Anga (Limbs) and texts
c.200 BCE	Mahabharata
c.100–200 BCE	Manu Smriti
c.100 BCE	Bhagavad Gita (composition until c.100 CE?)
c.300–400 CE	Probable compilation of Artha Shastra
c.450 CE	Kama Sutra

Note: Sutras ('threads', explanatory manuals or aphorisms on the Brahmanas) and shastras (usually later, longer books of instruction) comprise the smriti ('remembered') or sacred texts, which set out laws and legends; the originally-oral Vedic tradition is the shruti ('heard').

---

doctrine of rebirth. Non-Vedic religions such as Jainism or Buddhism flourished, with their ethics of non-violence and public benevolence, along with folk and animist religions. They all contributed to a new synthesis in which Vedic texts became authorities for philosophical treatises. A third phase accompanied the wider development, during the first centuries of the Common Era, of state and economic systems, of the priesthood, and of deities-in-temples. The dominant cultures took the form of theistic religion, as a major instrument of the spread of an 'Indian' civilization across the subcontinent, an evolution from court and city to community and countryside. These three broad stages provide the frame for the discussions of this chapter.

The expansion of Aryan culture is supposed to have begun around 1500 BCE. It should not be thought that this Aryan emergence (though it implies some migration) necessarily meant either a sudden invasion of new peoples, or a complete break with earlier traditions. It comprises a set of cultural ideas and practices, upheld by a Sanskrit-speaking elite, or Aryans. The features of this society are recorded in the Vedas. Firstly, they imply warrior-leaders, deified in the form of Indra – possibly marking the subjugation of the Dasas, meaning either separate tribes or lower social orders who resisted the Aryans. Secondly, the Vedas imply specialist priests (*brahmans*, those who pray), their role demanded above all by the fire-sacrifice (*yajna*), and reflected in a pantheon of gods, sun-worship and other rituals, especially those involving the hallucinogen, *soma*. Thirdly, the Vedas recognize traders, craftsmen and other workers. At some stage these roles ceased to be necessarily occupational but became hereditary. A dialogue from the *Chandogya Upanishad* begins with a father telling his son that no one in *their* family 'is unlearned in the Veda and remains a brahman only by family connections' – unlike others, we may assume.[1]

The basis of this differentiated society may also be guessed from the texts. A warrior model is compatible with the polity of military clan or migratory tribe; there is evidence of so-called republican systems, with clan assemblies. An emphasis upon domesticated animals and animal products suggests pastoralism: reliance on horses, cows, goats and sheep. Even in the great creation-sacrifice of Purusha the metaphors are of clarified butter and sacrificial grass.

During the first millennium BCE, however, the Aryan civilization spread eastwards, and became focused upon kings and assemblies, cities, merchants and settled agriculture (possibly learnt from earlier cultures). The Vedic hymns thus may suggest folk memory rather than current experience: the heroic pastoral tradition of an increasingly agricultural or urban people. By now a notion of political territory existed. Many geographical and political units are mentioned in ancient texts, as well as clans or peoples organized under a leader or by kinship. These territories, whether confederacies, kingdoms or empires, were typically controlled by local rulers or rajas and, to different degrees, by laws and officials. There are very early mentions of dynastic succession, as also of courts, councils and advisers. Well-established kingdoms included Kosala (present-day eastern Uttar Pradesh) and Magadha (Bihar south of the Ganga). Ancient India had political – even international – history.

Agriculture and a division of labour lay behind the political developments. Cultivators and their needs are not obviously important in the *Upanishads*: though these make some references to wealthy men, villages and food-grains, their major rustic images are of cows and forests rather than crops and fields. At some time during this period, however, agriculture came to be regarded as underpinning society. The Buddhist canon clearly reflected the political and economic conditions of the day when it included a myth of cosmic evolution centred on rice cultivation and the management and control of agriculture. In the words of one scholar, 'it is significant that the renouncer was the opposite, conceptually, of the householder'[2] – that is, an ideal of propertylessness implies a concept of property. One legend, in the *Digha Nikaya*, described the transition from a bounteous world without work or generation into one in which cultivation was needed for subsistence.[3] In the last stage of the bounteous world, rice had appeared without the labour of sowing or harvest; but then, men and women having become distinct, some people began to store grain to avoid the bother of collecting it daily, which led to a division of the rice fields between men, and a need for tillage. This created property in land and its produce – 'let us divide the rice fields, and set up boundary marks' – and hence the possibility of theft, and a need for punishment or protection. These led in turn to rulers by popular consent (Kshatriyas), and to those who rejected property in favour of meditation (some of whom then settled and became teachers or Brahmans), and then to other social divisions: craftsmen and traders (Vaishyas), and menials or hunters (Shudras).

If such origin-myths reflect the conditions experienced by those who composed them, then, firstly, rulers were establishing order, applying administration and a judicial system as well as military force. Megasthenes, the Greek ambassador who visited the court of Chandragupta Maurya (r. about 322–298 BCE), reported harsh punishments and a strongly interventionist as well as an expanding state in Magadha. (This degree of state control may have been an exception: by contrast, much later, the Chinese observer, Fa-hsien, around 400 CE, commented on a general freedom of movement and a lack of government interference.) Secondly, the focus was on settled land. Thirdly, the state was implied as existing in relation to necessary roles in society. We will examine land and society in greater detail, before returning to political authority.

LAND

Land settlement produced notions of title, use and benefit. Manu says that land belongs to those who first cleared it. The *Artha Shastra* attributed to Chandragupta's minister, Kautilya, urged royal protection (and proper rituals) for agriculture, while Megasthenes claimed that cultivators were numerous, and exempted from military and public service; they kept to their fields and produced large harvests. Even allowing for some exaggeration of royal prerogatives in the special circumstances of Chandragupta's rule (and for possible Greek misunderstandings), this and much other evidence support the existence of land rights and patterns of land use in villages of settlement and production. Despite some indications of claims to general sovereignty over waste and forests, land was not universally 'owned', and would not be expected to be, except where population was fairly dense and states effective. But land title, implying inheritance and historical status, was important in order to legitimize possession, in addition to cultivation or long, continuous and uncontested occupation. Some land rights were superior to others, including possibly a distinction between permanent and temporary landholders that was long to be observed across India. There is very early evidence too of the sale, mortgage, gifting and leasing of land, and of land measurement.

These are indications of private property; but there are also many assignments of land by kings and others to temples or to individuals (state officials, for example). The implication, as also because of a separate revenue head (*sita*), is of categories of royal or state as well as private land. There are references to the state's right to claim revenue from all land, either in return for the ruler's protection or by virtue of his overlordship. In addition there were community rights, for example over pasturage or water; villages and headmen had a role in approving access to land, and managing the taxation of its produce. A concept of private land, therefore, did not mean unqualified ownership. Nor did it necessarily imply individual property rights: the unit in many accounts is plainly the household, implying co-operative production by kin groups.

Though land grants were an important means of securing services, states clearly had the ability, on occasion, to pay officials in cash or kind (described for example in *Ramayana*, *Mahabharata* and *Artha Shastra*). State revenue – an early general term is *bali* – came from the land (as *bhaga*, a customary royal share of the harvest and other produce), quite possibly on the basis of an assessment and measurement of separate holdings, and also from tributes and presents, mines and irrigation, trade and commerce (*sulka*), and forest products and other supplies (*bhoga*, contributions to a local chief's or an overlord's subsistence). On occasion there seems also to have been some kind of head-tax, and there were many instances of obligatory labour. It is noteworthy that most of these taxes were treated as shares in produce (often in precise proportions), and that they seem to have been available to rulers at all levels, from village-lords to kings. It is also probable that they were originally conceived not as a separate category of surplus regularly extracted by the state (there is no evidence of this in the Vedic sources), but rather as a variable complex of social and religious roles, gifts and obligations. By the time of the Buddha, when town and country were also clearly distinguished, these agrarian dues had become recognized as a form of taxation from landholders (*gahapatas* in Pali). A regular revenue required some notion of property.

SOCIAL ORDER

Society too had acquired more complex needs. For example, a Jain text, the *Uttaradhyayana Sutra*, while expressing typical hylozoist sentiments (belief that life pervades all matter), refers not only to hunting and fishing, but also to carpentry and metal-working.[4] Differentiated social roles were important to the state. As recognized in the Buddhist *Digha Nikaya*, agriculture provided for specialized occupations, permitted lordship roles (and sometimes required them, as for irrigation or military protection), and hence necessitated new kinds of political order.

Early markers of courtly, urban and leisured life were the caste-like features that appeared around 1000 BCE. In India as in other early agrarian cultures, social divisions (like land rights) were almost certainly organized and preserved over time through households, groups of real or notional kin that specialized in certain social functions or items of production. The division of labour was backed by the city-states and by moral sanctions, quite possibly needing to be reinforced among nomadic and semi-nomadic peoples during sustained periods of settlement and expanding production.

The *varna* theory, as recorded in the texts that have come down to us, was arguably an abstraction from such practical needs, as the agricultural frontier advanced, and cities and elites developed. (It was not necessarily due to the desire of advanced 'Aryans' to subjugate primitive indigenes, or 'Dasas', an interpretation that accorded with nineteenth-century theories of race.) A settled and surplus-producing society is also suggested by the sophistication of Vedic cosmology and belief, and, in particular by its reflective and speculative character from the time of the *Brahmanas*. These philosophical and religious explorations may also be interpreted as responding to practical or political as well as metaphysical problems.

The four *varna* were conveniently related to the cosmic order, not only by the analogy with the head, arms, torso and feet of Purusha, but also because they were the site for, and the expression of, *karma* (fate, representing spiritual attainment through past actions) in the cycle of *samsara* (reincarnation) on the way to *moksha* (salvation). This associated a division of labour with a hierarchical moral classification and an ideology that explained the entire material and metaphysical world. Birth, rebirth and rewards for merit consistently justified lives devoted to supposedly higher or lowly tasks, and then, by an abstraction of heredity, high or low ritual status regardless of actual employment. A continued partnership of such self-serving teleologies (over many different philosophical schools) may also help explain the longevity of caste-like ideas.

Social distinctions, and income accumulation by leisured classes, are implied also by the accepted branches of knowledge and conduct, namely *dharma*, *artha* and *kama*, corresponding to the religious, material and sensual: the first is metaphysical and intellectual, the second covers all economic, political and social life, and the third is the realm of pleasure and entertainment. By most accounts *dharma* was the highest goal, and it was achieved by renouncing *artha* and *kama*. This meant that ascetics and then priests followed superior callings, and that other functions, including those of kings and warriors, were best served when not valued for themselves. The priorities favoured the leisured and learned elites, and implied the eternal exclusion of others because of their servile work or impure social roles.

COMMUNITIES

There had to be more to it, however, if this philosophy was to help perpetuate *interdependent* communities. The cycle of reincarnation, for example, explained status, but also demanded that the world be rejected in order that the cycle be escaped. The later classical age clearly needed some way of accommodating a mystical, yogic stance with the practical needs of political and economic life. A pragmatic basis for the great controversies of the thousand years from about 600 BCE may be found in this need. A full range of philosophical positions on human existence sought to reconcile the needs of asceticism and of society. Some persistent strands of Brahmanical thinking reflect on and even celebrate practical aspects of everyday life; arguably the growing importance and acceptability of the 'fourth' *Atharva Veda* indicated this trend. A summary in *Digha Nikaya* offers the following, as other examples of alternative philosophies, alongside Jainism and the Buddhist Middle Way: a belief in fate not works, an atheistic materialism, a theory of physical elements (easily preceding Greek speculations on atoms), and a virtually 'postmodern' scepticism – from Sanjaya Belatthiputta on the existence of another world: 'I do not say it is so; I do not say it is otherwise; I do not say it is not so; nor do I say that it is not not so'.[5]

Religious and social ideas had to be popularized if they were to be of any political and economic use. Even naked Jains still needed food; and indeed Jainism developed particularly strict and elaborate rules for laymen. Every Buddhist monk was necessarily a *bhikkhu* ('beggar' in Pali), and Buddhists sought adherents and built monasteries, even though they preached renunciation and concentrated more on the duties of monks than of laymen. The great emperor, Ashoka, who called for a modified Buddhism to be followed throughout his empire, intended it to achieve social as well as metaphysical ends. He, the conqueror of Kalinga (modern Orissa), called for peace and order, and espoused the less cynical principles of ruling from the *Artha Shastra*. He instructed his representatives not only to judge and punish but to seek the affection of men, because (to quote his edict, written in Prakrit, and preserved, among other places, on a stone near Bhubaneshwar, in one of the conquered territories) he desired that all should 'obtain welfare and happiness both in this world and the next' – as if the two goals were after all compatible.

The *Bhagavad Gita* (Song of the Lord; probably second century BCE) provided the most important of the answers to these contradictions: it preached that *karma*, meaning all the actions of material life, is necessary to man, and that the cycle of rebirth can be broken not only by knowledge and by renouncing worldly acts but also by performing those acts in a pure selfless spirit. Arjuna, the Pandava prince and main interlocutor of the poem, raises the issue by doubting that he should fulfil his role as a warrior, fighting his brothers: 'a heavy sin have we resolved to do, that we strive to slay our kin from lust after the sweets of kingship!'[6] Vishnu replies, reaffirming rebirth and hence the eternal, metaphysical being of man and god, but adding that to a Kshatriya 'there is no thing more blest than a lawful strife' and that 'if thou wilt not wage this lawful battle, then wilt thou fail thine own law and thine honour'. 'Holding in indifference alike pleasure and pain, gain and loss, conquest and defeat,' he ordered, 'so make thyself ready for the fight' (II. 31, 33 and 38). Such 'works' are a sacrifice that comforts the gods (III. 3–14), and 'works arise from Brahma; Brahma is born of the imperishable; therefore Brahma, the overlasting, who abides in all things, has his seat in the sacrifice' (III. 15).

But how will one perform well, if wholly detached and without desire? Arjuna objects that man is fickle (VI. 33). The answer is that he may succeed through ritual and devotion (*bhakti*), ultimately expressing or discovering his essential unity with god (VIII. 5–7) – a god, moreover, redrawn as the all-powerful guardian of laws that all men must obey. Arjuna, in the middle sections of the poem, accordingly expresses his devotion to Vishnu, and describes him in terms to inspire awe: 'For as I behold thee touching the heavens, glittering, many-hued, with yawning mouths, with wide eyes agleam, my inward soul trembles, and I find not constancy nor peace, O Vishnu' (XI. 24); 'As moths with exceeding speed pass into a lighted fire to perish, so pass the worlds with exceeding speed into thy mouths to perish' (XI. 29). Vishnu then assumes a more reassuring 'manlike shape' (XII. 51) – the aspect offered to the devotee (XII. 54) – and provides further lessons on the nature of the world and on true conduct. The *Bhagavad Gita* is much more, of course, but it is not ridiculous to see it, in one respect, as harnessing religious faith and fear in order to maintain social hierarchy and to discipline labour.

KINGSHIP

It used to be supposed that kingly authority was weak in India because priestly authority was strong. This seems to give undue weight to the priestly origin of so many of the sources. Read differently, the sources imply that political power had to be accommodated in the priestly theories. The king's religious functions were vital – even if not necessary to the performance of ritual, kings had a sacred quality in their persons that was often seasonally and periodically reinforced by ritual, and they had practical importance for Brahmans or other religious orders, especially as the priestly role came to be regarded as properly distinct from the role of the warrior.

Conversely, an important task of religious thinking was increasingly to reconcile all authority with a broader population outside the court and priesthood. The rise of the cults of Shiva and Vishnu, and of new ritual, also implied a need for public involvement, while *bhakti* meant *personal* devotion. These imperatives popularized the values implicit in the ranking of *dharma*, *artha* and *kama*, without refuting it or offering an alternative political and social framework. The king was expected to endorse the priority of *dharma*, which in turn supported the king. Its relationship with *artha* and *kama* was interpreted in practical ways, but kings, priests and philosophy were still united as means of control.

Contributing to the need for authority was the dependence of courts, towns and temples upon productive workers, and the increasing political importance of merchants and commerce. Around 450 CE, the *Kama Sutra* of Vatsyayana would state that there could be a *proper* enjoyment of earthly pleasures, and (Manu says the same) that all three forms of conduct and knowledge were necessary to happiness. But Vatsyayana still acknowledged that *kama* was a 'result' of *dharma* and *artha*. It was the courtly citizen who was able to devote himself to pleasure, *after* having acquired learning and wealth, and *before* trying to achieve religious merit in old age. The citizen, a civilized and hence urban man (*nagaraka*), could 'take a house in a city, or large village, or in the vicinity of good men, or in a place which is the resort of many persons', and devote himself to festivals, social gatherings, drinking and other amusements, and to love. His house and garden would contain different compartments, and flowers and perfumes, furniture, ornaments, musical instruments and games.[7] In short, this was a world dependent upon servants and the work of others. It follows that it was also a world in which quite small groups of elites needed to coerce productive subordinates, and to maintain order.

Political as well as ideological means were found to maintain authority. Some of these, and hints of the problems facing states, can be deduced from various political rule-books. Mostly they suggest that control may be kept by moderation and by promoting moral standards. Buddhist thought, for example, recommended that public assemblies decide on policy, that new laws be avoided, that respect be shown to elders and to religion, and that women and girls should not be held by force. We may assume therefore that tyranny, innovation and oppression were not unknown. Ashoka's edicts expressed his regret at the horrors of his conquest of Kalinga, and argued that the state should eschew violence, murder and social disruption, and provide uniformity of justice and impartial punishment. Ashoka none the less engaged in conquest, and, though opposed to arbitary government, he permitted his governors to act on their own initiative. He recorded that he had carried out great public works – providing travellers with shady banyan trees, mango groves, ponds, wells and shelters – and claimed that 'the kings of older times [also] have worked for the welfare of the world'. Early post-Ashokan inscriptions make similar commitments. Good works and exhortations against killing had (Ashoka asserted) encouraged the people in greater obedience to parents and teachers, and increased kindliness to Brahmans, ascetics, the poor and weak, slaves and servants.[8] The effect of good government, then, was to perpetuate a socio-religious and political system with ambitions for tight control over people's behaviour. *Artha Shastra* and *Manu Smriti*, and many other texts, proposed a great regulation of all aspects of ritual and social life. They make a presumption (quite different from the Vedic texts) that the state should have a monopoly of force, as part of a general promotion of courtliness, benevolence and religious perfection.

A broad description of government early in the Common Era may be deduced from the *Artha Shastra*, which gave precise and pragmatic prescriptions for the conduct of kings.[9] The king was a personal ruler, who needed to be well-born, intelligent and energetic; but the state also had six other constituents: ministers, the country, forts, treasury, army and allies. The king consulted his ministers in council, and through correspondence; he made plans for conquest with his commander-in-chief. He also had his own household to manage, and department heads and other officials from whom he received reports on law, administration and finance. He needed reserves against disasters. He gave public audiences, received information from spies, and needed to be knowledgeable about religion, sciences and the economy. His duties included ritual observances. His ideal country was readily defended, rich and compliant (having many industrious producers under 'stupid masters', those unlikely to challenge the king's authority). An inept king would produce a 'kingdom divided within itself, the army disintegrated, the civil service headed by ministers disorganized'. In short, the classical norm included a structured and record-based administration;

multiple sources of information; legitimation through descent, personality and religion; and frequent internal and external threats.

Apart from any internal pressure from social subordinates, the two main threats were external invasion and fragmentation. The first was often a catalyst of change: invasions from the north-west repeatedly affected India, from the Persians to the Mughals. The second was expressed in the long rivalries between Jain, Buddhist and Hindu kings and doctrines, between neighbouring dynasties and alliances, and between central and local power. Ultimately the development of regional polities marked the transition to the mediaeval era in India.

INVASIONS AND EMPIRES

In historical time the movements of armies, peoples and influences from west to east began with the Achaemenid emperor of Persia, Cyrus, who conquered parts of north-western India in about 530 BCE. Takshashila (Taxila), the capital of the Achaemenid province of Gandhara, became a centre of trade – coins survive – and of Indic and Persian culture. In the time of Darius III, some 200 years later, the Macedonian conquerer Alexander campaigned in north-west India for two years, defeated the Persians and occupied Takshashila. He penetrated as far as the Punjab, and founded short-lived Greek settlements. Trade followed both of these two conquests: evidence of it has been found right along the Ganga and into central India. The Greeks returned under Seleucus Nicator, but were defeated by Chandragupta Maurya in about 305 BCE. Further invasions, by Greeks from Bactria, followed Mauryan decline in the second century BCE. The Greeks, known in India as Yavanas, conquered much of the north-west, and at one stage, possibly under Milinda (or Menander, r. 155–130 BCE), reached as far as the Mauryan capital, Pataliputra (present-day Patna in Bihar). They brought some Greek influences but also interacted with Indian, especially Buddhist, culture.

In the first century BCE they succumbed in turn to the nomadic Shakas or Scythians who had been driven from central Asia by other nomads excluded by the Chinese and the Great Wall. The Shakas renewed Iranian and central Asian influences in terms of administration and culture, as did their successors, in the first century CE, the Yueh-chi who became or were followed by the Kushanas.

Starting under Kanishka, probably early in the first century CE, the Kushanas established a kingdom that lasted for about 150 years, and stretched from the north-west as far as Banaras and Sanchi.

Their conquests had the effect of pushing the Shakas south and eastwards. One section controlled north-west Deccan by around 100, ousting the Satavahanas, and another Shaka dynasty ruled in Gujarat and Malwa from that time until about 390. The Satavahanas, local chiefs mentioned in Mauryan times, had founded a powerful kingdom under Satakarni (r. 128–10 BCE). They were in turn forced still further east, into present-day Andhra where they became pre-eminent. Some later invasions had a similar effect. Hunas (Huns), centred in modern Afghanistan, ruled large parts of north-western India in the fifth century, and played a part in bringing an end to the Gupta empire. The Chalukyas who dominated the Deccan were overthrown by the Rashtrakutas in the eighth and ninth centuries, partly because of the Arab threat they had faced from the west. The invasions thus played a major part in shaping the political structures of north and central India over 500 years until about 300 CE and then again in later centuries.

Hosts of local lineages eventually dissipated the vigour of the invaders, as they would undermine successive pretenders to central power. Invasion imposed unusual pressures, but also represented acute versions of the underlying problems of centralizing kingdoms, the challenge of the localities. So too would rival kingdoms constantly vie with each other, but power also oscillated between petty chiefs and larger political forces. The localities provided a basis on which empires could be built, and, once built, challenged.

The Guptas took advantage of an accretion of local power after 320 CE, with the rise of Chandragupta I in Magadha. An empire was established by his successor Sumadra Gupta (r. 335–76). He subdued smaller kingdoms across north India, including much of Bengal, and achieved some kind of suzerainty or influence as far west as the Indus river, and over most of central and eastern India, as far south as Kanchi. His son Chandragupta II (r. about 376–415) also subdued the Shakas in western India.

Nevertheless the Gupta empire remained more of a confederacy than a centralized state. By around 550 it had succumbed to invaders (the Hunas, as mentioned), local insurrections, and the collapse of tributary alliances. Some of its feudatories were re-established as independent kingdoms. Four main successors to Gupta power were in place by the seventh century: a new Gupta dynasty in Magadha,

Box 3   Kingdoms of ancient and early mediaeval India

North-western   **North and north-eastern**
Harappa (2700–1700 BCE)

————————————— ARYANS (1500–600 BCE) —————————————

Cyrus of Persia (519 BCE)

> MAGADHA (542–458 BCE)
> Shisunaga (413 BCE)
> Nandas (362–21 BCE)

Alexander (327–5 BCE)

> MAURYANS (322–185 BCE)
> Chandragupta (321–298 BCE)
> Ashoka (268–31 BCE)

Yavanas (2nd century BCE   Shungas (185–74 BCE)
   to 1st century)   Kharavela (1st c. BCE)
Shakas (1st century BCE)

Kushanas (1st–2nd century)

> GUPTAS (319–540)
> Chandragupta I (319–35)
> Sumadragupta (335–76)
Huna invasions (454 & 495)   Chandragupta II (376–415)

Maitrakas—Pushyabhutis—Maukharis—Guptas (6th century)
————————————— HARSHA of KANAUJ (606–47) —————————————
Arabs in Sind (711–15)   Pratiharas (Bhoja, 840)   Palas (760–1142)

Western   **Central**   **South-eastern**

> SHAKAS (100–390)   SATAVAHANAS (128 BCE – 121)
> Rudradaman (150)   Satakarni (128–10 BCE)
>   Gautamiputra (86–114)
>   Vasishthiputra (114–21)

>   PALLAVAS (300–888)
> CHALUKYAS (550–753)   Aditya I (870–906)
> Western (7th cent.)   Eastern (630–970) Parantaka I (906–53)

> Rashtrakutas (757–973)   CHOLAS (907–1300)
> Chalukyas (973–12th century)   Rajaraja I (985–1014)
>   Rajendra I (1014–42)

Note: Many dates are approximate; they are CE unless stated otherwise. The position of each heading roughly corresponds with the territories (left to right, west to east).

Map 1   Early India

the Maukharis of present-day northern Uttar Pradesh, the Pushyabhutis of present-day Haryana, and the Maitrakas in Gujarat.

From 606, Harshavardhana of Kanauj re-established a central
authority over most of north India and Bengal. Harsha was
descended through his grandmother from the second Gupta line,
and through his father from the Pushyabhutis. His sister was
married to the Maukhari king at Kanauj. Harsha succeeded to both
the Pushyabhuti and Maukhari thrones, after his elder brother and
his sister's husband were killed in battle with the Guptas.

Harsha's empire, like that of the first Guptas, depended upon
a series of alliances, and on the energy and influence of its ruler.
When Harsha defeated Shashanka, king of Bengal, he reinstated
one of the second Gupta line as ruler in Magadha. He followed
the same strategy after defeating the Maitrakas in Gujarat. But
Harsha's empire did not survive him, and in the later seventh
century the north was dominated by a revival of the second Guptas,
and by other short-lived kingdoms. Between the eighth and tenth
centuries the Palas reigned in the east, while the Gurjara-Pratiharas
dominated the west, resisting Arab incursions. Eventually Pratihara
power was once again dissipated among more local chiefs, who
succumbed to the first of the Afghan invasions in the early eleventh
century.

South and central India had followed something of the same
pattern of centralizing and decentralizing power. Dynasties vied
over control of the vast dry plateau of the Deccan, and of the great
rivers leading into the Bay of Bengal, especially the Godavari and
Krishna. The Deccan was the site for flourishing kingdoms, as was
the eastern or Coromandel coast. In the sixth century, as successors
to the Satavahanas and Vakatakas, the Chalukyas ruled large territories in central India from an original base in Mysore. Harsha did
not succeed in a campaign against them, under Pulakeshin II. In
the eighth and ninth centuries (as already mentioned) they were
succeeded by another dynasty from the same region, the Rashtrakutas.
A branch of the Chalukyas revived and ruled the Deccan again
between the tenth and twelfth centuries. The south-west of the
peninsular was controlled, meanwhile, from the seventh century,
by the Pallavas, based in Kanchi, and great rivals of the Chalukyas.
They survived until the ninth century when they were ousted by
the Cholas, who remained dominant until the thirteenth century.
In the late tenth and early eleventh centuries their power reached
even to Sri Lanka and south-east Asia.

CULTURE AND ITS TRANSMISSION

There was not a single tradition in early India, but some tendency for separate traditions to coalesce. Brahmanism readily accommodated the *Upanishads*. Buddhism was more difficult to digest. Mahayana Buddhism in particular – the form exported to China and Japan – flourished separately between the first and seventh centuries CE. On the other hand, it also acquired ideas which went beyond the individual acquisition of merit to the possibility of mediation by a compassionate, suffering pantheon of Bodhisattvas. Though atheistic, Mahayana Buddhism developed some idea of links between this pantheon and the universal essence that was *brahman*. Though centred upon detachment, Buddhism also sometimes became involved with tantric sexual and mystical practices. By the seventh century, when the more austere Hinayana Buddhism was almost extinct in India, Mahayana Buddhism was also in decline. In the eighth century a new version, Vajrayana (Vehicle of the Thunderbolt), was developed and exported to Tibet. However, it was not remarkable that by then the Buddha should also have taken his place in Hindu thinking as an incarnation of Vishnu. Over centuries, as the *sangha* (Buddhist order) became more powerful in commerce and land-owning, it was increasingly engaged in controversy with Brahmans; but Buddhism was also gradually being subsumed within Hinduism.

Among Hindus, there was a greater tendency towards incorporation. First there was a conflation of categories quite unlike the binary separations familiar in modern times. Further elaborations on the ancient texts, in the early centuries of the Common Era, continued the earlier combinations of legend *and* instruction, of narrative *and* philosophy *and* ethics. So *Mahabharata* and *Ramayana* took their place as sacred writings. Secondly, many developments in religious ideas and allegiance also tended towards mutual incorporation. Three were most important: cults of Vishnu, of Shiva and of the goddesses. All drew in earlier and local deities, mainly by regarding them as many incarnations of one original. Vishnu, the benevolent protector and lord of all, appeared in many forms – as Krishna of course; as Rama, hero-king of *Ramayana*; and (as said) as the Buddha. There were various incarnations too of the destroyer and creator, Shiva, a fertility god, descendant of the Vedic Rudra, his cult focused on the phallic symbol or *lingam*. Through the idea of incarnation, each of these apparently opposed versions of Hinduism could regard the other as another, lesser expression of the one divine principle. Female goddesses too – very important for embodying localized, non-Hindu worship – were mostly regarded as the consorts of the male, as Parvati was for Shiva, or Sita for Rama. They embodied *shakti*, a female principle which represented the inner strength of the corresponding male.

At the same time that Brahmans became more and more concerned with purity and caste rules, they were also increasingly patronized by states and involved with a public – so that their beliefs and practices often consolidated local customs and other heterodoxies. Though many schools of philosophy can be identified in this period, they too overlap, as if they were merely different ways of looking at the same questions (as already seen in the *Digha Nikaya*): so *nyaya* (logic or analysis) was related to *vaisheshika* (physics; the atomic theory) and *samkhya* (counting; ideas that creation resulted from the inherent nature of all matter); while *yoga* (spiritual discipline) and *mimamsa* (inquiry) were also means towards *vedanta* (the end of the Vedas), with its emphasis upon meditation and the world's essential *maya* (unreality), as developed by Shankaracharya around 800.

In the south, as part of the convergence, there was a Sanskrit-based Brahmanization of religion. Shankara's work was important because, adapting a Buddhist model of organization, it encouraged further development of temples and centres of learning (*mathas*) and extended Brahmanic influence in the south. It was important also because it clarified the principles of *advaita* (monism) inherent in so much of Indic thought, and because it elucidated and combined strands from both ascetic and pragmatic traditions.

It is true that even this powerful influence was resisted by (and partly directed against) early Tamil cults devoted to Vishnu or Shiva that embodied Buddhist and Jain elements and were less concerned with caste. Such forerunners of later *bhakti* movements were the religious equivalents of the local political and social power which states had to accommodate. But even these heterodoxies can be seen as now falling within a broadly 'Hindu' frame, and indeed as spreading it from the closed Sanskrit world of Brahmans, kings and ceremonial sacrifice, into a vernacular realm of personal worship, popular celebration and song.

The ideas and practices which supported the political system and characterized the civilization were thus transmitted through worship, intellectual debate and textual exposition. Transmission was also achieved through buildings and images, formal education, and social rules. We shall briefly consider each of these in turn.

Buildings and other structures enunciated rules and ideas to an ever-wider public over time. Columns, often sculptured and inscribed, were erected to celebrate kings and battles. More consistently the culture was embedded in the landscape through sacred places, and in buildings which resembled caves and mountains. Low rounded hill-like structures, or *stupas*, recalled, and originally were, burial mounds. But, as time went on, and donations from adherents increased, the *stupas* acquired elaborate carvings and gateways (most famously at Sanchi), each with narrative or presentational purpose; some of the carvings show crowds of worshippers. Elsewhere, caves and mountains themselves were carved into buildings and statues. The greatest of these is probably the magnificent Kailasanatha cave-temple at Ellora, near Aurangabad, ordered by the Rashtrakuta king, Krishna I (r. 756–73).

From the Gupta period, free-standing temples survive. Increasingly – though still recalling mountains – they became elaborate guarded spaces, expressing the elements of ritual and the universe in microcosm. Within impressive portals (later reaching a climax with the massive *gopuram* of southern temples, as at Kanchipuram or Madurai), were to be found enclosed courtyards and pillared halls, teeming with images of gods and daily life, and finally an inner sanctum, typically small, hidden and mysterious. Like a ceremony or ritual cast in stone, such architecture both invited public participation, and commanded respect through its grandeur and its secret reserve. These developments imply an architectural history that was increasingly looking to a public while also regulating it, as when Shudras were excluded from temples which none the less incorporated popular deities and were designed to project an image of spiritual and temporal power. One example, indicating the continual processes whereby 'tribal' or folk traditions were incorporated into the mainstream of Hindu culture, is the Jagannath cult and temple in Orissa.

A similar story is revealed in arts and crafts. Especially in the earlier periods, the sculptured human and divine images were often youthful, contemplative, serene and detached. Later imagery added fear and excitement and passion. Carvings of battles, processions, love-making and everyday life seem to link mythology and courtly life with much wider, popular experiences. As at Ajanta, some paintings, though stylized, are marvellously humanistic. From Mauryan times, statues became so numerous as to seem mass-produced even in stone, and they *were* so later, especially in bronze and as miniatures. Characteristic ornamentation was then repeated on vases, ivory boxes and textiles; and of course in dance and music, the higher forms of which preserved and communicated particular emotions and narratives to large audiences.

More direct transmissions of knowledge were also provided through education. High-caste boys were supposed to learn the Vedas by rote from a *guru* or teacher, just as farmers, merchants and craftsmen learnt their trades by apprenticeship within families. Brahman boys would begin to study reading at about four or five years of age, and became *brahmacharin* (celebate students) after their childhood had ended with a 'second birth' or *upanayana*, when they assumed the sacred thread, aged about eight. Kshatriya and Vaishya boys were supposed to follow similar patterns, with the *upanayana* ceremony at age ten or twelve. Much of the teaching was domestic or individual, but Kashi (Banaras), Takshashila and later Kanchi all developed as centres of education, with colleges containing dozens or even hundreds of students. Monasteries, such as the Buddhist one at Nalanda in present-day Bihar, and, later, Hindu temples also became centres of learning. There was little stress on female education, though there are known instances of educated women.

As noted, one key to the transmission of social rules was kinship and inheritance. The Hindu joint family, already evident in ancient times, was patrilineal and could be polygamous. Richer households contained several generations, including cousins and half-siblings, as well as adopted children, students, slaves and servants. The authority of the male family head was paramount. In theory it permitted few private as opposed to family possessions. Joint-family partitions were formal and difficult affairs. High-caste families were then grouped into (properly speaking) exogenous *gotra*, literally 'herds of cows', or clans claiming a common line of descent.

Families and *gotra* ensured the continuity of custom through marriage, the birth and management of children, and the proper performance of roles at different stages of life. One important example of their influence is the subordination of women. This may possibly have been greater in Aryan prehistory, considering the Vedic emphasis on Kshatriya virtues, and the insignificance of the few Vedic goddesses. Over the centuries from Ashoka to Harsha, erotic texts and images recognized women's sexuality; there were warnings against the ill-treatment of women by men; and there is much evidence of free association between the sexes (as well as some indications of high-class seclusion of women). Indian art too plainly celebrated and enjoyed the female form. Even so, family structures and customs restricted women's independence, and ensured that their status was defined by that of men.

For the higher castes (at a time before child marriage was common for boys), the ideal union was between a man of over 20 and a girl one-third his age who had not yet had her first menstruation. A wife was entitled to some personal property in the form of clothing, jewellery and even money, but she invariably 'belonged' to the husband's family, to whom she had had to bring a dowry. Many were the exhortations to her to fulfil her religious duties towards her husband. Marriage was indissoluable, and widows could not remarry. Lower-caste women certainly worked, in agriculture, as weavers, and as prostitutes – these were regulated by the state, and later (as *devadasis*) by temples. For some, no doubt, work did mean independence and even wealth, but the rule of subordination seems likely to have been set by higher-caste norms.

PRODUCTION (SLAVES, RICE AND BANKERS)

The crops and methods of production of ancient India would have seemed broadly familiar to the early nineteenth-century observer, except for the introduction by that time of New World crops such as the tomato, chilli and potato. Meat was certainly eaten, but seems to have become less prominent in the diet, probably under Jain and other religious influence, and possibly due to a decline in pastoral production and the increasing use of animal-power for agriculture. Rice was the most important crop, in several varieties, the finest being reserved for the rich. Wheat and millets were also known, with wheat increasing its importance from the north-west towards the east during the first millienium CE. Many pulses were grown, as also gourds, sugarcane, oil-seeds and betel. Garlic, peppers, ginger and other spices were produced, and various fibre crops: cotton, silk (though not from the mulberry worm), hemp, flax and jute. In the north-east heartlands of the Mauryan and Gupta empires, three harvests were recognized, then as now: winter (November–December), spring (March–April) and summer (May–June). Principles of husbandry were recorded, including multiple ploughings, fertilizing, sowing at auspicious moments, weeding, methods of harvesting (by scythe), and threshing on a special harvest floor. There was some irrigation by wells, dams, reservoirs (tanks) and canals, under the general authority of great or local lords, who received tribute in return. The annals of properly run regimes recount successful irrigation schemes, and those of more disturbed times just as predictably bewail their neglect and decay.

Agricultural labour seems to have been organized in households, but households included slaves. Vedic sources refer to gifts of slaves and to prisoners being enslaved. 'Dasa' (of the non-Aryan 'tribes') also means slave in this context, and 'Shudra' often seems to mean much the same. Later it is clear that slaves were bought and sold, and that people could be born as slaves. Slaves performed household work, but also worked in the fields, for example as ploughmen. As it is recorded that hardship or famine could force people into slavery, cultivators' households must also have included free workers. The implication is of three levels of agrarian worker: the slave, the peasant family-member, and the lord. Intermediary roles are also implied for overseers, accountants and officials.

People of different types could take up various occupations – for example, Brahmans becoming traders by necessity – but artisans and merchants (like others) were generally hereditary professions, their activities being based around people who were related to each other. As the law code of Narada put it: 'if a travelling merchant... suddenly dies, the king shall preserve his goods until his heir comes forward. If no heir comes..., he must hand them over to his other relatives.'[10]

On the other hand, unlike the agriculturists (on the whole), the craftsmen, bankers and merchants, or at least those in towns, seem also to have operated through corporations or guilds: there is plentiful evidence in the seals and coins they issued. Commercial and craft guilds regulated and supported activities from prices to personal conduct. They played important political roles and sponsored religious foundations, especially (at this period) Buddhist and Jain monasteries. They concentrated their residence in particular quarters, set rules for themselves, lent and borrowed money, organized markets, and recognized craft or occupational leaders (called *setthi*, *jetthaka* and so on). They became part of the social panoply to be protected by the king. Co-operation helped long-distance trade, by providing contacts, information, and resting-places, and by securing protected routes for caravans and boats.

Such arrangements were needed, for there was considerable specialist processing of agricultural and other products. There is early evidence also of some very large-scale individual enterprises engaged in manufacture and distribution – pottery, and cotton and silk textiles in particular. Within India, and beyond, there was a good deal of land-, river- and sea-borne trade. It is impossible to measure the quantities, but the range is plain, implying networks that stretched from Gandhara in the north-west to Bengal in the east, and from north Bihar to the southern coasts of India – horses from the north-west; elephants from Assam; coral, pearls and sandalwood from the south; gold and iron from south Bihar; and so on. Satavahana power in the Deccan probably increased the north–south trade from the second century BCE. A spice trade with the Roman empire was long important along the west coast; Indian as well as Arab traders plied the western Indian ocean as far as Africa; in the south the Pallavas and even more the Cholas were noted for their navies and for maritime commerce. In the Kushana period, contacts with Afghanistan and central Asia were strengthened. The Palas in Bengal had links into Tibet and south-east Asia. Duties on trade were important to Indian rulers, certainly from at least the time of the Mauryans, and they sought to regulate aspects of commercial business. The Mauryans (though few of their successors) even seem to have fixed market prices; all kingdoms built or managed roads and river or sea-ports.

Bankers, who were also merchants, played an important part in securing the political order, and in facilitating trade, because, outside the towns, this was not a highly monetized society. Cows appear in texts as a standard of value, and rice (*dhanya*) seems to have been widely used as a means of exchange. Cowrie shells were used, too, over the millennia. But for small, rural and personal transactions, barter and other non-monetized exchanges were important (and continued to be so until very recently in India). The fact that barter was so common, for both goods and services, may possibly have reinforced the ritual importance accorded to gifts. Thus bankers not only provided credit, but also, possibly more importantly, acted as conduits between different means of exchange. They translated from an economy of slaves, forced labour, subsistence and barter, into ones of surplus, kingly courts, leisure, long-distance trade, and money.

Alongside states and great magnates, the bankers were users and coiners of the metal currencies, in gold, silver and copper, that operated widely from about 600 BCE, and probably earlier. The number of coins in circulation appears to correlate closely with the stability and effectiveness of political authority. The Mauryans, for example, produced characteristic punch-marked coins in silver and copper, but there are fewer coins from the ensuing Shunga period. The Kushanas issued gold and copper coins, marked with images of deities, the Buddha and so on; their wide distribution across India is a mark of the extensiveness of trade in this period. The Guptas too produced huge numbers of coins in gold, silver and copper; they contained smaller proportions of precious metal over time, possibly as the dynasty's fortunes declined.

This and other indications imply a decline in trade and surplus agricultural production in periods of political upheaval, for example in north India after the death of Harsha. On the other hand, even in such times, coins probably continued in use, in the larger or urban transactions for which they were always mainly intended. In the long term, mercantile activity and the growth of towns imply a gradual though not uniform widening of the scope of economic and political life. Subsistence cultivation and small-scale exchanges (such as raw materials and food in return for manufactured commodities), within families, villages and regions, were being supplemented by very long-distance trade and specializations of production. From time to time unfavourable conditions would scale down or even prevent distant and large-scale transactions; when they reappeared, however, they were often more extensive than before.

EMPIRES, RELIGIONS AND REGIONS

This chapter has suggested that rulers, social norms and production followed broadly similar patterns over long periods. This certainly exaggerates the similarities and continuities between particular cases. It follows the trail of characteristics that were widely shared and thus constituted 'Indian' civilization. It is true none the less that at the highest levels, but also at the lowest, there *were* common features and trends.

The village and the extended family remained the basic social, economic and political units, but they were so because externally involved. It used to be said that the norms of locality and kin group, especially caste, allowed a Hindu civilization to survive under the vagaries of weak rule and feeble economic development. Almost the opposite seems true: the norms survived because of their involvement with vigorous large-scale systems of thought and belief, of politics and economy. The highly cultivated areas of many parts of the subcontinent were separated by mountains and jungles, but trade routes, conquerers, monks and tax collectors penetrated the barriers, and thus spread the customs and ideas which predominated in the region.

The norms included economic roles, influenced by caste, and also patriarchal authority. They provided for the very numerous life-stage rituals, and for gender behaviour, especially for those of higher status. Some of the extant descriptions – forty rituals marking stages of childhood and adulthood; eight kinds of marriage; and so on – reflect the categorizing passion of the writers of texts. It cannot be supposed that these rules were strictly observed at all times. But it cannot be supposed either that they, and the habits of thought which lay behind them, were without influence.

For rulers, pomp and great titles were important – the horse sacrifice, for example, was practised to invoke the divinity of kings, although these ceremonies died out gradually after the Guptas. Military power and conquest were other vital marks of kingship, and many kings also travelled constantly – securing alliances, enforcing obedience and gathering information. In addition, kings did rely on more settled forms: on cities such as Pataliputra or, after Harsha, Kanauj (north-west of modern Kanpur), and on both collective and formal government (ministers, councils, laws). All states pursued some kind of territorially divided administration, with provinces (*desha*) and districts (*pradesha*) under designated officials, paid either in cash or by land grants (*agrahara*).

At the lower levels, the local bodies also were formalized and persistent in form: villages with headmen and assemblies, and towns with councils, and merchant and artisanal guilds that provided not only forms of self-regulation but also specialist knowledge and training. In the first millennium of the Common Era the power of these local forces was probably exaggerated by the reliance of the rulers upon land and upon pre-existing institutions. The administration of the Guptas and of Harsha rested in part on local bodies established in both town and country. In the south, too, despite the 'decimal' (ten-village) administrative system of the Deccan, or the Tamil districts (*nadu*) under provincial officials, the core of practical authority remained with local institutions and assemblies (*sabha*) that were at least semi-autonomous.

Religious rivalries similarly helped shape the states, but did not establish long-term political divisions. Like Ashoka, the Kushanas embraced Buddhism, as did the Palas; the much later Hunas opposed it. Kharavela, who ruled in Orissa in the first century BCE, favoured Jainism; the Rashtrakuta king of the Deccan, Amoghavarsha (r. 814–80), was another notable Jain patron. But also in the Deccan the Satavahanas had promoted a Brahman orthodoxy; Gautamiputra (second century CE) was said to be bent on destroying the pride of the Kshatriya Shakas. In the seventh century, Shashanka, the Shaivite king of Bengal who briefly conquered Magadha, was fiercely anti-Buddhist. The worship of Shiva was also importantly fostered in the south by the conversion of the Jain king of the Pallavas, Mahendravarman I (r. 600–30). There were continuities, however, partly because hard political and religious divisions failed to develop out of such local differences. This was not because religion was unimportant to kings or to states, but because states were not consistently centralized, and because in most areas religions also coexisted or even overlapped, and (as we have seen) tended towards merger and complementarity.

To see these effects as allowing for continuities is to go against and not to support earlier interpretations, as has already been indicated. In the nineteenth century, European scholars developed theories about the Indian past which they thought explained why 'Hindus' had succumbed to foreign domination. They noted that ancient Indic and early Hindu society purported to be more concerned with *dharma* (religious merit) than with *artha* (material success). Accordingly they pictured early India as unchanging and unpolitical, dominated by religious norms and caste, by fatalism, and by a cyclical theory of history.

However, we have seen that myths took linear or narrative form despite an emphasis on the cycle of days, harvests, lives and ages; so too worldly concerns had to be accommodated, and governments did have the power to influence conduct and produce change. Indian thinkers devoted much effort to defining the proper roles of kings. Theories of renunciation and sacrifice might seem to diminish the importance and responsibility of kings, but kingship seems to have relied firstly on a series of connected relationships expressed in gifts or boons, and secondly on the performance of roles which accorded with their *dharma*. The first of these had the tendency to diffuse authority throughout the kingdom, and the second bound royal power to the religious order of the universe and to that of the Brahman.

As said, kings could project religious and regional distinctions (in the case of Jain, Buddhist and, later, Muslim kings) but long-term in the early periods they were engaged in generalizing and standardizing what became Hindu traditions. They could do this because they were visible to the people through officials and agents, through coins and inscriptions, and through ritual, symbols and buildings. They – and other rulers, village chiefs or household heads, in microcosm – could do this also because charged with maintaining social hierarchy and economic well-being. Many texts also noted that kingly rivalries, greed or weakness could produce political and economic crises. The result was not a lack of politics, but an ebb and flow of power, both imperial and regional.

It may be assumed, tautologically, that some form of strong government was characteristic, if only briefly, of all the regimes that have been remembered in the records. Their extent varied greatly: in two millennia only the Mauryans and the fourth-century Guptas achieved broad and lasting empires. They were comparable in territorial range to the Romans or the Carolingians in somewhat similar periods of Western European history. Europe and India were both appended to the Asian land mass, and, in both, the fortunes of empires and states were influenced by intruders as well as by local rivalries. In the long run Indians were more often subjected to imperial suzerainty than Western Europeans. But, in both cases, the fact that empires were unusual did not preclude successful smaller regimes; vigorous local states frequently dominated large and populous regions.

Arguably the wrong question has been asked about India's early political history. The issue is not whether fragmentation was produced by its peculiar religious and social character, but why its central authorities were so often powerful. Religious and regional rivalries generated strong local regimes, which until the advent of the Mughals (and again more briefly in the eighteenth century) might have seemed likely to become consolidated into regional nations. That this had not occurred, for most of the subcontinent, by the year 2000 was a legacy of those latter-day empires, the Mughals, the British and the Indian. On the other hand, in the mediaeval and early modern periods, it was not India that was thus unusual but Western Europe. Nowhere other than Europe experienced such early and continuous development of small independent states and cultures that also, through violent and peaceful revolution, became 'national' and responsive to public and private interests – producing of course a very mixed legacy, of civil society, law, democracy, imperialism, racism and slaughter, but one largely denied India by the disruptive power of 'imperial' forces.

We turn next particularly to this incomplete regional development. It too needs to be analysed with caution. Recent interpretations of early mediaeval India challenge older notions of imperial break-up, decline and 'feudalism', and suggest, rather, expansions of states and their roles. In early India, as at all times, there were clearly different degrees and types of central jurisdiction, and more highly developed political cultures and economies in some places than in others. All kingdoms, like all villages, would have had outlying reaches over which they had claims but only intermittent control. But in the end there was a secular increase in population, cultivated area and political authority; and in that sense continual 'growth'. That is to say that the increases were not continuous, and yet it seems that in the long run they spanned periods of economic and political contraction as well as expansion. The more important early mediaeval story, therefore, is probably one in which scattered polities and religious centres, with their courtly or monastic life, sometimes in isolated places, were developing into a greater number of political, economic and ritual centres, located within and accessible to the countryside they controlled, with the potential for developing consistent regional identities. Nevertheless, as said, the next chapter, which tells this story, also shows how the regional focus of such developments was interrupted by the standardizations of empire, which they also permitted.

3

. . . .

Mediaeval India

REGIONALISM

Regional states characterized the mediaeval period in India. We
encountered aspects of their history in Chapter 2, and it will be
useful to recall the situation around the year 1000. In the south the
Cholas, ruling from Thanjavur (Tanjore) between about 900 and
1300, vied with the second dynasty of Chalukyas that dominated
the west and central Deccan between about 973 and 1189. Much of
north India was ruled by other competing dynasties, the Pratiharas,
important in Rajasthan from the eighth century, and the Palas who
controlled Bihar and Bengal from the same period, until overtaken
by the less-successful Senas in the eleventh century.

Once again there were three dynamic influences on these states:
rivalry, fragmentation and invasion. Some of the rivalries have just
been mentioned; later, other dynasties too aspired to wider power.
In the Deccan, between the twelfth and fourteenth centuries, the
Chalukyas were replaced by some of their former tributaries, namely
the Yadavas (clans who supposedly traced their descent from
Krishna) in the north and west, and the Hoysalas (originally hill
chieftains near Mysore) in the south. The Hoysalas had also gained
power during the thirteenth century at the expense of the declining
Cholas, along with more local chiefs and states. After 1336, in place
of the Hoysalas and Kakatiyas, the empire of Vijayanagara developed,
centred on a city of that name in what is now Karnataka. It dominated southern India, combating many local rivals, including new
Muslim states in the northern Deccan.

The fragmentation was either of long standing, or was caused by
the weakening of larger, already decentralized regimes. Many smaller

Box 4   States and empires of mediaeval India

North-western

North and north-eastern

Rajputs (9th c.–)

Bengal: Palas (760–1142)

Senas (11th c.)

GHAZNAVIDS (1021–1186)
Mahmud of Ghazni *c*.1000

GHURIDS
Muhammad of Ghuri (1192–1206)

Qutb-ud-din Aibak (1206–11)

DELHI SULTANS
Iltutmish (1211–36)
Raziyya (1236–65)
Balban (1265–90)

KHALJIS
Ala-ud-din (1296–1316)

Orissa: Gajapatis

TUGHLAQS
Ghiyas-ud-din Tughlaq (1320–5)
Muhammad bin Tughlaq (1325–51)
Firuz Shah (1357–86)

———————————— Sayyids (1398–1451) ————————————

LODIS (1451–1526)
Ibrahim (1517–26)

———————————— Mughals: Babur (1526–30) ————————————

Central and southern

Chalukyas (973–1189)   CHOLAS (907–1300)

Yadavas (12th–14th c.)   *Andhra*: Kakatiyas (12th c.)

Hoysalas (12th–14th c.)

BAHMANIS (14th–16th c.)

Sultanates:

Ahmadnagar — Bijapur — Berar — Bidar — Golconda

VIJAYANAGARA (1336 to late 17th c.)
Sangamas (1336–14)
Tuluvas (1505–50)
Aravidis (1550–86)

Kerala: Cheras   *Madurai*: Pandyans

Note: The position of each heading roughly corresponds with the territories (left to right, west to east).

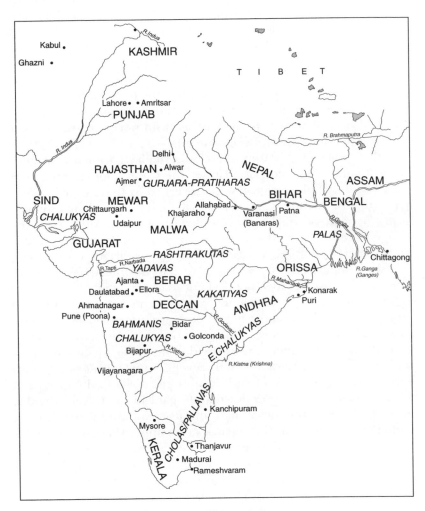

Map 2 Mediaeval India

realms operated at the fringes of the greater powers. In Kerala the Cheras kept hold of a distinct kingdom, subject to some Arab, Christian and Jewish influence, while in the far south-east the Pandyans sustained a similar semi-independence around Madurai. Various clans of Rajputs became powerful in the north-west from the ninth century, campaigning against each other particularly vigorously in the eleventh and twelfth centuries. Other smaller kingdoms arose in the north too, for example in Kashmir, Nepal, Assam and Orissa. Other examples were of states newly separated from broader systems. In the east, present-day Andhra was ruled by the Kakatiyas from the late twelfth century; they secured independence from the Chalukyas who had been defeated by the Cholas (who were themselves then too weak to reimpose a central control).

Within states at this time there was similarly evidence of both fragmentation and solidarity. Under the Cholas, for example, the villages, though hierarchical, were governed by the tax-paying residents (that is, excluding agricultural labourers) through an assembly or *ur*, for some of which very complex constitutions survive. (If the village were Brahman the assembly was a *sabha*; if a trading centre it was a merchant guild or *nagaram*.) Groups of villages were autonomously combined into *periyanadu* (or, if Brahman, *brahmadeya*), representing co-operative political and economic units.

Nevertheless, by establishing regular lines of authority and reporting, the Cholas at the height of their power (say, 985 to 1070) established a central bureaucratic control, reducing the power of local chiefs or assemblies. They divided the territory into administrative districts (*mandalam*) and revenue units (*valanadu*), with appointed state officials at each level, right down to the groups of villages. Land taxes (*kadamai*), mainly paid in kind, were divided into village dues (the lower share or *kilvaram*) and proportions set aside for particular external agencies (the upper share or *melvaram*). State taxes were thus separated, at the harvest, from village, community or temple dues. In the core areas of the kingdom, the tax-rates were determined by a land-revenue department which tried to standardize rates according to land area and output. Though some collections were still made through the lineages which dominated the irrigated river valleys, or through the *nattar* (assembly of *nadu* leaders) which managed the dry lands, it seems that much of the state's income-collection was in the hands of its own officials. An alternation of strong centres and strong peripheries was typical of the age.

The third factor, invasions, became significant again from around 1000, when Punjab, Sind and the north Indian plain were once more attacked from the west, this time by the mobile Afghan armies of the Turk, Mahmud of Ghazni. He and his immediate successors (after his death in 1030) established a Ghaznavid principality in the Punjab. It survived between 1021 and the arrival of the Ghurids in 1186; Muhammad of Ghuri was another Afghan Turk invader. He established a much wider control in north India. The Rajputs were unable to resist him, following his defeat in 1192 of Prithviraja III, king of the Chauhans, a Rajput clan based south-east of Delhi. Before his assassination in 1206, Muhammad set up a state relying upon both Turkish and Afghan nobles, a division that continued to plague his successors, Qutb-ud-din Aibak, of the so-called Slave Dynasty, and Iltutmish, the first of the Delhi sultans (r. 1211–36). Thereafter a series of struggles between Afghans and Turks (a new element in Indian politics) was interposed with conquests and further invasions.

EMPIRES: THE DELHI SULTANS

The earlier mediaeval period's regionalism was interrupted by two large empires. The rise of the Delhi sultans and of Vijayanagara, by the fourteenth century, marked the start of another transition. Both began to construct more elaborate states within the limitations set by local fragmentation and external threat.

The Delhi sultans' power ranged from Punjab to Bengal. Deploying cavalry, they plundered the lands to the south, and succeeded from time to time in giving effect to imperial ambitions in the Deccan; but their dominion was always fragile. Iltutmish imposed his authority over his factious nobles and generals in order to campaign against the resurgent Rajputs; but he was unable to prevent the Mongol attacks which began in the Punjab in 1229. He was succeeded by his daughter, Raziyya, who was murdered in 1265. Her successor, Balban, consolidated Turkish power once again, although (or perhaps because) cut off from Afghanistan by the Mongols. In 1290, Balban was succeeded by leaders of one of the Turkish factions, the Khaljis, the greatest of whom, Ala-ud-din, first campaigned successfully against the Yadavas in the Deccan, and then took the throne in 1296 after arranging for the killing of his uncle, the then sultan. Ala-ud-din died in 1316, and was followed by a quick turnover of weak rulers, including a Hindu convert, and then by a usurper,

Ghiyas-ud-din Tughlaq (r. 1320–5), who conciliated the nobles by reducing taxes. His successor, Muhammad bin Tughlaq (r. 1325–51), set about reconquering the Deccan from a new capital at Daulatabad (near Aurangabad), formerly the Yadava centre, Devagiri. His short-lived conquests prepared the way for local Muslim dynasties in the Deccan, the Bahmanis and their successors who ruled between the fourteenth and sixteenth centuries, as the great rivals of Vijayanagara.

The sultanate soon returned to Delhi, suffering attacks from Rajputs, a revolt in Bengal, and further Mongol plundering. After 1357, the new sultan, Muhammad's cousin, Firuz Shah (r. 1357–86), effectively conceded Bengal's independence, and made land and religious grants to secure the Muslim elite's support. The Tughlaqs eventually succumbed to the Sayyids, originally puppets of the Mongol, Timur (Tamerlane), who had invaded in 1398. Gujarat, Malwa and Jaunpur took the chance of breaking away. In 1451 the Sayyids were ousted in turn by a local Afghan dynasty, the Lodis, the last of whom (Ibrahim, r. 1517–26) was to be defeated and killed by yet another invader, Babur, a descendant of Timur and the first of the Mughals. Babur succeeded by making alliance with some of the Rajputs, and by taking advantage of yet more quarrels among the Afghan nobility.

The Delhi sultans introduced the new element of Afghan and Turkish infighting, and certain Islamic ideas about modes of governance and the role of the state, notably the distinction between believers and infidels (as in the *jiziya*, a head-tax, theoretically only on non-Muslims). Of the other three types of revenue permitted by the *shari'a* (Muslim law) – namely booty from conquests, special taxes for Muslim religious and charitable foundations, and a tax on agricultural production – it was the last, the land tax, that was the mainstay of the regime, rising at times to a notional half of the produce. Even had there been no other considerations, this would have implied that the Muslim states became 'indigenized', as they did from the time of Muhammad Ghuri. Sultanate administration rested upon village headmen (*khots*, *muqaddams*), superior landholders (*maliks*), and an older ruling class (*rajas*, *ranakas*) who, by the six-teenth century, became known as *chaudhuris* or *zamindars*. Instances of rebellion indicated that these figures were often able to mobilize local resistance.

On the other hand, they were none the less being incorporated into a centralized structure. All of them were responsible for collect-ing the land revenue (*kharaj*) and poll-tax (*jiziya*). In return they either received concessions on their own liabilities or were permitted to retain a proportion of the collections. Officials (*mutasharrif*) were appointed to record and supervise. The sultans' own resources, and cash pay for soldiers and officials (from the time of Ala-ud-din), came through the treasury, both from taxes and from the more direct income of the sultans' own lands (*khalisa*) – which were located in areas around Delhi, and grew as the empire expanded. Ala-ud-din introduced a greater degree of central regulation than before, forbidding additional cesses, setting the amounts of assessment, and punishing embezzlement. Muhammad bin Tughlaq, who greatly increased taxation, applied this same system from Gujarat to Bengal. He began the division of civil and military administration, distinguishing between revenue-collectors and the *amirs* and *khans* (army commanders). His successor, Firuz, faced with crisis, agreed to make a new assessment of the revenue demand (now called *jama* for the first time) and then, after four years' preparation, fixed it for the remainder of his reign; but he maintained the right for the rates to be settled by the finance department (*diwan-i-wizarat*). This was still the practice under the Lodis.

By that time, the land was divided into *sarkars* (provinces) and *parganas* (districts) – terms of Indian origin. Much earlier, under Iltutmish, the sultans had adopted a practice of making temporary land grants (*iqta*), in lieu of salary payments, to military commanders, and also to officials and supporters – including Hindu allies. In this way they paid for local governors (*muqtas*) who ran the regional administration. Similarly, tax-free grants (*amlak* – the plural of *milk*) were provided by written authority (*farman*) to Muslim religious and educational foundations and as rewards for services. Firuz Shah was forced to grant *iqtas* on more favourable terms, to accept that they might be inherited, and probably also to reduce the *khalisa*. The broader structures of sultanate administration were thus notable for their centralization and record-keeping, but also for indigenization, and for the risk that power could become fragmented.

Muhammad bin Tughlaq's experience illustrated the limits of central intervention even in the core lands. His very large increases of taxation provoked a rebellion of the local population in the Delhi area in the 1330s and 1340s. It was brutally repressed; famine ensued. In response, Muhammad introduced loans (called *sondhar*, an Indian term) – later more familiar as pre-harvest grants or *taqavi* (strength-giving) – to promote agricultural development and extend cultivation. Local *maliks* almost certainly had done likewise, but

Muhammad seems to have been the first of the sultans to try to manage this centrally. He established a ministry (*diwan*) for agricultural improvement, complete with field officers. The measures were apparently not a great success, and Muhammad's death in 1351 put an end to the experiment.

EMPIRES: VIJAYANAGARA

The second empire, that of Vijayanagara, was built out of the disruption caused in the Deccan by Muslim attacks and by the continuing rivalry among the Hindu kingdoms. The dry region of Karnataka had escaped the worst of the raids, which were directed more at the richer plains and valleys. There were three main Vijayanagara dynasties: the founding Sangamas from about 1336 to the late fifteenth century, the imperial Tuluvas (after a brief interlude) from 1505, and the Aravidis from 1550 (or effectively 1542) notionally to the late seventeenth century. Early in its expansion, Vijayanagara conquered Tamil kingdoms and their fertile plains to the east; late in the fifteenth century they drove back the Gajapatis of Orissa and gained control of all of Andhra, as well as the southern Tamil country as far as Rameshvaram. Vijayanagara's expansion to the north was thwarted by the success of the Bahmani sultans – descendants of Zafar (Bahman) Shah, a former governor for the Delhi sultanate – during the fourteenth century. Relations thereafter comprised occasional attacks or defence, plus diplomacy and, after 1538, shifting alliances among the five successors to the Bahmanis, at Ahmadnagar, Berar, Bidar, Bijapur and Golconda (Hyderabad), whom Vijayanagara sought to keep apart. An eventual coalition of Ahmadnagar, Golconda and Bijapur – all at one time allies of Vijayanagara in wars against each other – led to the sacking of the city in 1565, and the collapse of the empire.

Before coming to power, the Sangama princes, including Harihara who would become the first king of Vijayanagara, had supposedly fought for several of the regional powers who were resisting Muslim power. They served with Kampiladevaraya (a king based near the future city of Vijayanagara) in the battle in which he was killed, against Muhammad bin Tughlaq in 1327, and later joined the Hoysalas, and possibly the Kakatiyas of Warangal (Andhra). Five of the princes – so legend has it – were captured by the Tughlaq army in a battle against Warangal, taken to Delhi, converted to Islam, and then sent back to rule reconquered regions for the sultanate. Having gained power in Karnataka, however, Harihara is said to have rebelled in his turn, and had himself proclaimed a Hindu, king, and the earthly deputy of the local deity, Virupaksha. The Vijayanagara dynasties later projected themselves as successors to the Chalukyas, and also proclaimed a 'dharmic' kingdom, after a campaign of 1365–70 against the Muslims (more Tughlaq rebels) who had captured Madurai.

It is anachronistic to represent Vijayanagara's kings as protectors of 'Hinduism': they fought against many Hindus; they employed and gave protection to Muslims; their architecture is often an eclectic Hindu-Muslim mix. But, like the other regional kings whom they resembled, they did make use of Hindu symbolism. In Vijayanagara, a vast fortified city with up to 100 000 inhabitants, they built many temples, and formed ceremonial spaces, so that the capital presented itself as a celebration of the sacred character of the dynasty – especially the great platform on which the king would appear to receive homage. The king's person was re-consecrated annually in a ten-day festival (*mahanavami*) held in September/October to worship the city's tutulary goddesses. Across the region, as temples promoted urban growth, similar rituals would be repeated.

Manpower was as important as symbolism. The city contained barracks and kitchens for large numbers of retainers and soldiers. In its military expansion, Vijayanagara employed Brahmans and 'peasant warriors' (Vanniyar, Reddis and Velamas) as commanders – Brahmans being very numerous, and there being few 'true' Kshatriyas in the south – and also mercenary troops, including Portuguese, Muslims and local hill-people. To reduce the power of regional lords, the greatest of the Tuluva dynasty, Krishnadevaraya (r. 1509–29), bolstered up the position of petty military chiefs or poligars (in Tamil, *palaiyakkarar*; in Kannada, *palagararu*). These posts were often filled in the Tamil lands by Telegu warriors, who survived in the area long after Vijayanagara power had waned.

Vijayanagara had also learnt from the Kakatiyas their systems of *nayankara* or *amara* (military tenure) and *ayagar* (paid village servants). *Nayaka* was originally a Sanskrit word for a (military) leader; *amara* meant (military) command. Vijayanagara was a militarized state, but provided for its local commanders by means of lands on which the beneficiaries were entitled to specified shares of output. The *ayagar* system developed similar arrangements for village officials, and also artisans and service-providers, by means of a form of land tenure. This was new to the irrigated Tamil lands though not to the dry hinterlands where land was less valuable. In place of entitlements to shares of the harvests of the villagers, servants and officials were allotted land for their support.

The third strand of Vijayanagara's local government was the fort, placed under Brahman commanders, perhaps to counterbalance the Telegu poligars or *nayakas*. They too had designated villages for their support, as did the fourth prop, the temples. Both temples and forts also benefited from the growth of the towns which became attached to them. These were interventions by the state, unlike the *brahmadeya* villages set up as locally organized communities under the Cholas and sometimes developing into temple towns. The Vijayanagara state was helping build up new local rights, as well as securing its own power. When successful, such measures made a major contribution to order, though they did not solve all the problems of control or resources.

Such attributes make the empire seem in part a collection of feudatories, in part a confederation. Outside its heartlands, Vijayanagara's administrative capacity was limited. It depended upon alliances, and upon tribute from its conquests. When the kings placed provinces under appointed commanders, at the extreme they were merely delegating power to great magnates, with obvious dangers. The strategy produced tribute readily enough for a successful and feared military campaigner such as Krishnadevaraya. There are reports of large sums, one-third or one-half of that collected, reaching the king from provincial commanders. Among several such assignments, however, the greatest was made in 1510 with Saluva Narasingha Nayaka, called Chellappa, a Tamil Brahman general who was set up to govern most of the Tamil lowlands, with his own huge army, revenue-collectors, and religious patronage. In 1531 Chellappa rebelled against Krishnadevaraya's brother and successor, Achyutadevaraya, in alliance with other Tamil magnates, and thus threatened to cut off Vijayanagara from the riches of the Tamil river valleys. His successor, though a kinsman of Achyutadevaraya, rebelled in turn in 1543. Earlier a general sent by Krishnadevaraya to subdue the Madurai area had proclaimed himself its ruler. He was replaced by his own son, who remained loyal until 1565, when he too set up an independent kingdom.

Such provincial chiefs created by the kings (as most of the greater ones were, at the expense of existing local powers) were vital to its extended control, but also its greatest weakness. (The same was true of the Bahmani sultans, who also delegated to provincial chiefs.)

Rebellion repeatedly threatened the Vijayanagara dynasties, and the state's resources. Similarly, alliances with successful generals, sometimes reinforced by marriage ties, also helped secure Vijayanagara power, but equally built up potential rivals. The greatest rival of the Tuluvas in the sixteenth century was Aliya Rama Raja, Krishnadevaraya's son-in-law (*aliya*), a successful general of the Aravidu family who was pretender to the throne in 1529, and regent, effectively king, from 1542 to 1550, when he seized the throne in his own name. He ruled until his death in battle in 1565. Rama Raja himself strengthened the autonomy of regions, placing them under his sons and maintaining unity through kingly rituals and family loyalty.

The empire collected more land tax than its predecessors, helped by a growing monetization of the economy and an expansion of agricultural production through investment by chiefs and temples. Its core region was large and productive of cotton and livestock. But, with its low rainfall and dependence on tank irrigation, there were limits to its capacity to increase agricultural output. Moreover, the decentralized political and administrative structure restricted the proportion of revenue that reached the centre. Vijayanagara needed the tribute from the richer lands to the east.

There was another source of income. Control of the western seaboard gave Vijayanagara access to the growing Arabian sea-trade, sponsored by Islamic power, in pepper, textiles, sandalwood and other Indian produce. Customs and commercial dues were collected at ports and in the cities. Vijayanagara itself was noted for its merchant houses and warehouses. Important though this income was, however, there were limits to it also. Richer merchants had wide connections, and often could move their centre of operations at will. Many of the traders were organized into corporations (*nagara* and *settikara*) which became strong by dominating the trade in particular commodities. Artisans too frequently were organized into co-operative groups when producing for distant markets. The state had to moderate its demands, and seek the support rather than the opposition of these interests as they gained in wealth.

STATECRAFT

Four main kinds of state are referred to in the historical debates. Arranged in descending order of centralization, they are unitary-bureaucratic, military-patrimonial, feudal, and segmentary. Arranged historically, and taking centralization as the marker of modernity, the unitary-bureaucratic is sometimes said to have declined into the feudal or segmentary, and then developed towards the military-patrimonial under the Delhi sultans and Vijayanagara.

The unitary-bureaucratic state had a consolidated territory directly controlled by state officials, loyal to a ruler who in some way embodied the kingdom. In so far as such states existed in early and mediaeval India, they should be distinguished from the 'modern' state on largely technological grounds. The early state's resources did not yet allow its institutions and structures to be systematic and comprehensive in their knowledge or power. The military-patrimonial state also depended on personal loyalty to a dynasty, but achieved a high degree of military and bureaucratic control over vital functions and groups, and over a core territory, while relying otherwise on looser or indirect authority.

The feudal state had its unity sustained by hereditary loyalities and obligations, but qualified by a hierarchy of intermediaries. On the whole the centre did not penetrate to the base. Key features were the permanent alienation of land, implying a weakness in the centre, and the serfdom (the lack of general rights) of the bulk of the people who were dependent upon their lords. This feudalism is supposed by some, since the pioneering work of R. S. Sharma and others, to have been characteristic of mediaeval Indian states, evidenced by the increasing use of land grants to reward intermediaries rather than of money to pay officials. (Contrary arguments that such grants imply state power or that India's fertility allowed a free peasantry seem unconvincing, given the prevalence of hereditary chiefs and agrarian slavery.)

The segmentary state is supposed to have comprised levels of authority arranged in a pyramid, and unified mainly by ritual and ideology. Its main characteristic was the replication of independent institutions and powers at different levels, each entity being a 'little kingdom' with its own bureaucracy and rules, and not a unit constituted by a greater authority. The segmentary state did not differ absolutely from the feudal but did so rather in the way that modern federal constitutions differ from one another, in terms of residual powers. The feudal state, in the Indian usage, tends to be seen as having originated the structure, even when it had to incorporate pre-existing chieftains, whereas the segmentary state was multi-centred and constituted by its parts. At its base were differentiated but co-operative peasant producers and property-holders organized into local corporations.

Though much ink has been spilt in trying to characterize particular states and periods within one or other of these categories, it seems better to consider them as ideal types, sets of characteristics that were to be found to varying degrees in the states of the time. Certainly, it is hard to trace an even development in state-types associated with one period or another (even assuming such periodization to be valid) – that is, the early state as unitary-bureaucratic, the mediaeval as feudal or segmentary, and the early-modern as military-patrimonial. States might almost be seen as going through the stages repeatedly, according to their own prescription, as they strengthened and declined. Regional differences can always be found, and also varying combinations of central and decentralized institutions at any one time. Eventually, of course, there *was* a development of modern states.

The features that can be identified in most of the political systems over many centuries, borrowing in turn from each of the models, include ritual and ideologies of kingship, hereditary land- and office-holding, local autonomy, and centralized revenue-collecting and military capacity. We shall consider these further.

KINGS AND SULTANS

Kinship – that is, dynasty – continued to matter for kings (as for joint-family households), though of course there were palace coups, insurrections, and, on occasion, royal election or appointment which also often implied treachery. Harshavardhana had been invited to Kanauj by a council of nobles, though his accession probably resulted from intrigue. Sultanate succession, frequently called for by violence, also depended on intrigue among the nobles. Given the importance of its large army, it is unsurprising that the changing Vijayanagara dynasties marked the success of great generals, from chiefly families, such as Saluva Narasimha who seized the throne in 1485, or Isvara Nayaka whose son Narasi was the first of the Tuluvas; the Aravidis too descended from a successful commander, father of Aliya Rama Raja. Similarly the sixth-century Maitrakas had been generals to the Guptas, and eighteenth-century Mughal commanders would often discover they had pretensions to a crown.

Nevertheless it was strong *dynasties* that succeeded in retaining power for long periods. Vijayanagara power made much use of family ties and marriage alliances. Earlier, members of the Chola royal family and court also played an important part in administration. Inscriptions at the height of Chola power included detailed preambles recording the diplomatic events of the king's reign. The importance of dynasties led to some elaborations of the ideas about kingship and its legitimation. Superior kings were regarded as 'anointed' and took elevated titles. Subordinate chiefs were usually the heads of dominant local clans or castes (both military and agricultural), but they often assumed titles that recognized an obligation of loyalty to the king, and the associated royal claims over resources. In the later mediaeval period, kings were often semi-deified. They became the exemplification of their kingdom's tutelary gods, usually Shiva. They marked this role by large donations to religious foundations, and the building of monumental temples. These included the Rajarajeshwara temple in Thanjavur and the Kandariya Mahadeva temple in Khajaraho (in the eleventh century), the Jagannatha temple in Puri (twelfth century) and the Surya temple at Konarak (thirteenth century). Vijayanagara's royal ritual followed and extended this pattern, though interestingly for what it suggests of ideas in flux, one of Krishnadevaraya's titles (assumed in 1510) meant 'Hindu sultan', while his coronation name identified him as an incarnation of Krishna.

The notion of the virtuous king, which we saw with Ashoka, also continued to be advocated. Jain precepts provide a good example; they were particularly influential between about the eighth and twelfth centuries, especially in the Deccan. An extreme formulation was that of Hemachandra (r. 1089–1173) who urged complete *ahimsa* (non-violence), which the king was to command in his subjects; but he was also to influence them by showing respect for their property, redeeming their debts, and so on. Hemachandra was sponsored by the Hindu Chalukya king, Jayasimha (r. 1094–1143), and by his successor, Kumarapala (r. 1143–73), who converted to Jainism. Other Jain texts also expected the king to be frugal and honourable, and to set such an example as would change people's conduct. The king, said one (by Somadeva), 'is the maker of his times'.[1]

The duties of the king were important to Muslims too, and began to be enunciated in India only during the sultanate period. The first Muslim incursions into India, less than a hundred years after the death of the Prophet, occurred when his followers were still divided into rather inchoate sects. They brought little influence. (Rather, through these contacts, Indian astronomy and mathematics – numerical and decimal systems – were translated into the Arab world.) The much later Ghurid invaders were mountain chieftains and Turkish adventurers. It is doubtful that they were familiar with the finer points of Islamic thought, or had a philosophy of government appropriate for the empire their successors were to build in India. Scholars, the *ulama*, were not important in India until after the Mongol invasions of Iran and Iraq, when many sought refuge in Delhi.

The Delhi sultans made use of these immigrants as *qazis* (religious judges), to enforce the *shari'a*, and support their rule. The key to Islamic virtue was obedience to the laws of Allah, a religious duty which applied as well to sultans as to subjects. Kings had to display and also to enforce the piety required by belief in the one God and acceptance of Muhammad as his last Prophet, as expressed in the *hajj* (pilgrimage to Mecca) and by the giving of alms (*zakat*) and religious endowments. In turn they could also rely on Islamic law. Muslims looked for guidance on conduct (*hidayah*) to the Qur'an and the *hadith*, interpretative traditions based on the *sunna*, or 'model behaviour' of the Prophet, which had become accepted as authoritative from the ninth century. For Shi'a, these authorities were supplemented by that of an infallible guide, in each generation, the Imam.

Some authorities denied the legitimacy of the Delhi sultans, and most sought to apply some limits to their authority over their Muslim subjects, but on the whole the Islamic legal doctrines and religious obligations were employed by Muslim rulers in India to attach Muslims to their rule, which was represented as a partnership between divine law (and its representatives) and regal authority. At the same time the sultans evolved ideas and pragmatic policies which meant that they could mostly also come to terms with Hindus, treating them as tolerated unbelievers (*zimmis*). The later scholars had brought in the great Sunni schools of Islamic jurisprudence (named after their founders in the eighth and ninth centuries), especially the Hanafite. They also began the introduction of Persian epic poetry and a host of practical manuals of instruction, from war to gardening. About the same time Persian history-writing (*tarikh*) was imported – a tradition of biography, starting with the Prophet, to edify the reader and also (when applied to kings) to instruct the sovereign. The greatest of these writers in the sultanate period was Zia ud-din Barni, the Sunni companion of Muhammad bin Tughlaq, writer on the theory of government, and chronicler (*c.*1357) of the sultans from Balban to Firuz Shah.

LORDS, OFFICIALS AND LOCALITIES

In addition to ideologies supportive of dynasties or kingship, there were hereditary and hierarchical structures of rule ('feudal', by analogy with mediaeval Europe) that were crucial to the Indian regional states, especially from about 800 to 1200. Administration, revenue collection, and (after about 1000) military service, all relied upon hereditary landholders as well as or instead of cash-paid officials or subordinates. These lords professed a personal allegiance to the king, who surrounded himself with royal symbols, ceremonies and titles designed to encourage such support. In turn the lords commonly commanded similar loyalty from smaller lords arranged in a hierarchy. Brahmans, and (later) *ulama*, like the mediaeval Christian church, both served these local kings and lords, and maintained wider connections as scholars and theologians. There are clearly similarities between these 'feudal' regimes and some aspects of the more centralized power of the Delhi sultans and Vijayanagara.

The lords, with some exceptions (including the Pala, Sena and Chola trade with south-east Asia), drew their somewhat limited wealth largely from cultivation that was conducted by their Shudra dependants. At all levels land rights tended to become ever more entrenched through laws which limited individual rights and preserved communal or family shares, notably for sons who were guaranteed inheritance of joint property either on the death of their father (*dayabhaga*) or during his lifetime (*mitakshara*). Agricultural surplus was spent upon warfare, and on local consumption designed to impress – on palaces, temples and servants. Merchants declined in influence, as trade declined and the coinage was debased (though revenue continued to be collected in cash in some places, for example Sena Bengal). The revival of production and trade from the fourteenth century did not remove all of these regional and agrarian features.

Localities, even within strong states, alternatively could show elements of 'segmentary' independence. Such elements were indicated most clearly by the example of the Cholas, especially in the early and later stages of the kingdom. The Tamilian localities were more autonomous than those in the north. Most states had to work through institutions that could be harnessed either for central control or for local independence. A grant of tax-free land to a temple, for example, could increase the allies and enhance the standing of the king; but equally it could be a device to exclude a weak royal authority from meddling in local interests. Similar arguments could be applied to the *inams* granted to mosques by the Delhi sultans, or to Vijayanagara's land grants to *nayakas*, Brahman fort-commanders and temples.

On the other hand, all successful states had local bureaucracy and central authority. Most managed a close control over core areas – and such centre–periphery distinctions applied even when the states were strong. States became more powerful when they were able to specify rather than react to local rights and categories. By that token, Chola administration was more centralized than most, at its height. Local institutions could then become instruments of central patronage. One stage was the issuance of written orders, for example in granting tax-free privileges as was often done for temple lands. Whether merely recognizing or newly creating their local beneficiaries, such orders also advanced royal claims. The granting of honorific titles, too, sometimes was merely a gloss on existing local power; at other times it implied the appointment of a state functionary; but at all times it recognized a royal role. Orders, grants and titles usually involved some tactical acquiescence on both sides.

An ambivalence is to be seen particularly in regard to temples in south India. They supported state power, but also were closely implicated in their localities, through land-ownership, taxation and donations, and because temple-towns had often grown out of *brahmadeya* (Brahman villages). They provided local as well as regional sites of ritual, learning and education. They were major centres of local consumption and employment (not least for building and maintenance, as temples became ever more elaborate). Southern Brahmans were notably aloof, excluding Shudras from the temples and thus encouraging populist cults, but paradoxically they were also active in commerce and land-owning. Like the military grant-holders, the religious foundations were caught between prebendial-ism, deriving their land and power from the state, and independence, deriving their land and power from local grants or their own prestige and wealth.

The later empires required superior statecraft to succeed, but, as suggested, they too were mixed in character. Vijayanagara achieved a central system of military mobilization and control, directed its power to the localities through temples and associated towns, and raised additional revenue through duties on an expanding trade. On the other hand it did not fully suppress or incorporate local chiefs, nor did it control its own subordinates, large and small, who had to be rewarded through land rather than cash salaries. The Delhi sultans attempted a more centralized form of administration, notably in the revenue reforms of Ala-ud-din. But this power depended upon dynastic loyalties and the support of factions of nobles; these, and hence 'feudal' tendencies, were kept in check only while the sultan commanded respect and loyalty (through personal ties, military success and redistributions of booty), and so long as the *muqti*, or holders of land grants (*iqta*), could be transferred at will. These elements of the polity make it still 'mediaeval' in the sense in which the word is being applied here. They draw attention on the one hand to the need for regional or imperial ideologies, and on another to the shortcomings of the states' economic resources, subjects which the remainder of this chapter will discuss.

CULTURE AND BELIEF

In this period, regional characteristics were encouraged by political localization. Dynastic histories and royal biographies began to be written. Local languages were developing alongside the continued importance of scholarly Sanskrit. Several were developing out of earlier vernaculars or Prakrits, notably Marathi with Yadava patronage, or Bengali under the Palas and Senas. In the south too, Tamil, Kannada (around Mysore) and later Telegu (in Andhra) grew in importance, also with political backing. Often these languages were linked not only with regional kingdoms but with religions or popular cults.

As politics were becoming localized, religious developments were also encouraging regionalism. Creeds were or became divisive when focused on particular communities. Thus Jainism became associated mainly with regions such as Rajasthan, Gujarat and Mysore, and with merchants. Zoroastrianism, too, which had had some indirect influence in India since the third century BCE, was observed only by the Parsis (that is, Persians), a community of western India, originally refugees from Arab attacks in the early eighth century (CE). The religious 'mainstream' too became exceedingly fragmented.

While Jainism lost its general importance, and Buddhism virtually disappeared, various non-conformist and protest cults arose among Hindus – those devoted to the many mother goddesses, or a more playful, pastoral and erotic Krishna, or newly popular deities such as the elephant-headed Ganesh. There were Shaivite Lingayats who worshipped the *lingam* and questioned Vedic and Brahmanical authority. From the eighth century several mystical Tantric sects gained in importance. Tantra, usually practised in secret, involved the worship of *shakti* and the mother image, and mystical diagrams and rituals, some involving sexual acts. These cults professed to observe no bar of caste, and to be open to women as well as men.

On the other side of the coin, there were common trends in heterodox religion, in addition to regionalism and sectarianism. The radical cults tended to share an egalitarian and devotional emphasis, and hence to be directed against Brahman conventions, which preferred ritual hierarchy and detachment. Among the orthodox, there were attempts at reconciliation. The scholar Ramanuja (supposedly 1017–1137), who converted the Yadava king Vishnuvardhana from Jainism to Vaishnavism, fostered a kind of counter-reformation, against popular and 'protestant' reactions, by favouring temple-entry for Shudras, and promoting religious devotion above the discipline and self-knowledge advocated by Shankara. His influence provided a reply to the regionalism and community divisions of the age. Partly through trade, and because later mediaeval government was stabilized for some periods over large areas, generalizing influences were able to work. It helped that local deities could be readily equated with the Hindu pantheon, and adopted when necessary by 'outsiders' – Brahmans or rulers. Thus Vijayanagara kings and commanders sponsored Tamil gods in the Tamil lands they conquered.

The later developments once again had both local and general aspects, with the general always falling short of achieving hegemony. From the eleventh century, Shi'a *sufi* teachings spread from Sind and Punjab across north and central India. Sufi orders gained in influence, the Chisti active in north India, the Suhrawardi in Sind and the Firdansi in Bihar. They brought teachings designed to express the experience and rapturous love of god, culminating in reverence for saints and for the holy places associated with them, just like the *bhakti* traditions of Hinduism. Indeed, there were concerns among orthodox scholars of Islam that Sufis were too accommodating to Hindu belief and practices. Generally, Islam wore both inclusive and iconoclastic faces.

With Muslim influence, a host of Indic beliefs began to be identified as indigenous, distinct and different, as 'Hindu'. Some Brahmans sought stricter observation of the sacred rules, including caste. The temples kept their vital task of preserving and developing Hindu

ideas, not least because of their growing roles in land-owning, trade
and moneylending. As already discussed, the later mediaeval
period was notable for the growth of temples and their associated
towns. They became major administrative and pilgrimage centres.
They benefited from political patronage, large-scale gifts and tax-free
lands, often emerging as entrepreneurial land-owners, employing
agents, scribes, accountants and bankers as well as priests and
temple-servants. Temples recorded and displayed moral precepts,
religious epics and regional history, through their sculpture, teaching, scholarship, pageants and ritual. The larger temples attracted
devotees from long distances, especially for great festivals. The
establishment of sacred sites and the shared sense of their significance were important indicators of religious unity as well as of
distinctive regional identities.

Vaishnava reformers continued to be important, especially in north
India – Chaitanya (1486–1533) being most influential in Bengal –
and typically they joined in the teaching against caste restrictions
and in favour of personal devotion. From the fourteenth century
several of the mystical and protestant elements were recombined in
the Bhakti or devotional movements. Both of the most influential
thinkers associated with these, Kabir (1440–1518) and Nanak
(1469–1539), nevertheless ultimately founded yet more separate
sects or religions (the Kabirpanthis and Sikhism).

PRODUCTION AND SOCIETY

As noticed in Chapter 2, there seems to have been a decline in trade
after the fall of the Gupta empire. Certainly, fewer coins were
minted, and there is less evidence of trade guilds. The southern maritime trade apparently fell away from the twelfth century. We need
to be cautious, however, about assuming a loss of productive skills
or even of trading activity from mere lack of evidence. The tendency
is always to underestimate the sophistication of cultures that are
different, and it was tainted historiographies that called the early
mediaeval era the 'dark ages'. Throughout the period, some long-
distance trade persisted. Moreover, vast temple-building and considerable irrigation works show that very large resources were
sometimes able to be marshalled by states and elites. As noted earlier, the fact that fewer new coins were produced does not tell us
necessarily that there was a comparable reduction of the number in

circulation. Salt was produced and distributed, as was iron. By the sultanate period Indian swords were celebrated, and being exported. Gold, silver and horses were significant imports. It is probably true to say that no age, from palaeolithic times onwards, has been without specialist production and trade. 'Primitive' and 'backward' economies are for ever being shown to have exchanged goods at 'surprising' distances. What change over time are modes of production, ease and speed of communications, and levels of prosperity – and these changes too are often hard to identify for more distant periods.

Part of the argument about Indian feudalism, for example, concerns the relations of production, the suggestion that, in a time of economic hardship, struggles between priests and warriors, and political fragmentation, the landholders and cultivators *became* more differentiated. The appearance of a more complex terminology is held to imply the subjugation of peasant cultivators of many kinds, under intermediaries or overlords. In ancient times, so this argument goes, landholders each had their own land, under the king, and state officials or temples extracted surplus from them as taxes or gifts. Now local lords were claiming rights over all land and all of its produce, either exclusively or jointly with the cultivators. They often also acquired seigneurial rights – to punish wrong-doers, to enforce work, and to exclude external scrutiny. The refusal of orthodox Brahmans to hold the plough, or of upper castes to transplant rice, is sometimes said to be traceable to this social division of labour.

Yet the situation is too complex to be reduced to labels. In the Chola domains, for example, landholdings were known as shares (*pangu*), and agriculture was subject to communal decisions on water, labour-use and even cropping. On the other hand, land-control or 'overseeing' (*kani*, from Tamil *kan*, to see) was the equivalent of private ownership for individuals or corporations such as temples, though subject to joint-family and community obligations. *Kani* implied a duty to pay the land tax, and could be inherited, sublet or alienated – though there is little evidence of a land market, and rights to cultivate or to share in output could persist after transfer.

An even development from a tribal or peasant-proprietary into a feudal economy seems unlikely, not least because of the immense variety of environmental conditions in India. Rice was much more labour-intensive than wheat, but everywhere seasonal variations made for uneven labour demand over the agricultural year. Together these factors provided strong incentives for the command of labour. Multiple and not only feudal means were adopted. Nowhere did society comprise only lords, overseers and serfs, for the agrarian workers included slaves and forced and hired labourers. On the other hand we mostly do not know whether or not the cultivators enjoyed any autonomy of agrarian decision-making, or had control over the reproduction of agriculture. We know that lords or communities managed much of the artificial irrigation. But we often cannot be sure who decided which crops to grow, or who held the seed, and owned the bullocks and ploughs.

Some long-term characteristics of regions and their peoples seem to have had ecological origins. There were differences in particular between wet, semi-dry and arid zones. In the wet areas, the predictable water-supply and pattern of cultivation, the production of surplus, and the labour-intensity of artifical irrigation and rice cultivation, encouraged high population densities and a hierarchical society. In the southern river basins, for example, one found *kaniyatchiyars* (land-holders), *kudimakkals* (cultivators) and *paraiyas* (bonded labourers). Managing skills were at a premium. In the semi-dry areas, where wells and tanks, and responsiveness to seasonal conditions, were needed to raise millets and livestock, there was less room for hierarchy. Cultivating aptitude was most valued. In the arid zones, where agriculture and stock-rearing were unable to sustain large populations, and anyway vulnerable, widely scattered settlements and clan-like social structures were the norm. There was most call for mobility and military prowess. In north India this sequence represented a transition from east to west. In south India it marked the differences between river lands of the east (plus the thin coastal strip on the west) and the progressively drier central hinterlands. This is not to imply an ecological determinism; other social and political experiences and ideas also need to be added to explain varied local outcomes.

Though trade and production have sometimes been pictured as persisting in India more or less despite government, in fact the fortunes of states were the most important of these variables. Successful regional powers mostly promoted successful regional economies. The growth of the empires of the north and south from the thirteenth century was accompanied by economic growth. In the time of the Delhi sultans, textile production and weaving were considerable industries. Expensive items of cloth and carpet were produced in large workshops (*karkhanas*), in addition to simpler output from households and villagers. Production may have bene-fited from technological innovation around this time. At some stage, cotton came to be extracted using the carding-bow (*kaman*) rather than by hand-beating with a stick (called *mushta*); and the spinning-wheel (*charkha*) – the earliest reference is from 1350 – replaced the hand-spindle. Little is known about looms, but treadles may have been in use at this time. There was also much silk production, by now based on the mulberry silkworm (imported from China). A change noticeable from the fourteenth century was the availability of paper, another Chinese contribution, which, though remaining expensive, led to an expanded profession of copyists.

Between the fourteenth and sixteenth centuries there is also evidence of rural prosperity. Prices rose, especially for irrigated crops such as sugar and paddy, for most of the period between the thirteenth and sixteenth centuries. In the Doab region (between the Jumna and Ganga rivers), the once-extensive forest lands were cleared and an expansion of cultivation occurred, organized by villagers and menial workers, producing two crops a year, with some double-cropping. The cultivators mainly used wells, but there were also state-built irrigation canals, especially under Firuz Shah. The geared Persian wheel (though still made of wood, with leather or pottery buckets) was certainly in use before the sixteenth century. In Vijayanagara territories, both temples and local chiefs operated as rural entrepreneurs, and there were special tenures to encourage development, for example through tank construction, by ensuring shares in future output for investors, overlords, artisans and workers.

The increased incomes were not universally shared, however. Cultivators were liable to flee excessive taxation, given the availability of land, but most were probably dissuaded from doing so by the cost of land reclamation and (under the sultans) by laws requiring absconders to be sent back to their *maliks* (landlords) in order to protect the land-revenue collections. Under the earlier sultans, too, slaves, seized in military raids or in internal campaigns against refractory villagers, were exported in significant numbers – tens of thousands also being in the employ of the sultans themselves. (Numbers of slaves began to decline after the fourteenth century, possibly due to growing supplies of cheap free labour.)

Once again rulers maintained or built roads and resting-places. Vijayanagara territories were noted for their good roads, though caravans of pack oxen continued to be used for long journeys rather than carts. The sultans employed horse relays for the ready despatch of news, and there were also private postal arrangements. From the thirteenth century, many towns appeared or grew, implying the sale of food and other produce by merchants. The cash payment of revenue under the sultans (except in the early sixteenth century) affected at least that proportion of the demand which reached the treasury, and meant that crops were forced on to the market. The availability of money also assisted trade. From the mid-thirteenth century, the sultans struck gold and silver coins from the very considerable hoards gained in plunder. There was a standardization of value, and in the ratio between silver and gold. Copper coins and cowries were used in smaller transactions.

Even in the fourteenth century, however, despite a much increased level of monetization, money shortages were also restricting trade. At least some of the gold and silver coins were commemorative and not intended as a trading currency. Muhammad bin Tughlaq issued a token currency of brass and silver, copying the idea from Chinese silk or paper notes of credit. His problems were caused by his military expenses, and a shortage of precious metals, the latter being due to exports of specie to west Asia instead of the more usual imports. The situation was worsened by steep price inflation between the 1320s and 1360s, and also by the loss of Bengal (for some reason, an important importer of silver). Conversely, a sixteenth-century fall in prices led Sultan Ibrahim to order that revenue be collected in kind, which reduced the *cash* incomes of the treasury and of the collecting officials as they took their share. No gold and silver coins seem to have been minted by the Lodis.

A contraction of cities from the mid-sixteenth century suggests a similar decline in the Vijayanagara dominions. Earlier, a curious feature of the obvious involvement of Vijayanagara in international trade had been the dominance of foreign merchants, even for such vital military supplies as horses, muskets and cannon. Local production was inadequate in quality or quantity, and Indian merchants played little part in securing imports, which were in the hands of Arab or other Muslim traders and the Portuguese. Perhaps this was because the empire was based so far inland; and yet even the east coast's trade, despite Pallava and Chola example, increasingly was in the hands of Muslims from the thirteenth century, and later controlled by Europeans.

REGION VERSUS EMPIRE

For nearly a thousand years, India is supposed to have been wracked by conflicting petty kingdoms, and then yoked to impressive military empires which however did not have the economic or bureaucratic resources to prevent further fragmentation. Empires seem often to be regarded as preferable and superior to regional states. But, to return to the point reached at the end of Chapter 2, perhaps the history should be described not as failed empire but as thwarted regionalism – that is, the most interesting feature was not imperial weakness, but the regional discontinuity caused by empires.

Arguably the most significant development of the mediaeval period was the growth of regional identities. After the empires waned, regional political units re-emerged to match some of the local cultures which had continued to evolve. Building on Pala and Sena precedent, Bengal briefly threw off the dominance of the sultans, before succumbing again to the Mughals and the British. Tamil power, on bases established by the Pallavas, Cholas and Pandyans, appeared whenever Vijayanagara's power collapsed – again, until Muslim and British rulers intervened. Telegu and Rajput identities also reasserted themselves politically from time to time, but often only temporarily or in subordinate roles.

The fragility of such regional states is apparent at the level of cities as well. Of course many Indian towns do have continuous or at least repeated occupation. Delhi is the most obvious example as the capital of many different regimes (though seldom on quite the same site), and there are many others – religious centres, places with geographical advantages, and so on. But apart from Delhi not many ancient cities survive as political capitals to the present day, just as only a selection of the early religious centres have retained their importance. Urban disruptions were frequent.

In Europe, for whatever reason – accidents of geography (presumably the Mediterranean and Atlantic seaboards), or kings and churches, or clerks and merchants – regional state formations and (a different point) 'national' cultures seem to have focused at remarkably early times on particular urban centres. Such features often remained more geographically diffused or more discontinuous in India. (By contrast many west and east Asian cities were very ancient, but sustained common as much as local cultures.) Typical of the Indian experience was Lahore, sacked in 1241 but not rebuilt until the fourteenth century, or Daulatabad, once almost as large as Delhi and now little more than an impressive but ruined fort in a wilderness. Most telling is the appearance and disappearance of Vijayanagara, founded in one generation, the symbol and economic focus of an empire, and then – somewhat over two hundred years later – looted, abandoned and apparently forgotten.

Over the mediaeval period, then, there seems to have been a relatively weak association of peoples with places, and also of rulers with peoples (in terms of identity). In Chola times, Tamil agriculturists colonized the drier hinterlands as far as Karnataka. From the thirteenth century under Hoysala rule – arguably an example of a failed regionalism – Kannada-speakers spread southwards from Karnataka. Similarly, Telegu-speakers had migrated into the heartland of that region, bringing irrigation technology, from the twelfth century, and later spread into Tamil Nadu. These are the kinds of pre-modern migration which mostly had ceased by the eleventh century, within western Europe.

In India from about this time more stable political and linguistic units did begin to emerge, in almost all regions; but most of them were quite soon absorbed into larger generalizing empires. Important and influential though the regional states were, therefore, few of them experienced an uninterrupted and independent existence. On the contrary, in many areas, there was a marked discontinuity of borders and regimes, caused by political rivalries and imperial expansion, much of which brought in rulers foreign to the regions. This was true of many parts of the Vijayanagara empire, but even more evident with the Delhi and Bahmani sultans and the succession of lesser Muslim rulers who dominated most of India by the sixteenth century – a starting point for the next chapter.

4

Early Modern India I: Mughals and Marathas

THE MUGHALS

By the sixteenth century, India was mainly ruled by Muslims, despite the contraction of the power of the Delhi sultans. Some of the Muslim dynasties, such as that which had governed Bengal in the first half of the fifteenth century, were of Hindu converts. Of the major regions, Hindus ruled only in Vijayanagara, and in Rajasthan where there were a few Rajput kingdoms, most notably Mewar (around Udaipur), which was newly powerful under Rana Sanga after 1509. When the Lodis capitulated, and as Indian Afghan power eventually subsided, Babur and his successors were able to annex existing Muslim-ruled states, as well as subduing Mewar and the other Rajputs.

Zahir-ud-din Muhammad Babur was the Turkish king of Kabul. He won the battle of Panipat (north-west of Delhi) in 1526, after several earlier incursions, because of the superior mobility provided by his expert cavalry and his army's greater firepower. (Gunpowder was not used in warfare in India before the fifteenth century, and, apart from the Portuguese, Babur was the first to deploy firearms and cannon on a regular basis.) Rana Sanga, who had been ready to challenge the Lodis and had agreed to ally himself with Babur, did not launch an attack from the south as planned, but he was not needed. Babur took over the Lodi capital, Agra, and seized and shared out its treasure as booty. In 1527 he shattered the combined power of Mewar and other Rajputs. By the time of his death in

1530, he had conquered territories as far east as Bihar, and as far south as Gwalior.

His son, Humayun (r. 1530–56), had the difficult task of consolidating this empire. He distributed provinces to his four brothers as governors; they proved to have their own ambitions. He temporarily subdued Gujarat, and turned to confront the resurgent Indian Afghan power to the east. One of the Afghan nobles, Sher Khan Sur, had fled from Panipat to his base in southern Bihar, and from there he built up the main resistance to the early Mughals. In 1537 he attacked Mahmud Shah, the Arab sultan of Bengal. Humayun went to Mahmud's aid, but was unable to prevent an Afghan victory. Various skirmishing and negotiating ensued, until Humayun himself was defeated in 1539. Sher Khan proclaimed himself king (as Sher Shah), and Humayun went into exile, first in the Punjab and Sind, and finally in Iran. He launched a long war against one of his brothers, Kamran, who had defied him and continued to rule in Kabul. Kamran was eventually defeated, and blinded to prevent further rebellion; and then, between 1554 and 1555, Humayun reconquered north India. Sher Shah had died in 1545, and had been replaced by his son, a lesser man, and then by relatives who each ruled a region.

Humayun enjoyed his success only briefly, for he died in an accident in 1556, and was succeeded by his son, Akbar, who was not yet fourteen. The Persian regent, Bairam Khan, defeated most of the remaining Sur princes within a couple of years, and brought north India firmly under Mughal control. The backing of court and harem, and Sunni objections to Shi'a influence, helped Akbar assert his own authority in 1560, at the age of seventeen. The army and government were under Akbar's direct control before the end of 1561; he then transformed the nature of the regime and established Mughal power for generations. The story told of his final accession was that he threw Adham Khan, one of his foster brothers, from a balcony, and then, having had him dragged back up, threw him down again, killing him on the second attempt. Adham had been relieved of his army command following a massacre, and later had murdered the minister whom Akbar had appointed in preference to him.

The wars continued. Akbar made every effort in these early years to assert his prerogatives against his own commanders, and had to quell several revolts by governors. The most serious was among the Uzbek nobles, who had returned to India with Himuyan. They were supported by Akbar's half-brother, Mirza (Prince) Muhammad Hakim of Kabul. Under attack there himself, he marched the bulk of his army into India. Akbar, showing his skill as a strategist and commander, moved his forces to Lahore, made Muhammad Hakim withdraw, and then turned back to defeat the Uzbeks in a surprise assault. Not long after this, Akbar launched a holy war (*jihad*) against the Rajputs, who were defying Mughal power again at Mewar and elsewhere. After a long seige, the great fort at Chittaurgarh (Chittor) was razed to the ground. Its people, those who had not died in battle or by their own hand, were slaughtered in very large numbers. After losing other battles as well, the Rajputs were forced to accept Mughal suzerainty.

Akbar turned his attention to Gujarat, which was annexed in 1572, and finally subdued the following year after a revolt by its Muslim nobles. The very next year, Mughal authority had to be reasserted in Bengal and Bihar as well. After campaigns of fluctuating fortune, the eastern region was formally annexed, by 1580, as far south as Orissa. Again, protracted local resistance by Indian Afghans and Hindu rajas ensued, plus another concerted revolt, before the region was finally pacified. In the later 1580s, Akbar went back to the north-west, eventually re-establishing his power in Afghanistan (after Muhammad Hakim had died), and annexing Kashmir, Multan and Sind. The 1590s were taken up with attempts to subdue the sultans of the Deccan, success coming only after Akbar took command himself between 1599 and 1601.

In 1605, the emperor died. He had just quelled a rebellion by his son, Salim, but was reconciled with him shortly before his death. The accession of Salim as Jahangir (r. 1605–27) was disputed by a faction supporting the claims of *his* son, Khusrau, then seventeen – whom he eventually blinded for plotting against him. Jahangir completed the subjugation of the Rajputs, by military intimidation and then by persuading Karan Singh, the heir to Mewar, to accept imperial rank. Jahangir was not the general his father had been; and much power was exercised during his reign by Nur Jahan, whom he married in 1611, and her father, Itimad-ud-daulah, who became *diwan* (chief minister). During this reign (as also later) the Ahom rulers of Assam were contained rather than conquered, but the Himalayan Rajput chiefs were controlled, the Sikhs were suppressed in the Punjab, and the Deccan campaigns were resumed. Near the end of his life, Jahangir had to put down another rebellion, by the Iranian noble, Mahabat Khan, and a host of Rajput troops.

The greatest military successes of this period were achieved, especially in the south, by one of the royal princes, the ruthless Khurram. In the 1620s he too rebelled unsuccessfully against his father, first marching his army north to a defeat near Fatehpur Sikri, but later gaining control of most of eastern India, before being finally overcome near Allahabad. He had initially allied himself with Nur Jahan, and after his defeat was reinstated as governor of the Deccan, with his two sons as hostages at the imperial court. He had by then either killed or at least benefited from the deaths of two of his brothers, including Khusrau. Shortly after Jahangir's death Khurram became emperor (in 1628) against the wishes of the queen but with the support of her brother, Azaf Khan, the *wazir* (finance minister).

Khurram, as Shah Jahan, ordered that most of his other relatives who were actual or potential rivals should also be killed. He continued the campaigns against Rajputs and other local chiefs, and in the Deccan he defeated a last Afghan revolt, under Khan Jahan Lodi. In the 1630s his forces thoroughly subdued the sultanates of Ahmadnagar, Golconda and Bijapur, annexing the first and making tributaries of the second and third. The Deccan was twice put under the control of Shah Jahan's third son, the severe and pious Aurangzib. On his second term there, Aurangzib pursued a policy of aggression, attacking Golconda in alliance with one of its most successful commanders, Muhammad Said Mir Jumla, conqueror of the Karnatak and its coast. These attacks were opposed at court by factions around Shah Jahan's eldest son, the scholarly Dara Shukoh, who engineered a peace with Golconda. Not long afterwards, however, the emperor appointed Mir Jumla as his *wazir*, and allowed him as his *jagir* (revenue-estate) the whole of the Karnatak, which was now to be seized for the Mughals. Shah Jahan authorized a second invasion of Golconda, but again called it off at the point of victory, in return for the payment of a large tribute. Aurangzib turned his attention to an invasion of Bijapur.

The emperor fell ill, in 1657, while the withdrawal from Golconda was under way, and a war of succession broke out between his four sons, his children by Mumtaz Mahal, whose early death had inspired the building of the Taj Mahal. These brothers, except for Dara who had been designated the heir, commanded the great provinces of the empire: Aurangzib in the Deccan, Muhammad Shuja in Bengal, Bihar and Orissa, and Murad Baksh in Gujarat and Malwa. During Shah Jahan's illness, Dara took control at court,

Aurangzib was busy in Bijapur, but Shuja and Murad both had themselves crowned as kings. Early in 1658 Murad and Aurangzib agreed to divide the empire between them, if successful, and marched north to confront the imperial army, and then a regrouped force under Dara. Twice Aurangzib prevailed. Dara fled into the Punjab, and the ailing Shah Jahan became Aurangzib's prisoner at Agra – and remained so until his death in 1666. Murad was soon double-crossed and incarcerated (and some years later was tried and executed). Aurangzib had himself crowned in Delhi as Alamgir or 'world-seizer'. He had chased Dara out of the Punjab, but he took refuge in Gujarat, regrouped using Murad's resources, and again marched north. Dara was finally defeated near Ajmer, and some-time later was captured and put to death, with one of his sons. Meanwhile Aurangzib had turned, with a greatly augmented army and treasury, to confront and rout Muhammad Shuja who had refused to come to terms. He was eventually pursued into Bengal and took refuge in Arakan, where he was killed by the local king.

The triumphant Aurangzib returned to his policy of aggression and expansion. He reasserted Mughal authority in Bengal by appointing, as governor, Mir Jumla, who also annexed Kuch Bihar in north Bengal, and once again temporarily subdued most of Assam. Another governor was ordered to annex Palamau, a hilly tract south of Bihar that had been troublesome since early in the reign of Shah Jahan. Aurangzib himself organized expeditions to punish risings in Afghanistan and the frontier regions in the 1670s, and put down an extended Rajput revolt that was originally sparked off by his decisions in a case of disputed succession, and then aggravated by a Rajput alliance with Aurangzib's rebellious son, Muhammad Akbar. At this time, and for the remaining years of his life, Aurangzib was also embroiled in wars in the Deccan. He had three main object-ives: to annex the Deccan sultanates, to subdue the Marathas, and to remove the threat posed by Muhammad Akbar.

Aurangzib wanted to defeat rather than accommodate Bijapur and Golconda (tributary states of the empire since 1636) because they seemed a threat to the Mughals whether they were strong or weak. Under Shah Jahan their northern limits had been set, but could not be guaranteed if they became stronger, as had Golconda. If they were weak, as was the case with Bijapur in this period, they presented a different danger, that they would no longer contain local forces. The greatest of these were the Marathas under their leader, Shivaji Bhonsle (r. 1627–80). Shivaji, descended from chiefs in the service of the sultans of Ahmadnagar and Bijapur, had carved out a kingdom in the western coastal lands, breaking away from Bijapur. From the 1650s he struck eastwards into lands now held by the Mughals. In the 1660s he faced Aurangzib's reassertion of Mughal power, and in 1665 was forced to capitulate, becoming a tributary of the empire. The following year he was a prisoner in Agra, after a protest at a ceremonial audience, but he escaped. He was pardoned in 1668, but rebelled in 1670, and began again to plunder territories of the Mughals and of Bijapur. He had himself proclaimed king in 1674. Eventually he also annexed much territory in the Karnatak, after making an alliance with Golconda against Aurangzib. His policy was continued after his death by his son, Shambhaji.

Aurangzib's son, Muhammad Akbar, had fled from Rajputana to the Maratha court. He was a possible focus for disaffection, among nobles who disagreed with Aurangzib's aggression, and among those whom he was attacking, especially Hindus. In 1681 Akbar proclaimed himself emperor, and shortly afterwards Shambhaji made an audacious raid, in overwhelming force, north into Khandesh, sacking Burhampur on the Tapti river, some 300 kilometres inland from Surat (which his father had plundered in 1664 and 1670). Aurangzib's reaction was at first defensive: he strengthened the garrisons in the Deccan, and sent his own mobile raiding parties from time to time into Maratha territories. He then embarked on the conquest of Bijapur and Golconda, defeating both between 1685 and 1687. Shambhaji was captured in 1688, without a major battle, and brought to Aurangzib, who had him tortured and put to death. Muhammad Akbar fled to Persia. The Deccan sultanates, the Maratha kingdom and Karnataka were all annexed to the empire.

The Marathas, however, were not defeated. Local chiefs, the new king (Shivaji's younger son, Rajaram), and, after his death, Rajaram's senior widow, Tarabai, all continued to harry the Mughals. There were military successes for the emperor, and attempts to reach a negotiated settlement, but Maratha raids were not contained; indeed they spread to wider regions. The administrative structures of the empire remained strong enough to allow Aurangzib, for nearly twenty years, to pour his energy and treasure into his campaigns against the Marathas.

On his death in 1707, the empire passed to one of his three surviving sons, Muazzam, who ruled as Bahadur Shah, after a battle with his brother, Azam Shah. He then faced rebellions by the

Rajputs and the Sikhs, and a war with another brother who proclaimed an independent kingdom in Bijapur. Maratha raids continued, and local rulers began to pay substantial tribute to avoid them. In 1712 Bahadur Shah died, and, after further wars of succession, was succeeded briefly by Jahandar Shah (r. 1712–13), who was in thrall to his father's powerful paymaster and viceroy, and now *wazir*, Zulfikar Khan. Jahandar was quickly replaced by his nephew, Farrukhsiyar, who sought to secure his position by executing, blinding or imprisoning his remaining relatives. He quarrelled, however, with his most powerful ministers, and the empire then foundered in a bitter confusion of court intrigue and treachery. In the end Farrukhsiyar was murdered at the orders of the brothers, Sayyid Abdullah Khan and Sayyid Hussain Ali Khan, who were themselves killed in 1720, after the intervention of Asaf Jah (the Nizam-ul-Mulk) and other nobles.

The Sayyids had installed Roshan Aktar, grandson of Bahadur Shah, as the nominal emperor, Muhammad Shah (r. 1719–48). The confusion at court led among other things to a creeping independence for the Rajputs and a humiliating treaty with the Marathas. The capture of Kabul in 1738, and of Delhi in 1739, by the Persian, Nadir Shah, showed up Mughal weakness in the north-west. Afghanistan ceased to be the adjunct of an Indian empire. Other Mughal provinces also felt the effects of imperial decline, sometimes as anarchy, and sometimes as local defiance of central Mughal authority. Some able administrators far from Delhi or Agra, such as Murshid Quli Khan in Bengal and Mubariz Khan in Hyderabad (Golconda), began to re-establish the regional power which came to characterize most of the eighteenth century.

Muhammad Shah and his successors were unable to prevent this independence in the regions, and the Mughals' power contracted until it disappeared. Under Muhammad's son, the incompetent Ahmad Shah, they lost Gujarat, in 1750; and, in 1752, ceded Punjab and Sind to the Afghans. In the midst of these reverses a bitter struggle for effective power developed between Safdar Jang (the *wazir* and governor of Awadh) and the young Mughal noble, Imad-ul-Mulk, nephew of the previous *wazir*, and then allied to the emperor, Ahmad Shah. After his victory over Safdar, however, Imad-ul-Mulk removed and blinded the emperor, in 1753, and substituted the son of Jahandar Shah, Alamgir II. (He would murder him in 1759.)

In 1756 the Afghan, Ahmad Shah Abdali (or Durrani, the name he gave to the Abdalis), sacked Delhi in the fourth of his five incursions

Box 5   States and empires of early modern India

North and north-east

Rajputs (Mewar)

> MUGHALS
> Babur (1526–30)
> Humayun (1530–9)

> SURS (1539–54)
> Sher Shah (1539–45)

> MUGHALS
> Humayun (1554–6)
> Akbar (1556–1605)
> (Bairam Khan, 1556–60)
> Shah Jahan (1605–27)
> Jahangir (1628–57; d.1666)
> Aurangzib (1658–1707)
> Bahadur Shah (1707–12); Jahandar Shah (1712–13); Farrukhsiyar
> (1713–18); Muhammad Shah (1719–48); Ahmad Shah (1748–54);
> Alamgir II (1754–9); Shah Alam (1759–1806); Akbar II (1806–37);
> Bahadur Shah II (1837–57)

North-west	**Awadh**	**Bengal**
Nadir Shah (1739)	Shuja-ud-Daula	Murshid Quli Khan
Ahmad Shah Abdali	(1731–75)	(1700–17)
(1747–73)		Alivardi Khan
Ranjit Singh (1799–89)		(1740–56)

East India Company (1765–1858)

West, centre and south

Bijapur

> MARATHAS
> Shivaji Bhonsle (1627–80)
> Shambhaji (1680–9)
> Rajaram

> Golconda/Hyderabad
> Mubariz Khan (1713–24)
> Asaf Jah (see Chapter 5)

French East India Company (Pondicherry)

East India Company (Bombay)   East India Company (Madras)

> MYSORE
> Haidar Ali (1761–82)
> Tipu Sultan (1782–99)

Note: The position of each heading roughly corresponds with the territories
(left to right, west to east).

Map 3 India in 1765

into India, the others being in 1748, 1749, 1751–2 and 1761. At the invitation of Imad-ul-Mulk, the Marathas initially repulsed him in the Punjab; but they were defeated by him in another battle of Panipat in 1761, after which Delhi was left in the control of a Rohilla chief, Najib-ud-daula, who ruled there until 1770. By 1785 the Marathas, under Mahadji Shinde (Sindhia), again had control, with a new Mughal emperor, Shah Alam, who had been crowned as a fugitive in Bihar in 1759. He was blinded by the Rohillas when they temporarily recaptured Delhi in 1788. Though shortly afterwards restored to the throne, he and Delhi remained under the domination of Mahadji and (after Mahadji's death in 1794) Daulat Rao Shinde, until 1803 when the British armies reached Delhi. After 1803, the emperor, and his successors, Akbar II and Bahadur Shah II, remained pensioners of the British East India Company. In the preceding fifty years, the Mughals had themselves become just another struggling regional power, one less successful than most.

MUGHAL RULE

The Mughal state was geared for war, and succeeded while it won its battles. It controlled territory partly through its network of strongholds, from its fortified capitals in Agra, Delhi or Lahore, which defined its heartlands, to the converted and expanded forts of Rajasthan and the Deccan. The emperors' will was frequently enforced in battle. Hundreds of army scouts were an important source of information. But the empire's administrative structure too was defined by and directed at war. Local military checkpoints or *thanas* kept order. Directly appointed imperial military and civil commanders (*faujdars*) controlled the cavalry and infantry, or the administration, in each region. The peasantry in turn were often armed, able to provide supporters for regional powers, and liable to rebellion on their own account: continual pacification was required of the rulers.

Humayun brought with him some 51 nobles (*amirs*), more than half of them Turkish or Uzbek (and Sunni), and most of the remainder Persian (and Shi'a). Akbar appointed over three times as many, including many Hindus and some Indian Muslims. By 1595 there were some 1800 nobles and equivalent chiefs and officials. According to the *mansabdari* (office-holding) system, rank (*zat*) was calculated in terms of the number of troops nominally provided (from 20 to 5000 or even 10 000), which also defined pay and land-entitlements as officials and commanders. By the 1640s, when Shah Jahan's historian, Abdul Hamid, provided details, less than 6 per cent of the higher *mansabdars* were Afghans, about half were Persian or Mughal, about a fifth were Hindu (mainly Rajput), and somewhat more than one-sixth were Indian Muslims. The system produced a standardized but heterogeneous army – *mansabdars* were supposed to employ soldiers mainly from their own clan or religion, and could organize ranks and pay within the averages and standards that were set centrally.

The bulk of the empire's revenue went directly to these nobles through land-revenue assignments or *jagirs*. The nobles set up miniature courts, with domestic slaves and harems. They encouraged the development of local economies and of north India's largely Muslim *qasbahs* or market towns where servants' and artisans' huts surrounded palaces, gardens, mosques and *madrasas* (colleges). The Mughal system was thus decentralized, fluid and personal. But there were some checks. *Mansabdari* rank was individual, subject to change, and not heritable. The emperor could summon *mansabdars* and local chiefs to court. He could also change their *jagirs*, the lands of which were often not contiguous. The *jagir* was a right to collect revenue, and not a landed estate. The system gave the nobles an incentive to pacify territories, while rewarding their loyalty, and creating personal ties between them and the new dynasty.

The system was designed to incorporate as well as reward, which is why it was extended to the Rajputs. Akbar expanded the nobility to balance the Uzbeks and outflank the Indian Afghans; and he sought also to attach Hindu warrior-elites to his rule. He gave the Rajput chiefs (*thakurs*) who capitulated to him a *mansabdari* status, and on those terms appointed them to office, confirmed them in their lands, and protected the claims of their lineages. Uniquely among the *mansabdars*, they were permitted to hold on to their *watans*, or own lands. In return they chose to treat Akbar as a great Kshatriya. Similarly, after the conquest of the Deccan, later emperors, including Aurangzib, awarded *mansabdari* rank to local Muslims and some Maratha nobles – rather in the way that the Deccani sultans had made a point of employing Hindus in high office. However, Shah Jahan and Aurangzib were both too iconoclastic, and too much land was reserved to the centre rather than awarded to allies, for a thorough-going reprise in the Deccan of Akbar's policy towards the Rajputs.

Though military prowess was always most important and best rewarded in the Mughal times, yet it was crucial to their success that Akbar and his successors supplemented military control by a bureaucratic and intelligence structure, mainly paid for in cash. Such payments were possible, in addition to the huge proportion of salaries provided through *jagirs*, because of large inflows of foreign silver, treasure seized by an ever-conquering empire, large returns from the emperors' crown lands (*khalisa*), and increased imperial control over the currency. For a hundred years or more the empire had huge income and vast reserves. Akbar minted and re-minted pure copper, silver and gold coins, without charge to those supplying the metal but under close official supervision, and in such quantities that even poor workers in the towns could be paid in cash. Traders and moneylenders were among those who benefited from Mughal rule.

Akbar was thus able to reorganize the administration. He reduced the danger from overmighty subjects by doing without a chief minister, and dividing the government under four main heads, responsible for finance; army and intelligence; household (including communications); and judicial and religious affairs. A central treasury was established, manned mainly by Hindu service castes, to manage the salaries and *jagirs*, and audit expenditure, under the supervision of the *wazir* (finance minister) and the *bakhshi* (military paymaster). Governors (themselves *mansabdars*) were placed over each province (*subah*), with similar establishments – a *diwan* to manage the revenue and *bakhshis* to inspect and certify the quality of the troops. Officers were placed over each district (*sarkar*), and a judge (*qazi*) and a magistrate and police officer (*kotwal*) appointed in every town. Information was provided from every corner of the empire by runners and spies (*harkaras*) reporting to the *bakshi*, official news-recorders, and record-keepers. Paper documentation was newly significant.

Nowhere was the administration more fully developed than in Akbar's revolution of the land-revenue system. At all levels power rested both upon direct cultivation (often using forced labour) and upon taxing the output of others. It was expressed in control over and tolls upon land, markets, artisans, and the movement of goods and persons. In the localities, such control was held by dominant lineages and office-holders, including the often-hereditary headmen (*chaudhuris* in north India and *deshmukhs* in the Deccan). Successive rulers created posts and regulations to try to reach through the magnates and intermediaries directly to the actual producers.

The Sur kings had attempted to apply uniform rates of land tax, which was too inflexible a system. In 1580, therefore, Akbar instituted a major overhaul. His finance minister, Raja Todar Mal, began to collect statistics from the local record-keepers (*qanungos*), and to compile lists of prices according to standardized measures, within comparable assessment areas or circles. Survey parties were sent out to measure lands and to collect information on yields and prices over ten-year periods. These data were tabulated for each circle, and a final settlement of the land revenue calculated on the ten-year averages. The demand was set in cash terms, at the equivalent of about one-half of the food grains, and one-fifth of the cash crops such as indigo or cotton, plus set amounts for orchards, cattle and so on. Villages were required to accept joint responsibility for these settlements, under the supervision of their headmen and the revenue officers. *Jagirs* were then recalculated at the revised rates. Payments were to be made directly to the revenue officials, and records were kept of the remittances made for separate cultivating holdings. Local land-controllers and revenue-collectors, the *zamindars*, were allowed a fixed 10 per cent of collections. These rights, thus relatively standardized, became transferable as a form of property, and the landholders (of whatever origin) gained a recognizable and defined status with several grades.

Shah Jahan, faced with a immensely larger empire, succeeded in extending and modifying Akbar's system. He introduced further surveys to apply the revenue regulations (*zabt*) to new territories, in place of tribute payments or unregulated *jagirs*. In the Deccan the settlement was conducted for Aurangzib by the Brahman convert, Murshid Quli Khan, later to rule in Bengal. (Lower Bengal and Orissa, however, were not brought into the system.) Under Shah Jahan, the *jagirs'* liabilities were also reassessed in the regulation areas. Some were revised downwards to take account of variable returns because of harvest failures or disorder. But, overall, state income more than doubled in money terms from Akbar to Aurangzib, indicating the expansion of the regions under centralized administration and also of the economy. Conversely, from the mid-eighteenth century Mughal coffers were virtually empty, indicating the seepage of power to the localities.

Despite syncretic tendencies (discussed below), Islam was another important arm of the Mughal state. Akbar initially declared *jihad* against the Rajputs, supported the *hajj* (until 1580), and showed his devotion to the Sufi saint, Shaikh Salim Chishti (for whom he situated his new capital at Fatehpur Sikri). Though there is no evidence of his involvement in any Islamic observance after 1585, he claimed the status of Caliph (*khalifa*), and hence to be the ultimate arbiter of Muslim religious law, above the *ulama*. On the other hand, from the late 1570s, for political and economic reasons, and because of his interest in comparative religion, he began a series of moves against the *ulama* (many of them Indian Afghans) and towards religious tolerance. He began to resume any undocumented grants of land held tax-free (not unlike the British 250 years later) – much of it was held by Afghans and as religious endowments. Akbar abolished taxes on Hindus, including the *jiziya* (the property-graduated poll-tax), and permitted the building and repair of Hindu temples. He encouraged a process of cultural syncretism among Persian-literate north Indian Hindus and Muslims, which continued throughout the reigns of his successors, down to the mid-nineteenth century and beyond. However, the value of Akbar's early religiosity is indicated by the fact that his alienation of the *ulama* and his claim to be the *khalifa* contributed to a revolt in Bihar and Bengal in 1579–80 (put down by Todar Mal).

Akbar's successor, Jahangir, pursued more mixed policies, apparently governed largely by political expediency. He martyred the fifth Sikh guru, Arjun, and forced his son and successor to retreat to the hills; but he sought out for a long audience a Vaishnava ascetic, Gosain Jadrup of Ujjain, as had Akbar before him. He imprisoned the influential anti-Hindu Sufi, Shaikh Ahmad Sirhindi, but venerated the tomb, at Ajmer, of another Sufi, Khwaja Muin-ud-din Chishti. However, Shah Jahan took further steps towards Muslim orthodoxy, to accompany and assist a Sunni revivalism. He resumed patronage of the *hajj*. Rajputs, though still enjoying some privileges, began to decline in the imperial service and as a proportion of the *mansabdars*. Shah Jahan forbade the building of Hindu temples, and ordered some new ones demolished. In place of Akbar's somewhat eclectic architectural styles, he engaged in huge projects that were regarded as essentially Persian-Islamic in inspiration and which tended to conceal rather than reveal the emperor and his court – such as a new capital at Shajahanabad (Delhi), the Shalimar gardens in Kashmir, and the Taj Mahal in Agra. A similar spirit was intended in the huge production of Mughal miniature paintings at this time.

The succession struggle between Dara Shukoh and Aurangzib was in part a contest between Akbar's conciliation and Shah Jahan's iconoclasm. Aurangzib in his turn attempted to create a Muslim state. He too emphasized and rewarded conversion to Islam, and tried to reduce the numbers of Hindu officials. Brahman and Telegu chiefs who had served as officials in Golconda almost all lost their posts after 1687, and the state itself was renamed as the land of holy war (*dar al-jihad*), Hyderabad (Haidarabad) – the capital city itself had been founded in 1589 under the name of Bhagnagar. Aurangzib pulled down more Hindu temples, and reinstated the Hindu pilgrim tax and *jiziya*. In 1675 he executed the proselytizing Sikh guru, Tegh Bahadur, and thus deepened the strong enmity between the Sikhs and Mughals. He appointed Muslim censors (*muhtasib*) to check on public behaviour, and otherwise enhanced the power of the *ulama*. He sponsored an authoritative compilation of orthodox (Sunni, Hanafi) Islamic law, the *Fatawa-i Alamgiri*.

The revived Islamicization of the Mughal empire was one reason why, for all its powerful record-making and quasi-centralized administration, it did not develop into a fully objective bureaucratic state. Another reason was the importance of personality. Akbar promoted a cult of the emperor as having semi-divine inheritance and authority – set out in the *Akbarnama* written by Abu'l Fazl, and expressed in the discipleship of selected *mansabdars*. The majesty of dynasty, court and monarch was expressed in imperial audiences (*darbars*) and rituals of obeisance, in the vast tented entourage of the emperor on tour, in the building of fine cities, monuments and tombs, and in the patronage of painting, music and letters. Shah Jahan and Aurangzib tried to take this further, but particularly emphasized the private sphere. They promoted a notion of hereditary imperial service, and a loyal elite of courtiers.

None of the emperors could avoid such strategies, because the existence of the nobility encouraged revolt, the lack of a principle of primogeniture led to repeated wars of succession, and the emphasis on dynasty invited the rebellion of brothers and sons – as with Humayun and Kamran, Akbar and Salim (Jahangir), Jahangir and Khurram (Shah Jahan), Aurangzib and Muhammad Akbar, and so on. Of necessity, imperial policy vacillated between murdering rivals, keeping them at court, and entrusting large provinces to sons and brothers. The rulers' *personal* capacity, courage and following – and their knowledge – were necessary to survival, as their habitual blinding of rebels and rivals implied. Their achievement was that the empire lasted so long.

EARLY MODERN SOCIETY AND ECONOMY

Muslim texts propose an ideally harmonious world of divinely ordained social roles – of the pen, the sword, business and the soil. Even in the eighteenth century, South Asian Muslim commentaries still preferred such imported Islamic social prescriptions, although by then many military treatises or horticultural manuals, for example, had begun to reflect local conditions. Definite rules also governed the treatment and behaviour of protected unbelievers (zimmis); while conversion to Islam meant joining into quite different social groups, especially for marriage. (Converts were to be found among soldiers, administrators, court- and army-suppliers, slaves, low castes, and devotees of charismatic preachers.)

Of course social ideals do not fully describe an actual world. The Islamic 'community' which helped sustain Mughal rule was not a simple or unqualified inheritance. We saw aspects of this in Chapter 3. The first issue was Muslim division. Many less-acknowledged social distinctions were instrumental in politics and daily life. We noticed the discord between Afghans and Turks; there were gaps too between immigrant and converted Muslims. We saw how slavery was important; and slaves could perform any of the ideal roles. We noted how preachers taught Sufi mysticism and heterodoxy; they were spread further by the written records of lives and sayings. We saw there was controversy too, even among Sunnis, about the standing of Indian Muslims and their rulers in relation to the Caliph's authority.

After these divisions between Muslims, an even larger issue, however, was syncretism and assimilation. We remarked how, in the sultanate period, immigrant Muslim scholars brought new intellectual and cultural influences to India. In origin, these were Persian and even Greek as well as Islamic. As seen with the Delhi sultanate, and now with the Mughals, the state generally employed, tolerated and even protected Hindus (the status as zimmis). Akbar's policies exemplified this trend. More difficult, Hindu converts to Islam also often retained many of their old practices and ideas. Worse still was the closeness between Sufi and Hindu or Sikh mysticism; we have noted how the influence of Kabir, Nanak and Chaitanya, who had all condemned caste and idolatry, promoted further links between the Sufi orders and the Hindus.

Among Muslims, several compromises attempted to reconcile the varied traditions. Religious eclecticism flourished, and orthodoxy was often left to individual conscience. Moreover, private property, individual aspirations, devotional movements and legal custom made room for much practical co-operation, as well as rivalry, between different religious and social groups. Temple, mosque, pilgrimage, alms-giving and prayer apparently defined separate communities, but their practice often blurred the distinctions. Amidst linguistic plurality, there were shared traditions of debate and dissent, common literary or aesthetic movements, and economic and political partnership and exchange. Many Kayasthas (a Hindu writer-caste) were renowned for their elegant Persian. Even under Shah Jahan, Mughal architecture matched the archways, courtyards and gardens of Islamic tradition with the ornate solidity of 'Hindu' columns and audience chambers. Indian miniature painting combined the profile portraits, semi-formal settings and rich colours of Persian painting with the detailed depictions of plants and animals and the mythological iconography of Hindu art. Similarly shared were much music and poetry, elite pastimes such as hunting, and the popular ostentations and entertainment of fairs and festivals.

Meanwhile devout Muslims worried about these heterodoxies, especially in times of political turmoil and decline. They issued explanatory and defensive texts against mystics and to educate converts. Shaikh Ahmad of Sirhind (1564–1624) was one who argued against syncretism. However, the great Sunni reformer, Shah Wali-Allah (1703–62) summed up and helped reconcile the conflicts, for a time. He called for devotion to the Prophet, but translated the Qur'an into Persian. He also helped resolve Sunni–Sufi controversies, and preached tolerance. In most legal cases, he remarked, the truth 'lies somewhere between the two extremes', and in religion 'there is breadth and not narrowness'.[1]

Religious revivals and reforms, along with syncretic cultural developments, reflect the vitality and expansiveness of the age. This found expression also in the economic sphere. In Mughal times, there were many interruptions by famine and warfare, but on the whole the agrarian economy expanded. The stimulus came from the cash-based revenue demand, the increase in the money supply, the growth of towns, the settled order established in the countryside, and the growing foreign demand, especially for cotton, indigo, silk, saltpetre and sugar, augmenting the existing trade in spices. New crops were introduced, such as tobacco, maize and mulberry. Settled agriculture expanded markedly at the expense of pasture, waste and forests, for example as Sikhs and Jats developed the

Punjab valleys, using well-irrigation, or Rajputs and Bhumihars cleared forests and brought new lands under the plough in Awadh and Bihar, or Sufis and Hindu backers reclaimed land in eastern Bengal. Networks of travelling merchants (*banjaras*) and sophisticated systems of credit, insurance and accounting grew up to support the growth of commerce. Shipbuilding was important.

There was a growing demand for manufactured goods, and for the provisioning of towns and armies. Highly diversified types of cloth were produced, and high-quality indigo dyes developed, the latter especially round Agra and in Gujarat. Even in the country-side, specialist artisans were often able to sell their products, and were not wholly tied to service the village that fed them. Moreover, *aurangs*, or centres of concentrated craft production, became important during the eighteenth century in most of the cities of north India and beyond. The scale of communications and the very long distances at which goods and money could be exchanged imply a vigorous trading society; the size of the trade sponsored by courts, towns and armies should not be underestimated. On the other hand, despite specializations, most processing and manufacture remained rural, small-scale and dispersed. Most occupations remained caste-specific.

The Mughal empire was a major exporter into the world markets of its day, and the resultant influx of silver bullion added to its prosperity and (as said) to the resources of the state. But there were some special limits to internal demand in early modern India. Some may be traced to the great economic divides between classes in Mughal as in colonial India. Western observers, though familiar with the gruelling spectacle of eighteenth-century European cities, still frequently exclaimed at the feeble condition of most of the Indian poor. Land rights were jealously guarded, even when land might appear to have been in surplus; and marked differences in diet, income and the treatment of women and children existed between different classes of people. The rich nobles and courtly employees, and the growing middle-income groups of administrators, traders and moneylenders, certainly were able consume lavishly. But little could be bought by the lower orders of men, women and children, all of whom had to work for their food, and in many places ate only millets and pulses, once a day. (In Bengal and some other wet areas the poor did eat varieties of rice.) Oil and *ghi* (clarified butter) were important items of trade, it might be said, because fish and meat were rarely consumed at any level of society. By the same token there was a restricted demand for cloth and bricks where most people were very simply clothed and housed.

Another problem may have been that there was relatively little metal- or mineral-based enterprise, despite some exceptions of military significance, such as the cannon-balls produced in Golconda or the saltpetre of Bihar. Another may have been a want of information, expertise or capital. It was a remarkable testimony to trading networks, for example, but also a puzzle, that the flourishing silk-manufacturers of Ahmedabad and Surat in Gujarat drew their raw materials so largely, over long sea journeys, from distant Bengal (in return for cotton), and did not develop a more local supply; or that the rulers of Mysore, just like those of Vijayanagara before them, should have invested much effort in ensuring the long-distance trade that brought fresh cavalry horses from central Asia, rather than in local efforts to breed from improved stock.

Though European trade was still relatively small compared with indigenous markets, the European traders played a special role in encouraging production. They transmitted new demand, and financed the cultivation and manufacturing to meet it, importing bullion which they advanced to agriculturists and weavers. Thus, following the very long-established Arab traders, the Portuguese had developed the south Indian trade, especially in black pepper. A greater expansion of exports to Europe from many parts of the subcontinent followed the advent of the English, Dutch and French East India companies (the old East India Company in 1600, the United Company after 1702–8, the Verenigde Oostindische Compagnie in 1602, and the Compagnie des Indes Orientales in 1664). Indian cotton, indigo, silk and other products competed in Europe initially on price, but by the eighteenth century also on quality.

The Europeans gained against local and land-based long-distance traders because of their command of the seas, their enhanced ability to navigate (at least latitudinally), and their use of armed, purpose-built sailing ships manned by experienced captains and crews. They also benefited from privileged or monopoly access to the growing markets of north-western Europe, and from being able to raise capital in the European exchanges. They ran their affairs as organized companies under greater or lesser state regulation, while still spreading the risks by operating mainly through semi-independent contractors. The European settlements in India grew into small city-states, extending their influence to producers who were dispersed over much of the country.

The south Indian rajas and the Gujarati port of Surat were among the first to welcome the new sea-traders, but as early as the 1610s Golconda gave concessions to the Dutch and shortly afterwards the English, while Jahangir permitted the English to open inland depots (so-called factories) after the mission of Sir Thomas Roe in 1615. In eastern India, after the expulsion of the Portuguese by Shah Jahan, the Dutch and then the English traders further developed an already growing economy. The Mughals, concerned to tap this wealth, gave the Dutch exemption from local inland tolls from the 1630s, in return for an imperial customs duty of 4 per cent. Later the English Company secured a similar concession.

EIGHTEENTH-CENTURY POLITICS

Four kinds of state vied for territory in the extended eighteenth century, from about 1720 to the 1840s: regional powers, especially the Marathas and Sikhs; successors to the Mughal provinces, such as Bengal-Bihar, Hyderabad and Awadh; new Muslim adventurers, most remarkably Haidar Ali and Tipu Sultan of Mysore; and the European traders with their armies, allies and city-states, and eventually, in the British case, supremacy. This is not a chronological list; each of the above will be discussed more or less in the order in which they became important to the building of regional power, as Mughal authority waned. The fate of these states during the rise of British power will mainly be considered in the next chapter.

The Marathas might have seemed the most likely contenders to build an empire, arguably even at the start of the nineteenth century. Yet from the first they also showed some limitations. Their confrontation with Aurangzib (and at one time also with the Portuguese in Goa) had not only undermined their opponents; it also impeded a centralized Maratha state. Constant warfare sapped the local economy. It forced Shambhaji and his successors to seek alliances with a variety of local military elites (deshmukhs) and regional powers. It induced even Maratha chiefs sometimes to defect; and it encouraged the formation of small armed bands, that were successful against the Mughals but also could have fluctuating loyalties. When Shahuji, the son of Shambhaji, vied for the succession with Tarabai, he gained control (by 1718) effectively as the head of successful bands of marauders. Such bands evolved into separate military and political units, especially after the 1720s when Maratha deployments became much larger. The units in turn constituted the chiefdoms of a Maratha confederacy, acquiring their own core territories and spheres of influence. Notable were the Gayakavads (Gaekwads) in Baroda and Gujarat, the Shindes (Sindhias) in Gwalior, Ujjain and north India, the Holkars in Malwa and Indore, and the Bhonsles in Nagpur and Orissa.

These chiefs complicated the inevitable succession disputes which bedevilled the Marathas, among others. A further complication – though sometimes a solution – was the growing power of the chief minister, or Peshwa, who became the effective military and administrative head of the confederacy, based in Pune. Shahuji appointed Baji Rao (1720–40) as Peshwa to succeed his father, Balaji Vishwanath, and thus the office became hereditary for a line of Chitpavan Brahmans. The Peshwa took on the important role of trying to unite the confederacy, and became a major territorial power in his own right. He was further strengthened by an agreement made after the death of Shahuji in 1749. Under Baji Rao's leadership, and that of his son Balaji, known as Nana Sahib (1740–61), the Marathas spread their attacks from Rajasthan to Bengal, and from the Punjab to the Karnatak.

But the Peshwa also became a focus for dissension, much of which was really to decide which chiefs should dominate the confederacy. In 1761, after the disaster at Panipat, and the death of Nana Sahib, quarrels over the succession led to a war among the Marathas, drawing in outside participants, the Nizam of Hyderabad and the British East India Company. Raghunath Rao (known as Raghoba, or Dada Sahib) supported the accession of his nephew, the young Madhav Rao, with himself as regent. Raghunath was later pensioned off, and effective power passed to another Brahman, Balaji Janardhan, known as Nana Fadnavis (*nana*, the chief accountant). In 1772, when Madhav died, Raghunath claimed the office for himself, after murdering Madhav's younger brother. He appealed to the East India Company and was at first supported but then abandoned on orders from Bengal. (Company forces were subsequently embroiled again disastrously between 1779 and 1781.) Raghunath had been opposed by Mahadji Shinde, and others, and eventually defeated.

The cost of the civil war of 1773 was a fatal weakening of the office of Peshwa and hence the confederacy. Maratha fortunes subsequently depended on the prowess of individual chiefs, especially Shinde and Holkar, who struggled for dominance throughout the 1780s and 1790s. In 1792 Shinde prevailed, only to die within a couple of years. The suicide of the Peshwa Madhav Rao Narayan in 1795 sparked off yet another conflict; it was about a year before Raghunath Rao's son, Baji Rao II, was installed as Peshwa by Nana Fadnavis. Confused warfare continued between Baji Rao, Daulat Rao Shinde and Tukoji Holkar, especially after the death of Nana Fadnavis in 1800. Their quarrels prompted further Company intervention, with Wellesley forcing a subsidiary alliance on the incompetent and deposed Baji Rao in 1802. This led within a year or two to an almost complete victory for the British in the Maratha territories, until their progress was halted (temporarily) in 1804 by an inconclusive campaign against Holkar.

The Marathas' political divisions qualified the significant steps taken by them towards state-building. In an expanding range of core territories, and especially on the initiative of Nana Sahib, they evolved a regular administration along Mughal lines, with careful record-keeping, and a kind of district officer or *kamavisdar* who paid the taxation in advance of the collections. Many of these core areas remained stable, and experienced economic growth, in the later eighteenth century. The notable female regent, Ahilyabai Holkar, achieved success of this kind in her domains from the 1760s to the 1790s. It was possible too for new areas to be incorporated into the heartlands, as happened with Gujarat, Khandesh, Malwa and, for a time, Orissa.

It may be that, with a more concentrated leadership and without powerful opposition, the Marathas might yet have evolved as the Mughals had before them. Some of their administration was effective, and Mahadji and Daulat Rao Shinde accepted Mughal office and long dominated the kingdom of Delhi. On the other hand, outside the core territories, Maratha military raids merely produced booty. Increasingly this was transmuted into fixed rates of tribute (*chauth*, strictly a claim to a quarter of the government revenue), sometimes semi-institutionalized by treaty or Mughal sanction – as for Jaipur in 1748, Orissa in 1751 and Punjab in 1752. Yet such formalized tribute mostly did not evolve into regular government or even suzerainty, and punitive expeditions were often still needed to collect the payments.

The successor Mughal states also appeared strong at times, but they too never absolutely established their independence from the empire, or security from internal or external challenge. In Hydera-bad, when Mubariz Khan became *diwan* and governor, he installed members of his own family in key posts, stopped sending taxes to the emperor, and annexed the income from crown lands. He excluded Marathas from his administration, contrary to a treaty of 1717 (which had conceded to them the right to collect more than a third of the revenues). Mubariz was killed in 1724 in battle with Asaf Jah, then governor of Malwa, who was trying to found his own state in the Deccan. He became the first independent Nizam (though the title, meaning governor, implies a fiction of Mughal continuity), and ruled in Hyderabad until his death in 1748. His territories stretched, nominally, from Orissa to Thanjavur.

In Awadh (Oudh), independent power was achieved under the aegis of the imperial *wazir*, Safdar Jang, its governor after 1739, and his successor, Shuja-ud-daula, who was later dependent upon the British East India Company to preserve his kingdom from the Rohillas, an Afghan tribe. In Bengal, Murshid Quli Khan had ruled from 1713, adding Bihar to his domains in 1717. He died in 1727, but by then he too had established effective regional independence, subject only to the occasional tribute paid to the emperor. His son-in-law, Shuja-ud-din, took over in 1727, incorporated Orissa, and ruled until his death in 1739. His son was overthrown by Alivardi Khan, who remained Nawab or ruler from 1740 to 1756. (The title is another fiction, for *nawwab* is the plural of *na'ib*, meaning deputy.) These Nawabs were effective managers, and Bengal prospered, despite the Maratha invasions that occurred almost throughout Alivardi's reign. Pressed for resources, Alivardi gave up paying tribute to the emperor.

New states also arose where Mughal authority had been weak or indirect. Mysore was established as an independent state in the seventeenth century; it was extended under Chikka Deva (1672–1704). One of its subjects, of Punjabi origin but born near Mysore in 1722, was Haidar Ali, who rose in the service of the state while the original dynasty declined; and took over as effective ruler, after beating back a Maratha attack in 1760. He deposed the Raja in 1766. His son, Tipu Sultan, succeeded him in 1782. In Rajasthan, Jaipur's first raja was Jai Singh II, who died in 1743 and also was succeeded by his son. In the Punjab, the Sikhs survived in the hills, after their repeated struggles with the Mughals, but benefited from the collapse of authority following the invasions of Nadir Shah and Ahmad Shah Abdali, and the defeat of the Marathas in 1761. In the 1760s they occupied Lahore, and in 1767 founded the Patiala state. Their isolated war-bands became grouped into twelve *misls* (tribes), with a recognized leader. Ranjit Singh became this chief in 1792 at

the age of twelve. From around the turn of the nineteenth century
he was able to consolidate his power, in Lahore and then Amritsar,
subduing rivals among the *misls*. By 1805, he was at the head of
a disciplined army, by 1819 he had conquered Multan and Kashmir,
and by 1834 Ladakh and Peshawar.

MERCHANTS AND STATES

The view of the eighteenth century as a period of anarchy and
economic decline has long been exploded. There was certainly
much disruption from warfare, but also periods of considerable
stability and prosperity, especially in certain areas. A continuation
of the centralizing impulses of the Mughals, as tax collectors and
military administrators, was revitalized by alliances between landed
and commercial power in the regions. Both militarized states
and commercial centres were supported by these alliances.

India gives the lie to that part of Karl Polanyi's analysis in *The
Great Transformation* (1944) and elsewhere, which locates the market,
as an autonomous mechanism, as emerging only after the Western
European revolutions of the late eighteenth and early nineteenth
centuries. Trade was not marginal in eighteenth-century India, nor
was it wholly subservient to political power. The picture, however,
is much confused by general theoretical arguments and special
pleading. The colonial interpretations were related to British self-
confidence and self-interest; scholars have been trying to identify
the engine of economic growth, as merchant enterprise, technological
change, population growth, politics, or social attitudes. But many
now argue that economic conditions are *always* interrelated with
social and political ones, so that economic performance must depend
on the manner and not the presence or lack of such influences.

Close relationships between state and commerce seem to have
been the norm for the whole of the 'early modern' period being
considered in this and the next chapter. Records have mostly not
survived to provide a very clear picture of pre-colonial economic
life, but in some instances they are notably rich and detailed. One
such case is that of Jaipur state, the records of which indicate political
and economic interactions that may well have been typical over
much wider areas and longer periods. There, as in much of Mughal
India, cash revenue-demands were levied, but (as often also in
colonial times) this did not imply a purely cash economy in which

farmers sold their produce and then independently paid their dues in cash. On the contrary, various intermediaries, including the state, had to intervene in production and exchange, at almost all levels, in order to make the revenue and administrative system work. Service tenures and revenue-contractors enabled the state to pay for services in kind rather than cash, and state lands also reduced the immediate necessity to exchange produce for cash. Cash exchanges remained important, however, which meant finding ways of obtaining cash from the taxes on agrarian production (which probably amounted to up to a third of the total output).

The revenue was demanded at fixed dates, with interest chargeable on arrears, while grain sales followed a different timetable, related to the harvests. There were at least two possible consequences of this (very common) situation: either the revenue would be paid from credit, raised from moneylenders on future harvests, or payments would be accepted in kind at a valuation that was calculated in cash. Both of these methods implied interventions, if only in the division of the harvests, that could occur at any level – between cultivators and landlords or revenue-contractors, or revenue-payers and the state. In Jaipur the state itself acquired grain in this way, and hence was a major player in the grain trade. It even imported produce to take advantage of price differentials; but mainly it stored grain from year to year in its own granaries, and each year sold between 3 and 12 per cent of the estimated gross output. The prices were set at a standard daily rate, according to carefully recorded bazaar prices, for each district (*pargana*). They seem to have been negotiated with merchants, and to have reflected supply and demand, but of course the state was a very large seller, with large stocks of grain, and must have had an impact on the market. Its involvement was no doubt often expensive or inconvenient, and its officials (*amils*) who arranged the sales could readily collude with the merchants. But presumably it had no choice if it wanted to ensure that it would ultimately be provided with cash. Nevertheless, the evidence also suggests the existence of a large and vigorous grain market. Purchases from the state were dominated by few big dealers, but there were many very small buyers, some evidently merchants and others described as *patels* (headmen) or *raiyats* (cultivators).

Against the detailed background of such evidence, and also other findings showing extensive export trades, recent historians have painted a new picture of the eighteenth-century economy. It was focused on small-town gentry and merchants, including large-scale 'firms' with multiple interests in production, selling, insurance, transport, banking and revenue-contracting. The gentry and merchants were intimately involved with the regional states, such as Jaipur, as grain-buyers, providers of credit, military suppliers, and so on. They were also involved in large-scale and far-ranging markets for rice, cloth and other products. They were buyers of agricultural produce, of land and of services. Their activities, alongside those of the states, provided opportunities for upward social mobility and commercial enterprise. Their system was eroded, as we shall see, by the European dominance not only of the political system but also of many areas of commerce and trade.

RIVAL ECONOMIES ON THE EVE OF CONQUEST

The British conquest of India may be attributed to accident, allies and resources – and the greatest of these was resources. Here is a crucial moment at which we can observe features of the Indian economy, and the long and short-term origins of conditions which (arguably above all others) have shaped what India is today. It will be convenient to consider them now, paused as we are on the eve of the European dominance of India.

Huge questions are raised by the varied economic performance of India and Europe during the eighteenth and nineteenth centuries. The undubitable fact that England and not India became ever wealthier and more powerful, starting around the mid-eighteenth century and continuing throughout the colonial period, is one of those discrepancies that constitute the fundamental issues of world history – explained at one time on racist, culturist or climatological grounds, and nowadays traced to a host of proximate or long-term, even prehistorical, causes. Was indigenous economic progress thwarted by colonial rule? The emphasis of modern scholarship (and this book's introduction) on long-term trends rather than complete ruptures invites us to consider this as another narrative of loss: the question is phrased more sharply if one holds that India had hitherto experienced long if sometimes interrupted development.

A fully comparative approach might be expected, since the differences between Britain and India seem similar to those between industrializing Britain and the rest of the world in the earlier nineteenth century. However, the validity of that comparison is open to question. It is just as likely that India was a special case or variant within what may be a rather different contrast, over a much longer timespan, that between Eurasia (or its transplanted economies) and the southern and western hemispheres. On those grounds, as well as for practical reasons of space, this discussion will be confined to India and Britain.

The most frequent explanations of India's 'failure' are not general but specific: the imposition of British colonial rule on India, and the net extraction of Indian surplus, the so-called 'drain of wealth'. Both of these arguments will be discussed in later chapters. They imply immediate causes, even mutual effects widening the gap between the two economies. But they do not reveal more distant economic influences – why the British economy dominated the Indian in the first place, or (if it is debatable that it did, initially) why it was British merchants trying their luck in India, rather than Indian in England, between 1600 and 1800.

Institutions, capital and financial instruments, labour, and markets are four major areas in which there were similarities but also discrepancies between India and England around 1800. We shall look at them briefly. India had used money in the time of the Buddha, and from the sixteenth century, and at some earlier times, had large silver imports (almost all turned into currency, unlike gold). It had had some large manufactures, using hired labour, from the Mauryan age, and such workshops certainly existed widely in the eighteenth century, for military materiel, urban needs and exports. Internal and external trade had grown. As in Europe, warfare and political rivalries encouraged state attempts to mobilize production and information, and significant linkages between merchants and local gentry. Merchant guilds had operated in India from ancient times.

Yet early modern India did not have the multiple institutions of civil society that grew up from the sixteenth to the eighteenth centuries in England. Eighteenth-century India also had impediments upon trade – slow and dangerous roads and water-transport; local tolls, taxes and duties; and other local costs or inefficiencies due to the dispersal rather than concentration of production. India had credit notes and bankers, but nothing to match the explosion of easy paper credit that helped fund the industrial revolution. Nor could Indians tap into the agricultural, maritime, New World and colonial (including Indian) fortunes that underwrote this credit in England.

Between the start and the end of the seventeenth century, the Mughals' standard silver rupee in circulation had possibly increased threefold (with some fluctuation) while interest rates had fallen. New market towns flourished, cultivation was extended, and state revenues more than doubled. But apparently all this occurred without generating very much mercantile capital. Powerful Indian merchants lent to Indian states, but sometimes were repaid by taking over revenue collection, which rather trapped capital into the agricultural season than released it for further investment. Some great houses helped decide the survival of rulers, as the Jagat Seths did in Bengal in 1757 (unlike the East India Company which on the whole was kept at one remove from the ministries in England). But, even in the eighteenth century, the Indian merchants' vast profits seldom matched the scale and speed of those made by many British commercial entrepreneurs, from ventures at home and abroad.

Nor, as a rule, could prosperous Indian landholders match the long-lived surpluses of some of the powerful English landlords. English aristocrats presided over smaller gentry, tenant farmers and labourers; and gained from enclosures, investment, high rents and rising prices, at a time of population growth when little food was imported. In India there were important local markets for grain and other products; but nothing that compared with the population growth and consumption of eighteenth-century England. Even in the seventeenth century some 40 per cent of Britons lived in towns, and by 1750 more than half had non-agricultural occupations. The agrarian efficiencies which made this transformation possible and necessary were not replicated in India, even by the start of the twenty-first century. Agricultural production was probably improving there, from at least the seventeenth century, but more by extension than intensification. A high proportion of the population, at least 70 per cent, remained directly dependent on agricultural work. (In the colonial period, the proportion did not change greatly, and the man:land ratio worsened. Moreover, a sizeable proportion of agricultural profits was exported).

The eighteenth-century British economy took advantage of better ships, state backing, flexible labour, and convenient access to capital, raw materials, fuel, communications and markets – many of which resources were less readily available in India. In contrast with the labour flexibility of contemporary England, for example, and the increasing labour efficiency of English agriculture, most Indian labour could be found seeking subsistence from smallholdings of land, or locked into underemployment by economic and social controls, or kept for prestige and political influence rather than production. A poor labour force was unlikely to be a productive one, in the absence of mechanization; but there were few means and little incentive to increase labour efficiency. Both before and during colonial rule, Indian artisans and manual workers were notoriously badly rewarded, and living was relatively cheap. The English poor too were famously feeble, but over the eighteenth century English workers consumed more and more calories from meat and New-World crops (potatoes and maize), and they also gained the wages to buy cheaper items of mass production.

In eighteenth-century Bengal, it was probably most important that state revenue demand rose sharply, but not under conditions likely to enforce investment. Part of the increase occurred under East India Company rule, when rents could not easily be raised because the terrible famine of 1769–70 had so reduced the population that surviving cultivators gained bargaining power. The increases in taxation initially ruined many land-owners, even though some (or their intermediaries) later benefited from new property rights and security.

Moreover, not only was local consumption limited, but European and Indian traders artificially depressed many wholesale export prices. Rising prices could not be relied upon by agrarian investors, not even for food crops. Bengal rice prices, for example, probably more than doubled on average between 1700 and 1800, and other prices followed suit. But the price differential between country and town markets varied from about 150 per cent to less than 1 per cent, even in the last quarter of the century, while, for famine and other reasons, all prices fluctuated enormously from year to year and season to season. In lower Bengal common rice prices at least doubled temporarily, over short-lived periods in the early 1720s and late 1740s, around 1760, and in the later 1780s. By contrast they differed very little in some widely spaced years such as 1700, 1750, 1785 and 1794.[2]

The rational response in India was reflected in the outcome just described. It was to increase output extensively, by cultivating more land, a tendency to be noticed also in the large-scale movements of labour from east to west in China from the sixteenth century. By contrast the trend in England (already a densely populated island) was towards intensification and concentration, especially of labour and industrial production in the towns. Large cities developed in India too, and sponsored intensive production, and, in the colonial period, modern industrialization. But they remained exceptions – more commonly they were colonial-administrative and export-trade centres than cities of indigenous development.

If economic outcomes were very different in India and in England, then Indian conditions were obviously less favourable than those in England – less likely, say, to encourage producers to maximize profits through technical innovation or more specialized production at the expense of leisure and subsistence. But what is meant by 'conditions'? It will not do to assume either that economic behaviour and hence laws are the same everywhere and only material factors differ, or that economic behaviour is too various for general laws because it is determined by culture regardless of material factors. On the one hand, in India as a whole there is clear evidence of entre-preneurial spirit and the desire for profit, in expansions of agriculture, adoption of new crops, and price-responsiveness in production: so much in favour of a universal economic man. On the other hand, cultural inclinations or barriers do influence economic performance: colonial officials were fond of criticizing peasants who borrowed for 'unproductive' expenditure such as marriage or funerals – often perfectly rational investments producing social goods within Indian culture. Belief, custom and morality help define the possibilities and priorities of individual decisions in a given social setting. We can balance these opposing emphases by assessing behaviour, conditions and culture case-by-case, neither assuming universal priorities, nor recycling Hegelian and race-theory stereotypes about other-worldly Hindus and indolent Orientals. Then, I believe, culture *per se*, being anyway always negotiated and responsive, will be shown to be less influential than ecological and institutional environments.

This discussion suggests a range of factors that might have influ-enced the economic performance of India over recent centuries. They cannot be reduced to 'colonial impact' or 'indigenous conditions'. The colonial rulers deliberately tried to alter some of them, for example by improving transport, removing internal tariffs, and trying to create entrepreneurial landed proprietors or develop new items of production. But they continued or exaggerated other dis-advantages. They extracted capital, monopolized vital occupations and commodities, and favoured external over internal markets. We shall re-examine these points too in later chapters.

Most disparities between the Indian and British economies were not absolute, so that deeper explanations for their contrasting per-formances must be sought in differences of degree or combinations of factors. Some illustrative points of comparison have been offered here. They were mostly to India's disadvantage, as they would be (obviously) for other places too, at the moment when England began its industrial revolution. Even so, as also over time, most of the differences may have been ones of scale and consistency. For example, there frequently developed in India well-integrated or enterprising regions, many at least the size of Britain; but none of them enjoyed very long periods of continual progress and autonomy. Arguably this fact may help explain some of the particular differences to be seen, over the period when India fell to the East India Company and Britain expanded its industrial output and advanced in technology.

ADMINISTRATION, 1580–1765: SOME COMPARISONS

Earlier chapters showed that the state did not develop in India as a single process in one direction, but that there were characteristics of states at different times, as well as some important continuities over time. One useful measure of states was found in the degree and manner of central or single authority: how much was dispersed and how much concentrated; how far was the central authority effectively political rather than social or ritual or ideological – that is, did the commanding forces consist mainly in ideas, beliefs, symbols and imitated forms, or (in addition to these) in practical control over taxation, expenditure and conduct? Related was the question of how far control was subjective and how far objective. The means of coercion, alliance and record also made for significant variations between states. The early modern period in India was one in which there was a shift of emphasis between these various poles.

India had had well-established forms of authority, fulfilling many of the tasks of the state. They included castes and lineages, doctrines and laws, as well as more specifically political institutions. The roles of the state were carried out, but they were often *dispersed* rather than concentrated. As already remarked, the apparent lack of centralized control was often thought by foreigners to indicate government that was either weak or arbitrary – and either was possible – but there were also strong centralizing and normative forces. They existed particularly in the form of ideologies (religion, rules of social conduct, norms in regard to shares and processes) rather than in effective, bureaucratic interventions. Some such states were described as 'segmentary'.

As a result of the legacy of its past, in the early modern south the state roles were shared between rajas, temples, petty chieftains with police powers ('poligars'; *palaiyakarar*), and local communities – village heads, local priests, revenue officers, *chaukidars* (watchmen), and so on. In irrigated areas, control was exercised through very complex and detailed obligations and entitlements to harvest shares. In return for his share or tribute, a ruler was expected to assist, to arbitrate and to protect benefits and customs that were provided in terms of community and religion. Each other 'state' functionary at successive levels received shares and duties similarly.

Similar disaggregated administration and revenue distribution existed elsewhere in India, sometimes well into the nineteenth century – for example the *battai* (share) system of Sind under the Talpur *mirs*, whereby fixed shares of the crop were divided between government, zamindar and cultivator. The Mughals and then the emerging European powers fitted in with these arrangements up to a point. Even at the height of the Mughal empire, local power was significant, not least in the north and west heartlands where clans, brotherhoods and high-caste lineages dominated the countryside. Local clans and communities, such as the rising Jat groups of the Delhi region from the sixteenth century, or the Rajputs and Bhumihars of Awadh and Bihar, were able to co-operate on local defence, to provide soldiers in large numbers for outside regimes, or to take on new administrative roles. In many areas armed and entrenched lords controlled their localities, and a few leading households dominated villages. Hence, many lasting tenurial categories hint at long-standing rights. For example, cultivators were called *raiyats*, a Mughal word meaning something akin to 'subject', but they also continued to be divided according to whether they were ancestral (*khudkashta*) or non-resident (*pahikashta*) – terms implying inherited rights and status rather than, necessarily, dwelling-place. Raiyats too could be *pattidari* (paying revenue as ancestral co-sharers, kin-group communities) or *bhaiachara* (paying 'by custom of the brotherhood').

Concessions were needed to conciliate all the local power-brokers, whether new or old. In the heartlands of the Mughal empire, where tax-free land grants and religious patronage were used, the rise of the *qasbahs* marked the growing local power of the Muslim gentry. These and older elites were co-opted and rewarded as state functionaries. This was because, alongside the survivals of old power, the Mughals also attempted something quite different, starting with

Akbar's reforms after 1580: namely, centrally regulated and managed land-taxation upon standard principles. Thus, while they had to recognize existing local authorities, they also attempted to subsume them into their own system.

Whenever they could, the Mughals instituted checks against fraud and arbitrary power. They set up parallel bureaucracies. The military-criminal jurisdiction under a governor (*subahdar*) and his subordinates was supposedly co-equal with and separate from the fiscal-civil authority or *diwani*, and at best both were intended to penetrate to village level. The Mughals made great efforts to collect and record information. They legitimated office- and land-holding by written grants and land titles (*sanads* and *parcha*). They sought to manage public opinion, for example by grandiose building, history-writing, proclamations and ceremonies.

Particularly, however, they worked systematically, as with *mansabdari* ranks. They provided laws which applied to all subjects, or to all in particular categories (for example, in conception if not always in practice, the *jiziya*, abolished by Akbar and reinstated by Aurangzib), or according to standard principles, as in Aurangzib's compilation of orthodox religious laws. They ordered territory into subdivisions, districts and provinces (*parganas*, *tahsils* and *subahs*), measured land according to the quality of soil, and categorized it by holder and revenue-obligation, for example as revenue-paying (*malguzari*) or revenue-free (*lakhiraj* or *inam*); as *khalisa* (directly state-managed) or *jagir* (assigned to allies, agents and employees); as *zamindari* (directly managed by the lord or collector) or *raiyati*, managed by the cultivator. It was to register these complex details that the Mughals and their agents conducted their continual surveys of landholding and tax obligations.

From the late sixteenth to the early eighteenth centuries, even in regions subject to war, there were relatively stable systems of taxation, an indication of the degree of centralization that was being achieved. Sometimes the Mughals succeeded in replacing local powers with their own officials, ranked and disciplined, with distinct powers and obligations over land tax, military force, and so on: this was mostly true of the regulation (*zabt*) land-revenue settlements. At other times the arrangements seem no more than nominally to accommodate existing and local elites, as sometimes with the various levels of *zamindar* or land-revenue collector. But, in many cases, the effect was to start the building of classes with more secure and standard rights. This had social and economic consequences.

At all levels, in practice, revenue collections none the less continued to depend upon negotiation and on relative abilities to coerce, conceal or resist. According to a Dutch observer, Francisco Pelseart, even Jahangir was 'king of the plains and open roads only, for in many places you can travel only with a strong body of men or on payment of heavy tolls to rebels'.[2] *A fortiori*, then, Mughal decline was associated with a decreasing capacity to control and collect revenue from outlying regions and agents. A symptom of the failing of the empire was the breakdown of systems, temporarily during wars of succession, or long-term over the eighteenth century. The central imperatives retreated in face of growing local power, or were modified in return for short-term financial gain. In Bengal after 1713, for example, the *diwan*, supposedly an imperial officer, was treated as subordinate to the *nizamat* (governorship) of Murshid Quli Khan, who made settlements mainly with Hindu zamindars, several of them north Indian migrants, in his attempts to maximize Bengal revenues.

Under the Marathas too there were strong regional interventions. Like all the rising eighteenth-century powers, the Marathas drew upon Mughal precedents, as well as upon newer alliances between military force, territorial gentry and commercial capital. Their system was based upon a distinction between homeland (subject to regular administration), and external lands from which tribute (*chauth*) was demanded by military force. Shivaji collected the land tax broadly on the Mughal system, using collectors called *karkans*. We have already noted the role of district *kamavisdars*. In 1760, under the Peshwa Madhav Rao, there was a survey to record land rights and reassess the land tax, collection of which was the responsibility of hereditary village headmen (the *patel*) placed over cultivators (*kanbis*, also the name of a caste) who were treated either as hereditary residents (*mirasdars*) or as 'non-resident' (*uparis*). The former were jointly responsible for the land revenue, divided between them by the *patel* at customary rates (*rivaj*), apparently a survival of a system of shares. Both village and peshwari officials kept accounts and records. The *kulkarni*, for example, registered village and land-revenue payments; his accounts were superintended by another land-holding official, the *deshpande*, while district accounts were made up by the *daftardar*. All of these came under the jurisdiction of the hereditary district *deshmukh* who was both a police and revenue officer.

This pattern of administration, and many other features of the state, were continued under that other 'early modern' though gradually transformative regime, the East India Company, to which we now turn. Many of the same titles and offices persisted (as shown in Box 6), as did many of the alliances with local mercantile power, much of the emphasis upon armed force, and much of the reliance on personal ties and interests among the ruling elites, both European and Indian. The high officers of the Company, and its historians, presented the establishment of its rule increasingly as a decisive break – which of course it was, with hindsight. In its everyday affairs, however, it was necessarily and often deliberately gradual and partial in its innovations. Both Mughal and British empires intruded on and weakened local and regional entities, but did not replace them.

Box 6   Mughal–Maratha–British Indian polity

Area	Political/military	Revenue	Collection	Record
Province	Subahdar/nizam/ mansabdar Bakshi	Diwan	Mansabdar	
District	Jagirdar/zamindar	Zamindar/ kamavisdar	Malguzar/ deshmukh/ chaudhuri	Daftardar/ deshpande/ qanungo
Village/ estate	Patel/village zamindar Faujdar Thanadar/kotwal Chaukidar	Patel/village zamindar Raiyat	Krori Karnam/ kulkarni	Patwari

5

Early Modern India II: Company Raj

THE EAST INDIA COMPANY IN MADRAS AND CALCUTTA

European power expanded slowly from apparent weakness. The expansion can be best studied in the main cases, the south and Bengal. In the south, there were two centres of attention in the middle of the eighteenth century: firstly Hyderabad, and secondly the small states of the Carnatic which were under the nominal suzerainty of Hyderabad, though the Marathas also claimed tribute from them on the basis of past conquests. The British, centred mainly in Fort St George, Madras (Chennai), and the French at Pondicherry, seemed important initially because of the aid they could offer to participants in purely Indian struggles. However, under the governorship of Joseph Dupleix (1742–54), the French tried to create a south Indian empire, by intervening in regional and dynastic politics. Dupleix began this policy when it appeared that there was no longer any strong indigenous power in the south. The French had also taken Madras in 1746, an attack incidental to the Anglo-French war of 1744–9. Madras was restored to the British by the peace treaty, but the British position remained precarious.

Others also had ambitions in the south. By 1740 the Nawab of the Carnatic (or Arcot), Dost Ali, had taken over Tiruchirappali (Trichinopoly) and Madurai, and had also attacked Thanjavur, then under Maratha control. In 1740–1 Marathas invaded from the north, killed Dost Ali, and captured his son-in-law, Chanda Sahib.

Dost Ali's son succeeded him as Nawab of the Carnatic but was murdered by his cousin, who was ousted in turn when the Nizam of Hyderabad, Asaf Jah, intervened. The Nizam then appointed a ruler of his own choice, Anwar-ud-din. Thanjavur retained its effective independence under a Hindu raja.

Asaf Jah died in 1748. There was a disputed succession between his second son, Nasir Jang, and his grandson, Muzaffar Jang, who was supported by Dupleix. (Asaf's eldest son, Ghazi-ud-din, was imperial *wazir*, and, though he too later tried to claim the succession in Hyderabad, he died before reaching there, in 1752.) Nasir had gained most support and defeated Muzaffar, but was assassinated in 1750. The French advanced Muzaffar to be Nizam. When he too was killed in 1751, they backed yet another son of Asaf Jah, Salabat Jang. He ruled in Hyderabad with the aid of a French force, under the Marquis de Bussy. In 1755 the Nizam went to war, with de Bussy, against the Raja of Mysore, an ally of the French, who had already been attacked by the British. The Nizam was persuaded to come to terms by de Bussy, but this incident soured relations on all sides, and de Bussy was recalled. However, unable to return safely because harassed by Maratha attacks, he remained in Hyderabad and was able to help the Nizam defeat the Peshwa's forces (with whom the British East India Company had recently been allied in putting down pirates on the Malabar coast). This sequence of events cemented the French alliance with the Nizam. He ceded to them the coastal territories around Visakhapatnam (Vizagapatam) and Machilipatnam (Masulipatam). The French were now at the height of their strength in India, and the British were very much reduced in influence and manpower.

Further south the struggles had continued. Asaf Jah's replacement in the Carnatic, Anwar-ud-din, died in 1749, fighting Dupleix in support of the new Nizam, Nasir Jang. Anwar's son, Muhammad Ali, remained in Tiruchirappali with some help from the weakened British East India Company, and with the support of the Raja of Thanjavur. Muhammad Ali laid a claim to succeed his father as Nawab of the Carnatic, and was opposed by Chanda Sahib, now released and backed by the Marathas as well as Dupleix. In 1751, with the aid of Robert Clive and his daring diversionary attack on Arcot, capital of the Carnatic, Muhammad Ali resisted Dupleix's seige of Tiruchirappali. The following year, Chanda Sahab was put to death by the Raja of Thanjavur, and Muhammad Ali was made Nawab with British support.

Box 7   Mughal (Turani) nobles descended from Ghazi-ud-din Khan Firuz Jang, Aurangzib's Governor of Berar

1. *His son*: Mir Kamr-ud-din (known as Chin Qilich Khan, Asaf Jah, or the Nizam-ul-Mulk or regulator of the kingdom), Grand Wazir (1716–24), Vice-regent in Delhi (1738–41), Nizam of Hyderabad (1724–48)

2. *Asaf Jah's sons*: Ghazi-ud-din, Imperial Wazir (1741–52); Nasir Jang, Nizam (1748–50); Salabat Jang, Nizam (1751–62); Nizam Ali, Nizam (1762–1802)

3. *Asaf's grandsons*: Muzaffar Jang, Nizam (1750–1); Ghazi-ud-Din or Shahab-ud-din (Imad-ul-Mulk), Imperial Wazir (1753–9)

Dupleix was recalled in 1754. In 1758 news was received that the Seven Years' War had broken out in North America and Europe. The new French governor, a man of Irish extraction, the Comte de Lally, tried unsuccessfully to extort tribute from Thanjavur and to retake Madras. Meanwhile British East India Company troops, whom Clive had sent from Bengal, defeated the French garrison in Visakhapatnam, captured Machilipatnam, and came to terms with the Nizam, Salabat Jang. (He needed to secure protection against the fate which he was later to meet – when he was murdered, and replaced, by another of his brothers, Nizam Ali.) In 1760 de Lally too was defeated. Pondicherry was taken in 1761. It was restored to the French in 1763, but as an unfortified town. Robert Clive and other East India Company commanders had finally reduced the French once more to their original settlements. But by now the British Company and its armies were important players in the politics of the south. The British set about opposing or allying themselves with the other local states, as a territorial power.

The situation in Bengal was rather different, but the outcome was even more dramatic. By mid-century, benefiting from Bengal's productivity, the British East India Company, along with other European traders, had well-established trading settlements. The British had fortified Calcutta (now officially Kolkata) and maintained an army in Bengal. In 1756 Alivardi Khan's twenty-year-old grandson and successor, Siraj-ud-daula, quarrelled with the Company, objecting to the enhanced fortifications being undertaken at Calcutta, and also to the abuse by British private traders of the *dastak* (exemption from trade duties) that the Company had enjoyed officially since 1717. The Company had cause to fear French attack, and possible disorder in Bengal after the death of Alivardi Khan, plus invasion either by the Marathas or by the imperial *wazir* to enforce payment of tribute. It was already in touch with possible enemies of Siraj-ud-daula.

Siraj attacked Calcutta, defeated its depleted forces, and imprisoned some surviving British residents in a cramped lock-up or, colloquially, 'black hole'. There was a considerable loss of life, and thanks to later publicity by one of the survivors, a member of Council, J. Z. Holwell, this incident gained a disproportionate notoriety. News of the debacle reached Madras about the same time as that of de Bussy's success in Hyderabad, but a force was hastily sent to Bengal under Clive, with a British naval squadron under Admiral Watson. Clive landed successfully in Bengal, and retook Calcutta without difficulty. Siraj soon opted for peace. He was fearful of attack from Ahmad Shah Abdali, and proposed advancing to Patna, asking for Clive's support. Siraj's main army in Bengal was now under the command of Alivardi's brother-in-law (Siraj's uncle), Mir Ja'far. Clive's forces were tiny in comparison, and he also had valid concerns about possible French intervention. He embarked on a policy of intrigue. It was crucial, and (given the antagonisms common in periods of accession) not so very difficult, to neutralize Mir Ja'far, and to gain the backing of factions opposed to Siraj, and of Hindu financiers – Clive succeeded with the family of the Jagat Seths (Mahtab Rai and Maharaja Swarupchand). Clive first attacked the French at their settlement of Chandernagore; the Nawab failed to intervene. Clive then issued an ultimatum to Siraj and marched on Murshidabad, the capital of Bengal. Siraj was defeated, largely by superior cannon-fire and a lack of support from some of his own commanders, in a two-day battle at Plassey (1757). Mir Ja'far held aloof, but was installed as Nawab by Clive. Shortly afterwards Mir Ja'far captured and executed Siraj.

Mir Ja'far had made vast promises to the Company and its servants. These proved hard to honour. Clive had forced him to abandon all hope of levying duties upon European private traders; they prospered, as Indian merchants and the Nawab's revenues declined. Mir Ja'far tried to extort more income from local treasuries, at the same time as he needed to consolidate his power. Clive supported him in several minor military actions against local rebels, and also against attacks by Ali Gauhar (Shah Alam II) in Bihar; he also saw off an opportunistic Dutch expedition against the Company. But, after Clive's departure in 1760, Mir Ja'far was replaced by his son-in-law, Mir Kasim, on the basis of yet more promises to the Company. The revenues of three districts were assigned to pay for Company troops. The Company at first accepted a small duty on its servants' private trade, but this was soon abandoned. Mir Kasim then secured a direct hold on Bihar and its revenues, ousting the deputy nawab installed by Clive, and negotiating subtly with Shah Alam. He quarrelled, however, with the Company chiefs in Bihar and hostilities broke out in 1763, during which Mir Kasim killed his Company prisoners and their Indian allies at Patna. Mir Ja'far was restored to power in Murshidabad. Mir Kasim gained the support of Shah Alam and of Shuja-ud-daula, Nawab of Awadh; but his and the Awadhi forces were defeated by the Company at Baksar in west Bihar in 1764. This gave the Company effective command of most of north India.

At this point, in 1765, Clive returned to Bengal. He decided that the defeated Shuja-ud-daula should be restored to power in Awadh, but forced to form a defensive alliance with the Company, and to pay it a huge subsidy. Shuja was also made to cede the direct control of two districts to Shah Alam, who in the end had not joined in the battle of Baksar. The emperor in turn awarded the *diwani* (revenue collection) of Bengal to the Company, which began by administering it through a deputy, Muhammad Reza Khan. Mir Ja'far had died the same year, and was replaced by another Nawab. His powers too were mostly exercised by the Company's deputy, until, after some years of this indirect rule, the Company began to take over. The main dispute of these years had been over revenue, and, having tried different ways of extorting funds, the Company finally claimed the collecting rights in full, benefiting from its military success.

The Company was equally concerned to consolidate its power in the south, and did so by removing the French threat, subordinating Hyderabad, promoting British control over smaller states, and containing or defeating Mysore in four wars. It was initially less eager to extend its power against the Marathas. As we have seen, in 1775, the Company in Bombay (Mumbai) which was meddling in the Maratha civil war, was forced to abandon Raghunath Rao when overruled by the Governor-General in Bengal. It then went to war for him again in 1778 on instruction from England, and was defeated by Mahadji Shinde. Shortly afterwards it allied itself with him against Haidar Ali – leaving Shinde free to dominate the region around Delhi.

In Mysore, Haidar Ali had succeeded in creating a strong state and army, and in the 1780s an inept East India Company administration in Madras allowed him to form an alliance against them with the French, the Marathas and the Nizam. On that basis Haidar invaded the Carnatic. Madras was placed in more capable hands; and inconclusive warfare and Haidar's death led to a peace in 1784. The alliance between Mysore, Hyderabad and the Marathas was broken when the Nizam was attacked and defeated by Haidar's successor, Tipu Sultan. In the next phase of the struggle, Cornwallis, the new Governor-General (1786–93), formed an alliance against Mysore with Hyderabad. Tipu invaded Travancore, another Company ally, and was narrowly defeated. Finally, after the arrival of Wellesley, who had formed decisive views from official papers read on his voyage out, a final war was started with Mysore on the excuse that Tipu was communicating with the French. Attacks from the Company in both Bombay and Madras resulted in his defeat in 1799.

Hyderabad's alliance with the Company was formalized as subsidiary (that is, the Nizam was denied external relations but guaranteed in his internal administration except for having to fund Company troops). The Company continued to meddle with the Marathas, eventually imposing a subsidiary alliance on Baji Rao II in 1803, as the price for restoring him to Pune. This led to somewhat inconclusive wars with Shinde in 1803 and Holkar in 1804, and ultimately to a final war, mainly with the Peshwa and Holkar, which ended with Maratha capitulation to the Company in 1818.

The Company continued its expansion well into the nineteenth century, but the main outline of its empire was completed by the 1840s, in several stages. The end of the final Maratha war in 1818 left the British in undisputed command of central and western India. Sind was annexed from the ruling Talpur *mirs* by the violation of treaties and opportunistic warfare in 1843. The Punjab was absorbed, following the death of Ranjit Singh (in 1839), after two wars, in 1845–6 and 1848–9. Ranjit's rule had been personal, though based upon regular administration, the hold of the Sikh soldiery, and the incorporation of different peoples and religions. After the first war, the Company tried to keep the state as a buffer to the north-west, while subordinating it, claiming tribute, and making use of Sikh soldiers. Soon, facing disorder and resentment, and buoyed up by its overbearing claim to be a bringer of 'civilization', the Company found the excuse to annex the state outright. Further annexations occurred elsewhere, on similar arguments:

some areas already subject to British control, through subsidiary treaties, were taken under direct administration. On the other hand, a very large number of semi-independent states subsisted under British suzerainty throughout colonial rule.

The Company's disastrous intervention in Afghanistan in 1838–42, attempting to contain Russia and install an amenable ruler in Kabul, set the approximate north-western limits of its power (and henceforth of 'South Asia'), though this troublesome and ill-defined frontier and its independent tribes remained the major preoccupation of the British Indian army. (There were many frontier campaigns, and further Afghan wars in 1878–80 and 1919.) A treaty with Nepal after the Gurkha war of 1814–16 fixed the north-central extent of the Company's empire. Inhospitable terrain on the north-east slowed down its advance there, though Burma was conquered in two stages in 1852 and 1886. Map-making and force were applied to make these boundaries stable, and the limits of internal jurisdiction became even more precisely defined.

THE COMPANY'S RISE TO POWER

We have concentrated here on two illustrative examples of the expansion of European power, in the south and north-east. They were not identical. But in each case the Company worked through existing conditions: both the repeated dynastic and territorial struggles of Indian states, and the residual authority of the Mughal empire. The armies on which the expansion was based were recruited for defence against local disorder, and for offence against European rivals, as European wars were exported to India. European company settlements began to be fortified from the early eighteenth century; but the greatest stimulus to military preparedness was provided after 1740 by the sudden rise of the crown-backed French company.

In the end Clive and several other British commanders proved more decisive and effective strategists than de Lally or even Dupleix. But leadership, tactics and military technology were not the Europeans' crucial advantage against the regional powers. Apart from the many great generals of their own – Tipu, Mahadji Shinde, Ranjit Singh, and so on – the Indians employed large numbers of European soldiers of fortune, and quickly learnt the lessons of discipline and firepower which they had to offer. More significant was the European ability to pay for alliances and for mercenaries, backed in the case of the British by European investment. This was long attracted by stable dividends of 6 to 10 per cent; from the 1760s, when profits fell and the stock became speculative, it took the form of state loans and guarantees. The British also tapped hugely into Indian revenues and Indian investment. In Bengal in particular, the Company's strength came to be based on payments of tribute, and finally on control over the region's wealth. Yet, paradoxically, these would not have been secured if the Company had not originally had the military and economic strength to back its allies. It was significant that the European settlements were sea-based and dependent in the end on distant merchant capital, rather than landed states that drew wealth ultimately from agriculture through either taxation or plunder.

The British Company was the most successful of the Europeans, partly through luck, but mainly because it was the best suited to expansion. Its determination was enhanced by the selfish motives of private adventurers, and only at long intervals curbed by interference from a very distant Britain. Cautionary noises from home mostly were heard too late, and the Indian adventures were generally accepted after the event; indeed they benefited from the occasional, valuable backing of the British navy, army and state. After 1709, the Company had a local command structure, focused on the three presidencies of Bombay, Madras and Bengal, each with their governor and council. After 1773, by Act of Parliament, the administration in India was placed under the Bengal governor as Governor-General; and, after another Act in 1784, his authority was clarified over his own Council. Under an autocratic but bureaucratic government, and decisive leadership at key moments, the Company could mobilize resources, and each of the presidencies, though also often competitive, was able to support the others.

An additional factor was imperial ambition. This was arguably apparent in Clive and his contemporaries, but predominant by the end of the eighteenth century. The conquest of Mysore provides a good example. After the war that ended in 1784, the Company retained its possessions – a success of a kind, in view of the coalition against them. Warren Hastings, then Governor-General (1772–85), claimed that he had maintained the status quo. But territory was already at issue. Apart from Haidar's ambitions, Hyderabad's enmity at this moment had been prompted by the Company's resumption in 1779 of Guntur district, an area ceded following British success in 1758–9, but in 1765 given as a *jagir* for life to a brother of the Nizam. On the other hand, Hastings had handed

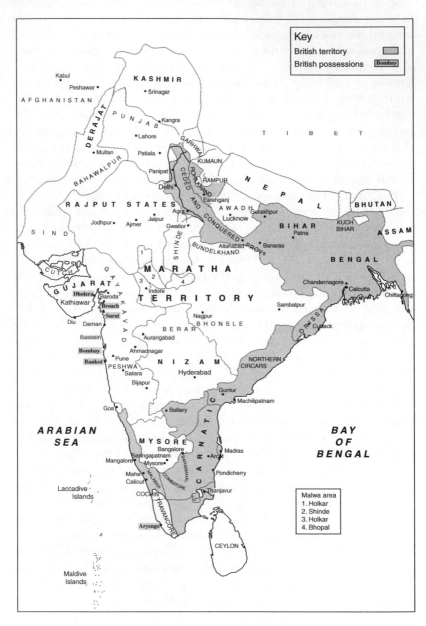

Map 4 India in 1805

back Guntur, to secure Hyderabad's neutrality in the war with Mysore.

Under Cornwallis, again, containment was claimed to be the Company's goal, but this time, after Tipu's defeat, the Company annexed a third of his territories. Nevertheless, under Sir John Shore (1793–8), the Company refused to help the Nizam against the Marathas. Then, after Wellesley (as Lord Mornington) became Governor-General (1798–1805), a treaty was engineeered with Hyderabad which, as noted earlier, ensured its permanent subordination, marked by the Nizam's agreeing to dismiss his French army officers. After the victory of 1799, even more of Mysore's territory was annexed, and the Hindu dynasty restored to a remnant of its lands. Tipu's demise earned Wellesley his new title, and became a cause for national celebration, at a time of popular mobilization against Napoleon. In this climate, though still officially banned from expanding Company territory, Wellesley found other excuses to annex Thanjavur and the Carnatic. The latter had already become hopelessly enmeshed in Madras politics by corrupt Company servants during the 1780s. Only military reverses prevented Wellesley from fulfilling similar ambitions against the Marathas.

This was a progression towards both territorial and (as in the subsidiary alliance with Hyderabad) indirect dominion. In some senses it was a mark of growing military and political strength, as the Company turned itself from a body of armed traders into an Indian power. But Wellesley's choices were made in the context of his having imagined the possibility of all-India supremacy for the British. He was eager to reduce all rivals to subservience not co-operation. He insisted on the subordination of the Mughal 'King of Delhi' in 1803. He took territory when possible under the direct administration of the Company. He wanted to build an empire rather than to consolidate a position or maximize immediate gain.

This remained more or less the policy of his successors, until power began to be transferred to Indians in the twentieth century. Lord Moira, later Lord Hastings (Governor-General, 1812–23), modified Wellesley's policies and instituted a mostly lasting compact with Indian princely states, promoting indirect rule over large parts of India. On the other hand, he and his successors also placed emphasis on pacification and the imperial order – through control of borders, development of the army and police, and measures against internal threats such as *pindaris* (armed marauders in central

India, 1806–15), or so-called *thagi* (thugs) and other 'criminal tribes', or, more generally, dacoity (armed robbery).

REVENUE SETTLEMENTS UNDER THE COMPANY

In the longer term, the administrative strengths of the successor powers of the eighteenth century served less to revive regional states and identities than to preserve compact territories capable of being dominated by the Mughals' successor, the British East India Company. Once again foreigners curbed the development of regional states. The Company first assumed responsibility for revenue and administration, within the remnants of the Mughal structure, in Bengal and Bihar after 1765. A few great zamindars, some local and some brought in from outside, had managed the affairs of the region, but its administration had come under stress, through the need to accommodate local land-controllers while raising additional taxation. As explained, the pressure came from the extension of warfare, the tribute paid to avoid Maratha raids, and various bribes for or debts to Europeans, and from the squeeze on revenue through European and Indian merchants' use of the Company's *dastak* (or pass) to avoid paying taxes upon trade. The means used to increase land-revenue receipts while appeasing the locally powerful included *ijaradari* (farming-out the revenue-collecting right to the highest bidder, usually on an annual basis), further assignment of *jagirs* (giving over the state's share of future revenue, often in return for a loan), and the alienation of *khalisa* (state land) to local zamindars.

The East India Company under Warren Hastings took over the revenue collection (*diwani*) directly in Bengal and Bihar in 1772, establishing a Board of Revenue at Calcutta and Patna, and moving the treasury records to Calcutta from Murshidabad. After 1773 the system was extended to the tributary state of Banaras under a Company Resident, as Awadh had ceded that territory by treaty. In 1774 district collectors were replaced by provincial councils (to prevent corruption) at Patna, Murshidabad and Calcutta, with Indian collectors in the districts. As not much was known about levels of assessment, a Committee of Circuit toured the districts to make a five-year settlement. It turned out to be little different in effect from the former annual farming-out of the revenue collections; but clearly, like the Mughals, the Company was seeking control through information and bureaucracy.

The permanent settlement of the land revenues of Bengal in 1793 was the earliest major example of socio-economic regulation under colonial rule. It was permanent because it fixed the land tax in perpetuity. At the same time it defined the nature of land-ownership. It gave individuals and families separate property rights in occupied land. Gradually over the next century or more, land measurements, court decisions and sales gave practical effect to the change. Land settlements were very different in other parts of India, but they shared this characteristic of creating landed property.

The East India Company had, as said, taken direct control of the land-revenue system in Bengal in 1772, beginning a series of experiments that ended in 1789 with ten-year settlements. The permanent settlement was designed to encourage political allies, social stability and economic advance, through the establishment of landed property rights. The permanance of this settlement distinguished it from others in India. It also singled-out rights *between* the state and the cultivator. Zamindars (whether land-tax collectors or local magnates or *parvenu*) were turned into landlords, retaining their old name but acquiring a new legal identity through a vast set of regulations. *Individual* title (whether held by household heads, co-sharers or legal corporations) was recorded with reference to *particular* plots of land, and also to forests, commons, reservoirs, roads and market-places. This was done without any survey or investigation or principle of assessment other than was provided by the Company's recent experience and by new or inherited records. All these features distinguished it from Todar Mal's survey.

Proprietary 'rights' were made definite and uniform in an 'objective' law. Certain other rights in land (tenancy and cultivating rights, for example) were also but much less clearly noted and defined, a neglect which, it was later argued, damaged those with subsidiary rights. Long afterwards such rights were also defined. Common, overlapping or contingent rights thus tended to be ignored or reformulated, a deficiency that mattered more as legal rights were enforced, land gained in value, and population grew. Thus began a legal and social change that would eventually be revolutionary.

The proprietary rights defined in 1793 were regarded at the same time as traditional, universal and necessary. The economic aim was to encourage investment by protecting private profit. The socio-political goal was to ensure or create aristocratic interests as a bulwark against popular unrest and corrupt or ignorant officials. The ultimate intention was minimal government and reliable income for the Company. Thus, though the settlement's initial demand was very high in many instances, theoretically it sought to prevent arbitrary exactions by the state, on the premise that investment depended upon security for landed minorities who supposedly had traditional rights and a potential for economic efficiency. The approach contrasted, it was thought, not only with the prevailing anarchy of Indian regimes, but also with the pragmatic policies previously adopted by the Company in Bengal – for example, short-term revenue contracts with the highest bidder.

On the other hand, the permanent settlement was also in some ways a transitional measure in its conception (as also its application and impact), befitting an 'early modern' state. The reliance on rural magnates was due to lack of information, fears about corrupt employees and administrative incapacity, as well as to pro-landlord sentiment and physiocratic ideas of political economy and a belief in minimal government. That the zamindars were given private property resulted from an accident of timing as well as a theory of economic development.

Moreover, starting between 1800 and 1818, there came a reaction against this gentrified model of society. It was based both on a rival ideology and on conservatism, a supposedly greater fidelity to Indian circumstances. It was held that there were large areas of India where no landlords existed; there were various kinds of over-lords and chiefs but the British refused to turn them into proprietors, persuaded by the advocacy of (among others) Thomas Munro, later to be Governor of Madras. A permanent revenue settlement was now said to invite indolence rather than enterprise. A different class, effectively of peasant-proprietors, was identified as deserving the privilege of property, still using arguments of tradition and efficiency. The outcome was a system of temporary settlements in which the 'occupants' of the land – 'raiyats' or 'actual cultivators' – became its proprietors. These raiyatwari settlements were introduced in the newly conquered areas of southern India from 1820 and then, with some modifications, in western India. The basis of the assessment – in this respect marking a return to the method adopted under Akbar – was a permanent classification of fields according to soil and produce, with average rent-rates fixed for the period of the settlement. The demand was determined annually in accordance with land use. Increasing exploration, information and bureau-cracy had given the Company the confidence to attempt closer administration, while claiming enhanced respect for Indian traditions, paradoxically bolstered by the Evangelical attack on Indian civilization and a Utilitarian eagerness for reform.

Variants of these two kinds of settlement were also developed, including settlements both with 'villages' collectively and on a temporary basis with 'landlords'. Most important were those of north India and the Punjab, the former based either on village-level settlements or on a 'restoration' of landlords, and the latter mainly on peasant proprietors. In north India and the Punjab, the officials declared that the local communities were 'still' vigorous (increasingly they were thought of as the original social form, an idea picked up by Marx and elaborated in the works of Henry Maine).

In 1822, after a Commission headed by Holt Mackenzie, it was officially required both that there should be no disturbance of pre-existing local rights in land, and that revenue demands should be set in accordance with local conditions as revealed and recorded after a full survey on 'scientific' principles. Under the Utilitarians' anti-landlord influence, a strict attempt was made to apply Ricardo's theory that rent was merely the net surplus, over and above prevailing rates of profit, obtainable on more favoured land. The conclusion was that the state could safely extract the bulk of this 'unearned income' and re-apply it more productively. Later surveys were forced to modify the application of this theory; so R. K. Pringle's settlement in the Deccan was quickly revised by George Wingate and H. E. Goldsmid (1835) who made a more formal separation between professional cadastral and revenue surveys, with the intention of basing the demand on a realistic assessment of the actual condition and potential of the land.

A basic divide remained between a permanent settlement with 'landlords' and temporary settlements with 'cultivators', and therefore between regions of minimal and closer government. But, in the late nineteenth century (as will be seen), there was some coming-together of the opposing tendencies, and this hastened as much as it interrupted the evolution of the state. All plans to extend the permanent settlement were abandoned, and instead special laws, more accessible courts, and surveys and records of rights were developed to regulate agrarian conditions, even in the permanently settled areas, and in particular (where the settlement was with landlords) to protect tenants by allowing the most privileged and successful of them to enjoy quasi-proprietorial rights. At the same time taxation was extended through political representation, special-purpose demands and fees. These changes contributed to the state's growing role as arbiter of the society and economy.

TRANSITIONS, 1770s TO 1860s: TRADE

The first half of the nineteenth century was a time of transition towards new political and economic conditions. Three elements are apparent. First was the continuation of earlier policies of qualified centralization based on the accommodation of local customs and power. Second were the ideological differences, beginning with James Mill's disdain for the aristocratic prejudices of the Bengal settlement. A host of modern historians have emphasized the importance of theory to the formation of policy – even though they admit that attention was paid to Indian practices, and attempts made to reduce the disruption of foreign rule. Third was the common ground between all the administrative systems, amounting to a transition to a new kind of state. More recently, for example, some scholars have realized that, despite the pretensions of Thomas Munro or the declarations of Holt Mackenzie, the land systems all misread Indian conditions, and imposed legal rights and distinctions which were novel in their degree of standardization and of state and judicial backing. All assumed 'ownership' and gave a priority to the 'occupancy' and use of land – that is, they focused on settled and commercial agriculture as well as on exclusive individual property. They all facilitated land transfer, by making the state and its records the arbiter of property rights (in theory if not immediately in practice). All embodied an important colonial input, an aspect of Western scientific methods and knowledge, at least in the estimation of colonial officials themselves, namely rational and objective categorization – norms, measurement and enumeration. Such measures were transitional, or still 'early modern', only because of inherited continuities, pragmatic practices, and delays of implementation or influence.

A range of other spheres followed the same pattern – a mixture of accommodation and transformation. It is apparent in trade and production; in the assertion of British supremacy and of colonial order, and the disarming of the population; in the introduction of other modernizing social, legal and administrative policies; and in the start of public works and investment. We will consider a few examples.

The acquisition of the *diwani* in Bengal in 1765 transformed the Company's trading policies, by largely removing the need for imports of bullion. Bengal revenues also helped pay for deficits and military campaigns elsewhere in India, as indeed they had in Mughal times, when the net loss of bullion by Bengal may well have been even more considerable. Over the last forty years of the eighteenth century, however, this double blow undoubtedly had an effect on the local money supply, and contributed to Bengal's unstable economic condition, soon to be further damaged by a sharp decline in the export of cotton goods under pressure from British protectionism. Similarly, control or closure of local mints, standardizations of the metallic content and exchange value of the coinage, overproduction of crops such as indigo that depended on foreign markets, higher taxes, and the export of treasure from India to Britain all contributed to economic downturns in the second quarter of the nineteenth century – a depression brought to an end after the 1850s, in part by worldwide increases in the supply of gold and silver, and by imports of silver into India to pay for railways and canals.

The changes in trade were most significant in the long term. Broadly speaking, between the 1780s and 1860s, India moved from being an exporter of processed goods and an importer of bullion, to being an exporter of raw materials and an importer of manufactures. The change reflected the opening of Indian trade to the British by the removal or reduction of internal checks, dangers and tolls, following the example of England and Scotland after 1707. The change also kept pace with the industrial development of Britain, and gained further impetus with the retreat from protectionism begun under Robert Peel in 1842.

In India the first stage was a tripartite trade that developed on the basis of the revenues and resources gained by the Company when it acquired the *diwani* in Bengal. It was an advantage in this respect that the Company (unlike the government in Britain) raised its revenue primarily from the land instead of from customs and excise. Indian silver, opium or cotton paid for Chinese tea and silk, which were shipped back to Britain along with Indian produce. This trade altered existing trading patterns within India. Some Indian regions such as Bengal and Gujarat were drawn into worldwide rather than regional relationships: so Gujarati cotton and piecegoods went to China and Europe rather than Bengal. Some regional connections were lost: for example, Bengal began to import cotton by land and river from central India rather than by sea from Gujarat, which was deprived of Bengal silk, while Bengal sugar was driven out of west-coast markets by south-east Asian imports.

The terms on which commodities were supplied also changed, as the Company established monopsonistic trading conditions for cotton and indigo, and monopolies in opium and salt. At first, production, trade, transport and towns all expanded markedly: Indians responded to new opportunities. But there were also changes in costs and profits, between producers and merchants, between commodities, and between regions. Export shipping, insurance and marketing were increasingly in the hands of European agency houses, paying advances to sellers and being repaid, with commission, after the sale.

Most important, Indian producers became vulnerable to contractions in international demand. The same bankers and bills of exchange (*hundis*) underwrote both internal and export trade, so that the economy as a whole was involved in any collapse in the export sector. From early in the nineteenth century, British protective duties and then cheaper manufactures damaged the market for Indian cotton piecegoods. In the 1830s the Agra and Bundelkhand areas were depressed by overproduction of, and falling international demand for, Indian raw cotton, in the aftermath of the ending of the Company's monopoly. This was symptomatic of a downturn that ushered in a quarter-century of economic depression in Calcutta and north India.

One qualification of the picture of an economy captured by colonialism, however, is the extent to which some activities remained in Indian hands, and to which even those that were dominated by Europeans retained aspects of pre-existing practice. Great Indian merchant houses continued to flourish, and *banjaras* (travelling merchants) still conducted the large interior trade. In Surat in western India, for example, the fortunes of the city were sustained, to an extent, by large and international dealings in pearls and in gold and silver wire and tinsel, even after the bulk of Surat's industry, including the processing of locally produced cotton and sugar, had moved to European-dominated Bombay. The Indian 'bazaar' economy was not confined to small-scale or local enterprise. Surat's surviving skilled and luxury producers were typical of those that remained largely outside the concern of government or European capitalists. Such production then sustained merchants who imported raw materials and commodities of consumption, especially cloth, from elsewhere.

Similarly, in the colonial economy, aspects of production followed Indian rather than European methods. In Gujarat raw cotton was obtained, for factory production or export, using the pre-existing networks of finance, buyers and intermediaries. In north India and Bihar, the Company's opium was obtained – despite a repeatedly expressed preference for direct production or direct purchasing – through local agents who were commonly also members of village elites; and the Company's output competed with so-called Malwa or native-state opium that was eventually brought under British control only by being exported through Bombay. The capital for opium cultivation was provided by government advances, and that for north Indian indigo through harvest loans from indigo speculators; but much other commercial production – of cotton, wheat, rice, sugar, jute, oilseeds, market vegetables, dairy produce, animal-rearing, leather goods, and so on – was supported very largely from local moneylending. If these goods found their way into European or Indian factories, it was often through the agency of travelling, often independent, wholesale buyers, frequently the same who had advanced the harvest loans. The resilience of local economies and customs, and the complexities of markets and landholding, made it difficult to impose the logic of European capitalism or commercialization throughout all of the stages of any production in India – even, later, on the European tea or coffee plantations.

Thus, trade developed from partnership with Indians towards an imposition by Europeans which none the less embodied features of Indian origin. Some similar patterns could be seen in other spheres. Between 1765 and 1772, the Company had deliberately operated a dual system of government, leaving details of revenue collection to its Indian deputies, and many other matters to the puppet Nawab. The Company was in financial crisis from the 1760s, needing cash for Indian costs, European dividends, and the mercantile investment. In 1769–70 there was a terrible famine in Bengal, but the land-revenue collections remained high. In the 1770s the Company began to incur ever greater costs from its wars, and its expansions of territory, administration and public works. It cut the Nawab's expenses from Rs (rupees) 3.2 million to 1.6 million and stopped paying tribute to the Mughal emperor. It embarked on a Europeanization and professionalization of its administration. Even much later, however, public and private concerns remained notably blurred. In the early nineteenth century, though standards of administrative probity were beginning to be enforced, the Company remained venal and arbitrary in practice, concerned to maximize private and public profit. Especially at lower levels, influential Europeans who were well known to be corrupt were still kept in office and even promoted.

LAW

At the same time the Company began to cover itself in a patina of regulation and legal process, and to support its policy proposals by expressions of concern for the public good, which marked a departure from Mughal norms. As early as the 1760s, the Company's government faced increasing scrutiny at home, and began to share in the reforms of administration which were occurring also in Britain as a gradual recession from the patronage systems created in state, army and church after the Revolution of 1688. In 1765–9, for example, Robert Becher (Resident in Murshidabad) was worried about the impoverishment of raiyats through excessive taxation. (It had increased from Rs 2.4 million between 1582 and 1722, to Rs 11.6 million by 1763, half of that between 1760 and 1763 under Kasim Ali.) The Governor, Verelst, agreed, and on that basis in 1769 appointed European revenue supervisors, the start of the attempt to get beyond the dual system. A little later the farming of revenue collection to the highest bidder was opposed by Philip Francis, as a member of Warren Hastings' Council, on the physiocratic grounds that it was damaging to existing proprietorial interests and to their future economic investment. This was a rhetoric of policy-making that was rather different from, say, that espoused by the Company's deputy *diwan* for Bengal, Muhammad Reza Khan, who saw his duty as partly to guard the Nawab's rights (and was arrested, effectively for that reason, in 1772). The Governors-General of the late eighteenth century – Warren Hastings, Sir John Shore and especially Cornwallis – espoused thrift and propriety, while early in the following century Wellesley sought efficiency (not very successfully in his more grandiose projects).

One can trace this slow change, in the operation of the law. Old systems continued to exist and evolve independently of central influence. They were based on the authority of local chiefs and zamindars, and on local tribunals (village, trade and caste *panchayats*),

and deployed community rules, physical coercion or moral persua-
sion (for example, *dharna* or *gherao*, sit-down strikes or passive
obstruction, where weaker parties would seek redress for grievances
by publicly shaming someone stronger). These levels of customary
law could be allied with and gain strength from higher forms, both
the state's revenue and criminal jurisdiction and the Hindu *shastras*
and Muslim *sharia*. But they did not form part of an integrated
system of law. There was no hierarchical relationship or appeal
between these informal legal processes and the Mughal courts
(*adalat*) – a Daroga Adalat al-Aaba for petty criminal and civil cases,
the *diwan* as judge in civil and military cases (Daroga Adalat Diwani),
and the nawab in criminal cases. Though legal and moral debates
thrived in the eighteenth century, the Mughals and their Indian
successors relied more upon personal decision and authority than
upon objective legal structures.

The East India Company began to alter this. In 1765 Francis
Sykes (the Resident) set up a High Court at Murshidabad, and this
was inherited by Becher under whom revenue supervisors were
supposed to look after justice as well as revenue. In Dinajpur the
supervisor set up subordinate courts. Above all, in Calcutta from
the 1770s the British introduced a full array of English legal instruments, including Supreme Court and Grand Jury; Equity, Requests,
Marine and Military courts; arbitration; coroners, magistrates and
justices of the peace. Under the Regulating Act of 1773 this system
of English law had jurisdiction over all British subjects, Company
servants and Calcutta residents. Key features in practice were the laws
of debt, contract and employment needed to help Calcutta function
as a growing mercantile centre. Indian residents – merchants, bankers,
shopkeepers, tradesmen, contractors, bearers, boatmen, labourers
and servants – were inevitably drawn into these courts both as
defendants and as plaintiffs.

The Company also began to take over and codify local laws and
practices. It developed the existing courts, setting up District (Mufas-
sil) Diwani Adalats (for civil cases) and Faujdari Adalats (for criminal
cases), the former under the European collector and Indian *diwan*,
and the latter under *qazis* and *muftis*. For capital cases there was a
Sadar Nizamat Adalat in Murshibadad (sentencing being reserved
for the Nawab); and there were appeals from the *mufassal* (country
districts) to the Sadar Diwani Adalat in Calcutta. Under Warren
Hastings, after 1772, all this was transferred to Calcutta. Hastings
too authorized the first codification of Indian personal laws (of

inheritance, for example) for use in the Company's courts, which employed Muslim *qazis* or Hindu *pandits*. *Qazis* had first been registered for this purpose by Rous in Rajshahi in the 1760s.

Struggles for jurisdiction quickly followed, between the Supreme Court under its first Chief Justice, Elijah Impey, and the Governor's Council, especially Philip Francis, and later Hastings himself. The Court held, for example, that it had jurisdiction in cases where district zamindars failed to pay debts to Indian bankers based in Calcutta. Matters came to a head in the Kasijora case of 1779–80 when the Council denied the Court's jurisdiction, a Court officer was arrested by Council, and the Court issued a writ of habeus corpus. To avoid future conflict, Hastings abolished the old indigenous courts, except for the Sadar Diwani Adalat, which he revived under the presidency of Impey himself.

Ultimately this was a dispute about the Company's role in India, as in the more famous quarrels between Philip Francis and Warren Hastings. Francis (as he wrote to Lord North in February 1775) thought the Supreme Court should have extended jurisdiction but without touching local customs or courts. In England, Edmund Burke too argued against applying English law to Indians who (he claimed) understood only despotism. On the same argument Francis wanted the landholders (as he termed the zamindars) to have lands as private property, in perpetuity. He proposed then to leave the people alone, placing the revenue collection in Indian hands, and taking only such tribute for the Company as would provide for defence. He opposed Hastings's military policies as expansionist rather than defensive. By contrast, Hastings, like Clive before him, favoured pragmatic interventions. It was as an attempt to resolve such conflicts, that the 1784 Act made the Governor-General supreme over his Council, and in regard to other Governors and the courts. This prepared the way for much greater interventions, and eventually to claims of the Company's political supremacy in India, to general legislation, and to the reform of Indian governance and law.

Thus, in government, the British began to impose their own ways. They did not, as some have argued, merely impose a doctrine of 'difference' on India, to justify more arbitrary or paternalistic policies. They frequently made relativistic arguments in policy debates, but just as often they applied universalist remedies. On one hand, therefore, they tended to insinuate European ideas into Indian conditions, as when criminal and civil laws were applied, in theory, equally to all persons, or, even when kept distinct (as for personal and religious law), were administered according to stand-ard procedures and assumptions. On the other hand, the British were concerned to attach or reconcile Indians to their rule by accommodating Indian preferences; and their impulses to change were restrained not only by anxiety about Indian reactions but also by limits to the government's capacity, just as for other early modern administrations.

EDUCATION

Different impulses existed in individuals but also can be traced to divisions of opinion and principle between Company officials. In education, for example, the policies which typified the early nineteenth century were associated on the one hand with so-called Orientalists, and on the other with the Anglicists who favoured Western teachings in English as a way of overcoming what they regarded as Indian backwardness and superstition. The Orientalist tendency comprised a policy of conciliation, and three related goals: to sponsor Indians in their own culture, to advance the knowledge of India, and to employ that knowledge in government. Thus, in the first case, Warren Hastings argued that the patronage of indigenous learning was proper in the 'seat of a great empire' and to the Company as successor to the nawabs – the promotion of knowledge being 'the Pride of every polished Court and the Wis-dom of every well-regulated Government', as he noted in 1781.[1] Accordingly, he supported the establishment of the Calcutta Madrasa, responding to a Muslim petition (which he may have drafted). Seminaries already existed under Muslim rule, most famously at this time at Firangi Mahal (Foreigner's House) in Lucknow (Lakhnau). Later, indeed, a new doctrine arose among Indians, in response to the continuing problems of a culturally alien government: namely that, to adopt the words of the rich, conservative, Bengali reformer, Raja Radhakanta Deb (1784–1867), it was the 'duty of the Rulers of Coun-tries to preserve the Customs and the religions of their subjects'.[2]

Secondly, it was argued that the Company should appease its subjects by going further (or being better) than its predecessors; on these grounds, in Banaras (Varanasi) in 1791, the Resident, Jonathan Duncan, founded a Sanskrit College. The Asiatic Society of Bengal, founded by William Jones in 1784, had represented a similar impulse, a desire to 'preserve' Asian knowledge *and* to promote knowledge about Asia. Surveys, mapping and description developed, on such arguments, through the intermittent patronage of the Company's government (though also, more notably, through individual scientific enthusiasm).

Thirdly, it was considered necessary to educate Company servants in the languages and cultures of India, so as to render them more effective as rulers. In 1800 Wellesley set up the College of Fort William with this aim. The most influential Company officials of the early nineteenth century (such as Thomas Munro, Mountstuart Elphinstone and John Malcolm) followed his lead, and believed they shaped their governance largely in accord with Indian expectations. Their ideas dominated educational policy in the 1820s, as marked by the formation of further Sanskrit colleges in Pune and Calcutta.

The quite contrary Anglicist impulse was represented by most Christian missionaries – excluded from Company territories until 1813 – and by evangelicals such as Charles Grant (1746–1823), oft-times Company chairman and Member of Parliament. Grant advocated a state education policy for India (twenty years before government took on that responsibility in Britain), with instruction in English, in order to bring Western knowledge and Christian belief to the Indians. This approach was aided by the Utilitarian influence, headed by James Mill, which dominated the Company's home administration. Believing in the moral efficacy of proper government and law, Mill also advocated the imparting of useful knowledge, not least in order to increase the employment of 'suitable' Indians in civil administration. The growing use of English, including the abolition of Persian as a language of the Company's government and law courts in 1835–7, was intended to aid efficient management, but was also, in the phrase of Lord William Bentinck (Governor-General, 1828–35), thought to be 'the key to all improvements'. Thus English education was advocated both to aid the government and progressively to 'improve' the Indians. These ideas were embodied in the celebrated Minute of 1835 written by the legal member of the Governor-General's Council, Thomas Babington Macaulay (1800–60).

But even the Anglicist policy was evolved in a dialogue with Indian opinion. By this time, some Indians were actively seeking Western knowledge, both in English and in Indian languages, as indicated by the formation in 1816 of the Hindu College in Calcutta. Attendance at such schools grew largely during the 1830s. The literate classes, as ever, took an interest in the culture of the rulers, and in new ideas and information, and in acquiring skills for gainful employment, without necessarily undervaluing their 'own' inheritance. An example was the scholar and religious reformer, Rammohan Roy (1772–1833). His advocacy of both English education and a text-based Vedantism was opposed by more typical defenders of Bengali Brahman orthodoxy, but they too were increasingly willing to sponsor English-language schools, in search of employment, while rejecting Christian 'contamination'.

It follows that the harsher British condemnations of Indian society, represented by Grant, James Mill or Macaulay, were counterproductive. In 1839 Lord Auckland (Governor-General, 1836–42) proposed a compromise, which continued or restored funding to both English-language and Indian-language institutions. His proposals, and an ideal of mass vernacular education, were substantially accepted, in a famous Education Despatch of 1854. This produced the ever-underfunded elementary and secondary schools, along with the English colleges which developed into the Indian university system. Together they are typical of the mixture of adaptive and reforming policies developed by the British government and its Indian co-adjutors. Similarly, a committee under Macaulay was responsible for the reform of the law codes and the introduction of a new court system from the 1860s, supposedly wholly inspired by 'English principles'. But in its operation and in the amendments introduced by legislatures in India, it was also susceptible to 'vernacular' modifications.

FEATURES OF COMPANY RULE

The Orientalist–Anglicist divide occurred at the same time as a series of other similar English debates about the proper role of government. In that context, rule by merchants was an anomaly that was remedied by turning the Company into an arm of administration, subject to Parliament. In England, more seriously, government legitimated by popular will was being set against government according to established principles – the issue of the Reform Bills (1830–2) – so that relativism vied with universalism in governance, and advocates of representation with those of tutelage. (The argument was refracted by the opposition between materialist, mechanical philosophies and the advocates of high culture and morality.) Division over what government should do was brought into sharp focus by

India, and by many other instances of perceived differences – especially critical in an empire – among places and peoples, or between ruling ethos and general culture, or high principle and common practice. Should the policy on slavery be the same in Britain and the West Indies? Was it the Christian duty of an Anglican government to force an established Church upon a Catholic Ireland (as upon England); or should it recognize a 'wrongful' faith by, for example, permitting Catholic Irish prison chaplains, or by disestablishing the Irish (or even the English) Church? To what extent should indigenous populations – Australian aborigines, Maori, Zulu and so on – be protected against European settlers and the onrush of their 'civilization'? How should the French and British be accommodated in Canada? – Lord Durham was despatched to report. *Mutatis mutandis*, these were the very dilemmas of British Indian administration, which therefore embodied both a desire to 'civilize' India and the wish to 'represent' it.

Greater realism and changing medical and racial theories soon saw off the dream of large-scale immigration by Europeans into India. But ideas of British supremacy came to predominate over much high policy, first to conquer and then to reform. The roving adventurers of the eighteenth century had often already evidenced remarkable confidence, an attitude which (as noted) became more obvious in political policy from the moment of Wellesley's arrival in 1798. According to a contemporary diarist, Richard Blechynden, Wellesley affected an 'appearance of vanity and affectation', and argued that Cornwallis had 'carried matters too far' by going about in Calcutta 'as any other person' – he had done so, Wellesley thought, as an example to 'curb the profusion and overbearing upstart manners of the Company's servants', but it meant that he (Wellesley) had to 'do many things . . . very unpleasant to himself' so as to restore his post to its 'due consequence'; he had 'to carry matters with a high hand . . . to support his authority'.[3] He declared that he gave orders to be obeyed not discussed; and his assertiveness over officials was applied by them to India as a whole.

It was in this context that General Lake was told to insist on symbolic equality when meeting the Mughal emperor in 1803; and that, even after softening Wellesley's subsidiary alliances, Lord Hastings pressed the Company's paramountcy on the Indian princes. Sind was conquered, arbitrarily, for its 'own good', earning Charles Napier a place in the pantheon of imperial heroes and a plinth in Trafalgar Square. The annexation of the Punjab followed on

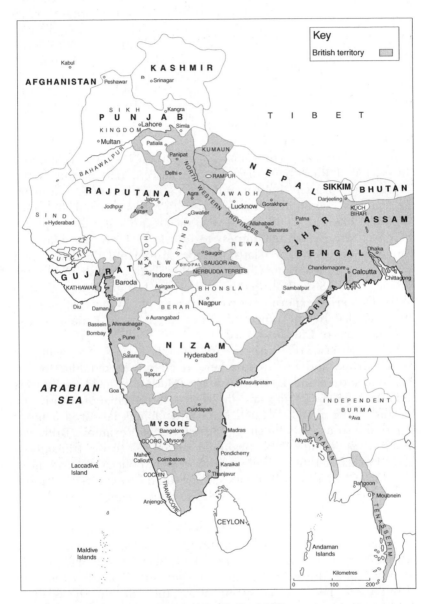

Map 5   India in 1837

similar arguments. W. H. Sleeman (though admitting that Indians seemed strangely to prefer Indian rule) argued that things were so bad in Awadh (in 1851) that the Company had a positive duty to intervene; and so Dalhousie (Governor-General, 1848–56) shortly afterwards found an excuse to annex the place outright, in defiance of treaties. Dalhousie applied the same reasoning also to smaller dependent states (Satara 1848, Jhansi 1853, Nagpur 1854, and others), developing his 'doctrine of lapse' – that is, technical excuses for annexing princely territory whenever the succession was not absolutely straightforward.

There were some contrary voices. James Tod, the celebrated chronicler of Rajasthan, discovered a nascent nationhood in the Rajputs, and argued that this put them on a different footing from the Mughals, who had failed for want of proper national allegiance to them. On the whole, however, racial and cultural prejudice increased the British willingness to interfere. Thus Macaulay was famously dismissive of Gladstone for supporting the ineffectual foisting of the Anglican Church on the Catholic Irish (*Edinburgh Review*, April 1839), but was the archetypical Anglicist in regard to India. Utilitarian experiments could be introduced there, apparently untrammeled by the powerful vested interests of Britain or the complications of European race.

There were two real curbs on ambition, however – that, being far from Europe and few in number, as already noted, the British feared disorder and lacked capacity. (Macaulay, incidentally, was consistent in favouring an indirect self-'reformation' both for Ireland and for India.) Such fears and failings favoured a more Orientalist strategy. Paralleling the Irish case, for example, Brahman cooks were permitted for Brahman prisoners. In the transitional period to about 1860, therefore, government policies did take more account of Indian susceptibilities than would be expected from the bravura rhetoric of empire. They did so on principle, by policy, and for reasons of expediency.

Instances when substantive change was introduced, either with or without Indian consent, included the rationalization of the bureaucracy according to best nineteenth-century theory. Landed property and the economy also saw major changes. Utilitarian public works began to be given importance, despite the reservations of *laissez-faire* political economy. Auckland began a push towards canal-building following severe famines in north India in the 1830s. Dalhousie followed up on earlier concern with roads and river-transport, and made a start with the telegraph and railways.

The results on law and education were more equivocal. A few apparently marginal social reforms were undertaken: the 'abolition' of *sati* (immolation of widows) in 1829, and of slavery in 1843, for instance. These had relatively little direct effect. As in many spheres, Indian practices and ideas persisted or became enhanced (including that of the honour of the wife sacrificing to her husband as to a god). But such measures also began a process of reconstituting social relations. 'Woman' became a legal category, in labour, property or marriage laws – not always an advantage, but a necessary prerequisite of campaigns 'for' women. 'Slaves' became *the* form of unfree labour, excluding the bonded agricultural workers or household members ignored by European definitions. At the same time, Western contract and property laws probably worsened the position of poor agricultural workers, while the complex position of household 'slaves' – eunuchs, concubines and children – was overtaken by a reconstitution of domestic and caste status, under such terms as 'Hindu', 'Muslim', 'married', 'legitimate' and so on, which diminished the legal rights of, or even rendered invisible, those who did not fall within those categories.

SOME EARLY MODERN INDIAN RESPONSES

The influence of British rule was immediately shallow but eventually profound. Indians responded to Western influences, to print, to Christian missionaries, and to representations and 'rediscoveries' of India's own past and character. A few embraced 'modernity' of thought, just as many more took up new economic opportunities; but most Indians reconsidered their heritage, or resisted change, in a host of religious or rural movements through to the great rebellions of 1857 and beyond. These influences fed into an existing complex of intellectual and cultural life which had developed in the courts and towns of Mughal and post-Mughal India, in centres such as Delhi, Lucknow, Hyderabad and Banaras. We shall consider these changes more fully in Chapter 8, but some of the earlier ones are also outlined in this section.

As noticed briefly in Chapter 4, the literate classes of north India – Hindu as well as Muslim – had become proficient in Persian during the seventeenth and eighteenth centuries, leading also to the development of a literary Urdu and to common participation in Hindu and Muslim festivals. These and other elites had also established a hold in the countryside, through office- and landholding, kinship, patronage and armed retainers. In Delhi, however, Shah Wali-Allah and his son Shah Abd al-Aziz (1746–1824) had prepared the ground for a revival of Sunni orthodoxy that stressed the importance of the Prophet's *hadith* to Muslim conduct, and criticized popular devotional religion and the worship of saints. In the nineteenth century, the problem was increasingly how to react to a Christian government and to changing laws, despite the Company's initial concern to respect Mughal forms. Shah Abd al-Aziz debated whether or not colonial India was *dar al-harb* (land of war, where Muslims were bound to oppose the infidel). A demilitarized countryside, the standardization of land as property, and an Europeanized higher administration all represented a growing challenge to the old order. Poets and soldiers lamented the loss of power. The Sufi-influenced but reformist Sayyid Ahmad of Barelwi (Rai Bareilly) (1786–1831) went to war against the Sikhs and Ranjit Singh, declaring *jihad* (holy war) in 1826; his followers, so-called Indian Wahabis, similarly resisted British rule as inimical to Islam. In eastern Bengal, the Sunni Hajji Shari'at-allah (1781–1840) and his son Dudu Miyan (1819–62) led a violent peasant uprising, the *fara'izi* (strict observance, dutiful) movement, in opposition to Hindu and European landlords and to popular syncretism. They combined peasant protest with Islamic puritanism and the suspension of Friday and festival prayers (*jum'a* and *id*). In western Bengal another puritan and anti-zamindar insurgency was led by Titu Mir (1782–1831).

The Islamic reformers were beginning to divide the Urdu-speaking elites, and attempting to separate the whole community, more distinctly along religious lines. Some Hindus reacted similarly. The Indian merchants, landholders, professionals and clerks of Calcutta began to form a layered society, as similar people had in older Indian cities. But they also began to acquire particular interests and characteristics as a result of living under Company rule. Among the Hindu *bhadralok* (respectable people) were those whose status was chiefly defined by their access to English education as well as by high caste: increasingly the Calcutta *bhadralok* was comprised of such 'babus' (learned men), in reforged knowledge-based professions, especially law, journalism, the civil service and education. Print – books, pamphlets and journalism – came to be a major means of communicating views. Another was the formation of societies and pressure groups. Thus Rammohan Roy was a pioneer of journalism, and also published Vedantic texts and commentaries, influenced by Islamic rationalism and Christianity. In 1828 he began the Brahma Sabha (later Samaj), as a monotheistic and reformist alternative to the Hindu practices of his day. Others began to organize themselves to protect orthodoxy, as they saw it. The Dharma Sabha (1830) was the most notable of those Calcutta societies. A little later, in 1838, a Landholders' Society was created, intending 'to embrace people of all descriptions, without reference to caste, country or complexion, and ... on the most universal and liberal principles' in order to represent the landed interest.[4]

All these societies were influenced in form and behaviour by the public and civic bodies set up by the Europeans; and thus were foreign to the image of a wholly caste-based Hinduism that was even then being constructed as the norm. They were not without precedent in Indian civic life, but they do mark the beginnings of 'modern' politics in India. This was because they were in large part the product of, and attempted to further, exchanges with a foreign government, and therefore were shaped by its procedures and expectations, as will be discussed in later chapters. Towns and other groups had long organized themselves so as to enter into a dialogue with their rulers; here they did so, at first, by holding meetings, electing chairmen, passing resolutions, and presenting petitions. Thus the forms and procedures expected by the state began to shape civic and even private as well as public life.

At the opposite extreme was the military and agrarian revolt of 1857–8, the 'Mutiny' that spread over much of north and central India. Yet it too revealed a mix of new and old features, albeit arguably more old than new. In part, it was just the most serious of several mutinies by Company troops, objecting to their conditions, at a time of reduced European manpower. The army had been irritated over issues of pay and service abroad, as settled in the General Enlistment Act of 1856. The annexation of Awadh, too, affected pay and privileges. Military leadership was poor, and British troops reduced in number because of the pacification of the Punjab and the Crimean war.

The mutiny was also yet another rejection of the disturbing force of British rule, and of its (by this time) possibly Christianizing agenda. Open proselytizing was being undertaken by certain evangelical officers, and the missionary presence was growing in north India, as a result of increased enthusiasm and organization in

Britain, of the relaxation of restrictions in India, and of charitable work during and after famines. Fear of conversion lay behind the objections of both Muslim and Hindu soldiers to the introduction of the new Enfield rifles, which required greased cartridges in gelatine-stiffened paper. These offended not only for their potential of actual pollution for both Hindus and Muslims, but also for the very thought of it, among a body of high-caste sepoys who could be observed by camp-followers and families, and were often close to their home districts. Just before the principal mutiny at Meerut, soldiers were disciplined for refusing to drill even with cartridges of the old issue or according to a modified procedure. Similar fears explained later attacks on Christian buildings, including orphanages initially built during famine. There were calls for *jihad* (Muslim holy war). The British belief in their 'civilizing mission', their confidence in the benefits of their rule, and their slowly growing willingness to interfere, help explain both the extent of the violence by Indians, and the spirit of revenge behind the brutality with which the rebellion was suppressed.

The outbreak also consisted in a host of local revolts. In part, these were an assertion against the centre by local groups, as so often in the past – for example among the Jats and Gujars, who were dominant in particular districts, and took the opportunity of rebelling, as their ancestors had whenever earlier regimes were weak; or in the case of Kuar Singh of Jagdispur in Bihar, one of very few permanently settled zamindars who rebelled (though many had done so in the past, both before and after 1793). In part it was a final upheaval of the old order in north India, reacting to the cessation of formal tribute to the Mughal King of Delhi (1844) and the gradual decline of the old elites, and to the peremptory annexation of Awadh (1856) and a new land settlement there with village zamindars which sought to bypass the local chiefs or taluqdars (*ta'alluqdars*). Elsewhere there were attacks on moneylenders and Bengali officials. The mutineers of Meerut turned to Bahadur Shah in Delhi, and popular uprisings elsewhere revolved similarly around deposed or discontented pensioners or rulers – around Nana Sahib, adopted son of the Peshwa, Baji Rao II; around the remarkable Rani of Jhansi; around Birjis Qadir, a son of the Nawab of Awadh, and Hazrat Mahal, his mother; or around Khan Bahadur Khan, last independent Muslim ruler of Rohilkhand (annexed by the Company in 1801). These were not all eager leaders but more often opportunists; they played their part as representatives of power that had been waning, and of controlling elites who were still able to mobilize large numbers of people, Hindu and Muslim.

The British explained the uprisings with a stereotype of fanatical Muslims eager to fight for their faith (though a majority of those involved was Hindu). As said, religion and religious leaders *had* influenced the revolt; British commentators inflated their part into a general Islamic conspiracy. Strident calls came from Britain for Muslims to be punished in person and through property. As British rule was restored, there were summary executions and some symbolic destruction. But the Governor-General, Canning, resisted vengeance. Due sentences of death were passed on convicted 'rebels'. Otherwise, though at first many pensions and lands were forfeited, large proportions were reinstated after review, and a policy of appeasing men of influence was re-established, taking into account the 'lessons' of 1857. The revolt cast a shadow of apprehension over succeeding generations of colonial rulers, but did not divert them from their course. Belief in the impossibility of common cause between Indians of different religions was shaken by events, but reaffirmed as a mainstay of policy.

The various reactions and the organized resistance to Company rule had had much in common. Leaders in 1857 both evoked Mughal forms, and instituted command structures on the model of the Company's army and administration. Local loyalties remained to the fore, despite some larger claims. Arguably the focus of revolt upon a few hubs, such as Delhi or Lucknow, and the failure to consolidate across wider areas except through alliance with lesser centres or power-brokers, repeated a tendency of the pre-colonial regimes, and facilitated the colonial reconquest. 'India' did not rise, nor was a 'national' revolt conceivable. Such ideas would emerge later, mainly in towns, from a mix of earlier civic traditions and a newer public culture, and of indigenous allegiances and borrowed concepts. Part of the prerequisites for the change was the building of larger standardized identities, of classes and castes, which provide an important subject in the following chapters.

6

....

Modern India I: Government

The remaining chapters of this book will analyse the emergence of modern India. It is a tale of empire and decolonization that is in many respects exemplary of its age. It is a saga of nation-building and emergent democracy. It is concerned with the growth of a modern economy, and of wealth and poverty. It is an account of transforming traditions and of global flows of goods and ideas. It is one of the great stories of history.

But it cannot easily be told and understood as a single narrative. Therefore the following chapters divide it into many different, overlapping aspects. The divisions are artificial and may seem somewhat unlike the ways in which topics are usually grouped. The argument is that they allow distinct elements of a very complex whole to be given their due weight. This sixth chapter will discuss the creation of modern forms of government under colonialism, considering various policies to show how the state grew. Chapter 7 will turn to Indian politics, tracing, in turn, anti-colonialism, religious nationalism and popular protest, eventually reaching the transfer of power. Chapter 8 will look at changes in society, including women's, low-class and religious movements. Chapter 9 will consider the economy, focusing not so much on the undoubted distortions of colonialism or the considerable triumphs of recent growth, but on the continuing problem of rural poverty. These different aspects are of course parts of a single whole. It is hoped that, after completing the four chapters, the reader will be able to draw together the different strands to form a view of how modern India was made.

MODERN GOVERNMENT

The 'modern' India which emerged after the middle of the nineteenth century was different from the Indias of old; at the same time it was contiguous with them. The concept of modernity has been discussed several times in this book, and caveats about it were recorded in the introduction. Now, these themes will be drawn together and elaborated. Though some of the changes were replicated among the hundreds of semi-independent Indian states, notably Mysore and Hyderabad, for reasons of space the discussion will be limited to British and then independent India.

As we have seen, all the eighteenth-century regional powers had continued some Mughal offices and titles, though without imperial control. At first, the East India Company ruled as little more than a collection of regional powers; and many Mughal relics were always to be found in its government also. From the 1790s, however, it was becoming strong enough, in military force, alliances and administration, to think of dictating events. The result was a new imperium. By the middle of the nineteenth century this regime and its influence may be described as 'modern'.

What made it so? All the states discussed in this book were surrounded by (and involved with) larger or smaller regions occupied by hunters, pastoralists and swidden or mainly subsistence cultivators, but they also had cities, writing, ideologies, rituals, settled agriculture, specialist occupations, and hence trade, money and social classes. This was true of the East India Company, but also in ancient times. Over five thousand years the great world empires rose and fell, their urban centres by the Nile or Indus, in Mesopotamia or China. They too had centralized bureaucracy, taxation, records and armies. They too had religious and intellectual traditions, long-distance connections, and means of extracting and storing wealth. We have discussed the examples of the Mauryan emperors of Magadha, and their apparently 'modern' ambitions, as prescribed by Kautilya or the edicts of Ashoka. How then should we distinguish modern states from all other kinds?

The most familiar answer, downplaying any continuities, is a narrative of evolving state capabilities, drawn from European history. This traces the slow separation of the royal household, the sovereign's person and the state, and the extensions of the king's law and sovereignty – as in the thirteenth century, under Philip IV of France and Edward I of England. Many accounts discuss the emergence of private rights out of feudal property, for example after the aristocratic reaction of the fourteenth and fifteenth centuries; and hence the development of the king's contract with his subjects, of objective bureaucracy, and of consent and representation. These topics are related in turn to national interest and national rivalries, to 'internal colonization', as in Britain and France from the fifteenth to the nineteenth centuries, and then to the creation of citizens, through regulated conduct, language and education, and through improved internal communications. A growing tax base from expanding production and trade also enabled increasing, or better-regulated, state responsibilities.

Others eventually shared the experience. The Ottomans under Sultan Abdulhamid II (r. 1876–1909) sought a renewed state control of language, religion, information and national symbols. In Japan the Meiji restoration of 1868 increased uniformity and professionalism in administration, emphasized national loyalty and liberty rather than interpersonal ties, and sought the growth of a national economy and of 'civilization' and 'enlightenment'. But Europe most commonly defines the criteria of modernity, an assumption partly justified by its direct influence. In eighteenth- and nineteenth-century England, for example, war, trade and empire sponsored an investment in people – facilities for orphans, public health and education – and in institutions such as equity markets, banking, standard currency, more certain law, departments of state under Treasury control, salaried officials, and so on. The East India Company assumed that similar measures were proper for India. The bureaucratic framework begun with Pitt's customs office, for example, was replicated in India under Cornwallis in the 1790s.

Another justification of Eurocentrism may be that Enlightenment science – emphasizing visibility, empiricism and progress – seems crucial to the state's modernity, though in this respect influences went from India to Britain as well as in the other direction. In an alien land, there was a specially strong incentive for a foreign state to acquire knowledge, through surveys, reports, and categorizations, methods which found favour increasingly in Britain as well as abroad. 'Inscrutable' India was the India thought most in need of (or alternatively beyond) 'improvement'. There were also particular Indian problems of non-standard law, ethnography and official incompetence or corruption. Legal, social and civil-service reforms were copied and recopied from one country to the other.

On these arguments, the elements of a state's modernity seem to be objectivity, scrutiny and inclusion, the forms of each differing between cases. In India, the colonial state assumed such modernity, firstly, when it offered the post-Enlightenment ideal of objectivity in the rule of law, impartial bureaucracy, and empirical knowledge (the scrutiny of 'experts' and official inquiries), in place of other views of legitimacy such as the divine or the just monarch. Secondly, it employed technologies of standardization: categorizing law; setting out administrative and legal responsibilities; defining and measuring classes, rights and languages; deploying print and records – none of which was really unprecedented except in speed and scale. Thirdly, it presented itself in terms of 'national advantage' and 'public duty'. To rule over people and territory was to express the mutual responsibility of state and citizen, in order to promote improvement. The state not only sought to incorporate peoples through rituals, rules and symbols, but it justified itself to them as an agent of progress. The people were combined as if in making a public petition, which then defined the state's task – a metaphor that frequently had its counterparts in reality. The advent of representative councils formalized the process, again providing the rhetoric with some credibility.

It is true that the colonial Indian state's modernity was largely imposed and incomplete. The British insisted on India's variety and disunity as well as its territorial and cultural integrity. They demarcated areas where the state's sway was minimal or indirect, often applying special regulations to, or abstaining from intervening with, 'tribals', tenants, rural workers, women, family, religion, custom and so on. The state's modernity in such cases was to be found only in the formality of the exemptions. In nineteenth-century England too, classes and regions were distinguished for different treatment, and the state made similar but smaller abstentions respecting married women and privacy; there was freedom of conscience and Catholic emancipation. For a colonial government these exceptions were inevitably large, among both its subjects and its policies. It created an English-knowing and Western-influenced class of clerks and servants, and it endorsed public and civic roles, but also it was detached from many of the Indian institutions between household and state.

Nevertheless, the most important unifying factor in India after about 1850 *has* been modern government. The modern colonial state used objective legal rules and institutions, and penetrated more

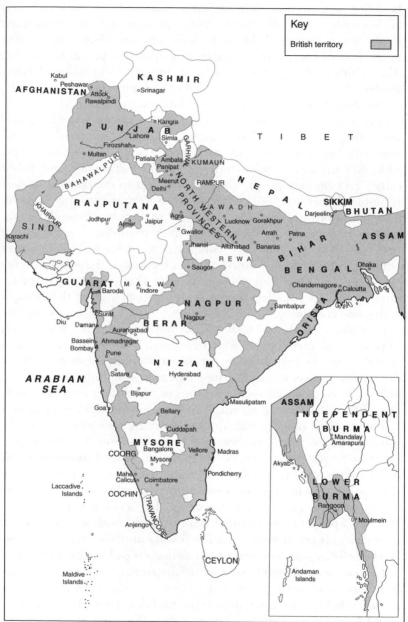

Map 6   India in 1857

directly through society with its taxes, records and information, and its larger agenda of interference and control. It reflected ideas of nationality, national history and national interests, seeking the expected modern mobilizations of an entire population within a measured territory, for example through law codes and gazetteers. It re-created the modern fictions of homogeneity of culture and history.

COUNCILS AND DEPARTMENTS

We will now consider some of the state's features in more detail, beginning around 1859, when the Company was disbanded and Crown rule instituted through a Government of India (with executive councils in the Presidencies of Bengal, Bombay and Madras). In many respects this change merely confirmed the situation that had obtained in practice since 1834, after a distinct central government was established, which in turn repackaged the pre-eminence (dating back to 1773) of the Bengal governor and council over the Company's other governments. In 1858 the Indian government was even more firmly subordinated to the Westminster Parliament, under the Secretary of State, than the Company had been to the Board of Control and through the periodic Acts of Parliament which renewed its charter. But neither Westminster nor Whitehall could possibly cope with the quantity of legislation and regulation required. Hence British India also gained (in 1861) an extended power to make laws, through the establishment of legislative councils. During the 1860s also new penal and civil codes, laws of evidence, and High Courts were introduced, on Benthamite principles of legal rationality, following the recommendations of Macaulay's law commission. Later, from time to time, the number and accessibility of local courts were also increased. Indians principally ran and used these courts.

The central and provincial legislatures were advisory extensions of the executive councils, and this constitutional limit (as also the overriding authority of the Secretary of State, in the British Cabinet) remained unchanged in constitutional terms until 1919. But the legislative councils were from the first augmented in membership so as to give voice to unofficial views. They had a prospect of becoming representative. Indians were not excluded from local bodies that were set up for towns and, later, districts, bodies that gained powers of local taxation after 1850. A system of local self-government was extended first under Mayo, and then, more substantially, by Ripon in 1885. The intention was to create active local interest groups, and also to help pay for more extensive public investment in education, public health, roads and municipal development, without increasing direct taxation.

In 1892 elected representatives of these local councils were included in legislative councils, and in 1909 (after consultation by the Secretary of State, Morley, and the Viceroy, Minto) this principle was greatly enhanced, through direct election (on very restricted franchises), with a possibility of non-official majorities in the provincial legislatures. At the same time, the executive councils were expanded to include Indian appointees. As the legislative councils remained in theory advisory, though modelled in fact as quasi-parliaments, the outcome (it was said) was power without responsibility.

In 1919 the Montagu-Chelmsford reforms took the first explicit steps towards Indian self-government at these higher levels, by creating enlarged territorial constituencies, and transferring limited provincial responsibilities to Indian ministers (alongside executive councillors, a so-called 'dyarchy') under a version of parliamentary government on Westminster lines. From 1920, nominated or elected Indians formed a majority also in all executive councils, controlling departments and their European officers – a great shock to diehard opinion. From 1937 (after elections under an Act of 1935), responsible government by Indian ministers was established in the provinces of British India. This system and the further reforms planned for the central government were interrupted by the Second World War, but aspects of the 1935 Act were preserved in the Constitution of independent India promulgated in 1950.

A full scheme of departmental administration had been evolving in India since at least the 1820s, with members of executive councils assuming particular portfolios. The higher bureaucracy had been created on the initiative of Cornwallis, and embodied in the Charter Act of 1793, when posts paid over £500 a year were reserved for (European) covenanted servants of the Company, and civil posts were distinguished from military appointments. This separation was significant, though not always observed, especially in the frontier areas, including the Punjab. From the 1830s and 1840s, discipline was provided through hierarchies, delegated responsibility, standardized reporting, and a career structure. Utilitarian influences were thus added to a long-standing recognition of the need for administrative efficiency, responsibility and honesty. The civil service provided its own training, first by examining the cadets in Persian and other subjects after they reached India, then by instructing them at Wellesley's College of Fort William (1800), and later, when its role was reduced, at the East India College, Haileybury (1806), and by secondments with experienced officers, and further examinations, after appointment in India. The recruits were selected by competitive examination after 1853, a precursor of civil-service reform in Britain. Haileybury's monopoly was ended at that time, partly as a result of lobbying by secular reformers at Oxford.

The promise of equal treatment for all the government's subjects, implicit in the principles of the introduced English law, and in the Charter Act of 1833, had again been proclaimed as the basis of imperial administration in 1858. After this, few legal measures were overtly discriminatory against Indians – despite the impression given by the Vernacular Press Act (1878–82), the Arms Act (1879) and the unofficial European protests about the extensions of Indian magistrates' powers under the so-called Ilbert Bill (1883–4). On the other hand, until a progressive Indianization in the twentieth century, practical means were found of keeping Indians out of the higher reaches of the army, and of restricting their appointments to the Indian Civil Service (ICS) to a mere token (starting with Satyendranath Tagore in 1863).

At lower levels, as the administrative structure grew, with more and more departments and ever wider responsibilities, millions of Indians entered government employment. Government of India expenditure rose from £21 million in 1840 to £75 million in 1901. The expansion and increasing specialization of administration created problems of manpower that began to chip away at the exclusiveness of the ICS, well before there was any political will to respond to Indian criticisms and reduce the European domination of the higher administration. A statutory service was created in 1879, allowing the nomination of 'suitable', meaning aristocratic, Indians. This was a failure and abolished in 1887. Instead a fifth of ICS posts were opened to persons promoted from the provincial (uncovenanted) services. Manpower shortages continued, despite the very generous salaries and conditions of ICS officers; and hence further effective Indianizations continued, a process encouraged officially by the Public Service Commission of 1912. The Montagu-Chelmsford Report of 1918 proposed recruiting in India for one-third of the ICS posts, and increasing the quota by 1.5 per cent per annum,

---

Box 8   Major rulers in India from 1772

East India Company Governors-General

Warren Hastings, 1773–85	Amherst, 1824–8
Cornwallis, 1786–93	Lord William Bentinck, 1828–35
Sir John Shore, 1793–98	Auckland, 1835–41
Wellesley (Mornington), 1798–1805	Ellenborough, 1841–4
Cornwallis, 1805	Sir Henry Hardinge, 1844–8
Sir George Barlow (acting), 1805–7	Dalhousie, 1848–56
Minto, 1807–13	Canning, 1856–8
Hastings (Moira), 1813–24	

British Viceroys and Governors-General

Canning, 1858–62	Curzon, 1888–1905
Elgin, 1862–3	Minto, 1905–10
Sir John Lawrence, 1863–9	Hardinge, 1910–16
Mayo, 1869–72	Chelmsford, 1916–21
Northbrook, 1872–6	Reading, 1921–6
Lytton, 1876–80	Irwin (later Halifax), 1926–31
Ripon, 1880–4	Willington, 1931–6
Dufferin, 1884–8	Linlithgow, 1936–43
Lansdowne, 1888–94	Wavell, 1943–7
Elgin, 1894–8	Mountbatten, 1947

Prime Ministers of India

Jawaharlal Nehru, 1947–64	Chandra Shekhar, 1990–1
Lal Bahadur Sastri, 1964–6	P. V. Narasimha Rao, 1991–6
Indira Gandhi, 1967–77	Atal Behari Vajpayee, 1996
Morarji Desai, 1977–9	H. D. Deve Gowda, 1996–7
Charan Singh, 1979–80	I. K. Gujral, 1997–8
Indira Gandhi, 1980–4	Atal Beharee Vajpayee, 1999–
Rajiv Gandhi, 1984–9	
Vishwanath Pratap Singh, 1989–90	

(Minor appointments omitted; peers listed without their titles.)

---

pending a further review at a later stage. Similarly Indians were admitted to army commissions in 1917 during the First World War, and after the war as a deliberate, albeit gradual, policy.

Over this period, the roles of government increased and became more technical. The East India Company had set up many investigations, aware of its own ignorance and responding to individual scientific enthusiasms. Though limited use was made of much of the information created, yet methods of survey, classification and enumeration became the commonplace of government decision-making. Land surveys and records, a rationalized legal system, and bureaucratic regulations and public inquiries also formed an interface between foreign procedures and the Indian peoples, many of whom were eager participants: a host of individuals and institutions responded to the agenda implicit in the state's own structures and priorities. Tenants and landlords sought written leases or title-deeds; even humble workers sometimes sought to protect themselves in the courts; middle classes formed societies for education, science, museums, and social or agricultural improvement. Chambers of commerce and ratepayers' groups were set up in towns, landholders' societies in the countryside. Lawyers joined bar associations for each of the provincial High Courts; doctors formed medical associations, and sought to improve not only their own status but also public health or conditions in farms and factories.

FINANCIAL PROBLEMS

The professionalization of government (and public life) did not run smoothly, of course. Shortage of money limited most initiatives, especially as the public debt grew, building on the expense of suppressing the Indian uprisings of 1857–8. In the later nineteenth century, the cost of the state's payments in Britain, for pensions, office charges, interest on loans and so on, also rose as the rupee lost value against sterling. (In 1873/4, payments of £13.5 million equated with Rs145 million, but in 1892/3 payments of £16.5 million amounted to Rs265 million.) The permanent settlement, fears of rural disaffection in temporarily settled areas, other politically motivated reluctance to raise taxes, and unwillingness to cede significant power to Indian representatives, all reduced the possibilities for increasing the government's income.

Nevertheless, tax revenues did increase, from around Rs360 million in 1858/9 to about Rs4400 in 1946/7, far outstripping price inflation over the period – as good a measure as any of the growth of the state. How much and where the tax grew were, as ever, very political questions. The agrarian interest was effective in limiting its contributions. Gradually from the late nineteenth century, the land revenue – anyway susceptible at the margins to famine or epidemics – declined as a proportion of state income, some 50 per cent of which was derived from the land tax in 1858/9 but only 26 per cent in 1920/1. Land revenue also declined markedly as a proportion of average agricultural incomes, which rose much faster than the revenue between 1860 and 1900. When income tax was finally introduced in 1886, after several aborted experiments, agricultural incomes were exempted.

Other political influences also came into play. As the taxes upon trade rose in importance, this gave increasing leverage to businessmen and industrialists. On the other hand, taxation hardly promoted a large public, involved in scrutinizing policy. It would be hard, for example, to consider opposition to the salt tax in that light. The tax represented 2 to 16 per cent of government revenues (declining after 1900). Regulation damaged independent salt production, and the tax fell disproportionately on the poor. But it was low per capita, equivalent to a sixteenth or an eighth of a rupee per annum, and its rate was raised only in emergencies, and reduced as soon as possible. Protests against the tax, culminating in Gandhi's famous salt march in 1930, were occasional and often symbolic.

Income tax too remained only a low proportion of the total, between 4 and 12 per cent; and was seldom increased except in wartime. Above all, it was paid only by a very minute fraction of the population (perhaps 0.1 per cent). These facts are an indication of the nation's poverty, of the inequality of incomes, and of the comparatively low rates of overall taxation. They reinforce the argument that political and economic exigencies limited the options of both the finance and the spending departments. They left a legacy for the future. Problems of distorted budgets, inadequate public resources and skewed distribution continued to affect Indian governments throughout the twentieth century.

James Wilson, the Finance Member, had placed the fiscal system on a modern footing after 1859/60, at the cost of a straitjacket of rules. Inheriting the centralization that began under the East India Company, the regional governments had little fiscal independence between the 1850s and the end of the nineteenth century. The Government of India had control of all revenues, and much expenditure, and itself was kept under tight regulation by the Secretary of State, whose sanction was required for quite trivial recurrent spending and hence legislation. Provincial governments were permitted to set their own priorities in very limited areas of policy. Financial devolution began in 1870, coinciding with a budgetary crisis; it was intended to encourage the governments to make savings on items such as education and medical services, on which they were now given greater discretion.

After 1877 five-year contracts distributed revenues between centre and province. Excise, stamps and court fees (at centrally approved rates) were allocated directly to the provinces in addition to central grants. At the same time important heads of administration were partly devolved, greater discretion was permitted over expenditure, and provincial governments gained a more elaborate departmental structure following the model of the Government of India. As the division of revenues was reassessed between the 1870s and 1920, the provinces' share of expenditure rose around threefold, to about 30 per cent. It was very unevenly distributed, with Bombay in particular receiving a disproportionate share per head of population, and Bihar and Orissa faring particularly badly: the impoverished Gangetic heartlands of Bihar contained much the same population as Bombay Presidency excluding Sind, but enjoyed only a fraction of Bombay's spending. Public investment in infrastructure (railways, canals and so on) was also markedly higher per capita in the Punjab and in the cotton-growing areas of central and western India than elsewhere.

After 1919 the provincial settlements were revised to take account of the impact of 'dyarchy' under the Montagu-Chelmsford reforms. It was decided to allocate entire heads of revenue and expenditure to either centre or provinces, each being able to decide the level of tax. The centre retained income tax and customs, and the provinces the land revenue and some other receipts. As this left the centre with a likely deficit, at least in the medium term, it was subsidized by the provinces – effectively almost wholly by Madras, Punjab and the United Provinces. Bengal and Bombay made very much smaller contributions from revenues than would have been expected, but their residents contributed three-quarters of the income tax. The new arrangements proved unsatisfactory. Almost at once the centre's income began to grow, while that of the provinces, responsible for most of the development expenditure, was proportionately in decline. In 1935 the provinces were allocated a share of the centre's income tax and export duties, on terms favouring those provinces where they had been collected or where the taxed produce had been produced. Two main conclusions follow. Firstly, the centre–province settlements between 1870 and 1920 were generally to the disadvantage of the provinces, and hence of more progressive expenditure. Secondly, they also tended to exaggerate the difference in benefits or disadvantages that existed between India's richer and poorer regions.

These disparities existed also between different heads of administration. Partly because of financial pressure, limited investment and low pay, the capacity developed at the highest levels was often notably absent at the lower, where cruder forms of power held sway. The police, for example, evolved only slowly from forces to combat itinerant raiders and armed gangs (*thagi* or 'thugs', and 'dacoits', especially in the 1840s and 1850s), and from the systems of village and town watch, some inherited and some introduced or reformed. An arrangement of *thanas* (police stations) and *darogas* (local officers) was formalized in 1793 in Bengal, where an Act of 1856 and later measures also tried ineffectually to regulate *chaukidars* (local watchmen). As the system of police developed, the oppression, ignorance, lawlessness and incompetence of its lower orders became notorious. Several commissions of inquiry sought in vain to improve the standing and quality of the service, for example by appointing Inspectors-General from Britain, and improving the pay and prospects of constables. Moreover, only in a weak sense was the police a detective force before the twentieth century: at best its roles were exemplary and reactive. The maintenance of order relied on military force, on the carefully constructed prestige of the ICS officers, and on territorial and community leaders, implying categorizations of the population as a whole. Early in the twentieth century, moreover, it was only the government's demand for a scrutiny of 'seditious' politics and political violence that led to wider recruitment of informers and the development of criminal intelligence and investigation departments.

At the other extreme, the well-funded military services developed professional standards by training, specialization and promotion on merit, though they too had special features which reflected British priorities and attitudes. After 1859 the Bengal army was reconstituted on the basis of recruitment from classes not implicated in the revolts. From being a high-caste Hindu and elite-Muslim body, it became one based around supposedly loyal 'martial' races, especially from the Punjab. The ratio of European to Indian troops was set at 2:1 in 1867, and at first there was an attempt to mix Indian 'races' in each regiment so as to discourage collusion between them. But a commission in 1879, which recommended the unification of the three presidency armies, also proposed concentrating for recruitment upon particular, approved categories of people. Frontier campaigns needed adaptable and independent fighters such as Pathans or Gurkhas. A policy developed therefore, of building regimental loyalty around 'castes and tribes' in certain areas, as with Irish, Scottish and Welsh regiments in Britain.

BENEVOLENCE AND INTERVENTION

British rule in India was always shaped more or less by imperial self-interest. On the one hand, policies of protection and improvement suffered most from financial limits. In general, apart from the shortage of money, *laissez faire* assumptions and fears of disorder or disaffection also placed a partial curb on many activities. On the other hand, a desire to reward supporters, and to promote the prestige and security of the colonial regime, meant that the colonial state was bound to profess goals of economic growth and material well-being for India. Technology was taken as a measure of success; but also nineteenth-century thinkers (Carlyle, J. S. Mill, Arnold, Ruskin, and so on) espoused organic society and a civic gospel, what Coleridge described as the 'heart' and 'duty to be just'.

By the later nineteenth century, belief in the inevitable benevolence of British rule was being challenged, even among civil servants, as well as nationalists. But this increased rather than discouraged state interventions. Exceptionally severe famines, in north-west India (1861), Orissa (1865) and south and north-east India (1876–8), and devastatingly widely around the turn of the twentieth century, became matters of political contention among officials and the educated Indian public. Government was often held responsible too for epidemic and endemic diseases, which struck with appalling effect (often exaggerating famine death-tolls) – worst were malaria, cholera, typhoid, plague, and influenza in the pandemic after the First World War.

Laissez faire – which, it should be remembered, was devised as a means of maximizing public and economic benefits – stated that governments should not intervene in markets. Some theorists, who also claimed to espouse the greater good of India, made the Malthusian argument that (to quote George Couper, Lieutenant-Governor of the North West Provinces in the 1880s) it was damaging and wrong to secure the lives of 'men so low in intellect, morality and possessions' that they could not flourish, and whose numbers, if sustained, would be a drain on the general well-being.[1] (Couper

was arguing against the opposite view of the 1880 Famine Commission; Ripon later refused his request for an extension of his term of
office.) These, and other such maxims, set up a four-way conflict
between local distress, the demands of petitions, pressure groups
and public opinion, the local officers facing the distress and in
receipt of those demands, and the rule-books or rigid instructions
of governments and Boards of Revenue. In every famine of British
India these tensions were evident. Ideology – for example, the fear
that interfering with the 'normal course' of trade would do more
harm than good – was a severe drag on policy, and probably cost
millions of lives between the 1860s and 1901.

Ultimately, however, those who advocated intervention won the
argument, at first saying that the laws of political economy should
give way to urgent necessity, and then suggesting that the laws
required modification. Officials and others mostly sought to avert
the Malthusian crisis, as population seemed to outstrip food supply.
The result was additional pressure to modernize the administration, to modify the law, and to intervene and invest in Indian
society. The two major types of state intervention were the economic
and the 'scientific'. Public works – especially roads, bridges, railways
and canals – and the communication services (printing, post and
telegraph, and later radio and television) represented the most
concentrated efforts made under state sponsorship, with education,
medical and scientific services (geology, cartography, archaeology,
metereology, agriculture, and so on) developing more patchily. State
expenditure on public works rose from around £200 000 in 1840 to
£30 500 000 in 1901.

Between the mid-nineteenth century and the early twentieth,
moreover, Indian economic policy stopped being largely restricted
to infrastructure (communications, security of trade and property).
John and Richard Strachey argued, from the late 1860s, that it was
financially sound to pursue 'uneconomic' projects, for example on
railways or canals, if they protected against famine, preserved the
revenues, and reduced exceptional expenditure on famine relief.
The state now concerned itself more directly with production; it
also began from around 1900 to intervene in industry and commerce
as well as agriculture. From production and export boards in the
early twentieth century, the state moved on to wartime price and
supply controls in both 1914–18 and 1939–45.

The Famine Commission of 1880 had laid a new emphasis on
agrarian statistics. It encouraged tenancy reform (in Bengal in

1885, following earlier measures such as for Punjab and Awadh in 1868). It promoted agricultural experiments, as well as more systematic famine-protection and relief works. Some of these interventions were attempts at social engineering. Ripon's government (1880–5) placed a special weight upon educational development, as did that of Curzon (1899–1905). In the latter's time too the Punjab Land Alienation Act of 1900 and the Co-operative Societies Act of 1904 sought to undo the supposed stranglehold of moneylenders in rural areas. In the 1920s and 1930s, these concerns were expressed again in Provincial Banking Inquiry Commissions and a Royal Commission on Agriculture.

At first, few measures were directed at urban industry, though Factory Acts were passed in 1881 and 1891, partly under pressure from British industrialists who feared Indian competition. There had been some intrusions by the state into labour relations, through master–servant and contract law, providing criminal sanctions against labour and civil against employers. Disorder, disaster and disease also led to state interventions to regulate conditions in various industries, including indigo, tea and coal-mining; factory or labour commissions were set up in 1875, 1884, 1890 and 1908, gradually imposing scientifically based standards for workplaces and workers, under the scrutiny of experts, in line with measures in Britain, and internationally after the Berlin Conference of 1890. Indian 'exceptionalism' was proclaimed on the basis of climate, marriage age, inscrutability; Eastern 'culture' was contrasted with Western 'efficiency'; and there was more evasion than observance of the rules. Still, regulation defined a formal sector of industry according to numbers of 'workers', who were then divided into men, women and children, skilled and unskilled, and so on, and accorded appropriate minimum wages, maximum hours, and 'rights'.

By 1900, British officials were pessimistic that increases in agricultural productivity could keep pace with population. A policy of guaranteed state-purchasing assisted the development of Tata steel production at Jamshedpur early in the twentieth century. During the First World War, military failures in Mesopotamia, partly attributed to shortages of supplies, prompted the establishment of the Indian Industrial Commission (1917). In the aftermath of the war, economic questions also became more strongly political. For a generation Indian nationalist publicists had been critical of British economic and fiscal policies, but now increasingly organized lobbies sought tariff protection, price regulation, workers' rights, and so

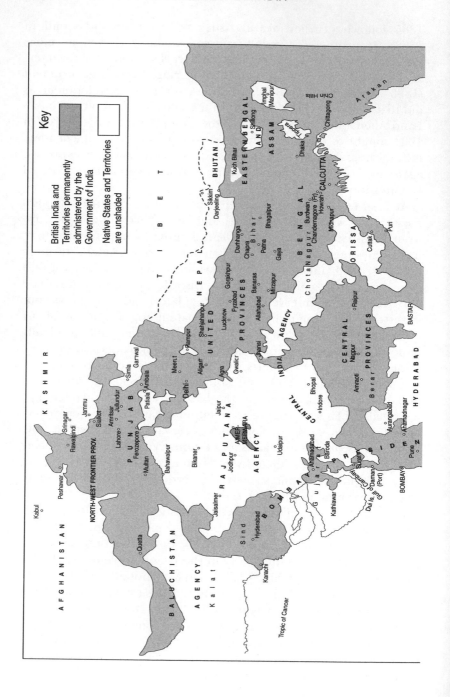

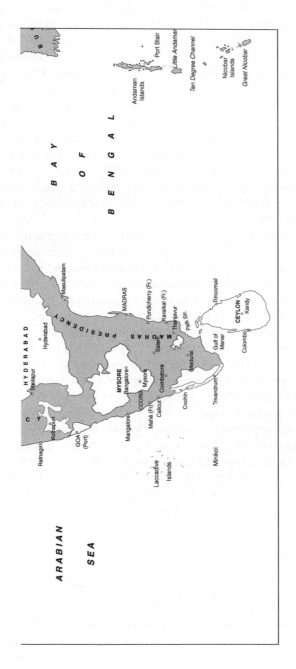

Map 7 India in 1909

on. Cartels, such as the Indian Jute Mills Organization or various planters' associations, had been formed to retain control over and to represent the different industries. Claims for *swadeshi* (the purchase of home-produced produce) were first articulated during Bengal's anti-partition agitation of 1905; they later took various forms, from Gandhi's campaigns for hand-production (*khadi*) to the National Planning Committee (1939). Trade unions, feebly established before the First World War, began to be objects of political ambition: socialists, nationalists and employers all sought to recruit to their own bodies. These developments, and government fears of Bolshevism, led to regulation in the Trade Union Act of 1926. Strikes of the late 1920s led on to the all-India organization of labour, which gained further importance with extensions of the franchise after 1935.

In general, nineteenth-century concern over the standards and marketing of products, for the imperial markets, intensified by the political developments of the early twentieth century, led the state in stages to an increasing involvement in trade and commerce, matching its fiscal interests. Together with wartime pressures and changing fashions in policy, these precedents helped produce the mixed but state-dominated economy of independent India in the third quarter of the twentieth century. By contrast, as we shall see, there was relatively little colonial intervention in social policy, despite the prominence of the controversial Age of Consent Bill of 1891, and of the contentions of the twentieth century over issues of religion, untouchability and marriage.

Education again provides a marker. It was repeatedly argued that famines and poverty could not be reduced without a diversification away from agricultural occupations, and hence that investment and vocational training were vital to Indian progress. But, though universities grew and were reformed in the first decades of the twentieth century, widespread training in new skills, that oft-repeated goal, was not achieved. An outcry soon arose at the large numbers of unemployed graduates. Nor was access widened sufficiently. In the last two decades of the nineteenth century, the number of secondary-school pupils in India increased from over 200 000 to nearly 560 000. Put another way, however, this meant that mass education, the professed aim in 1854, was nowhere near being achieved; the main reasons were underinvestment in the primary sector and an excessive reliance on private initiative for secondary schools. A Government of India that accepted that 'the active extension of primary education is one of the most important duties of the State', also admitted (Education Resolution, 11 March 1904) that 'Four villages out of five are without a school; three boys out of four grow up without education, and only one girl in forty attends any kind of school'.

In the late 1930s a basic education scheme was endorsed by the Central Advisory Board of Education, developed from a conference of Congress Education Ministers held in Wardha and chaired by Gandhi. This controversial and utopian programme sought to realign Indian education towards craft-training and away from an imported academicism. Implementation was precluded by the Congress resignations after the declaration of war. In 1944 the Board proposed a national, free and compulsory system designed to enable all children to earn a living and 'discharge their duties as citizens'. It also proposed to reorganize the high schools, and to double the number of places in the universities, while directing attention away from over-popular arts and law courses. The outcome, given continued financial and other impediments, was neither 'national' nor universal education, but an extension of changes that had already occurred.

At the turn of the century, Lord Curzon, though fiercely critical of actual emphases and achievements, had declared that a major contribution of colonial rule was the replacement of narrow, socially exclusive, religious, theoretical, informal teaching by a more open, organized, scientific and utilitarian system. This meant education in formal places and times, for certain age-groups, with publicly trained and regulated teachers and stipulated curricula and examinations; but for very limited sections of the population. One of the few fundamental alterations to this pattern over the twentieth century – though of course an important one – was an evening-out of the proportions of boys and girls in education. Class and town–country divides were little changed.

POLICY GOALS: BRITAIN AND INDIA

The allocation of state expenditure reflected imperial priorities, in the high proportion devoted to the military, and, arguably, in the subsidy to British capital represented by state-guaranteed returns on major railway and irrigation projects. The cost of administration too was relatively high, partly because of the employment of well-paid British officials. Military expenditure was not wholly unproductive – there was a policy of preferring Indian suppliers which had some marginal impact, for example, and military incomes helped the expansion of Punjab agriculture in particular – but if the military budget could have been reduced to the same percentage of the whole as in Britain, then spending on education could have been more than trebled in most years. Education and health together accounted for less than 5 per cent of expenditure in 1900/1, when the military took one of its lowest proportions at around a fifth, about the same as the British average, and when administration took almost a quarter (half on collection costs). In the twentieth century, reluctance to face a hostile legislature caused the British to cap military spending, at some cost to efficiency. Tax-collection costs too were reduced, and education budgets greatly increased; but they still fell well short of the minimum needed to achieve mass literacy.

More telling still, perhaps, is that Indian military expenditure was *not* exceptional as a proportion of national income. The real problem of colonial priorities was that, as far as can be judged, Indian tax revenues remained safely under 10 per cent of gross national product throughout British rule, and total public expenditure reached no more than 16 per cent even in wartime. Meanwhile the advanced economies were increasing tax revenues and state spending very greatly, often to several times those proportions of national income. This was the major qualification of the British Indian state's modernity.

Colonial rule bore the main responsibility for this pattern of costly defence and bureaucracy, underinvestment and low taxation. True, the British achieved some successes. Often cited are the Indian railways' more than 56 000 kilometres, 44 billion net metric ton-kilometres of freight, and nearly 70 billion passenger-kilometres by 1945/6. But the British also shaped such productive state spending as there was: they geared the railways to exports and strategic interests, not to transport needs as a whole; they preferred railways to irrigation; they promoted large-scale revenue-producing canals rather than smaller-scale projects to secure regular and clean water; they favoured urban over rural health; and so on.

It might be said that they made errors such as are made by states, and that some such errors would have been made by any Indian government – state guarantees for foreign capital-investment were probably then unavoidable, for example, and doctrines of political economy and norms of state policy spread irrespective of frontiers or nationalities. But imperial self-interest was an additional element that focused and exacerbated the inevitable shortcomings. In particular, as said, the state tended to raise charges in India (from taxation, railways and canals) in order to make payments in Britain, for salaries, pensions, capital and supplies. It was noteworthy how little capital was raised for major projects within India, and how much expenditure, especially for heavy machinery, was incurred in Britain. Whether or not there were sufficient benefits to balance this expenditure is hotly contested. Indian nationalists and many economic historians regard it as a 'drain of wealth', an idea that contributed to the emphasis in independent India upon self-sufficiency, import substitution, protection, and heavy capital-intensive industry.

'L'histoire', wrote Voltaire in *L'Ingénu*, 'n'est que le tableau des crimes et des malheurs' (history is but a portrait of crimes and misfortunes). Much of the colonial record – and not a little of India's other history – could be read as illustrating this aphorism. Nevertheless, why and how far India suffered, and indeed how far British interests alone were expressed, are complex issues. One reason for the complexity is the part played by Indians; another is the existence of various motives within British colonialism itself. India, though not very often politically contentious, became significant in British finance and business, and in ideas and imagination, because of an aura of military exploits, the glamour of the tiny ICS, employment in the other Indian services for so many British families, the occasional secondment to India of distinguished British political and intellectual figures, and the enormous if often unacknowledged importance of India to British prestige, wealth and influence. Partly because of India's importance, however, distinctive Indian government positions arose on most issues, leading at times to quarrels with the authorities in Britain. Though the latter usually had their way, except sometimes when the India Office in London sided with the Government of India, yet the distinct Indian voices were increasingly heard.

Foreign policy questions, especially in central Asia or on the use of the Indian army for imperial wars, looked different from Calcutta or New Delhi than from London. Currency and exchange questions were troublesome for at least sixty years from the 1870s. Under doctrines of free trade – initially so convenient for British manufacturers – tariffs too were contentious between India and Whitehall. Debates began before Ripon abolished protective tariffs in the 1880s.

They continued as parity was maintained between Indian import and excise duties, until after the introduction of differential rates in 1917 to the advantage of Indian production.

This last was originally a wartime concession to a cash-strapped government, intended to facilitate a war loan to Britain. It hardened into a new policy. It marked the reduced importance to British manufacturers of their exports to India, and a decline in British capital investment in Indian infrastructure, changes which help explain the convention of Indian fiscal autonomy that obtained from 1920, and the full provincial self-government, subject to political and financial safeguards, enacted in 1935. British interests still prevailed in some respects – for example, promoting so-called 'sound money' policies, using Indian gold reserves to back the international role of sterling, and effectively controlling the Indian Reserve Bank set up in 1935. But the United Kingdom government no longer held the main levers of power, and Indian budgets were increasingly subject to Indian voters. The influences on economic policy became more diverse, more indigenous and more urban. After about 1920, a policy of tariff protection was recommended, and import substitution was endorsed, with some apparent success (discussed in Chapter 9).

The colonial backing for indigenous national interests was paradoxical. The country's anomalous status was repeatedly exposed – in her participation in the peace conferences after the First World War, in the League of Nations, in the International Labour Organization, and in the Ottawa Conference of 1932. The modern Indian state had a colonial inspiration, but also involved a gradual indigenization that appeared in the policies well before it touched the higher personnel of government. On the other hand, and crucially, many British policy-makers and (even more) the British establishment as a whole failed to understand what was happening and what it meant, in India as in other parts of the empire – or if they understood it, they hated it. Political concessions to Indians were accompanied by a fall in the recruitment of Britons to Indian service; 'special arrangements' were made for officials 'unwilling' to serve under Indian ministers.

Pragmatic or even principled concessions to Western-educated Indians coexisted with the reflex of sneering at their alleged moral shortcomings. Recognitions of Indians' claims to be heard were frequently buried under a racialist paternalism that infanticized them. Many were the 'Orientalisms' in evidence here: ones that admired and respected Indian history, knowledge and culture; ones that believed in 'appropriate' laws and policies; ones that denigrated Indians' moral, physical and intellectual capacities; ones that 'loved' India but diminished it by romanticism or sentimentality, by making it picturesque (as in the painting used as a cover for this book). Certainly there were also universalisms, of citizenship and civic rights, but prominent as they were, and influential in the eventual denouement of empire, yet they were usually outweighed by the dross of 'biological' superiority which the Europeans so thoughtlessly and effortlessly expressed. These contradictions of policy and attitude were bound to provoke Indian rejections of the raj, if not of all its works.

POLITICAL POLICIES UNDER COLONIALISM

Colonial policy walked a tightrope between control and appeasement. The British suppressed rebels and practices; they measured, categorized and taxed. But they also defined areas and subjects where they refrained from interference or modified their policies; they rewarded allies. Accordingly the colonial regime depended, about equally, on structures of law and administration, coercive force, and collaborators. Predominant among the last was the rural interest, especially before the First World War; competing measures sought to secure and reward in particular either landlords or peasant proprietors. Starting with the permanent settlement, a series of policies tried to create and preserve clear and unencumbered property rights for what came to be regarded as hereditary propertied classes. The larger land-owners were rewarded with quasi-feudal titles, organized in associations, and provided with 'appropriate' education; they were expected to eschew force but to support district administration through active civic leadership and social prestige. Also to be appeased were those recognized and endorsed as leaders of religious communities, despite the official avowal of either Christian principles or religious neutrality. Colonial rule in the Indian princely states, though even more indirect, developed into another version of this strategy, one which was also elaborated upon in other parts of the British empire, notably in Africa.

A few urban groups, such as the Bombay *shetias* (merchants), especially Parsis, were similarly involved with European officials (and commercial interests) and were also wooed and rewarded by the state. So too, initially, were 'loyal' members of the new professions. All these groups came to depend quite heavily on the government – not just property-owners with their need to collect rents and to secure their lands, but also many lawyers for their briefs, teachers and doctors for their training and posts, and journalists for their information or for advertisements.

Such political policies as these rested on complex orderings or imaginings of Indian society. The role expected of, say, landlords or religious leaders made assumptions about particular Indian social relations and priorities. 'Responsible' *ashraf* (high-class) Muslims were recruited to control their 'fanatical' co-religionists. Village communities, castes or tribes were identified as units to be maintained (or if necessary created) and then co-opted. The lesson drawn from the uprisings of 1857–8 (and reinforced in decennial censuses from the 1870s) was that such groups were real and effective, and also dangerous if challenged. Accordingly, in the later nineteenth century, the Bengal zamindari model and the compact with the Indian princes (both of which largely stood the test in 1857) provided a blueprint for a new policy towards landlords in Awadh, and led to a long debate about possibly extending the permanent settlement. On the other hand, the loyalty of the Punjab in 1857, under its new paternalistic, militarized colonial regime, supported arguments for the extension of a coparcenary and peasant-proprietary model. This formed the rationale for later military recruitment, as has been said, and was introduced elsewhere through tenancy legislation, most notably in the Bengal Tenancy Act of 1885 which tried to encourage a secure and enterprising independent peasantry.

There was an inevitable conflict between both of these 'traditional' or 'customary' modes, and the promised cultural, economic and legal reform that was also supposed to justify colonial rule. This was not because any policies were genuinely conservative, but because of a conflict between promised improvements and political expediency. In the one corner, for example, were advocates of the likely impact of European rationalism upon Indian 'superstition' or of the bracing influence of property and contract-law on economic efficiency. In the other corner were jeremiads which warned of jacqueries, and insisted on gradualist policies attuned to Indian conditions. The outcome was inevitably mixed.

In the Punjab, for example, when the British took over from Ranjit Singh's successors, they immediately sought to appease military and landed interests. While professing to maintain the pre-existing system, they created secure and alienable property rights on the basis of continuous occupancy, for agriculturists and especially members of the demobilized army of the Sikh kingdom. After 1857 they reinforced this implied alliance by supporting not only the village communities of the central and eastern districts, but also the larger landlords of the south and south-west. They thus matched the reassessment of aristocratic models that was also applied elsewhere, though the peasant proprietor remained the Punjab orthodoxy and certain 'agricultural' castes provided the bulk of military recruits. On the whole (despite innumerable disputes between the officials) the alliances with all these groups, in the Punjab case, were consolidated by the paternalistic rule of the district officers and commissioners, by an emphasis on customary law rather than the abstract rules of a universalist jurisprudence, by politically motivated limitations of the land-revenue demand, and by privileges granted to favoured castes on the newly irrigated lands of the canal colonies. An image was created of sturdy martial peasants who needed to be treated well, and protected from the contagion of urban moneylenders and urban politicians. The former danger was the rationale of the Punjab Alienation of Land Act of 1900, which prohibited the transfer of land to 'non-agriculturists' (defined by caste and community), and the latter was the justification for controls on the press and the deportation of the politicians, Lajpat Rai and Ajit Singh, during what were largely rural disturbances in 1906–7. Policies in other parts of India took a different shape, in that the British focused on other sections of the population. But the pattern of defining categories of people and trying to co-opt them was repeated, as were efforts to restrict the flow of information (including a Press Act and a Seditious Meetings Act) and to inhibit contacts between supposedly distinct sectors of the population, such as peasants and politicians, or secular leaders and religious communities.

There were faltering attempts to come to terms with the educated politicians. Some provincial governments more than others developed working relationships with local political leaders on a range of civic issues, especially education and municipal affairs. The centre occasionally intervened on the side of the politicians; for example the Viceroy, Minto, and the Secretary of State, Morley, overruled the Punjab government's characteristic hostility to urban politicians during the agrarian disturbances in 1906–7. But in general any compact with the educated classes depended upon the moderation of their political demands, and on their avoidance of religious, social and agrarian controversy. Exceptions to these rules were thought illegitimate because of the gap between the urban educated and the rural masses, and were met with repression or censorship. Violence too could be similarly repressed, partly because it was eshewed by the mainstream of educated politicians – despite the attraction to some of them of anarchist cells and of political assassination (movements such as Bengal's Anusilan Samiti or the Punjab's Ghadr Party, that mirrored those appearing at the same time in many parts of the world).

British political policies always contained contradictory elements, but the emphasis before the First World War was on paternalism and on rewarding rural allies, with concessions to the educated mainly because they were noisy and also needed for administration. During the war, by contrast, the officials began to talk of 'awakening the masses' – in some ways the opposite of paternalism with its supposedly passive clientele; the words are from the Montagu-Chelmsford Report on constitutional reforms (1918). This policy was an extension of earlier experiments in appeasing political ambitions and recruiting allies, but it was also novel in that it marked, for the first time, an acceptance that overall self-government might one day be suitable for Indians as well as for Europeans.

In the event, it did not overturn the various patterns of inclusion and exclusion established by local governments, nor did it really involve ordinary people actively in the country's governance, though that had been promised, through information and elections, and the British continued to gesture towards developing 'appropriate' government and an indigenous political environment. For the most part, after the Montagu-Chelmsford reforms, the British began to use the methods and political vocabulary of the Western party system and even of nationalism. They set up Westminster-style constitutions, and effectively treated the nationalist politicians as representative leaders. They tried to avoid making martyrs of popular figures, and issued their own official propaganda. They helped organize princely and landlord representation, recognized separate political parties for 'non-Brahmans' and others, and built up the Muslim League as the 'established' leadership of a 'community'. But they also had to acknowledge the increasing popular appeal of urban, educated politicians, and adapted structures from Europe that suited such leaders well. Eventually, after independence, the leaders were able to develop the institutions they inherited, and also to pursue policies that to an extent grew out of those of their predecessors (Indian and British).

DECOLONIZATION

To consider these events fully, we must turn to the many-faceted history of modern Indian politics, and indeed to social and economic change. Still, it will be convenient to end this chapter with a few words on Indian decolonization from a broad perspective, reflecting its implications for the development of states and government. The transfer of power in India applied elements established worldwide over the preceding two centuries. In Europe national states had been increasingly defined, from the French revolution to the Treaty of Versailles. In North America between 1775 and 1783, Britain's colonies had claimed settlers' rights over land and government, both of which then expanded by purchase, cession or conquest until 1867. In South America from 1808, settlers demanding rights over bounded states and subject peoples had prevailed over weak or distracted metropolitan powers. Similarly, in the remaining British empire of settlement, local dominance over territory (and indigenous populations) had gradually evolved between the Durham Report (1839) and the Statute of Westminster (1931). In India similar change was hampered for racist, social and institutional reasons, but Indian independence eventually took the same path, paving the way for the nationhood of other parts of Britain's subject empire. Worldwide, the tendency was reinforced, amidst American rhetoric, by the defeat of the twentieth-century imperial or colonial ambitions of Germany, Italy and Japan, in Russia, Africa and Asia.

India was established as a nation of citizens and territory, most of the consolidation having taken place during colonial rule, with additional incorporations after 1947. India's definitions of nationality were inclusive, guaranteeing citizens' rights to all those 'native' to the territory, an idea that had emerged during the nineteenth century, for example over the issuing of passports to pilgrims and other travellers, or the definition of treason; it was embodied on principles of equality in the Indian Constitution of 1950.

The extension of settler independence to a subject people marked the victory of one set of ideas over another – a discourse of nations and rights over one of race and empire. Tellingly, it had already been reflected in the concept of mandate territories under the League of Nations. It had featured in the dismemberment of the Austro-Hungarian and Ottoman empires. A Britain weakened by world wars, and by trade rivalries, was finally unable to resist these trends; many on the left did not want to try, unlike the earlier Liberals and populists, who had come to terms with empire.

However, finally, hindsight should not be permitted to endow these momentous changes with an air of inevitability. India did not have the complication of settler interests that encouraged imperial expansion in the Americas and Russian Asia, and worked against decolonization in much of Africa; but individual European concerns in plantations, business and pensions still proved stumbling-blocks, and attracted a disproportionate amount of attention. Attlee introduced the bill for India's independence, in the House of Commons, as the noble culmination of a benevolent plan: he spoke not as an historian but as a propagandist seeking to outflank malcontents in the country and in the party of that imperial diehard, Churchill. The generality of the constitutional change does not reduce the importance of the struggle for national independence in each individual case. When fears for prestige and residual interests could unite to protect even the least viable European outposts – Goa being a case in point for India – it is obvious that independence movements, both bourgeois and popular, were vital to decolonization. More than this, a prerequisite seems to have been the development of varied political ambitions and organization across a wide front, encompassing different classes and interests. These are the subjects of Chapter 7.

7

Modern India II: Politics

The modern history of India is not only about colonialism and the opposition to it. This chapter makes the point that there are differences (as well as connections) between the politics of nationalism, religion, class and protest. If there are several stories there cannot be a single narrative line. This approach has a cost – preventing a ready appreciation of the ways the stories are interwoven, and even at times of the chronological sequences. The reader is asked first to consider bourgeois nationalist politics as if they were separate from other forms, and then some other fields of politics as if they too were distinct, and only then to appreciate how much they all affected and fed off each other.

MODERN POLITICS

The partial retreat from colonialism that occurred after the first decade of the twentieth century may be attributed mainly to the growth of the state and the articulation and organization of Indian opposition. Both of these relate, in turn, more to the system's failures than to its successes. In the final analysis, India remained subject to some imperial priorities so long as it had British rulers. We saw this in the balance of military and educational spending, and the relatively low proportion of national income harnessed by the state for productive expenditure or to reduce poverty. We concluded too that government policy, distorted by colonialism, was more oppressive and inefficient at lower than at higher levels, and more feeble in its developmental than its coercive aspects. It centralized and standardized but also tended rather to increase than to diminish disparities between regions and classes. None the less it also expanded, and intervened increasingly. It had its supporters and admirers, but it is hardly surprising that it inspired hatred and resistance.

This opposition was articulated under specific conditions and according to particular ideologies. It was not only a 'natural' response, because it was different from the resistance that had always arisen against centralizing states. It contained the fairly novel idea that rulers should be of one's own kind and notionally representative; it was called into being by the conditions of colonial rule. Both collaborators and opponents were affected by the state's 'modernization'. Thus Indian politics and modern parties developed in parallel with government, and colonial rule helped produced its own nemesis, nationalism.

Such accounts (as just offered), and indeed the very existence of a process of modernization, are disputed by some scholars, but they remain convincing within their limited perspective. We will begin to consider Indian politics, therefore, with an all-India narrative that owes more to the colonial inputs than to evocations of cultural identity. This deliberately defines Indian nationalism in a restricted way, and focuses on particular theories of identity and political rights. No doubt, in other senses, the 'nation' has a history in India that could be traced back to *Mahabharata* and *Ramayana*, not unlike the way that the Old Testament contains a narrative of the Israelites that was borrowed by Christian peoples and states in Europe. For our present purposes, however, it seems sensible to retain a precise meaning for the word 'nationalism', rather than to conflate it with other forms of identity, patriotism and political theory.

This nationalism admits a debt to English education and the political ideals it transmitted. It invokes the Orientalist reinvention of the Indian past, and also refers to more recent histories of France, Greece, Germany and Italy, and most of all of America and Ireland. Its advance was basically institutional, starting with the early rate-payers', land-owners', educational and reform societies, and was concerned with organizing meetings, resolutions and petitions, and ultimately with mobilizing supporters into movements and parties. In short, we place the nationalist movement as one example of a developing modern politics in India.

Politics are modern ideologically (that is, in addition to new technologies and goals) when they rest upon the attribution of rights to nations, religions, classes and individuals. A discourse of rights implies reifications of category and regulation by law. In India rights were not universally claimed, but increasing came to be asserted, in legislation, administrative practice and political propaganda; in regard to working conditions, income, health and well-being; on behalf of custom and belief; and for 'races', castes, languages, men, women and children. As a guiding principle such rights were both beneficial and pernicious: they provided an explanation of why colonialism was wrong, and arguments against injustice or on behalf of the weak, but they also framed religious and sectarian conflict, and weakened the sense of collective responsibility, duties of care within and across broad communities.

Imperial (or emergent) nation-states and anti-colonial resistance had this modern nationalism in common. Both identified peoples by culture (categorizations of ethnicity, language and custom) and history (narratives of origin and descent), and assumed them to be entitled to self-determination or self-government within given territories. Both preferred to associate nationalism positively with democracy, rather than negatively with political, ethnic or religious conflict. Theories, first enunciated in these terms in the West, attribute such nationalism to Western social and technological change. Adopting familiar terms,[1] the change may be described as being an evolution *away* from internally contiguous and structured communities, dominated by clerisy or cosmologies; and a movement *towards* politicized, scientific, secularized and industrialized cultures and societies, represented and imagined in print and mass media. Europe, seeking to facilitate flows of both political and economic resources, transferred these models to the remainder of the world, sometimes bestowing them on units of people and space that Europe itself had largely defined.

Of course, political awareness and organization also evolved over far wider fronts. The 'modern' politicized classes formed very small minorities within India. To become effective, they had to harness larger, but mostly more localized, popular forces which also were undergoing change and employing new means to achieve solidarity. These forces also used Western technologies, reassessed identity, location and history, and adopted Western-influenced concepts of race and religion. But they drew as well upon much older unities and connections. These will be discussed later.

The resultant blend of old and new, elite and popular, is well conveyed by the text of the song 'Bande Mataram' which (set to music) became an anthem of Indian nationalism. It is taken from *Anandamath*

(1882) by the Bengali novelist, Bankimchandra Chattopadhyay.
The book tells of an ascetic-military (*sannyasi*) leader, Satyananda,
who is victorious over the Muslims, and then has a vision of God
who tells him to stop fighting, even though the infidel British still
prevent a Hindu dominion. The vision tells him that the purpose of
British rule is to revive the true Hindu faith, and to bring the
Hindus necessary knowledge of the physical world – a possibly
ironic mirror-image and a certainly expedient echo of the rulers'
own claims. Some key passages in 'Bande Mataram', as translated
by the radical nationalist, Aurobindo Ghosh, are as follows:

> Mother, I bow to thee!
> Rich with thy hurrying streams
> ...Dark fields waving, Mother of might
> Mother free...
> ...Mother, I kiss thy feet,
> Speaker sweet and low,
> Mother, to thee I bow.
> Who hath said thou art weak in thy lands
> When the swords flash out in seventy million hands
> And seventy million voices roar
> Thy dreadful name from shore to shore?
> ...Thou art wisdom, thou art law
> ...Thou art Durga, Lady and Queen
> ...Thou art Lakshmi lotus-throned.

Here one may note that the ideal of freedom and the magic of
number, which arguably became items of public consumption during
British rule, were combined with images of strength and solidarity
which replied to colonial and racist denigrations, and also with
appeals to landscape, ritual and tradition, including the modesty
and power of women, and the personification of India as Mother.
Bande Mataram's implicit promise is of an order that is Hindu,
strong, wise and prosperous (the realms of the goddesses, Durga
and Lakshmi).

Harnessing disparate elements into an appeal to all-India and
all-Hindu sentiment runs counter to the political and linguistic
divisions of much of the preceding centuries. The British too had
a self-interested bias against almost any kind of all-Indian identity.
As already noted, their influence first helped develop regional and
sectional identities by modern means. Effects can be seen, with

relatively few all-Indian elements, until the later nineteenth century – for example in various regional associations, such as the Indian Association of Bengal, the Bombay Presidency Association, the Pune Sarvajanik Sabha, and the Madras Mahajana Sabha. But, as also said, the Indian state was becoming more objective, better resourced and more interventionist than its predecessors. It also laid claims to inclusive territory and exclusive citizenship, in ways that prepared for national identity. Scrutiny and control were achieved, through formal bureaucratic structures, over more and more of the activities of citizens and institutions. Unwittingly, therefore, the British imposed a national unity of sorts, from their own governmental structures and policies, and from the boundaries they invented or reinforced, and within these, they could not prevent indigenous attempts at nation-building. Because Indians were implicated in the developments from the start, they too began to imagine a new political significance for India as a territory, and for themselves as a people. Indian nationalists, though with mixed success, tried to subdue regional and religious differences, and to build up national similarities: 'from shore to shore' as in another emerging, heterogenous, subcontinental nation, the United States. All-India politics and economic interests, and Indian professional, business and intellectual identities, began to be formally articulated. Indians used the vocabulary of Western thought, referring to nations and peoples, to national economy and the national interest, and to individual entitlements and self-determination.

It was regarded as a project. The Bengali leader, Surendranath Banerjea, entitled his political autobiography, *A Nation in Making* (1925). Many of the practitioners of this nationalism thus saw themselves as creating a new India. They were the lawyers, journalists, teachers and public servants indebted to the colonial system, including some of the 1400 to 2000 graduates produced from the universities each year by the 1890s. They often expressed a politic gratitude to the West. Their education had been supposed to be 'wholesome, and adapted to the crude understanding of Oriental students', to quote the Secretary of State for India (1897) – that is, intended to enlighten them and make them useful, while confirming their supposed inferiority. But in practice, of course, it often encouraged them to re-evaluate Indian achievements, and made them perfectly familiar with the legal, sociological, liberal and democratic debates of contemporary Europe. Such Indians became, in the eyes of some colonial officials, half-educated babus (or learned men; here a term implying the ineradicable frailty and 'Indianness' of Indian intellect). Then, in that revealingly English phrase, they proved 'too clever by half'.

Many of the new professionals, and also urban merchants who were involved in the export trade and with factory production, began to engage in public life in close association or in parallel with Europeans. They became accustomed to representing particular interests on a host of educational boards and charities, and on other quasi-public bodies such as the Bombay Chamber of Commerce (1836). With rising incomes and ambitions, they formed their own pressure groups to serve their communities and to lobby government, replicating the European societies' constitutions, subscriptions, officers, meetings and minutes. In the early 1880s they witnessed bitter controversies among non-official Europeans over the Ilbert Bill and the Bengal Tenancy Act, and noted again how government policy could be modified by orchestrated campaigns; they believed British Liberals susceptible to such pressure from Indians. They were supported by increasing numbers of Western-educated young men, frustrated at lack of opportunity, and by the growing readership of newspapers, tracts and novels.

The colonial state constituted 'British subjects' and 'Indians'; and by its own centralization encouraged them to combine. As is common enough among those in positions of relative weakness, early nationalists tried to turn the colonial state's protestations against itself, even to the extent of internalizing many of its assumptions. In 1898 the British Indian Association, by now largely representing lawyers and other professionals, defended their preponderance in representative bodies with the claim that 'men of property and position, with their oriental notions of propriety, as a rule, keep themselves aloof from ... elections'. The colonial state provided yardsticks against which its colonialism could be judged and found wanting – its promises, for example, of 'effectual and impartial administration of justice', and that it would 'remove ... every judicial disqualification which is based merely on race distinctions', the language of the Ilbert Bill. Dadabhai Naoroji, the Parsi nationalist and one-time Liberal member of the House of Commons, owed his reputation partly to a famous attack on British Indian economic policies: not only were they destructive because colonial (reversing the free-trade orthodoxy, as others did too); also they were destructive, he said, revealingly, because they were 'un-British'.

THE INDIAN NATIONAL CONGRESS

The first avowedly all-India bodies were the British Indian Association in Calcutta (1851) and the East India Association in London
and Bombay (1855). They were followed by the 'true' start, the
foundation of the Indian National Congress, in 1885. The Congress was an organization of the intelligentsia and the new professionals, with some backing from princes and merchants. It could
not have existed without the English language, the telegraph and
the railway; a nucleus of its leaders had met while studying in
London. It professed empire loyalty and admiration for Western
technology and British liberties. It espoused the class interests of
those who sought government jobs and a voice in law-making. It
also advanced ideals of representation, of the elite's responsibilities
to the public, and of the national interest, especially in regard to
fiscal and economic policy – stressing official culpability for famines,
for example, and objecting to the high cost of the army and the home
charges. It located itself in regional associations and urban centres,
and long had no real permanent existence in India, other than
what was provided by its secretary (1885–92), the former ICS man,
Allan Octavian Hume. But, by moving its once-a-year sessions
around the country and drawing the attention of a growing press
and public, it began to build personal reputations and all-Indian
connections for a few leaders – Parsis such as Pherozeshah Mehta
(1845–1915) and Brahmans such as Gopal Krishna Gokhale (1866–
1915), who between them dominated Congress in Bombay.

   Milestones for Congress include the administrative partition of
Bengal into two provinces (1905–11). The Congress then temporarily
repudiated popular agitation, following a split at Surat in 1906, but
the ensuing period saw more active opposition, both constitutional
and terrorist, which popularized the nationalist linkage between
territorial boundaries, political identity and self-determination.
The same connections were promoted by issues in foreign and
military policy, and in regard to Indians abroad, in South Africa
and as indentured plantation labour in other parts of the British
empire. The political situation was transformed during the later
stages of the First World War, by growing resentment at economic
difficulties and political restrictions, by the British promise of
progress towards Indian self-government (1917), by Muslim outrage
at the peace terms being offered to Turkey, and by the fall-out from
the Punjab disturbances in 1919.

The cause of the last of these was largely local, but the occasion was a widespread protest against the two Rowlatt Bills (one of which was passed, though never invoked) that would have allowed detention without trial and other executive sanctions in areas declared to be disturbed – a proposed continuation of wartime measures deployed with some success against political terrorists, but also used against politicians. (The British at this time persistently confused advocacy with violence, as a means of ruling out nationalist ambitions.) The repression of the anti-Rowlatt protests and the ensuing disturbances in the Punjab seemed merely harsh when largely hidden under martial-law restrictions in 1919; during 1920 they came to be regarded as 'satanic' – Gandhi's word – following the revelations of a Congress investigation and an official inquiry. Most damaging was evidence of the callous and illegal conduct and vindictive motives of General Dyer who, having assumed authority at Amritsar, perpetrated a terrible massacre upon a non-violent crowd, hundreds of whom died, at the Jallianwala Bagh (garden). Dyer was dismissed, but lauded in certain sections of the British press and parliament. Many Indians took this as a proof of British bad faith, as they reassessed the very qualified offer of self-government made in the Montagu-Chelmsford reforms.

In 1920 a revised constitution, agreed at Nagpur, turned the Congress into a permanent political opposition to the British raj. Post-Nagpur, the Congress sought wider participation, better organization and more uncompromising political demands, policies that had been foreshadowed, not only in various local agitations, but also on the national stage by Home Rule Leagues founded during the First World War – one by the Maharashtrian leader, Bal Gangadhar Tilak (1856–1920), and one by the Irish Theosophist, Annie Besant. After 1920, to encourage popular involvement, the Congress permitted the use of Hindi as well as English, and reduced its annual membership fee to four annas (a quarter of a rupee). Permanent organization was sought through a hierarchy of local, provincial and all-India Congress committees, a decision-making Working Committee, and a full-time, annually elected, president. Fund-raising, professional workers and Congress volunteers also allowed the organization to function. It was thus prepared for Gandhi's non-violent protest movements, and also for other Congress-members' participation in legislatures and government (notably by the Swaraj Party of 1923–7, the Congress ministries of 1937–9, and the Interim Government of India in 1946–7).

Gandhi's mass movements (Rowlatt in 1919, non-cooperation in 1920–2, civil disobedience in 1930–4) were based upon passive resistance or, as he called it, 'truth-force' (*satyagraha*) and a Jain-influenced non-violence (*ahimsa*). His view was that colonialism was as demeaning of its perpetrators as its victims, and could be resisted by example; one's suffering would shame and convert the enemy. Gandhi's activism and idealism appealed to young volunteers, local leaders and many established all-India politicians as a means of confronting the British without risking violence or violent reprisals.

He had built up support with indigo cultivators in Champaran and mill-workers in Ahmedabad, and a host of other local campaigns, some political and some social, that widened his prestige and his base of supporters. Initially seen as a popular champion with the ear of the government (after his campaigns in South Africa, his Kaiser-i-Hind medal, and his participation in government conferences and commissions), Gandhi developed an image as national hero and *mahatma*, great soul. His quixotic points of principle sometimes alarmed or enraged his colleagues but they added to his saintly image. His self-discipline, suffering and sacrifice (*brahmacharya*) were expressed in repeated fasts (often a weapon to impose his will on others), in model communities (*ashrams*), and in speeches and in print (endless moral homilies on diet, health and everyday conduct, as well as politics). He advocated 'bread labour' and spinning as a mark of humility and of commitment to work for the common good. He asserted India's superiority in its achievement of 'mastery over mind and passions', an attack on Western materialism (in the tract, *Hind Swaraj*, 1909). He extolled the interdependent life of an imagined village community – despite being allied to some great merchants and land-owners. He professed the equivalence of religions and classes, initially attracting Muslim support through his endorsement of the Khilafat campaign against the Turkish peace terms. But he also backed Hindu pride, with his selective use of sacred symbolism, and his advocacy of Hindi as the national language.

He appealed to a great mass of Indians even while he insisted on a single incorporate body of 'Hindus' (inevitably dominated by the rich and the high-caste), and on a somewhat ambiguous valuation of caste, assuming it could be shorn of its 'imperfections' such as Untouchability and fear of pollution (the indignities of labour). He thus alienated the 'Untouchable' leader, Dr B. R. Ambedkar, who thought Gandhi understood little of the economic and social deprivation of those he called *harijans* (people of god) and who are now known as *dalits* (oppressed).

Gandhi's Congress undoubtedly hastened the tardy concession of Indian independence, though not all of his leadership was wise or consistent, especially when it came to detailed negotiation. There was a major contribution too from the younger generation including Vallabhbhai Patel, Jawaharlal Nehru and Subhas Chandra Bose (the last ousted in the late 1930s after quarrelling with Gandhi). The Congress was able to maintain a wide support-base, from businessmen who became more attracted the closer the party came to power, to peasant activists who used and were used by Congress. Evidence of popularity came in the Congress victories in the 1937 elections, not only in general constituencies, but in scheduled-caste (*dalits'*) seats, except in Bombay, and even, where they contested them, in many Muslim seats. The outcomes were clear Congress majorities in five of eleven provinces, with not far short of half the general seats, and a huge boost in recorded Congress membership, by nearly 50 per cent, to 4.5 million. The cost of this support, and of unity among the senior leadership, was a subordination of class and local issues to the national cause, and the shelving of difficult questions of political purpose and philosophy. Right-wingers, religious zealots, social reformers and socialists drifted in and out of the Congress in hope and frustration. The argument of the central leadership was that ridding India of the British was more important, because the British were responsible for most of India's ills.

A mirror image of Gandhi and the Congress constitutionalist politicians was provided by revolutionary terrorists, in a resurgence that also began during the 1920s. They are written out of some histories and arguably played only a minor role in moving the colonial government towards concessions; but some of them, such as Bhagat Singh and Surya Sen, also gained huge popularity. Like Gandhi they were celebrated partly for their self-discipline and self-sacrifice – the Bengali, Jatin Das, for example, died after a long hunger strike in prison. Like Gandhi, too, they had uneasy relations with more conventional politics. Bhagat Singh was executed for his part in the murder of an officer responsible for a police charge (in 1928) in which the veteran Punjabi leader, Lajpat Rai, was killed. Bhagat also espoused socialist ideas, in his writings and as a leader of the Hindustan Socialist Republican Army. Surya Sen, who planned a famous raid on the Chittagong Armoury in 1930, had been secretary of the district Congress Committee. Unlike Gandhi, however, such men (and women) represented a strand of violent activism, to be traced back to a newly militant god Ram, or to vengeful goddesses. In an alternative narrative of the independence struggle, they are commemorated as heroes by the people and by nationalist historians, and not least by governments that make modern claims to a monopoly of force for the state.

POLITICAL ISLAM

Muslims, so the censuses revealed, made up about 20 per cent of the population of British India, but were unevenly distributed, ranging from almost 100 per cent of the population in north-west Punjab to under 3 per cent in the Central Provinces. In the United Provinces (UP) Muslims made up less than a tenth of the total, but nearly a third of those living in the towns. By contrast, two-thirds in East Bengal were Muslim, as were around half in the whole of Bengal, but fewer than one in 25 in the towns. In south India as a whole they made up around 5 per cent, but a quarter in Malabar. Muslims might be peasants, artisans, merchants, land-owners or professionals; distinctions were made between the decendants of 'converts', between different castes, and among the elite (*ashraf*), the Saiyids, Shaikhs, Mughals, and Pathans. Most Muslims were Sunni, though many in the north were Shi'a.

It was often argued that South Asian Muslims were a race, nation or culture. Attempts were made to define them as a single community, though they were so divided by class, region and custom. The British tended to treat them as a single category, and gradually distinctively Muslim political interests began to be widely articulated. This process was not peculiar to Muslims. The population at large was generally identified and counted, in law and censuses, according to caste and religion. As already noted, a theory of India's essential divisions and communities influenced the government in everything from the recruiting of military and civil-service employees to appeals to 'natural leaders' to promote law and order. Separate electorates for Muslims after 1909 marked an extension of this policy as the constitution began to include representative elements. Muslims were considered a useful and potentially conservative or 'loyal' counterpart to Hindus, because necessarily opposed to them – even though they were often also feared as fanatical, in the aftermath of the uprisings of 1857, attributed to Muslim resistance, and of the assassination of the Viceroy, Lord Mayo, in 1872. Muslims too adopted these ideas about themselves, and promoted them, leading to the assertion that India contained two historical nations, one Muslim and one Hindu.

In 1876 the historian-official, W. W. Hunter, wrote *The Indian Musalmans* in which he claimed that the Muslim aristocracy of Bengal was 'in need of a career' through its lost roles in government, the army, and civil employment. It was, he said 'shut out from official employ and from the recognised professions' because the British 'system of public instruction, which ... awakened the Hindus from the sleep of centuries and quickened their inert masses with some of the noble impulses of a nation, is opposed to the traditions, unsuited to the requirements, and hateful to the religion of the Musalmans'. Teaching was in Bengali, not Persian or Arabic; it was secular and the teachers were mostly Hindu. In the Punjab too, during the 1880s, a settlement officer, S. S. Thorburn, painted a picture of social disruption and impending disaster, based upon his notion that traditional Muslims, used to distributing land amongst themselves according to Pathan tribal principles (*vesh*), were becoming embroiled in the clutches of Hindu moneylenders because of ill-suited laws of property and contract. By the 1890s such were the commonplaces of Punjabi arguments that justified the Alienation of Land Act of 1900.

Such advocacy contributed to a consensus that colonial rule had particularly disadvantaged 'the' Muslims. Some earlier Muslim reactions had certainly promoted the idea that true believers could live only under Islamic rule; Shah Abd al-Aziz and Sayyid Ahmad Bareilly, for example, were mentioned in Chapter 4. Some Company policies too had certainly affected Muslims' interests, such as the Europeanization and demilitarization of administration, the award of fixed land-rights, and the resumption of revenue-free holdings. Arguably these changes could be linked to protests (also mentioned earlier) such as the risings of Titu Mir or Hajji Shari'at-Allah and Dudu Miyan in Bengal.

On the other hand, throughout the nineteenth century some Muslims retained privileged positions. In the northern Indian heartlands of the Mughal empire many were still influential and active in public life. They were initially less involved in modern politics (as described here) than their counterparts in the great presidency towns, but that applied equally to others in those regions. True also, the expansion and redirection of trade benefited Hindu trading castes and some towns grew at the expense of declining *qasbahs* (centres of Mughal nobility, with their markets, mosques and madrasas). But still the Muslim literate classes continued to be over-represented in government jobs and land-owning. Their predominance was reflected among Hindu elites by a shared Persianized culture and the use of the Urdu language.

After 1857, however, this supremacy began to be challenged, by quotas in government service, by Hindu revival and chauvinism, and by language and script controversies. A specifically Muslim identity came to be asserted (and stretched to include the lower classes). As will be discussed more fully in Chapter 8, a new awareness was encouraged too by renewed orthodoxy and respect for Qur'anic authority, prompted at least since the eighteenth century by conditions of political stress, and encouraged by the growing influence of *ulama* trained at the seminaries at Firangi Mahal (founded 1694) in Lucknow and at Deoband (1867). Specifically Muslim interests were evoked in two main ways: attempts to 'modernize' Islam within India, and efforts to establish universal Islamic solidarity. The work of Sayyid Ahmad Khan (1817–98), and his movement to found and develop Aligarh College, represented the strongest impulse to accommodate a reformed Islam to modern science and Western government. Pan-Islamic sentiments were encouraged by the Indian tours in 1879 of Jamal al-din al-Afghani (1838–97), and by pro-Turkish and pro-Caliphate sentiment channelled through the Red Crescent Society and other means, in the early twentieth century, by figures such as Abd al-Bari (1878–1926).

Though often mutually antagonistic, these different movements shared the assumption that Muslims formed a single community of belief and political interest. Many Muslims continued to participate in general bodies, including the Indian National Congress, of which the Bombay notable, Badr al-din Tyabji, was a founding member; but they came to think of themselves as representing 'Muslims', and many also began to promote societies restricted to Muslims alone. These included the National Muhammadan Society founded in 1877 by Sayyid Amir Ali, and the Muhammadan Educational Conference (1886). The logical extension – largely a combination of the aristocratic and Aligarh-educated – was the Simla deputation to Lord Minto and the formation of the Muslim League (1906), which pleaded for and embodied the separate political representation of Muslims in the forthcoming legislative councils.

By the First World War some younger figures, including Wazir
Hassan and the 'Young Party' in UP, were repeating Tyabji's earlier
pleas for 'common cause' with the Congress. This rapprochement
was reflected in the Lucknow pact of 1916 (accepting the principle
of separate Muslim electorates) and in Gandhi's co-operation with
Muhammad Ali (1878–1931) and his endorsement of the Khilafat
campaign against the Turkish peace terms (1918–24). All the
co-operation, however, was on the basis that Muslims were a distinct
political entity. Many more were thus attracted into political activism
but *as Muslims*, including some of the *ulama* who formed their own
associations to pursue political as well as religious aims, during and
after the Khilafat campaigns. This pattern was especially characteristic of certain elite politicians and of the UP, but it had its counterpart in populist religious reform movements among the laity (to
be discussed below). By the 1940s it was not to be deflected by the
continued importance of Muslim Congress leaders such as Ab'ul
Kalam Azad, nor by the long dominance of apparently secular or
non-separatist parties, led by Muslims, in Muslim-majority areas.
(Notable were leftists in Bengal such as Fazl-al Haq, the landlord-
dominated Punjab Unionist Party under Fazl-i Husain, and the
pro-Congress 'Red Shirts' of Abd al-Ghaffar Khan in the North-West
Frontier Province.)

POPULAR PROTEST

One way of considering Indian politics under colonial rule, and
after it, is as a failure of both regional and all-India inclusion. A great
deal of mobilization occurred at different levels of society. Many
fierce struggles reflected local and sectional interests, and there were
many attempts to bring them together into larger campaigns – within
regions and countrywide, and on a range of religious, social and
nationalist agenda. But sectional or local politics often remained
distinct from the elite or bourgeois arena, limiting the possibilities
for integration, either in any one region or in India as a whole.
Indian politics contained a complex series of fractures, over which
were ranged competing ideologies and loyalties. On the whole the
situation seemed to replicate the kinds of regional–imperial divide
discussed earlier in this book. To illustrate this argument, we will
now consider some of the popular protests of the period, and some
attempts at political consolidation.

Indian people displayed natural resistance as well as natural deference; they both accepted and contested authority. Individuals and localities would support social norms and political leaders, but also try to avoid scrutiny and taxation. The oppressed might endorse their oppression by explaining it, for example attributing Untouchability to an ancestor's 'mistake', or while modifying it, for example claiming higher status within the existing system. Equally they might oppose the very basis of existing hierarchies. Some have argued that Indian labour lacked the means of solidarity enjoyed by the English working classes, given their different pre-industrial experiences; but Indians did not lack other means of protest, either autonomously or in conjunction with social and political superiors. What changed during the modern era were the ideologies, the groupings and the technologies of both protest and acceptance.

For all the local varieties of custom and belief, regional loyalties and cultural identities had long embraced whole populations, forming them into self-recognizing 'communities' that were bound by institutions as well as tradition. This assisted those with the most power, but, as we have repeatedly noted, an important part of the unity was an explicit compact between ruler and subject. Indians had long had ideas about social equity and state responsibilities, alongside justifications of hierarchy and arbitrary power. A code of political ethics underwrote sovereignty, but transgressions of the code also justified rebellion, both political and social. Thus military and religious leaders repeatedly arose to challenge, improve and replace existing orders. Rebellion occurred frequently against 'unjust' kings, whether Hindu or Muslim, and also against social and caste exclusions.

Protests of the modern era therefore had a ready vocabulary available to them. As in the past they were led by millenarian preachers and magical figures, who invoked devotion, appealed to proprieties of conduct, and expressed social and regional solidarities. Many such activists appeared, some 'from the people', and some from outside, or influenced by modern education. Some remained focused in a few villages, where they are still revered as saints; many toured the countryside, speaking in market-places and villages, gathering bands of devotees, spreading ideas, organizing protests. These preachers re-employed very old religious magic, and political methods, in diverse causes: religious and social orthodoxy, cow protection, tenant rights, nationalist aims. Often they introduced new concepts – legal rights as a kind of personal property; pride in one's class or religion; the representative nation-state; and so on – but there were always existing socio-political ideas on which these could be grafted. Vaishnava teachings, for example, proved widely important – such as for upwardly mobile agricultural castes in north India, or low-class cult leaders in Gujarat, or the millenarian rebellion led by the visionary prophet, Birsa (1874–1900), among the Mundas of Jharkhand (1898–1900).

Elsewhere there were many similar millenarian movements (that is, those based on belief in the coming of a divine leader who will rule during an era of happiness and prosperity for a chosen people – by analogy with the supposedly promised thousand-year reign of Christ). They are usually interpreted as reactions to outside disturbance, as phenomena of disjunction. For example, among the Bhils in Surat district, Gujarat (so David Hardiman's recent study reveals),[2] a movement developed in the 1920s in which individual people of low status, and even children, were possessed by a goddess. In direct and indirect ways this movement reflected the situation in which the Bhil *adivasis* ('tribals', original people) then found themselves. The British had conquered Surat between 1800 and 1817, and spread state authority in the usual way, through officials and ruling units (chiefs, headmen, villages, districts), and also through taxation and commerce (settlement, land scarcity, labour recruitment, timber-felling, deforestation). Meanwhile, the Bhils suffered increasingly from outbreaks of malaria, and experienced intrusions by Christian missionary educators, and Parsi moneylenders, liquor-contractors and land-owners. The Bhils reacted in particular to state regulation of alcohol production and consumption. They had attributed important social, religious and medicinal roles to alcohol, and responded by smuggling and illegal manufacture; but also by taking up new ideals of abstinence, which they came to associate with prestige and virtue, along with cleanliness and vegetarianism (a mixture of Christian, Vaishnava and Gandhian influences).

The protest movements associated with possession by the goddess represented another aspect of their reaction, and were directed against those interlopers seen as responsible for changing their lives, including their access to alcohol, for example the shopkeepers, moneylenders and land-owners. Together such experiences helped define the Bhils as a distinct social group, opposed to others. They protested not only because government and the money economy affected their lives, but also in order to re-establish forces of cohesion that had been disrupted.

This provides a useful model of developing social consciousness. We should not see everything, however, in reductionist terms of attack, defence and loss. Events and sentiments are not merely the products of certain instruments – such as colonial rule, legal intrusions, economic interests – for they all contain many origins and aspects, ideological as well as material, internal as well as external. Nor should we imagine peasants, village communities and *adivasis* as living in a unique social and ecological harmony, until disrupted from outside. Fully isolated, self-sufficient, homogeneous, self-supportive communities did not really exist. Rather they contained specific relations of power that could be changed by internal or external forces. Indeed broader solidarities may be more the product of modern than of earlier conditions.

With these arguments in mind, five kinds of resistance can be distinguished under colonial rule, apart from the nationalist movement. To set them out, however, is to show how far they overlapped. The first was based in protest at change in or interference with local authority. The East India Company had fired rebellions as it tried to dispossess or redefine the rights of various chieftains and magnates – the Sivaganga poligars (*palaiyakarars*) in 1799–1801; zamindars and peasants in Bengal variously from the 1760s, or in the Khandesh in 1852; and so on. Such resistance was not just a feature of the establishment of rule, however: it continued throughout later periods.

Related to this, secondly, was local or social resistance to economic and political incorporation, as also occurred throughout Indian history. During British rule, apart from the instance of the Bhils in 1920 (and also during the nineteenth century), there were examples on the fringes of Awadh and in central India, in Gwalior and Rewah, among the Bundela Rajputs, or Kols (1829–33), and also in north Bihar, Assam and the Bengal hills. The Santhal rebellion of 1855–6 was one of the most notable of such insurrections, but resistance of this kind continued after independence and to the present day.

Thirdly, there were religious movements: remonstrations against Christians in the 1840s and 1850s in north India; Hindu–Muslim disturbances breaking out initially around the cow-protection movement from the 1870s; fighting among Sikhs associated with the Akali movement in the early twentieth century; and many others. Arguably problems over caste status fall into this category – there was a host of campaigns about temple entry, name changes and status.

Fourthly, there were riots of opportunism or hardship. In this category fell some banditry, as by marauding Pindaris (1806–18) or dacoits (armed gangs, including so-called thugs or *thagi* and supposedly 'criminal tribes', especially from the 1830s to the 1870s), or by the gangs of the low castes there labelled as Baraiyas, who engaged in social banditry in Kheda district, Gujarat, in the early 1920s. Also noteworthy and sometimes related were grain riots, such as in north India between 1833 and 1838, or in the Madras area in 1806, 1833 and 1844. Protests at changing conditions of agricultural production may be considered here as well, such as those over indigo (the 'blue mutiny' of 1860–2, and decades of Champaran protests culminating in 1917), or those against landlords and rents (among thousands of examples, Pabna in 1873), or against moneylenders (such as the Deccan riots of 1875).

Fifthly (and often an element in both economic and religious quarrels) were protests around class issues, ranging from landlords and ratepayers to rural labourers and trade-union strikers. Notable among low-class protests (of which further examples will be given in Chapter 8) were the non-Brahman movements. These occurred among Marathas, Malis and Mahars – especially Jotirao Phule and the Satyashodhak Samaj (truth-seeking society) – in western India after 1873. In the Tamil lands, too, they were found in the nineteenth century among Vellalas and Chettiars, so-called Dravidians, including, by 1925, the 'self-respect' campaigns of E. V. Ramaswami Naicker. In the twentieth century there were the many popular agitations in the countryside. Obviously they were partly about hardship, but also they were about asserting new demands. They were class protests, even though almost always seen through the prism of caste. It is true that social and working conditions delayed class organization by reducing solidarities and emphasizing factions or groups, not only in the countryside but in factories. There workers long kept up rural ties, and were recruited and managed by contractors or intermediaries (jobbers) who had been promoted often from among people more or less of the workers' own kind. Trade unions did none the less develop, and workers began collectively to demand improvements in wages. Tenant-rights movements too arose, inspired for example by such travelling preachers as Gauri Shanker Misra and Ram Chandra, who were implicated in the Faizabad disturbances of 1921. There were attempts to assert the dignity of agricultural work, such as by Swami Shahajanand who (with others) organized peasants into *kisan sabhas* (peasant societies). The All-India Kisan Sabha, founded in 1936 under the leadership of Shahajanand, developed a programme that included demands for the abrogation of zamindari rights, replacing land revenue with agricultural income tax, the abolition of forced labour, and the restoration of certain common privileges in the country-side.

Class and interest-based combinations had been occurring increasingly among higher tenants. In the Pabna uprisings of 1872–5 richer raiyats, with rights of occupancy, resisted their landlords. The Deccan riots of 1875 seem to have been sparked off by an interruption of credit; moneylenders were attacked by cultivators, who often were successful producers of cotton for the Bombay and international markets. In Bihar between 1933 and 1942 richer peasants combined to quarrel with landlords, partly over the control of labour. In the Mappila (Moplah) rebellions of 1836 to 1921 in Malabar, class solidarity also may be discerned. Characteristically the government saw only religious fanaticism, spasmodic outbreaks to kill as many non-Muslims as possible, or (in 1921) an organized uprising aroused by the Khilafat agitation. The Muslim martyrs did share in a growing religious sentiment. But they were usually poor, and, in addition, support for them was often shown by richer, upwardly mobile peasants, some of them rent-receivers, who were seeking security of tenure from superior landlords.

In the twentieth century such protests seem to have developed successfully at ever-lower levels of the agrarian hierarchy. In Awadh between 1918 and 1922 larger landlords were opposed by peasants over security of tenure and forced labour. In Bardoli in 1928 landless labourers resisted dominant peasants. In Bengal between 1938 and 1950 share-croppers and smaller occupancy tenants and poor landlords repeatedly rose up against higher landlords, seeking better terms and security from eviction. Similar motives lay behind risings in the Central Provinces in 1946–7 and Andhra in the early 1950s.

Peasant movements reflected religious and social concerns, and responded to changing economic and legal conditions and to a discourse of rights. In their class aspects, they expressed grievances over oppression and exploitation, but the weakest people were naturally often unable to respond directly. The most obvious targets were not always attacked. The colonial state and Europeans were not assailed as frequently as might have been expected, considering that revenue demands, legal innovations and restrictive contracts often lay behind the problems. However, sometimes the necessary cross-class solidarities were achieved. In the 'blue mutiny' small landlords, moneylenders, and poor peasants combined against European indigo planters; while richer peasants, moneylenders and outside publicists repeatedly resisted the planters in the Bihar indigo campaigns between 1860 and 1920.

By now, however, the connection was more often being made, by political preachers and peasants, between land-owning and the state, between rents and taxation. In Kheda, Gujarat, in 1917 and 1934, rich and poor Patidars (the dominant landed caste) united in refusing to pay the state's revenue, amid agricultural hardship. In the UP in 1930–2 no-rent, no-revenue campaigns were conducted by richer peasants and small landlords uniting against larger land-lords and the state. These grievances aided the nationalists' attempts to co-opt local protests for the anti-colonial struggle: as said, the Congress sought to focus on the British without alienating the landed classes.

POPULAR NATIONALISM

The Congress from the end of the First World War, and the Muslim League at the start of the second, managed to harness popular protests to the nationalist campaigns. Here we will sketch in some aspects of the process as far as the Congress was concerned. The impression given in British police and political records, and the histories largely based upon them, was that there was a politicizing of spheres and people hitherto isolated or quiescent: such were the assumptions too of British policies at the time. Many more local campaigns did become attached to central ones after 1920. They were particularly severe and widespread in coincidence with them. The people involved, at all levels of society, were influenced by national leaders and issues, as well as by news of struggles elsewhere. On the other hand, as we have just seen, local protests were not new. Similar outbreaks occurred both in the past and in future, often quite independently of any nationalist agenda. Nor were link-ages unprecedented: many existed before, between protests, across castes and communities, from town to country, and between leaders and followers. Finally, local movements were not necessarily created by or subservient to a central plan even at the height of the Congress campaigns.

Thus, the non-cooperation movement of 1920–2 had several components under Gandhi's leadership. Some parts were directed at a largely 'middle class' audience, as the anti-Rowlatt agitation also had been, with its notions of *habeas corpus*, due legal process, and constitutional liberties. In this aspect, non-cooperation comprised a boycott of elections, titles, state schools and the courts. Many title-holders, teachers and lawyers joined the movement, and some set up new, rival institutions. (Some survived after the campaign, the most celebrated probably being the Jamia Millia Islamia now in New Delhi and the Kasi Vidyapath at Banaras.) The idea of boycott appealed enormously to students, many of whom became Congress volunteers, but also to some with business interests who contributed to Congress fund-raising. The programme implied a degree of discipline. Many more or less reluctantly complied, even when the campaign was peremptorily called off by Gandhi, in protest at violence, after the murder of policemen in a riot at Chauri Chaura village in the United Provinces.

Boycott was a key weapon not only against British rule, but also in a *swadeshi* (own-country) campaign against foreign products, in market closures and general strikes (*hartals*), and in the social ostracism of people who refused to comply with aspects of the campaigns – especially the anti-liquor agitations. With these and other socio-economic issues, the movement moved into causes semi-detached from Gandhi's, and only loosely within the purview of central Congress leaders. These questions were often immediate and specific, rather than nationalist. Labour strikes occurred over wages and conditions in the mills of Bombay, Calcutta and Madras, amidst accusations of wartime and post-war profiteering, and in a host of other industries – indeed, from rickshaw-pullers to tea-garden workers. Many rural grievances were aired: against Union Board establishment and the resultant taxes in Midnapur district (Bengal), or against forest laws in Andhra and elsewhere, or, most notably, in Faizabad and other parts of UP, where there were attacks on land-lords, merchants and moneylenders. No-revenue campaigns were begun, more or less without Congress authority. They had been included in the programme but as the penultimate non-cooperation (the final one being withdrawal from army service) in a graduated list, to be invoked as and when Gandhi required.

However, the collapse of the movement in 1922 meant that many of these local movements also lost prominence and support. It was becoming ever harder to distinguish between central and local issues, as the government's own policies now reflected, not least because of the power of communication and imitation. There was movement too on the other side, as it were, in what constituted high politics. Issues behind the apparently peripheral parts of non-cooperation were now increasingly relevant to legislative politics, into which some Congressmen entered through the Swaraj Party, ending their boycott to contest elections under Motilal Nehru and Chittaranjan Das. The 1920s also saw a would-be radicalizing of Congress attitudes, not least because of the influence of younger recruits attracted during 1920–1, for example on religious or socialist issues. Little came of their programmes within Congress itself, but a palpable result of their radicalism was its formal acceptance of a goal of *purna swaraj* (complete self-government) in 1929. This followed a period of debate over the meaning of British promises, as the existing British Dominions were becoming more obviously independent. The Viceroy, Irwin, proclaimed that the British goal *was* dominion status in that extended sense; British Conservatives demurred.

The Great Depression, and the collapse of commodity prices and rural credit, caused distress in India, but, even before this, there was ongoing labour and rural unrest. In 1930, as previously mentioned, Gandhi chose the issue of the salt tax as the centrepiece of a new civil disobedience movement. He marched a long and circuitous route through Gujarat from Sabarmati ashram to the coast at Dandi, to commit the symbolic illegality of salt-making. Similar marches took place elsewhere. Often they generated local support and focused local protest; sometimes, as in the march organized by C. Rajagopalachari, the southern Congressman, they resulted in violence.

The civil disobedience movement too was abruptly halted, and hence divided into two parts (1930–1 and 1932–4), but not on the issue of violence (which this time was sidestepped). Gandhi called the pause to take part in meetings with the Viceroy in 1931, and then to attend the second Round Table Conference. The Gandhi–Irwin talks produced no tangible concessions on the government side, but were a victory of a kind in that they raised the standing of Congress to one of implicit equality with the raj, a prominence reinforced by the subsequent sensation of Gandhi's popular reception as he visited Britain (then embittered by its own socio-political divisions). Similarly in 1932, when the new Viceroy, Willingdon, proscribed the Congress and started imprisoning leading Congressmen (tens of thousands had been imprisoned overall), both civil disobedience and its related movements petered out.

These facts, and a degree of management of the rural agitations, give the impression that civil disobedience was more rigorously controlled by the Congress than non-cooperation had been. But, if so, it was partly because Congress leaders rushed to the head of existing popular movements. Over the civil-disobedience period as a whole, the Congress's nationalist campaign encompassed a long list of separate local concerns. More anti-forest law agitations broke out, this time in the Central Provinces and Maharashtra. The rise of the pro-Congress Red Shirts of Abd al-Ghaffar Khan led to rioting in the North-West Frontier Province. Peasant and Hindu urban parties rallied against the Unionists in the Punjab. As already mentioned, no-revenue campaigns broke out widely – in Guntur (Madras); in Rai Bareilly and Gaurakhpur in UP; and in Kheda and Bardoli (Surat) in Gujarat where a prolonged revenue strike forced the government to moderate or abandon its attempt to enforce large increases in the demand.

The advent of Congress governments after 1937 none the less strengthened the hand of the party's central leadership once again, partly by the exercise of executive authority to woo supporters, and partly by organizational changes (sponsored by Vallabhbhai Patel in particular) that gave the central leadership a tighter control over party and regional members. The Quit India movement of 1942 then started off with the familiar pattern of *hartals*, strikes and passive resistance; students were to the fore again, more than in the early 1930s. Soon this developed into the most violent and disruptive of the Congress campaigns – if such it was, for the escalation occurred after all the senior Congress office-holders had been arrested.

Congress and nationalist elements may seem few in the 1942 outbreaks. Again, there were economic and social grievances, this time exacerbated by the dislocations of war. The movement, in its extreme forms, was very localized. It was mostly confined to eastern UP, Bihar, Midnapur, Orissa, and a few parts of Maharashtra and Karnatika, and occurred mainly in relatively poor areas, many of which had had earlier agitations. It was a series of rural rebellions, producing severe but district-level rather than all-India disruption; similarly localized was the pattern of those arrested as the disorder was brought under control. On the other hand, the picture was still of growing nationalist sentiment being infused into specific grievances and interest groups. In the Quit India rebellions, the *inspiration* was overwhelmingly nationalist. This was a reflection of a world of wider publicity and propaganda, which were challenging the certainties of colonial domination, and making available a new range of explanations and ambitions. More specifically, the agitation took strongest hold in large measure where there was a reaction against the harsh official repression of initial protests. Colonial rule was thus doubly the grievance.

COMMUNAL SEPARATISM

Despite long coexistence and much mutual influence, there was always the potential for antagonism between Muslims and Hindus, over such issues as cow sacrifice or the musical or other defilement of mosques. As sections of the population became more organized and as activists sought to standardize attitudes and beliefs within communities, so these antagonisms increased and flared more frequently into violence. By the 1920s, despite an appearance of harmony under the inspiration of Gandhi and anti-colonialism, the religious 'communities' were already polarized politically. An ideology of cultural and even ethnic separation, in a nationalist climate, naturally gave rise to demands for a political 'homeland' which would express and preserve these differences; the poet and Muslim League president, Muhammad Iqbal, argued as much in a celebrated speech in 1930. Moreover, the nearer the goal of democratic representation came to being achieved, the more demography began to count. Accordingly minority interest groups began to seek special treatment. Elite UP Muslims, in a permanent minority, claimed a legislative membership appropriate to the historical contribution and socio-economic importance of their 'community' rather than its numbers. Bengal Muslims, though at a slight numerical advantage, asked for extra allowance to make up for their 'backwardness'.

A constitutional consultative committee had been set up by the Indian National Congress under the leadership of Motilal Nehru, as a riposte to the British parliamentary investigation under Sir John Simon. Nehru's committee reported in 1928, directing itself more to convincing British sceptics of Indian readiness for self-government than to generating the broadest possible consensus among Indian opinion. Its principles were popular sovereignty, territorial constituencies, responsible self-government, equal civil rights, and state responsibility for the economic and physical well-being of the public. It envisaged a Supreme Court, and regional governments based on linguistic provinces. It made proposals on Muslim representation but advanced a secular inspiration for Indian government.

These proposals were rejected by Muhammad Ali Jinnah and others. The All-India Muslim Conference of 1929 went to the root of the disagreement when it declared:

in view of India's vast extent and...divisions, the only form of Government suitable to Indian conditions is a federal system with complete autonomy and residuary powers vested in the constituent States, the Central Government having control only of such matters of common interest as may be specifically entrusted to it.

Moreover, even under such a constitution, it would be necessary for reserve powers to be vested in the religious *communities*: separate electorates would persist, with at least a third of the central seats reserved for Muslims, and legislation on (undefined) 'inter-communal matters' would be subject to communal veto. The state should not be neutral on religion; rather the constitution ought to 'embody adequate safeguards for protection and promotion' of Muslim education, languages, law and charities.[2]

This was a time (after the collapse of the Khilafat campaign) of division and uncertainty for Muslim politicians; but also of the hardening of the separatist position and its theories of the state. Now too there appeared the organized Hindu chauvinist parties. V. D. Savarkar's presidential address to the All-India Hindu Mahasabha in 1931 extolled national strength and economic self-sufficiency, but also the need 'to see that the Hindu peasants, the Hindu traders and the Hindu labourers do not suffer at the hands of non-Hindu aggression', and the need to resolve 'the conflicting class interests among the Hindus themselves'.[3]

Muslim separatist arguments were encouraged by the government's stereotypes and by its failure to keep to its own policy of developing territorial constituencies. The Indian disagreements also became vital parts of the British narrative of constitutional reform, exemplified in the Round Table Conferences held in London between 1930 and 1932 in an attempt to settle the terms of the next stage. In his speech to the second conference (the only one he attended), Gandhi explained that everyone there represented sectional interests, and Congress was treated as one such party. But 'Congress alone claims to represent the whole of India'. It was 'a determined enemy of communalism in any shape or form'; indeed, it represented 'all the minorities' better than they did themselves; and, anyway, their present enmities were just a by-product of British rule.[4]

Bitterness was increased in the UP and at the all-India level by the resounding Congress victories in the provincial elections of 1937. Not only did the UP Congress refuse to give effect to a pre-election pact with Muslim League members (except on insulting terms), it also set about enhancing its popular support, among poorer Muslims as well as Hindus, by a 'mass-contacts' campaign. Jawaharlal Nehru attacked Muslim separatists as 'feudal' exploiters and their dupes; by contrast he professed socialist principles, at least for the future – they were opposed by Gandhi, and weakly if at all pursued by Congress governments at this time. In turn Jinnah, returning to active Indian politics from a period in England, proclaimed the resignation of the Congress ministries in 1939 as a 'day of deliverance'.

PARTITION

The standing of the Muslim League under Jinnah was greatly enhanced during the 1940s. In 1938, though he retained his own patrician style, he had at last followed the Congress example and reconstituted the League on a more active, organized and populist footing. He strove to impose discipline upon nominal adherents of the League such as Fazl-al Haq, leader of the Krishak Praja (Peasants' and Workers') Party, which had been in decline in Bengal since 1937, or to encourage separatist sentiment and support for the League through volunteers and the influence of *ulama*, as was achieved in the Punjab in the face of a collapse of Unionist Party support. This rise of the Muslim League was revealed when it won nearly 90 per cent of the vote in Muslim seats in the elections held after the war, to the accompaniment of increased bitterness between higher-level Congress and League politicians, and of street-level violence that culminated in the Great Calcutta Killing of 1946. For Muslims, political issues had sometimes had a religious dimension; now, for a majority, religion was necessarily political. The League's success implied that regional distinctions, and the provinces' various class-based or non-sectarian political elements, were hidden under the cloak of religious identity.

The British continued to regard Muslims as a united political interest set among irreconcilable communities, and they looked to the League for support, especially when they were at odds with the Congress. In the early 1940s the problem was Congress opposition to the war effort, instituted under Gandhi's influence, and initially because of a quarrel with the Viceroy, Linlithgow, over his declaring war without consultation. Hostility culminated, as already noted, in the Quit India movement (1942), when the government arrested senior Congress leaders, after which their followers and local malcontents rose in many districts, bringing British authority to a temporary halt. In this context, Linlithgow, who believed in the 'two-nations theory' advanced by separatists, deliberately elevated the League to become an equal party with the Congress in the negotiations which ensued, a distinct simplification of the complex balancing act attempted unsuccessfully in the Round Table Conferences. The later negotiations in India (notably the Cripps Mission in 1942 and the Cabinet Mission in 1946), the strenuous and more flexible efforts of Linlithgow's successor, Wavell, and the partition settlement brokered by Mountbatten in 1947, all had Congress–League disagreements at their core.

The federal structure of the central government, proposed in 1935, had proved unworkable (partly because the Indian princes declined to co-operate) so that the basic constitutional question had remained open. In the late 1930s, strongly encouraged by the British, the League had debated ways to entrench separate Muslim interests and weaken what they regarded as Hindu dominance. Most members advocated some degree of autonomy for provincial states under a weak centre. In 1940, a wordy and ambiguous version of this goal was endorsed by the League meeting at Lahore. It called for sovereign, autonomous and independent Muslim-majority areas; and hence was open to the interpretation that it envisaged what some activists had already called for, as 'Pakistan', namely a completely separate state or states. Others could accept the resolution while opposing 'Muslim Raj here and Hindu Raj elsewhere' (in the words of Sikander Hyat Khan, the Unionist leader of the Punjab).[5] Jinnah's own commitment to complete separation has been doubted. His ultimate position on the issue (during and also before the 1940s) was kept deliberately vague as a bargaining tactic. Certainly he neither expected nor wished to achieve the actual outcome of 1947: a 'moth-eaten' Pakistan whose borders followed the strict logic of self-determination and included only Muslim-majority sub-districts; producing two entirely separate countries of India and Pakistan whose division on religious grounds was exaggerated in the event (despite the huge numbers of Muslims still in India) by tragically violent transfers of population.

A variety of political perspectives had been on view. The British professed to offer and eventually conceded territorial representation and responsible government, but had hidden behind a theory of primaeval communities that required a federal solution – and, until it was achieved, British overlordship; and after it, British guidance. Among separatist Muslims there were theocrats who wanted an Islamic state, and personally secular politicians such as Jinnah who sought a cultural homeland or the expression and protection of Muslim political interests. Among other Indians, there were Gandhians who would dissolve the state into villages, and who equated self-rule with individual and social self-control; there were Nehruvian socialists who promised to use an independent state as an instrument of economic and social development; there were centrists who regarded the state as a bulwark against regionalism and disorder; and there were devotees who looked to the state to constitute a Hindu order.

After independence, India continued elements of British colonial policy towards religious and other minorities: professing neutrality (with symbolic appointments to high office) and defusing violent confrontations, but also reaffirming distinctions and categories, and employing them on occasion for political advantage. The British had conceded separate elections for Muslims, partly from a view of the world which equated religion with community and political interest, as well as with culture and character. They had conceded them also for political advantage, arguing that Muslims, at least for a time, would provide allies against more assertive Indian-nationalist demands. The Congress government used Hindu symbols *and* wooed Muslim votes even as it proclaimed its secularism. Nehru's government not only modified its civil code in response to Hindu critics, but also perpetuated religious personal laws in order to palliate orthodox Muslim opinion. Just as problematically, the Hindu laws effectively stood in for a common code.

COMMUNITY AND CLASS

From the later nineteenth century onwards Indian politics developed to express both community and class perspectives – 'community' meaning identities and interest groups based upon 'biology' or faith, and 'class' meaning socio-economic affinities. Nationalism was one ideology that increased its popular recognition and allegiance from about 1920, but it sent out confused messages in regard to community or class allegiances. It was a platform and an end in itself rather than a programme for government. It attempted to subsume all other, sectional political identities: the priority of the anti-colonial struggle was unity and independence rather than any class agenda or any one political philosophy. Businessmen were corralled with trade unionists, and landlords with tenants. The Congress railed against community politics as a feudal vestige, but its alternative, secularism, was flawed.

Other interest-based ideologies were on offer, especially from socialists and communists. Yet, as seen with Indian Muslims, it was 'community' that became the dominant mode of political identity. There were some strong reasons for 'community' politics, in the nature of popular allegiances, the importance of religion and caste, and in modernizations that strengthened and standardized these identities. Many class-based groups – peasant associations, movements among peasants and workers, even movements for status and solidarity among professionals or in commerce – turned out on closer examination to be dominated by particular castes, or even to take on the form of caste or community identities, as among literate Kayasthas or commercial Marwaris, or with the Ad-Dharm and Adi-Hindu movements (discussed below) and a host of caste *sabhas* (societies) that sought to organize and improve the condition of low-class groups from the 1920s.

On the other hand, communalism always vied with some non-communalist alternatives. In the 1920s, when the Indian Communist leader, M. N. Roy, lived in Moscow, the Communist Internationale allotted funds to 'communize India', and the colonial government fretted over Bolshevik infiltrations whose importance it seemed to overrate. But political leaders and supporters from many different backgrounds *were* becoming more interested in socialist ideas. In Bengal many Muslims were numbered among the early socialists, including Muzaffar Ahmed (tried in the Meerut conspiracy case of 1929) and of course Fazl-al Haq, leader of the Peasants' and Workers' Party. After the First World War, and especially in the 1930s, as union and socialist activity encouraged an increasing number of strikes in cotton and jute mills and other factories, and on the railways and in railway workshops, larger organizations and possible common ground began to emerge among bodies that represented economic classes. An All-India Trades Union Congress was formed (on the model of the Congress in Britain). We have already noted that movements of the agrarian left gained a national profile with the establishment of the All-India Kisan Sabha (also linked with Congress). From the late 1930s, too, the then Communist Party leader, P. C. Joshi, sought an anti-colonial front with the Congress, a compact that continued at lower levels even when the Communists joined the war effort and formally attacked Congress opposition.

All this time the communalist parties flourished, but they were never unchallenged. There were even signs during the 1930s that non-community politics were gaining ground. Gandhi undertook a 'fast to the death' at Pune to oppose the recognition of the depressed classes, under Ambedkar, as a distinct community with separate electorates. At the other extremes, the Hindu right, unlike a similar splinter group in 1926, did poorly in the UP elections in 1934 under the aegis of the Congress National Party of M. M. Malaviya and M. S. Aney; while the Muslim League won less than a quarter of the Muslim seats (109 out of 482) across India in 1936.

If communalism none the less was always significant, and if it dominated everything in the 1940s – that is, at one crucial moment, rather than by becoming the sole form of political identity – then attention is drawn (as above) to the emphasis placed upon community by the colonial government. The British dictated the frame within which the constitutional negotations took place. The Cripps and Cabinet Mission proposals gave priority to resolving what they saw as the basic problem, the 'Hindu–Muslim divide'. Without this influence, the partition of India might not have become central to the transfer of power.

Low-caste parties' fortunes contrast interestingly with those of the Muslim League in the 1940s. They can hardly be said to have been united – their fractious organizations had to run through the full gamut of titles, from 'association' to 'party' – but they did consistently seek to address the distinct political interests of the low castes and 'untouchables'. The All-India Depressed Classes Association had been formed in 1926 under M. C. Rajah, and then a separate Depressed Classes Congress under B. R. Ambedkar in 1930. Ambedkar called for *dalits* to be regarded as a socio-political identity. They are, he said to the Round Table Conference in 1931, 'a minority which comes next to the great Muslim minority, and yet their social standard is lower than the social standard of ordinary human beings'.[6] After Gandhi's Pune fast thwarted Ambedkar's

ambition, reserved seats were conceded alongside common electorates; but the Congress and other parties generally hampered the
institutionalization of the *dalits* as a political community. Rajah agreed
to common electorates, and joined Gandhi as he embarked on his
intensified 'harijan' campaign. That failed to redress the *dalits'*
economic and social disabilities but provided another political option
in 1935 with the inauguration of the All-India Depressed (later
Scheduled) Classes League under Jagjivan Ram. Ambedkar responded
by forming the Independent Labour Party, in an attempt to bypass
the caste issue; it won almost all the reserved seats in Bombay in the
1937 elections. Rajah, who had been elected in Madras on a
Congress ticket, became disillusioned at the failure of his Temple
Entry Bill, and joined in Ambedkar's All-India Scheduled Caste
Federation formed in 1942, again on a separatist agenda.

The Cripps and Cabinet Missions recognized the Federation as
representing *dalits*, but in the end refused them the status they
accorded the Muslims. In these discussions only religion was
considered a proper marker of minority identity. The problem with
the Scheduled Castes (as the Secretary of State had put it in 1942)
was that they were 'neither one thing nor the other'; they did not
have the 'courage' to convert to Christianity or Islam but remained
a part of the 'Hindu system', and hence they would have to take
their chances on social uplift as Hindus.[7] Ambedkar continued to
insist that he represented a third force, after the Congress and the
Muslims, and he was repeatedly invited to join in deliberations
(and indeed the government) on that basis without ever carrying
his main point into the constitutional proposals. Ambedkar's Federation and various other *dalit* groups then protested vigorously in
a *satyagraha* campaign in 1946.

But what was the consequence of this denial of political recognition? In the 1945/6 elections the Federation had generally lost out
to the Congress in the battle for the votes of its 'community'; indeed
it had fielded very few candidates. Many *dalits* at this time followed
the example of the low-caste Namasudras of Bengal who (it has
been argued) belatedly endorsed the defection of some of their own
leaders, and chose 'Hindu nation' over caste or class solidarities.
This fatally damaged Ambedkar's attempts to persuade the British
to reopen the question. He was forced to seek a *rapprochement* with
the Congress, which in turn endorsed constitutional and legislative
proposals to improve the *dalits'* situation. Special provisions of the
1950 Constitution then helped create new political interest groups

on the basis of caste rather than economic status. However, for at least a generation many of the oppressed continued to support the Congress, or (as in both east and west Bengal after partition) the various socialist parties. Ambedkar himself sought to convert his followers to Buddhism, thus preserving them as a distinct community, but this did not attract the bulk of India's *dalits*. At the very least it can be said that British, Congress, socialist and Hindu-rightist influence all coalesced to confuse low-caste consolidation into a political 'community'; whereas similar efforts may be said to have *promoted* that effect for Indian Muslims on the eve of partition.

India was arguably disposed, as a mostly pre-industrialized society, to mobilizations on the basis of religious and social identity. But, as argued above, the colonial state ensured that community would remain the commonplace of politics. Other forces that might have resisted communal politics, from the Congress to capitalism, were weakened by British sociology and race-theory assumptions, and by deliberate colonial policies of divide-and-rule. It is impossible to disentangle degrees of responsibility – did colonial rulers emphasize religious community because it was an inescapable fact of Indian political life, or did it become such a fact because colonial rulers emphasized it? Either way, the outcome is plain. From a twenty-first-century perspective it appears that the ultimate legacy of the colonial era was not after all (or not only) a modernizing secularism, the rule of law and equitable theories of government and citizenship, but a politics geared to atavistic representations and social and religious division. Means of mass communication increased, and economic and social conditions seemed to promote greater class similarities; but, paradoxically, politics became fragmented into personal followings, special-interest groups, and communities, in India as elsewhere.

THE AFTERMATH OF COLONIALISM

Jawaharlal Nehru's Congress came to power in 1947 and set about developing India's federal Constitution, based on responsible government and adult franchise. Though built upon the reforms Act of 1935, the Constitution of 1950 and the resultant political system had some distinctive, even curious features. One was the merging of democracy and Cabinet government with the executive-officer model adopted from the ICS and now continued in the Indian

Administrative Service (IAS). Another was the apparent contradiction between the Westminster mode of parliamentary sovereignty
on one hand, and on the other the fundamental rights and directive
principles of the Constitution, which protected groups as well as
individuals *and* required social reform, and thus afforded a superior
and political role to the Supreme Court. A third anomaly was the
emphasis upon unity and centralization alongside a promise of
linguistic states and regional and sectional rights. The system has
produced much conflict, but has also worked remarkably well.

Nehru and others argued strongly that independence required
a new understanding of politics, in which loyalty and respect for law
were demanded by the state, separation was achieved between
party and government, and independence, accountability, responsibilities and rules of conduct provided for civil servants, courts, police
and army: accordingly a civil–political compact developed in India
(in contrast with the civil–military nexus in Pakistan). These ideas
were debated with a high degree of sophistication among India's
already experienced leaders and public. They implied a continuity in
many respects with the colonial state rather than with the anti-colonial
movement.

Nehru saw himself as building a modern nation, through politics
and planning. The advent of independence brought a further explosion of the state, government employees at all levels rising from
around 4 million people in 1953 to about 16 million in 1983. Still,
there were many areas of difficulty. Even central institutions did not
develop without argument. Various local and development agencies
came into conflict not only with party bosses anxious to secure
privileges, but also, as with the ICS during colonial rule, with the
elite executive officers of the IAS, jealous of their authority.

The Congress, especially under Nehru, was still less of a unified
party than a national forum embodying a range of interests and
opinions, and attracting opportunists. This made it difficult to
control. Nehru's rise initially threatened a conflict with Vallabhbhai
Patel, who dominated the party organization as Nehru did the country. The Congress presidency became a focal point of disagreement,
with the election of Patel's candidate, Purushottamdas Tandon, in
1950. Subsequently, after Patel's death the same year, Nehru forced
Tandon to resign, but Nehru's joint occupation of the offices of party
president and prime minister did not improve the party machine,
especially at local levels. His failure to resolve these difficulties lay
behind later crises of national leadership, and eventually undermined

Congress support with the electorate. It contributed, after his death, to the dynastic succession of his daughter, Indira Gandhi, and then of her son, Rajiv; but it also allowed further struggles for control of the Congress machine, most notably between Mrs Gandhi and the Tamil Nadu Chief Minister and Congress President, Kamaraj Nadar, who had originally helped engineer her succession. These arguments led to a split in the Congress in 1969, this time on the occasion of the election of the Union President, when Indira Gandhi's candidate, V. V. Giri, defeated the official Congress nominee, Sanjiva Reddy.

Nehru had strong credentials as a democrat, his legacy arguably illustrated by the remarkable advance of the electoral system, from a parliamentary electorate of some 173 million and a participation rate of around 47 per cent (1952) to an electorate of nearly 376 million and a turn-out around 63 per cent (1984). Unity was a key concern, and lay behind a whole array of policies, including the attempts to bring Ambedkar into government, and the Scheduled Castes and Tribes into the political mainstream. In practice, however, Indian politics continued to rely heavily on caste and community voting-blocs – that is, on vertical solidarities commanded by political bosses. There were few successful national parties based on class solidarities, though the Communist Party of India and, after 1963, the more militant breakaway Communist Party Marxist (CPM), sometimes were important, as were agrarian parties such as the north Indian Lok Dal of Charan Singh, founded in 1969. At the centre, on the whole, the chameleon, enveloping nature of the Congress, and Nehru's long pre-eminence, had the perverse effect of preventing the building of a credible two-party system. The Janata Party, a loose coalition, eventually ousted the Congress in elections of 1977, but collapsed in upon itself in 1979. It then seemed (misleadingly) to be business as usual, when Rajiv Gandhi's Congress won the elections of 1984, on a wave of sentiment following the assassination of Mrs Gandhi, with just under half the votes and almost 80 per cent of the seats.

Nehru was also not averse to repressing opposition, for example those Communists who were placed under preventive detention in the 1950s and 1960s. Among telling aspects of the government of Nehru and his successors was the marked growth of the state's means of coercion, in terms both of special units and emergency powers, and of overall manpower. The police numbered under half a million in 1951, but the complement had nearly doubled by 1980. The armed forces totalled about 400 000 in 1956, but some

1 260 000 in 1986, regularly consuming around 20 per cent of government spending. The authoritarian tendency reached its apogee, in terms of overt suspension of constitutional norms, when Indira Gandhi declared an Emergency in 1971, to face down a nationwide agitation led by the charismatic Jayaprakash Narayan, and a crisis created by the decision of the Allahabad High Court to cancel Mrs Gandhi's election to her parliamentary seat, on the grounds of irregularities.

In the aftermath of partition the transfers of population, though less marked in India than in Pakistan, had caused dislocation and also created opportunities, the effects in both senses being felt disproportionately by some regions and peoples. Sikhs were particularly disrupted, and fanned out across India and the world, but often became successful, especially in business or transport industries. West Bengal and Calcutta in particular came under immense pressure from continuing waves of Hindu migrants from the east, but these often-resourceful people also brought some benefits. Military and strategic rivalries were a more damaging legacy of partition. The short-lived invasion by China in 1962 over a disputed colonial border, and India's ambitions as a regional power, probably mean that military expenditure would have been high even in the absence of the Kashmir dispute (discussed below) and any threat from Pakistan. But the exceptionally hard barriers to regional trade and co-operation that were erected with the partition-boundaries cannot have helped regional economic development.

Another difficulty was the tension between regionalism and all-India concerns. Under both colonial and Congress governments, most political histories and movements either appealed to or challenged all-India traditions. Remarkably – probably a comment on the extent of foreign influence – even early nineteenth-century Bengal intellectuals had adopted 'Hindu' models and 'Indian' concerns as well as Bengali ones. The Hindu right and Muslim separatists did the same. Subsequent influences consolidated this unification: national radio and television, national elections, national sports teams, and international conflicts, especially the wars against Pakistan in 1965 and 1971. As said, independent India's Constitution too was strongly centralized in the colonial tradition.

Even so, political parties remained largely regional, and regional differences continue to grow. The British both defined and suppressed regions (for example, when collecting and spending revenues), but regional development was encouraged by modern features such as administrative and linguistic borders. Regional languages and literatures, and local associations of all kinds, delineated and developed regional identities. Historical, political and economic differences became more clearly and firmly defined between distinct regions, and political mobilization even at the height of the nationalist movement or of Congress dominance was basically regional and local. During and immediately after the Nehruvian era, only regional political parties had the ability to mount a consistent challenge to Congress dominance. Notable, among others, were the Dravida Munnetra Khazagham (DMK) in Tamilnadu, the Akali Dal in the Punjab, and the Assam Sana Parishad. Regional variations also help explain the success of the Communists in Kerala, and especially in West Bengal where the CPM led the governments after 1977.

After independence, linguistic identities focused several political conflicts that were diffused by Nehru's government through reluctant acceptance of separations, of Andhra and Tamilnadu in 1956, and of Gujarat and Maharashtra in 1960. Haryana, Himachal Pradesh and Punjab followed in 1966. Under Nehru and afterwards, tensions continued to increase between centre and regional state, and between state and state, and between areas within states. Centre–regional problems, though repeatedly brought to compromise, were not dissipated. They too impeded the emergence of effective national parties, and sometimes effective national policies. The national language issue, for example, most potent in Tamilnadu, was shelved by way of the three-language solution – Hindi, English, Tamil – as demanded by the DMK. This solution did not solve the problem, in either regional or class terms, of the continuing pre-eminence of Hindi and English as national languages. The status of English was supposed to end in 1956; instead it was arguably enhanced, through university policy, government practice and globalization.

Kashmir, the endemic crisis, was in many ways another of India's problems of regionalism and centralization. The precise terms of the accession of Indian states were left vague in 1947, but the question was mainly resolved by a mixture of *force majeur*, diplomacy and guile. Kashmir acceded to India by the Instrument signed by Maharaja Hari Singh in 1947, amidst an uprising and irregular invasion designed to force accession to Pakistan or the claim to Kashmiri independence. Two-thirds of the state remained in Indian hands at the end of hostilities in the Indo-Pakistani war of 1948–9. Under the premiership (1947–53) of Sheikh Abdullah, the Kashmir assembly had also ratified the accession, but on a promise of local

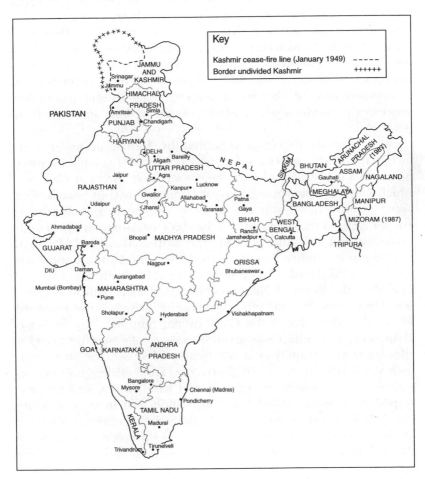

Map 8 India in 1980

autonomy to which effect was never given. Nor has a promised plebiscite ever been held. For Nehru the accession of largely Muslim Kashmir (complicated by non-Muslim Jammu) was as much as anything a tribute to the secular cohesion of India. He feared its loss as a blow to both his anti-communalist stance and to his struggles for Indian unity. For nationalists on all sides it became a rhetorical symbol of pride and strength, akin to the rival brandishing of nuclear weapons which latterly has accompanied the dispute. Kashmir itself has been the victim, many of its Hindus and Muslims killed, oppressed or ousted, in the cause of incompatible identity-politics. It remains one of the major imperfections in the incomplete processes of modernization which created nations and regions in South Asia.

Other serious problems inherited by Nehru in government included poverty, underdevelopment and social division. On policy, he made a qualified pact with the conservative forces in Congress, which helped delay the advance of Hindu chauvinist parties. Religious communalism was also directly combated and secularism encouraged, in the aftermath of Gandhi's assassination by a Hindu extremist, and following the temporary suspension of Indo-Pakistani disputes in the Nehru–Liaquat pact (1950). The Hindu Code Bill of 1951, and the Hindu Succession Act of 1956, both compromises, described the limits of Nehru's efforts to reform Hindu personal law. Untouchability was officially abolished, though not removed, under the schedules of the Constitution, reinforced by an Act of 1955. Very little effect was given to policies of reserving places in education and employment for depressed classes; at stake were both standards and entrenched privilege. Land ceilings and peasant rights were canvassed, partly to attract rural voters, and partly in response to provisions of the Constitution and to long-standing, even inherited pro-peasant rhetoric. Zamindari abolition, introduced by the states between 1951 and 1962, was supposed to (but mostly did not) reduce the disparities in ownership of and access to rural land.

There was marked economic improvement, including a 50 per cent expansion of industry between 1951 and 1959, and large increases in agricultural output, sponsored by the National Planning Commission, first established in 1950. But this was insufficient to counter the impact of the rise in population, by about one quarter between 1941 and 1981. Electricity, the communication networks and education did not improve sufficiently to secure better standards of living for a majority. Such improvements as were achieved were focused disproportionately on the elites and on towns. In many ways India found a new confidence and vibrancy with the end of colonial rule. In others, it continued to deploy old policies, and it continued to fail.

ROADS TO INDEPENDENCE AND TO MODERN POLITICS

The successful Indian independence movement had been a composite in which Westernized politicians, deploying modern concepts of nationalism and class, linked up with the masses in localities and communities with their own particular interests and ideas. As discussed at the outset of this chapter, this depends on a way of looking at history, privileging certain strands and criteria, replicating Europe; but it is appropriate to the decisions about independence and government, which were taken at that rarefied level. But, as also demonstrated, it would be wrong to substitute this partial story for the whole, to regard either the nationalist movement as homogeneous, or the masses as quiescent until brought into the light of the nationalist movement. Moreover, as said, 'anti-colonialism' was not identical with 'politics'.

In the Indian countryside, there were many influences at work and different responses in evidence. First, there was economics. Moneylenders, traders, landlords, cultivators, share-croppers and landless labourers were all involved, in different ways, in the marked growth of commercial production and consumption. They were also all subject to systematic legal and official labelling and enumeration. Many displayed 'passivity' in the sense that their responses were unobserved or were restricted by the control of others. British observers were often convinced of the fatalism and acquiescence of the countryside. Certain favoured groups, and most notably so-called 'martial castes and tribes', recognized the benefits bestowed on them by the imperial connection.

At different times, however, very many people took part in the large number of economic protest movements, often reflecting particular grievances against landlords, indigo planters or money-lenders, exacerbated by epidemics, famine and land hunger. Some ultimately became involved in organizations which purported to represent economic interests, especially zamindari or land-owners' associations, and (about a hundred years later) *kisan sabhas* or peasant societies. They became aware of a rhetoric of political and economic rights. The Tebhaga uprisings in north Bengal in 1946, the Telangana rebellion in Andhra in the late 1940s (which turned into Hindu resistance against the Muslim-ruled state of Hyderabad), and the Naxalbari or Naxalite violence in eastern India in the 1960s and 1970s, all had these features in common: a high ideological content, Communist involvement, and protests against large property-holdings or oppression by commercial farmers. All of them also, despite regional specificities in the form of caste or community, attempted to unite 'tribal' populations, small peasants, dispossessed share-croppers and poor labourers by means of argument, organization and violence.

Secondly, social and religious changes – it is hard to separate them – were experienced alongside the economic. Rising classes made claims to upward social mobility or protested against social disruptions, thus tending most usually towards a dominant orthodoxy (the mores of caste Hinduism or strict Islam), but also quite often challenging the existing order. We shall consider these movements in the next chapter, but of course they were clearly political in many of their aspects and results.

Finally we come to politics. There was a great deal of unorganized and unrecognized power. It operated in a world of 'corruption', networks and kinship which was barely visible to the British, but which provided important functions to very many people, and which possibly gained in strength and prominence as institutions declined after the mid-twentieth century. There was a rash of vernacular political movements, large and small, often closely integrated with religious or social organization. Lastly there were the rarefied and artificial worlds of largely English-language political leadership, both legislative and agitational – the arena which was once the only one considered because it supposedly 'delivered' national independence and shaped the successor nations' political systems.

Some accounts, having identified that it is wrong to equate elite and popular politics, also argue that they represent distinct and separate spheres. Arguments for autonomous popular consciousness and action are advanced (though not always illustrated).[8] A variant divides India vertically rather than horizontally, between an *outer*, material and political world imitating the West, and an *inner*, indigenous, cultural sphere of language, literature, family, religion.[9] However, while such distinctions may be made, as here, for purposes of analysis, and while each defined group or field obviously had its own peculiar characteristics and trajectories, in practice all of them were also involved with each other. One assertion is that lower orders and peoples were stereotyped as 'unruly' by colonial and nationalist elites. But they also *sought* popular support. (It was not necessarily a prejudice to note that people, of whatever class, like states, could be violent or irrational.) The political worlds interacted and over-lapped; 'modern' influences affected the lowly and the private as well as the high and the public. Moreover, the changes which we are discussing largely came from external influences – material, personal and ideological – with 'external' meaning either foreign or from other fields of life. For example, new forms of mass politics echoed the methods of Sufi preachers, of evangelical Christians and of political radicals (from the Anti-Corn Law League to Irish nationalists): these were imported techniques or they were indigenous practices applied in new ways or for new purposes.

Modern Indian politics included many new institutions, from the Indian National Congress with its mostly cautious middle-class nation-alism, to the militant primordialism of the Hindu Mahasabha, the social agitation (and internal bickerings) of the Communists, or the violent anarchy of the Naxalites. In public life generally, the range extended from literary associations to the Boy Scouts. Modernity had a seductive appeal, but most bodies also took on elements (to varying degrees) which appealed to conservatives and traditionalists. A complex array of institutions ostensibly rejected much that was new, but most organizations were or became hybrids, including not only language societies and peasant and labour organizations, but also the Congress, the Muslim League and most other political parties.

8

Modern India III: Society

CATEGORIZATIONS

Continuities from the past played a very important part in the social changes experienced in India from the mid-nineteenth century. On the other hand, the changes would not have occurred as they did without the context and impact of colonial government and economy, and the influence of Indians who reacted to them. This chapter will explore this aspect. In particular it will consider the importance of new ways of naming and belonging, new forms of community and identity, alongside the persistence of indigenous models.

Complex categorization and forms of rationality had been essential to Indian civilization; they had linked types of people to particular roles, customs and even ecologies. Time itself had its typologies: the present era was *kali yug*, an age of debasement. Alongside hierarchy and purity, a sympathetic correlation – linked to *advaita* (monism) – was to be found at the heart of these ideas. What characterized castes, also defined bodies, appetites, foods, work, leisure, kingdoms, soils, mountains, rivers and gods. In some respects this was a theory of humours, paralleling that in Europe. Indian Islam too had compatible ideas of social harmony. At the same time (possibly because of these pervasive echoes) Indians displayed a practical subtlety and fluidity, seeking balance, and responding to empirical observation and circumstance.

In the early years of colonial rule (as already mentioned) a different kind of taxonomy and history was applied in India, and became available to Indians. Its basis was binary distinction – definition by means of observed characteristics measured according to rule, the legacy of Linnaeus to botany. To this was linked an assumption of rational causation: everything had purpose and meaning, whereby and for which it had evolved. Interrelationships were interpreted as influences or forces, of one body on another, rather than as complementarities. The evolutionary tree was a recurrent model. Exclusive categorization of this kind emphasized separateness rather than unity. Each unit's external borders were hard, and its internal homogeneity was complete in the 'essentials'.

This scientific revolution, as is well known, formed part of a very general change in the ordering of knowledge and practice. It affected the separation and professionalization of disciplines, the periodization and empiricizing of history, the boundaries and remit of states and laws, theories as to the origin and status of peoples and languages, and so on. Moreover, categorization by objective external features was always (but perhaps increasingly) linked to subjective judgements about intrinsic qualities and purposes. Among peoples especially, but also for climates, landscapes and regimes, it was easy to equate physical with evolutionary-biological and moral nature. 'Race' theories of society and its evolution were added to India's hierarchical and genealogical obsessions.

European scholar-administrators played a crucial role. William Jones (1746–94) learnt about Indian civilization from Pandit Radhakanta and others, and also, distrusting 'native informants', from his own researches. He began the characterizing and explanation of 'Indo-European', in a decidedly modern view of languages, deduced from structural affinities, that was also implicitly ethnological. Jones helped institutionalize the collection of data about India through the Asiatic Society and its publications. Even earlier in recording and publicizing such findings (of varied reliability), were J. Z. Holwell's *Interesting Historical Events* (1767), Alexander Dow's *History of Hindostan* (1768–72), Nathaniel Halhed's *Gentoo Code* (1776) and Bengali grammar (1778); and Charles Wilkins' *Bhagavad Gita* (1784). In the early nineteenth century, H. T. Colebrooke too was famous for his Sanskrit learning, and the Abbé Dubois (though he plagiarized another priest, Gaston-Laurent Coeurdoux) for his studies of 'Hinduism'. Between 1816 and 1856, Francis Ellis and Alexander Campbell (assisted by Patabhirama Sastri, a teacher at the College of Fort St George) and then Bishop Robert Caldwell were largely responsible for the 'discovery' of 'Dravidian'.

William Jones had been concerned to relate India to Biblical ethnography and chronology, in terms of a rational Anglicanism. Christian missionaries too were always involved in the attempt to understand India. William Carey made a translation of *Ramayana* (1806); while Unitarians such as William Adam searched Indian traditions for a universal religion. However, as noted in Chapter 5, Evangelicals became increasingly contemptuous of India. In that context, James Mill's *History of British India* (1812) was only one among many which sought to explain and justify the British conquest by analysing India's past. On the other hand, these nineteenth-century Western writers established chronologies and interpretations which influenced future historians, and not least the first generation of Indian practitioners, writing on nation, peoples, locality, community or caste.

In more practical and quantitative spheres, exploration also gathered pace. From the 1790s until his death in 1819, Colin Mackenzie, aided by the South Indian Brahmans, Letchmia and Cavally Venkata Boria, collected local documentation and made detailed surveys and maps; he helped institutionalize such work in the Survey of India, where his notable successors as Surveyor-General included John Hodgson (1821–3 and 1826–9) and George Everest (1830–43). Among earlier pioneers of mapping was James Rennell who surveyed Bengal in the 1760s. Contemporaries of Mackenzie, just as important for technical or social observations, included William Lambton (1750s–1823) for the trigonometrical survey and Francis Buchanan (1762–1829) for socio-economic reports. Around this time too Indian *materia medica* were collected for assessment by Europeans developing theories of medical topography, as they faced what they now regarded as a hostile and typologically distinct 'tropical' environment. Geology, meteorology and climatology were other fields developing amidst Indian examples, and in Indian state departments, even under the Company. Later surveyors, for mapping, revenue-settlement, census or social enquiry, are too numerous to be listed. Among them, Lionel Place is credited with helping reinvent a sacral Tamil landscape; Denzil Ibbetson and H. H. Risley with rival ecological and biological explanations of caste; George Grierson with creating the first modern survey of Indian languages. Beyond such work there developed – also within government agencies – a range of techniques of social description, from finger-printing, through anthropometry, to ethnography.

State-led and scientific categorizations thus helped define new ways of perceiving and expressing identities. Solidarities were created within political and administrative units, and within other supposed or real boundaries of history, material culture and custom.

Pressure groups were spawned. Non-state organizations and identities were based on rules, stories, rituals and gestures, which defined and inspired their members. Identities became more definite and distinctive, more opposed to others, and more closely bound up with systems of belief – they were strongly differentiated according to caste and religion.

One persistent view of Indian society that emerged was of 'little republics' as defined by Charles Metcalfe and taken up by Marx among others: a society that was localized, isolated, self-sufficient and unchanging, and unconnected from the arbitrary powers which dominated it. This contained several half- or untruths. Communal land-ownership and production – joint responsibility for land allocations, services, and the reproduction of agriculture (capital, seeds, irrigation, labour) – were qualified by the influence of rulers, including the British, who appointed and sustained headmen and overlords, and took taxes at up to one-third or more of output. Specialization of production, labour movement, marriage networks and religious pilgrimage also implied connections with the outside world. And, without isolation, there could hardly be complete stability. True, land reclamation was hard and expensive; and there is much evidence of attachment to place, the land of one's ancestors. At village level this would have had effective meaning for the male half of the population, but even so villages were not really fixed and unchanging over long periods.

One can see why such simplifications would help those who wanted to understand and to rule. A closed, stagnating base and middle-level despotism also implied that the state (especially colonialism) could bring light and improvement. The British Indian state claimed legitimacy by pretending to a superior concern for the lower, collectivist, *original* forms of community and kinship, which it protected and perpetuated. Indians were supposed to lack individuation; community norms were their means of both oppression and support. Supposedly they engaged mainly in 'static expansions', meaning change by 'whole communities', to adopt the term used for South-East Asia by J. H. Boeke (1948). Concepts of 'Islamic modernization' or 'caste mobility' fit into this frame, and certainly Indians made use of the new 'traditions' in these ways.

The colonial state assisted through a combination of political need and intellectual tendency. The British were unable or unwilling to create allegiance as in the past, by exchange of gifts, through sacred identity and personal allegiance. They had demilitarized society, eschewed religious rituals, and replaced chieftains by bureaucrats, Therefore they tried to create, as if in a shadow-box or theatre, a new set of quasi-feudal allies and a system of precedence and honours. They engaged with individuals but also, more particularly, with representatives of communities or types. This led to a reconstituting of identities, which, as we saw earlier, then raised a host of other issues. Could a Bengali really be 'educated', or be a 'gentleman'? Should Afghans who left for the *hajj* through Bombay or Karachi have British Indian passports (a real question raised in the 1880s)? Should 'non-nationals' – or 'non-agriculturists' – obtain landed property? Indians at home and abroad were confronted by such questions. Clearly here were identities to which rights were attached. According to Western science and government, they existed within fixed boundaries and with continuous histories. Pressure groups, organized parties, and nationalist movements were one consequence, already noted. Reworkings of social relations were another.

NEW ENVIRONMENTS: CALCUTTA

Colonial scholarship brought new methodologies to India, while working very closely with Indian associates. Colonial rule also provided new environments in which Indians could react. There were schools and societies, print and publications. There were new kinds of city. Eighteenth- and early nineteenth-century Calcutta, for example, was dominated by rich Indian families, merchants and property-owners, who were characterized by their family connections and expansive social style (displays of consumption, elaborate rituals, funerals and weddings, nautches and other entertainments, patronage of functionaries and clients, and so on). People were arrayed in mostly multi-caste *dals* or factions, with their rich *dalapatis* or bosses (such as Dwarkanath Tagore; Nabakrishna and then Radhakanta Deb of Shobhabazar; or Ramdulal and his son, Ashutosh Dey). They lived and worked in courtyarded houses, in *mohallas* (gated lanes) and neighbourhoods. But new styles were emerging: for detached houses surrounded by gardens, for a separation of home and workplace, for middle-class social connections. The *bhadralok* or respectable people began to be identified amidst the 'aristocrats' (*abhijat*) and the householders (*grihastha*), roughly equivalent to the upper and lower middle-classes. As mentioned in Chapter 4, the *bhadralok* were mainly Brahman, Kayastha and Baidya by caste. Money had guaranteed status in eighteenth-century Calcutta (many of the great aristocratic families having doubtful origins), but relatively few from the lower castes gained recognition as *bhadralok*. (The merchant and social conservative, Motilal Seal, was an example of a Subarnavanik or 'unclean Shudra'.) Increasingly (it will be recalled) the middle classes were those engaged in service occupations and new professions, so that education rather than wealth came to be their most important qualification, and newspapers and public associations their most important means of communication.

Such people heard the descriptions of Indian history – the glories of the classical age, the notions of evolution and decadence – and the new theories of society, science and religion. The result in Calcutta was self-consciously described as a renaissance. Untypical were Henry Derozio, a young teacher (1826–31) at the Hindu College, and his followers in 'Young Bengal', with their iconoclastic enthusiasm for all things Western and modern (except, interestingly, outright denigrations of Indian civilization). At the other extreme, also modernizing but socially conservative, was the *abhijat* Radhakanta Deb, involved not only in the Calcutta School Society (1817) bringing modern education to Bengal, but also in the Dharma Sabha (1830) that sought to impose high-caste norms and to defend orthodoxy of custom and belief (including *sati*). Between the two extremes, was Rammohan Roy (1770–1833), founder of the Brahmo Sabha (1828). He developed an argument, as had Holwell, about the monotheism of *vedanta* (1815–17). He argued for Indian wisdom, as William Jones had, against increasingly hostile Evangelicals (for example, in *The Precepts of Jesus*, 1820–1); but he also campaigned against Indian customs such as *sati*, hook-swinging and Kulinism (polygamy). Similar in some respects was Akshay Kumar Datta whose articles in his journal *Tattvavodhini Patrika* stressed the rationalism of the *Upanishads* (1843).

Under the influence of his successors, Rammohan became retrospectively the founder of a sect, namely the Brahmo Samaj (1842) of Debendranath Tagore (1817–1905), with its emphasis on texts, church-like worship, and the superiority of Vedantic and Hindu beliefs. After a split, formalized in 1866 under the leadership of Keshub Chandra Sen (1838–84), the Samaj attracted new recruits and moved in a more radical reforming direction, distinct from Hinduism, opposing caste restrictions, and advocating inter-caste and widow marriages.

Literary developments also reflected a range of attitudes, for example the satirical poems of the conservative Ishwar Chandra Gupta (1812–59), the Sanskritized Bengali plays and blank verse of the Western-influenced Christian, Michael Madhusan Datta (1824–73), or the patriotic historical novels of Bhudev Mukhopadhyay (1827–1894). Translations from both Indian classical and European works made them available as never before, and increased the authority of texts as models of behaviour.

A whole gamut of consequences can be discerned. Female education was soon advocated (1822). Biographies and novels appeared. Many writers, for example Bhabanicharan Bandyopadhyay (1787–1848), satirized the *babu*'s (learned Bengali's) pretensions. In 1861 Rajnarayan Basu founded the Society for the Promotion of National Feeling. In 1867 he helped start an annual Hindu *mela* (fair) to show off Bengali crafts. There was established a sense of Bengali and indeed Indian identities and priorities, selected from Western and indigenous influences. Among these identities were new understandings of caste, to which we now turn.

CASTE AND CLASS

Standardizations and accommodations in Indian society, in this period, often took the form of status controversies between notional or kin groups rather than individuals, as already noted. Caste began to be reassessed. The outcome was both a development of harder and broader communities, *and* the persistence of pre-colonial norms. Influences had also included regional political mobilizations, Mughal and Company policies, and the specialized production and urban growth sponsored by long-distance trade. The changes were social as well as intellectual, affecting the upper levels of society first.

Remarkable caste-based subdivisions (of labour, marriage and custom) were already noticed, by seventeenth- and eighteenth-century European observers, among low-status servants and workers. Even so, most Shudras were still only vaguely identified by 1800. Among the agriculturist Jats, Kunbis and Vellalas, for example, caste and *jati* divisions often seem to have been localized and obscure to outsiders. By contrast, Brahmans, Kshatriyas and Vaishyas were commonly differentiated outside as well as within the localities, and hence some groups were widely accepted as belonging to a 'high' *varna*. Many achieved this, however, only after deliberate effort and changes in behaviour.

Broadly, in the early modern and modern periods, caste was being changed by the spreading of Brahman and Kshatriya norms among those who claimed that status, and among other aspirants for whom the norms had hitherto been unimportant or vague. There was a greater reliance on texts, increased religious piety, stricter barriers of pollution, and larger, more definite and organized caste and community identities. Similar processes of standardization and upward mobility occurred at different rates in different places. In the regions around Delhi, for example, the Jats were already rising in status *vis-à-vis* the Brahmans in the time of the Mughals: they could express their increasing prosperity and military pretensions as claims to Kshatriya status.

Economic and political contexts – insecurities and privileges – help explain the changes. This undermines Hegel's and Dumont's opposition between caste and state or economy (see Chapter 1). Caste was instrumental to states, and states behaved differently because of caste. Caste was also responsive to economic power as well as, sometimes, a brake upon it. Hence Mughal, eighteenth-century, British-colonial and post-independence states all played a central part in changing caste, with their laws, policies and categorizations. Western scholars and ethnographers were important too (though varied in their interpretations, and more consistent on race than caste). Vital were Indian intellectuals, publicists, leaders, and everyday practices.

Of course caste was not the only mode of assertion available. Jats could also develop their ambitions, for example, within alternative sects, such as the Satnamis or most obviously Sikhism. Non-caste values continued to be available to all groups in local syncretic traditions, through *bhakti*, Sufism, and so on. Nevertheless those who were (or chose to be) Hindu made their new claims most often in terms of caste, and thus strengthened it as *the* mode of Hindu identity. Brahman and Rajput norms were pre-existing vocabularies that were being reinforced. Again, the role of states was important to this choice. It mattered that Brahmans and Kshatriyas had high status in the Hindu texts. But important too were Mughal alliances with the Rajputs, or the eighteenth-century development of Hindu rule, especially by the Marathas, or the British colonial state which restored 'legitimate' Kshatriya lineages, applied Brahmanical scriptural rules in its law courts, and reified and counted 'castes' in its censuses. Because these interventions sought to clarify ambiguities, and in particular to relate *jati* to *varna*, a circular process developed: the more caste-like identities were generalized and ranked, the more contested they would be; the more they were contested, the more defined and organized castes would become. Gradually, it might be said, *jati* (in the sense of actual or potential kin groups) became augmented by caste, an imagined and impersonal association justified by ideals of kinship and (from *varna* rules) of conduct.

This tendency towards 'caste' limited the impact from innovations of British colonial rule – individual rights, uniform laws, religious neutrality, commoditization, private property, secure long-distance communications, and so on – which greatly appealed to some Indians, and might have been expected to encourage an alternative mode of identity, namely of economic class rather than caste. On the contrary, many of these changes were made to serve growing assertions of caste status.

Useful studies have been made of caste in many parts of India. One telling example comes from western India (Maharashtra), showing the role of both Rajput (Kshatriya) and Brahman identities. The former identity is traceable to the evolving meanings of the term 'Maratha'. It is used by modern scholars (and in this book) to refer to the peoples who speak Marathi, who predominate in Maharashtra, and who held sway over that region (and much besides) from the late seventeenth to the early nineteenth centuries. Shivaji Bhonsle, encountered in Chapter 4, was remembered as a 'Maratha' Raja of Satara who rebelled against the Muslim emperor, Aurangzib, and hence as the founder of a people's fortunes and the 'national' hero. Shivaji said he was 'Maratha' by caste, and meant by that something much narrower than the broader linguistic and regional identity just referred to (which was also sometimes in use in his day) – that is, he claimed to be a member of a Rajput lineage, a 'warrior' or Kshatriya by *varna*, and distinguished from both the Brahmans and from the mass of Shudra peasants or Kunbis (from among whom in fact he came). To prove his status, in this case, he required genealogical support and recognition from a Brahman; he also required appropriate behaviour among his ancestors and relations, behaviour that included military profession and attitudes, the observance of certain rituals (daily, and for marriage and death), the wearing of the sacred thread of the 'twice-born' higher castes, restrictions on dining, the seclusion of women, and so on. In the early nineteenth century the same process of 'Kshatriya-ization' was repeated, amidst great controversy, on behalf of Pratabsingh Bhonsle, installed as Raja of Satara by the East India Company.

For most of the eighteenth century, however, dominance in western India had rested more with the Brahmans, ranging from the Peshwas to a host of petty bureaucratic and village officials. The Company was also anxious to appease such dominant Brahman groups, and later came to use them extensively in its own administration. The Brahmans took to Western education as well as attending to their own religion, and became important leaders of Indian politics. They were divided into separate sub-groups, such as Chitpavans or Chitrapur Saraswats, probably clusters of different lineages brought together by pragmatic alliances during the eighteenth century.

Under later colonial rule, therefore, a Western-educated professional class or intelligentsia arose in western India that was also very largely drawn (apart from the special case of the Parsis) from high-caste Hindus. These people organized themselves in many societies and professional and political bodies (such as the Pune Sarvajanik Sabha, founded in 1870). A similar equation or confusion of caste and class developed also among lower-caste people, often directly or indirectly related to education that had been provided by Christian missionaries or government vernacular schools. Social allegiances, economic status and patterns of social behaviour were thus conditioned by the expectations of ritual and belief.

Four points may be noticed. Firstly, Kshatriya status was not directly necessary to Shivaji's or Pratabsingh's success: some rulers did not bother to assert it – for example (among 'Marathas') Shinde and Gayakavad who were of peasant castes, or Holkar who was of Shepherd or Dhangar caste. Secondly, the powerful could persuade others to endorse their claims to status: there was a degree of ambiguity and fluidity, not so much about the nature of the *varna* or the rules of conduct (though they too were negotiable up to a point) as in regard to the ranking of each *jati*. Thirdly, Kshatriya status was none the less important in the seventeenth as in the nineteenth century (particularly for a claim to be a king, or *chatrapati*). It served to distinguish an elite from both the bulk of the low-caste population and from Brahmans. In the case of Pratabsingh it served additionally to provide his family with a political and social role in opposition to the Brahmans, many of whom opposed this 'loosening' of categories lest it encourage wider social mobility. There was a growing tendency to see castes in a 'modern' way, in opposition to each other rather than as contributing to an interdependent whole.

Finally, caste-status claims, such as to Kshatriya *varna* for 'Marathas', depended upon particular behaviour and ideology that were held to be primordial. This was probably especially the case in the nineteenth century. In practice claimants collected information, created new rituals, and devised suitable history. Following the line of James Grant Duff, Resident in Satara (1818–22), Kshatriya claimants attributed Maratha decline to the rise of corrupt and unmilitary Brahmans. This was a status controversy using 'modern' weapons, including print, but to support claims that were thought to be old, and that were not at all directed towards Western notions of social category such as nationalism or class.

LOW-CASTE MOVEMENTS

Jotirao Phule later identified Maratha Shudras as the non-Brahman, majority community. He employed anti-caste rhetoric, but still used caste or *varna* labels. Elsewhere too lower-caste groups sought upward *caste* mobility to reflect changes in their economic status, the more prosperous commonly separating themselves off and changing their names. Even the most down-trodden seldom successfully escaped the logic of caste, despite the long availability of anti-caste rhetoric and vehicles for protest within 'Hinduism', through renunciation or devotion, and of alternatives in the form of local, heterodox or caste-specific rituals and deities.

From the 1820s, for example, Chamars ('Untouchable' leatherworkers) of Chhatisgarh in Madhya Pradesh flocked to join the Satnami (true-name, one god) movement of Ghasi Das (which has no connection with the movements of the same name that began in seventeenth- and eighteenth-century north India). Ghasi Das and his followers naturally opposed caste, but they also sought to respect cows and avoid meat-eating, in line with Brahman strictures. Later, after several schisms, they were identified as a single-caste Hindu or 'Untouchable' sect with its own priests and rituals.

Later, Chamars and other low castes in north India took a somewhat different route in contesting Untouchability, but arguably ended up at much the same point. Towns had grown and attracted low-caste labour while perpetuating the separation and subordination that existed in the villages. As often in the past, some sought the devotional route of *bhakti* to escape this discrimination, declaring themselves *bhagats* (devotees) and followers of Kabir, Shivnarayan or Ravidas. They also set up caste *panchayats* (councils) and made their own contributions to a spate of temple-building, celebrating *bhakti* gurus. Educated 'Untouchables', such as Swami Acchutanand (1879–1933) or Ram Charan (1888–1938), also began to add a second, related strategy which drew on the new histories and ethnographies of India. They declared that they were not outcaste Hindus at all, but Adi-Hindus (original Hindus), descendants of an indigenous race of people enslaved by the Aryans. This was an idea found also in the south (the Adi-Dravidas) and in the Punjab (the Ad-Dharm or original religion movement). The latter was founded by Mangu Ram in 1925, proclaiming that the *achhut* (Untouchables, *dalits*) were a separate religious community. It was active into the 1940s, and reappeared in the 1960s and 1970s. Several low-caste *mahasabhas* (associations) also were set up from the early 1920s.

In the 1920s and 1930s, Adi-Hinduism provided a doctrine of communal separateness, just as Hindu activists were increasing their campaigns for a common Hinduism on high-caste principles (notably in the Arya Samaj, which held some attraction for *dalits*, and in Sanatan Dharm, both of which will be discussed below). But the groups which followed either or both of these routes to self-esteem also sought to distance themselves from their traditional 'polluting' occupations, and to devise new rules of behaviour that conformed more closely to high-caste ideals. They appealed to ideas about equity and rights, but did not form a class movement with claims and solidarities based on their existing status and employment. They formed a movement for *caste* mobility; even their narratives of separate identity did not challenge the fundamentals of the caste system.

In another, successful transformation of caste, the Shanans of south India moved from 'unclean' toddy-tapping, and a controversy over the wearing of breast cloths (in the 1820s), through adoption of the sacred thread of the twice-born and disputes over admission to temples (1870s to 1890s), to the advocacy of the new 'Kshatriya' caste name of Nadar and of new political ambitions. Kamaraj Nadar became both Madras Chief Minister and President of the Indian National Congress. In the same region, starting at a later date, Palli agricultural labourers became Vanniyar, and organized in the Vanniya Kula Kshatriya Sangam and then as Tamilnad Toilers (1952). In 1957 they helped deliver election victory to the Congress of that other Kshatriya, Kamaraj Nadar. Acceptance of myths of hierarchy, though not of one's place in them, characterized very many protest movements among lower castes, if only as a means of escape.

In Malabar, similarly, dominant Nayar *tharavadu* (matrilineal households) dominated the countryside, managing cultivation and reclamation, drawing forest and low-caste people into dependence. The more important families also controlled temples, including the production on temple lands, but above all religious observances and festivals. These reinforced even while sometimes symbolically violating caste distinctions. Some shrines and rituals, however, were managed exclusively by lower castes, though under overall Nayar control. Often they expressed a sense of injustice, as in the performance of ritual dances called *teyyattam*. In the twentieth century such arenas of protest expanded, as some low castes benefited from education, government service, migrant work, or commercial agriculture. Tiyyas (toddy-tappers) in particular prospered, following a pattern set by the Ezhavas (also toddy-tappers) in neighbouring Travancore state. But the Ezhava caste association, the SNDP (Sri Narayana Dharma Paripalana) Yogam of Sri Narayana Guru, formed in 1903, claimed equality with the Nayars by adopting their standards of behaviour; so too the Tiyyas adopted 'purer' conduct, and set up their own temples to local deities in their more Sanskritic (Shivaite or Vaishnavite) guise. Some of them did begin to represent themselves as separate and non-Hindu, but, during the 1930s, involvement in the Gandhian Congress or with militant Hindu nationalism drew them back into a redefined Hindu community. It was one which still professed higher 'Brahmanical' standards, and therefore, inevitably, caste inequalities.

Another parallel – not least, interestingly, in the return to the Hindu mainstream during the 1930s – is suggested by the case of the Chandalas or low castes of Bengal, who turned themselves into the more respectable Namasudras. Christian missionaries had targeted depressed classes, in Bengal as elsewhere, contributing to their sense of distinct identity while providing means of mobilization, through education. The Brahmo Samaj's Depressed Classes Mission too was running some sixty schools in north and east Bengal by 1916. The upwardly mobile Namasudras who formed the Bengal Namasudra Association identified themselves as a community requiring separate representation during the Montagu-Chelmsford discussions of 1918. An alternative had already been available to them in the form of deviant Vaishnava sects. Bengali followers of Chaitanya, organized in the Gaudiya Vaishnava Sampraday and other movements, had always included lower classes, but in the mainstream they remained subject to the authority of Brahman gurus. Among others, Harichand Thakur (1811–78) of Faridpur had formed a body of anti-caste devotees, the Matua sect (from *moto*, drunk), celebrating through devotional songs, and following personal gurus. This movement too, however, advocated conformity with certain reformist and indeed Westernized ideals – regular marriage, abstemious living, hard work – and also with the idea of caste itself, dissociating the Namasudras from Untouchability rather than contesting its very existence. The Matuas rather rejoined than abandoned Hinduism. Harichand's followers deified him as an incarnation of Hari (Krishna) and his son, Guruchand, as an incarnation of both Shiva and Krishna. The dichotomous communities thus wore a recognizably traditional face.

ISLAM

Islam's solidarity was derived from learning as an act of worship – that is, from sources of religious authority in the Qur'an and *hadith* (sayings of Prophet), interpreted and transmitted by the *ulama* (as a universal learned elite), by means of *fatwa* (judgments) or in accordance with *ijma* (the sense of the community), to produce *shari'a* (guidance or law). As already remarked, most South Asian Muslims followed the Hanafi school of jurisprudence which allowed 'personal reasoning' (*ijtihad*). They were also influenced by Iranian *adab* literature (codes of moral and social conduct), and by a range of technical and scientific works. The tradition was embodied in shrines and buildings, as well as through the madrasas, where access to texts was largely through oral instruction and rote learning. It was perpetuated through public prayer, preaching and pilgrimage, and a calendar of festivals, sacrifices and processions that became increasingly generalized and militant.

As Sufi mysticism (the direct knowledge of God through devotion) was strong in India, and not confined to practising Muslims, there were also several proselytizing orders or sects that were celebrated for healing, spiritual teaching, or divine mediation. Sufism's warrior saints (*pirs*) and its concept of brotherhood also promoted community (*umma*), both local and universal; its shrines and tombs (*dargahs*) defined a sacred landscape; its devotional songs and poetry expressed cultural cohesion. Of course there remained a great variety among Indian Muslims, many of whom were unschooled in orthodoxy, and eclectic in practice. 'Muslim' might serve merely as a local marker of identity, as a *jati*-label, defining status and marriage patterns. But even this provided a basis on which reformers and unifiers could work.

The story of Indian Muslims in the modern era cannot be told in isolation. They shared in the experience of challenges and reverses for Islam, as also in Western Europe, Russia and China. Everywhere the reactions included reform, renewed orthodoxy, puritan movements, holy wars, Islamic revolts, and new Muslim states. Examples include the Wahhabi movement in Arabia (from 1740), Egyptian resistance to the French (1798), anti-Russian wars in the Caucasus, rebellions against Manchu rule in north and central China, and nineteenth-century African states such as that of Hajji Umar Tali in upper Senegal (1852–93), around Kano in northern Nigeria from 1804 (Sokoto), and of the Mahdi in Sudan (1881–98). We have already noticed similar political resistance among Indian Muslims to the advance of Hindu, Sikh and British rule. They also enjoyed the eighteenth-century intellectual revival that combined Hanafi and Sufi influences, emphasizing comprehension (not just rote-learning), and individual conscience and moral responsibility.

In the nineteenth century, a more 'Protestant' Islam developed in Deoband from 1867 foreshadowing similar developments of seminaries elsewhere, for example in Cairo and Indonesia as well as all over India. Deoband, founded by Muhammad Qasim Nanautawi (1833–77) and Rashid Ahmad Gangohi (1829–1905), took its curriculum from the earlier seminary of the Firangi Mahall in Lucknow, but also adopted the *practice* of modern Western education as its model. Students did not learn as an adjunct to their other religious observances, in a madrasa that was an antechamber to the mosque. They attended a formal residential college, with permanent staff and examinations. Funding was by public donation rather than endowment. Students were taught to know the *shari'a* and to follow the *tariqah* or path of religious experience, under the guidance of the *ulama*. Deoband was notable for the number and range of the *fatwa* it issued. It played an important part in the development of a unified and orthodox Islam in India.

Throughout the Islamic world, modernizers also emerged, such as Sayyid Ahmad Khan (1817–98) at Aligarh, but also Jamal-al-din al-Afghani (1839–97), Shaikh Muhammad Abduh (1849–1905) in Egypt, or, in Turkey, Namik Kemal (1840–88) and Mustafa Kemal (Ataturk) (1881–1938). Sayyid Ahmad Khan's contribution was an attempt to reconcile Indian Muslims to British rule and to Western knowledge, arguing that there could be no contradiction between the prior, ultimate knowledge that was the Qur'an, and the natural laws revealed by empirical science. The religious sense (*ijtihad*) could accommodate modern life. The college at Aligarh was designed to produce Muslims who could operate and serve their community in the new colonial world. It too was residential and supported by donations (and later by government grants). It promoted 'Islamic values' but followed a Western curriculum under an English headmaster, preparing students for the examinations of Allahabad University, until it gained university status in its own right. Rather than promoting deep scholarship or even examination success, however, it was most significant as a vehicle for political training, through its debating societies and student elections, in a general atmosphere of Islamic awareness. It was too controversial among the orthodox to promote Muslim unity, but it helped develop leaders of a Muslim political community.

Muslims were being defined and unified, then, on one hand by the spread of orthodoxy and avoidance of syncretic practices, and on the other hand by Islamic modernizations. Further efforts, in India as elsewhere, rested on the spreading of respect for the Caliph, and new steps to involve and inspire the laity. Especially in the north, the rise of Urdu as a 'language of true religion' was an important element. Muslims were led into confrontations with other religions or communities. A good example were the proselytizing Ahmadiyyas, founded by Mirza Ghulam Ahmad (1935–08). Popular in the Punjab, they were known for polemical clashes, both with other Muslims and with Hindus, Sikhs and Christians. In 1914 a segment of the Ahmadis broke away; the majority followed Ghulam's son, Mahmud Ahmad, and established themselves as a separate Muslim sect. It was noted for missionary work in many countries, based upon translations of the Qur'an and a rule for pure Islamic life (*tahrik-i-jadid* or new scheme, devised by Mahmud Ahmad in 1934).

Other important and long-lasting South Asian movements included the Tablighi Jama'at – lay preachers or inviters (*tabligh*) fanning out to spread the message of Islam – that was founded at Mewat in 1934 by Maulana Muhammad Ilyas (1886–1944), a Chishti. Another was the Jama'at-i-Islami, formed by Maulana Sayyid Abul A'la Maududi (1903–79), to promote Islamic universalism and an Islamic state and also an educated laity.

HINDU AND SIKH RELIGIOUS MOVEMENTS

After the first split in the Brahmo Samaj in the 1860s, Debendranath Tagore devoted his time to the Adi Samaj, concerned with ritual and with defending Hindu theology. A Brahmo convert, Bijoy Krishna Goswami (1841–97), later took *sanyas* (renunciation) and reverted to Vaishnavism, as a follower of Chaitanya. After the second split of the 1870s, the reformulated Sadharan Brahmo Samaj (1878) continued with social reform and Western-influenced adaptations of Hinduism. Keshub Chandra Sen moved towards populist devotionalism (*bhakti*) and a synthesis of rituals and symbols in a search for universal religion. These were the likely choices of religious reformers in the later nineteenth century.

In Bengal, Gadadhar Chattopadhyay (1836–86), known as Ramakrishna Paramahamsa, was a potent influence on Keshub Chandra and on many other followers, who sought him out as one who had thought deeply about different religions, and concluded that they all led to God – a way of defending Hindu orthodoxies. Most important of the followers was Narendranath Datta or Swami Vivekananda (1863–1902), celebrated particularly for his success in the West, his espousals of Indian spirituality, his criticism of 'degenerate' customs and beliefs, and his goal (following Ramakrishna) of selflessness and social service.

In the Punjab, similarly, a former Brahmo, Shiv Narayan Agnihotri (1850–1929) formed the Dev Samaj in 1887, proposing radical social reforms and new patterns of worship. More important was the Arya Samaj (Noble Society) begun in Bombay in 1875 and in Lahore in 1877 by Dayanand Saraswati (1824–83), who called for a kind of protestant Vedic Hinduism. He attacked idolatry, Brahmanism and pilgrimage, and advocated social reform, including widow remarriage. After his death, the Lahore Samaj and other societies he had formed across northern India came together to found a school in his memory, the Dayanand Anglo-Vedic College in Lahore (1886). This and other bodies helped unite the various societies, though educational issues also helped promote a split (in 1893) between more moderate and more radical members.

The first College Principal, Lala Hans Raj, backed by other moderates, favoured a mixture of English and traditional education acceptable to the Punjab University, to which the College had affiliated in 1889. After the split, the moderates greatly expanded the Arya schools and charities. The radicals, led by Guru Datta Vidyarthi, Lekh Ram and Munshi Ram (or Swami Shraddhanand), wanted to focus on Sanskrit and Vedic learning; they also insisted that vegetarianism was obligatory for Aryas. After the split, they established a girls' school and then a women's college (Kanya Mahavidyalaya, 1896), and later a Vedic men's college, the Gurukula Kangri at Hardwar (1902). But they concentrated on cow protection, *ved prachar* (preaching and proselytizing), and *shuddhi* (conversion or baptism).

Shuddhi was initially intended as a ritual to 'readmit' individual Hindu converts to Islam or Christianity, but later was used to 'purify' large groups of 'Untouchables' and Muslims (on the argument that their ancestors had been 'Hindu'). The radicals became more and more antagonistic towards Muslims, especially under the influence of Lekh Ram, who was assassinated in 1897. Caste prejudices also remained, despite condemnations from leading Samajists, and despite increasingly active *shuddhi* campaigns. As already noted, some *achhut* (Untouchable) followers dissociated themselves from the Samaj.

The Arya Samaj was a movement chiefly among urban commercial castes (Aroras, Khatris and others), often educated and prosperous. They were creating an organized, regulated and proselytizing Hinduism that was (like the Brahmo Samaj) akin to the churches and communities of a revealed religion – that is, a disciplined body of the faithful and the book. There were more conservative reactions too, of similar kind, that were set up in defence of *sanatan dharm* (orthodoxy) – most importantly the Bharat Dharma Mahamandala founded in 1887 by Din Dayalu Sharma, with a programme of *varnasharmadharma* (religious duties) and cow protection. The society was well funded and well organized, with branches extending throughout India by the 1930s. Its work was advanced through regular conferences, paid preachers, public campaigns and schools. It looked after temples and pilgrimage sites, published largely, and set up widows' homes.

Among Sikhs too parallel developments took place; the period was one in which divisions between Sikhs and Hindus also became more formal. Baba Dayal Das (1783–1855) called for a return to Guru

Nanak's ideals (the origins of Sikhism), the pursuit of morality in ordinary life rather than by renunciation, the abandonment of idols and priests, and worship of a formless (*nirankar*) God. In the 1850s and 1860s the Nirankaris were formed into congregations, especially amongst the urban castes of the Punjab. Another puritan Sikh movement, the Namdharis, was founded in 1857 by Baba Ram Singh (1816–85). It too rejected Brahman authority, and challenged the hereditary custodians of Sikh *gurdwaras* (temples). It set up schools, employed preachers, and attracted agricultural castes and 'Untouchables'. Violent clashes over cow protection in 1871 and 1872 led the government to seize, execute or intern a number of Namdharis; Ram Singh was exiled to Burma.

Partly in reaction, Singh Sabhas began to be formed (from 1873), also to promote and protect a pure Sikhism. In Amritsar the Sabha was a organization of community leaders; in Lahore it became a vehicle for the inclusion of all social classes in opposition to the established *gurdwaras*. Together, in a variety of ways, the Sabhas sought to institutionalize, redefine and delineate Sikhism. Some regarded Sikhs as a Hindu sect; others as an entirely separate community. The latter view was strengthened by direct competition with Hindu reform movements. From the 1920s, when more radical Sikhs seized control of the *gurdwaras*, spearheaded by activists of the Akali Dal (army of the immortals), the talk was of Sikh separatism. Akalis participated in the non-cooperation movement of 1920–2. They gained control of the shrines following the Gurdwara and Shrines Act of 1925. They argued without avail for a separate Sikh state during the partition negotiations of the 1940s. Sikh separatists subsequently challenged successive Indian governments.

Not all religious change in colonial India was sparked off by alien rule and modernization. India had a continuous tradition of religious protest, reform and revival, on which all movements drew. Some important developments also clearly had pre-colonial origins. For example, the Swami Narayan movement, devoted to Krishna, had been established among followers of Ramananda Swami (1739–1802) and then spread in Gujarat from around 1800, by a Brahman from north India, Ghanashyam Pande, known as Nilakantha Brahmachari and then as Swami Shahajanand, later deified by his followers. This was a vegetarian puritan movement, especially but not exclusively attractive to the higher castes. Its adherents were divided into a laity and hierarchical orders of mendicants (of any caste), under the authority of a Brahman *acharya* (leader). The community became wealthy and began building temples. In more recent times, it has followed Gujarati migrants and spread abroad. Though its origins were pre-colonial, and its forms of organization autonomous, it did not (and does not) avoid modern appurtenances.

Whether as a process of imitation or in pursuance of indigenous trends, the binary categorizations favoured in the West were thus increasingly replicated within Indian society, in the form of castes, sects and religions. A form of 'Hinduism' as a whole found its socio-political voice in the Hindu Mahasabha founded by M. M. Malaviya in 1915. The 1920s saw a determined campaign against the secular politics of Motilal Nehru and the Swaraj Party; from about 1924, it saw a compact between the Arya Samaj and Sanatan Dharm in an expanded campaign for *shuddhi* and *sangathan* (organization) led by Swami Sraddhanand, among others, in order to assert Hindu and caste solidarity. In western India one legacy of Tilak's brand of Hindu populism was the formation in 1925 of the Rashtriya Swayamsevak Sangh (RSS) of K. B. Hedgewar and B. S. Munje. Under M. S. Gol-walkar after 1940 it developed paramilitary pretensions, as an armed Hindu orthodoxy, matching the Islamic militancy of Inayatullah Khan Mashriqi's Khaksars (1931).

In the processes of separation and unification, the very languages diverged. Print spread orthodoxies, and invited debates about literary style and vocabulary. Bengali became either Sanskritized or 'pure' during the nineteenth century. Bengali Muslims wondered if they should adopt Urdu, or if a 'Musalmani Bangla' could be developed. Sikhs later insisted upon Punjabi in Gurmukhi script. Across north India, Hindi and Urdu drew apart. The Nagari Pracharini Sabha, formed in the 1880s, equated a script (*devanagari*) with a language (Hindi). Literary men debated the proper regional standards: two main Hindi forms were available, *khari bholi* and *braj bhasha*. Bharatendu Harishchandra (1850–85) pioneered the use of *khari bholi* in prose; Mahavir Prasad Dwivedi (1864–1938) and the journal *Saraswati* (1902) sponsored it also for poetry. These too were movements of categorization and communalism.

WOMEN

Gender provided another vitally important area for debate and influence in modern India. As may have been apparent in earlier discussions, masculinity was contentious in very many ways. There were concerns about physical strength, sexual potency, patriarchal authority, the bearing of arms, and so on. For reasons of space, however, we will focus here on questions relating to women. They represent one of the most interesting developments of the modern era, the growth of theories of the separation of state and society – of domesticity and personal life, say, from law and government – at the same time as an increasing possibility that each sphere *would* impinge upon the other.

Women have always been labelled and defined, but increasingly the colonial literature presented Indian women as a single oppressed or vulnerable class. Nineteenth-century missionaries regarded them as victims of marriage, prostitution or seclusion; Katherine Mayo's *Mother India* (1927) redelivered the attack to a wider, twentieth-century audience. By such accounts, an Indian woman, if not murdered at birth to protect her family's caste status, was fated to be bought as a child-bride for her dowry, to serve as a servant to her mother-in-law, to rear sickly children as a child-mother, and to remain in ignorance, meaning in *purdah* (seclusion). As the slave of her husband, on his death she would either perform *sati*, the ultimate sacrifice of wifely duty and devotion, or survive as a widow, abandoned and despised. Unmarried Indian women could only be *devadasis* (temple-women), nautch-dancers and concubines – that is, corrupt and corrupting. Distorted reports of tantric sexual rituals, and of love poetry, including Persian *ghazals*, all contributed to a stereotype of the sybaritic Orient, in which once again all women were the victims of men.

In response, many Indian men harked back to a more 'civilized' age before the improper accretions of lust and oppression. Indian social reformers were impressed by Europeans who claimed the treatment of women was a marker of civilization, and they sought improvements for Indian women very much according to the agenda set out by the foreign critics, albeit by restating what was 'indigenous'. Offending mediaeval verses were suppressed; propriety of language and literary subject was sought. All major social movements of the nineteenth century advocated changes in the treatment of women – for example, the Brahmo Samaj of Debendranath Tagore and Keshub Chandra Sen, and the National Social Conference of Mahadev Govind Ranade. Several notable figures placed these questions at the centre of their concerns. In Bengal, Iswar Chandra Vidyasagar campaigned for widow remarriage, submitting a petition in 1855 that led to the Widow Re-marriage Act of 1856. He campaigned too for state intervention against the polygamy practised by Kulin Brahmans, though without success. He supported female education, notably in Bethune's school between 1849 and 1869. In Pune, similarly, D. K. Karve sought to solve two problems in one by setting up a school to train widows as teachers.

The fragility of these efforts, however, was often apparent, as illustrated by the controversy that erupted over the Brahmo Marriage Act of 1872. It provided for civil and inter-caste marriages for the adherents of Keshub Chandra Sen's Brahmo Samaj. One problem was that it defined Brahmos as non-Hindu (implying thereby that the restrictions on women were necessary to Hindusim). Another was that radical Brahmos soon sought further ways to raise the status of women, while Sen himself resisted change, and later abandoned the provisions of the Act in marrying his young daughter to the Maharaja of Kuch Bihar, precipitating another split in the Samaj.

The colonial state increasingly defined women within the legal system, in terms of property, family and labour law. The British made rules of administration which reflected a very early apprehension, reinforced by their own nineteenth-century assumptions, that Indian men were peculiarly sensitive about intrusions upon women; but they also interfered whenever they found an ethical case overwhelming and some Indian support forthcoming. In the latter category were the abolition of *sati* (1829), the Re-marriage Act of 1856 (which also restricted the joint-family inheritance-rights of widows), and an Act of 1891 further raising the age of female sexual consent, from 10 (in the Indian Penal Code) to 12 years. Lord Lansdowne, the Governor-General, enunciated the (somewhat incoherent) underlying principles in a speech on that last enactment, to the Imperial Legislative Council in April 1891. State interference, he claimed, could be justified in the interests of 'public morality or of public welfare'. Where a conflict might be supposed to exist between those interests and prevailing custom or religion, a distinction needed to be made between 'great fundamental beliefs' that were 'absolutely obligatory', and minor, 'accretionary dogmas that have accidentally grown around them'. In regard to the age of consent, many Hindus professed a basic objection to colonial interference in private practices, and to foreign arbitration upon religious questions, as well as to the potential for petty tyrannies in the operation of the new law. Some also expressed a more particular concern about the moral and social consequences should a girl not be married before puberty and her marriage not be consummated immediately after her first menstruation. But in that case the religious law was merely permissive, Lansdowne claimed, and the sanctions for transgression of the most insignificant kind.

With greater participation by Indian legislators these principles were gradually extended, for example with the Child Marriage Restraint Act of 1928 which forbade marriages for males under 18 years of age and for females under 14 (or the abetting or permitting of such marriages), with sterner penalties should the husband be over 21. Further bills between 1937 and 1939 sought to reform the Hindu and Muslim codes in regard to divorce and women's property, matters taken up also by the Rau committee in the 1940s, and in revisions of the Hindu Code in the 1950s.

None of these measures was thoroughly enforced, nor wholly enforceable; but together they amounted to a recognition of a body of rights for women, as a category. Thus law overrode distinctions between women of custom, caste, class, and in some respects religion. (Not in all respects, because, for example, weaker rights were accorded to Muslim divorcées under legislation in 1986.) For some women, this influence opened a space for greater independence, already being encouraged by other developments. As employment changed, for example, with new professions, factory work, even paid field-labour, and new kinds of mobility, urbanization and housing, many households were affected, and sometimes nuclear families replaced joint ones as the everyday norm. Companionable marriages began to be written about as an ideal.

In India as in Europe most women and men had performed separate but interdependent roles within patriarchal households. Ploughing tended to be men's work; transplanting, weeding and other field labour were shared between men and women; women engaged in work within the house and garden. There was nothing necessarily egalitarian about these households from the women's points of view, though of course as in all regimes women could be influential within their own spheres and from their personal power over or through their sons and husbands. In Europe a re-evaluation of the household tasks occurred with the expansion of market production and technological innovation, raising the relative importance of the male roles and preparing the way for the post-Enlightenment legally backed differentiations between men and women in terms of rights and supposed abilities. In India the same process was imported through law and Western government, to reinforce existing distinctions that were also encouraged by high-class aspirations, especially for the seclusion of women, made possible by higher incomes. Greater public opportunities for women, through liberal ideas, law or education, were then resisted in the name of orthodoxy. The males 'protected' the females who were paradoxically both weak and dangerous.

Women lost some roles in agriculture and processing, in India as in Europe, as a result of commercialization, mechanization and specialization (rice-husking, spinning, and so on). The rising prosperity and social ambitions of some classes probably did increase the numbers living in *purdah*. But, on the other hand, modern female education began to develop. Not only did more girls become literate, but also a new range of female occupations opened up. Many women made careers as educationalists from the later nineteenth century. Other professions also developed to provide services for women by women – sometimes in spheres which in their older Indian forms had been the preserve of men. In Western medicine, for example, there were not only attempts to recruit and train nurses and midwives, but also the Lady Dufferin Fund, providing medical-training scholarships from 1885, and the first Indian women doctors, who graduated in the 1880s.

Women's lives could now be celebrated: perhaps, despite a long tradition of male hagiography, the admiration for female heroines (such as the Rani of Jhansi, for her resistance in 1857–8) came easily to a society familiar with the exploits of powerful goddesses, and now governed by an almost iconic Empress. Women's voices began to be heard through the new print media. One of the first private biographies by a woman was that of Rassundari Devi (1876). It described her struggle to learn to read; she had to overcome barriers that were seldom raised against higher-class girls in later years. The tragic case of Vijayalakshmi, a widow of Surat convicted of killing her illegitimate child, inspired Tarabai Shinde's Marathi *Comparison between Men and Women* (1881), with its sharp questions on the equality of treatment for men and women.

In the twentieth century, many organizations were formed by and for women. In 1917 the Madras Women's Indian Association (WIA) was set up among Theosophists and in order to join the deputations that were meeting the Secretary of State and Viceroy (Montagu and Chelmsford) on their tour of consultation about constitutional reforms. From the WIA there developed the long-running All-India Women's Conference (1927); its campaigning journal *Roshni* was started in 1947. In Bombay, in 1925, Mehribai Tata, the wife of the industrialist, set up the National Council of Indian Women, one of several instances in which wealthy women followed the example of men and sponsored public bodies to represent particular interests and to undertake good works. All these bodies engaged in campaigns for 'women's rights'. Especially from the 1930s, women also began to take an active part in politics, not just as the wives and sisters of male politicians (many of them imprisoned) but also in separate organizations, for example as members of the Desh Sevika Sangha that developed out of the Rashtriya Stree Sangha led by the poet and associate of Gandhi, Sarojini Naidu; or of the more militant Mahila Rashtriya Sangha founded in Bengal in 1928 by Latika Ghosh, with the encouragement of the nationalist leader, Subhas Chandra Bose.

Images of women gained even greater prominence with the advent of printed pamphlets and journalism: among Hindus, rules were inspired (as already noticed) by the key symbols of Mother and Perfect Wife. High-caste norms were expounded as a means of promoting communal identity and unity. Concern about child marriage and over child-rearing reflected eugenic theories that were linked to a cult of male physical strength and designed to refute the colonial racial stereotypes about weak and emasculated Indians. By the 1920s, amidst moral and demographic panic, widow remarriage was being justified as a means of reducing so-called abductions by Muslim men, and an allegedly burgeoning Muslim birth-rate; though celibacy and family or public service were still considered more 'meritorious' for widows. Much of this intense activity – even when it stressed the power of women – can be interpreted as a means of enhancing male authority. The economic, social and political changes prompted some men to ever sterner denunciations of female depravity and more elaborate exhortations as to proper conduct.

Gandhi, like Vivekananda, regarded women as a regenerative force. He repeatedly addressed women in his political and social homilies; he permitted and even encouraged their active participation in politics and public life, especially after 1930. On the other hand, the roles he expected for them (not least his own relations and admirers) were as mothers and supporters of men, and as exemplars of self-sacrifice and non-violence, as spinners of *khadi* (handspun cloth) who should sell their own jewellery (an important store of wealth) to show devotion to the nationalist cause, which was an issue for men. Gandhi considered women most worthy in their 'traditional' place; it was because they were weak and dependent that (in his typical love of paradox) they were strong. His praise was not so much for real women; on the contrary it was aimed at men.

Women in modern India have flourished in universities and middle-class occupations, in politics and the arts. Lower-class women continue to labour in fields, building sites and factories. Most women still suffer from many disadvantages: neglect as children, pressure from dowry demands and in-laws, poor health-care (especially for childbirth), and rejection as widows. There are regional variations in female mortality, with Kerala having the best record. A chilling statistic has repeatedly been revealed in Indian censuses: there are many fewer females than would be expected from the usual sex ratios (which have been shown to apply to live births). In north India the deficit can be as high as 15 per cent.

THE BRITISH RAJ AND AFTER

Especially in new centres relatively untouched by the revolts of 1857, but also even in northern India, the patterns of politics and social ambition became strongly influenced by Western ideas during the later nineteenth century. A language of communities and rights predominated. At the same time, the translation of society into classes, and of classes into nations, was incomplete. One reason was the persistence of alternative norms, of religion and status, as also of economy. Just as Indian traders continued to conduct flourishing businesses outside the limits of European-dominated commerce, but often using its methods; so indigenous religious, intellectual and social allegiances continued vigorously to evolve, often partly employing English education and modern technologies, and yet outside their purview. As mentioned, it has even been suggested that the Western dominance of certain public and political arenas, through ideas, law, economics and material culture, encouraged Indians to focus on the private, social and religious as sites of continuing, indigenous legitimacy and tradition – among other things, conflicts over the proper roles of women thus marked dissent from colonial rule as well as between religious communities.

Certainly atavistic appeals were made to supposed Indian (or Hindu or Muslim) norms, and particular objections to the rather limited state interference in customs such as *sati*, child marriage or female seclusion; they have their equivalents in the present-day Hindu rejections of 'modern' or 'western' in favour of 'indigenous' forms, as if cultures comprise unchanging essences. Such arguments are partly a way of blaming others for the divisions and antagonisms between different groups in India, appealing to an earlier, supposedly more harmonious age, whether in regard to religion, society, economic relations or the physical environment. On the other hand, in practice, Western and modern influences penetrated into all spheres, and were both welcomed and resisted in all; and it seems unlikely that colonialism had more than a marginal impact on the importance attributed by Indians to households, kinship, ritual, ethics or spiritual beliefs. The British raj merely pretended at forbearance from social and religious questions, and it merely attempted to gain hegemony over politics and economics.

The result was a series of different but overlapping arenas for social and political activity. At one point on the spectrum were organized political movements, concerned ultimately with elections, laws and policies. At another point were a host of vigorous intellectual publications and associations, whereby literati debated language, images, identities and traditions. At yet another were campaigns and agitations, mobilizing their public not only with words but through actions – sacrificing or saving cows, defending or reforming custom, marching or celebrating, striking, rioting. From these three kinds of process, new communities of interest and new practices were forged.

They took particular forms. The standardization of religious belief and social identity, as in late mediaeval and early modern Europe, required the identification, potential conversion or demonizing of non-members (such as Jews in Europe or Hindus and Muslims in India). These others defined and disciplined the socio-religious community. Conflicts increased as sites for them expanded, with print and transport; growing government, bureaucracy and law; urbanization and mass politics. Later, slights, quarrels and atrocities – real or invented – were 'remembered' as caused by and explaining difference. Efforts were made to extend exclusivity across everyday life, a process assisted by reductions of necessary interdependence. For Muslims as well as Hindus, the end of Muslim rule reduced the need to coexist. Muslim elites no longer sought Hindu allies and agents among Indian subjects. Later they could dispense with Hindus amidst pan-Islamic sentiment, communal cohesion or colonial collaboration. So too Hindus, gaining education and and political and economic strength, had little need of Muslim patrons.

The British, moreover, denigrated Muslim 'fanatics' even as Hindu chauvinism was emerging. They eschewed all interest in projecting non-Christian religious or social norms. When they appealed to social or religious leaders, it was only to co-opt their influence over 'separate' communities. The British endorsed democratic representation, and so it seemed to Muslims and other minorities that they were being swamped in a sea of caste-Hindus. But the British espoused a politics of interests too, and so it seemed to many Hindus that Muslims as a community were merely artificial agents of conservatism and colonialism, brought into existence in order to be pampered by the state. A similar view is expressed by some Hindus today. Other groups seeking constitutional privileges from the British (including Indian princes, *dalits* and *adivasis*) were also subject to criticism. Particular, local and less communally structured allegiances became unpopular or expendable; they lost out to hegemonic but narrower, competing identities and interests.

Since independence, while both Indian nationalist and all-Hindu identities have grown, many grass-roots organizations have flourished, espousing causes from Sikh or *adivasi* separatism to environmental conservation. Middle-level identities have also strengthened, pitting regional states and local peoples or broader interest-groups against each other.

9

Modern India IV: Economy

DECLINE AND EUROPEAN DOMINANCE

The great economic event of the modern era for India was its involvement in new forms of production and long-distance trade, triggered by colonial rule, but continuing after independence. The growth of output and in trade was remarkable. This benefited many Indians but worsened the lives of many more (a difference on which this chapter will concentrate). Moreover, despite the strong upward trends in India's economy, they were dwarfed by those of the developed world, so that, in world trade and in domestic wealth, India suffered a massive decline in comparison with the most successful economies. There are some puzzles about this performance.

One is that the changes wrought by colonialism and worldwide capitalism were more limited than might be thought, partly because of the mixed methods whereby capitalist enterprise tapped Indian production. The huge expansion of agricultural exports depended not only on cultivators responding to market opportunities, but also on landlords and other intermediaries who used share-cropping, traditional labour-dues and caste prestige to capture and subjugate the cultivators. This benefited the capitalists but also marked a limit to their ability to enforce changes in landholding, peasant priorities and agricultural methods. Similarly, well into the twentieth century, even modern factories attracted, organized, managed and paid their labour through foremen-recruiters or 'jobbers', rather than through any kind of labour market.

These intermediaries, and advance payments for goods and services, may have been crucial to the nature of the economy in

India, by restricting the availability of capital and labour, and by reducing indigenous demand. In a different kind of economy, one in which materials and labour were generally paid for in arrears, the costs for credit were lower. They fell mainly upon producers and retailers, and hence were factored into prices for consumers. The suppliers of capital and some providers of services tended to gain. In much of India, however, as producers were heavily reliant upon intermediaries and advance payments, the costs and probably the risks of credit were higher. They fell initially upon the lenders; but, where the lender was also the wholesale buyer, as so often in India, he gained from his double role, and was often able to transfer the credit costs very largely to the producers, through high interest rates and low wholesale prices. The loss which the producer sustained could be transferred, if necessary, to consumers, sustaining markets and keeping prices low. In such ways too, rich countries have been able to secure supplies cheaply from poorer countries. One should see this situation as the product of interlocking circumstances – law, landholding, information, capital-distribution, social power, and so on – rather than as a ploy by agents free to devise an optimum system in their own interests. (Of course such niceties hardly matter to those at the bottom of the pile.)

As international trade grew, as markets became more competitive, and as production became more dependent on capital, none of these facts of itself changed the situation. One would expect competition to force down the ultimate consumers' price, and for different parts of the supply chain to be squeezed according to their relative socio-economic power. Monopolistic producers would raise prices, so far as any cartel held and political or consumer pressure could be resisted. On the other hand, monopolistic retailers would still tend to be able to reduce the returns to producers. In much of India, this logic applied, and very often it was the producer who bore the pressure. The more international trade there was, the more the local creditors, as the last link in an ever more important chain, impinged on 'ordinary' cultivators. The more price competition there was, the greater the incentive to use socio-economic power to protect the returns to the monopoly creditor-buyer. This aspect of the Indian economy reminds us, then, to consider the differential impact of capitalism or colonialism.

Another anomaly, almost the opposite of this skewed capitalism, was that market-orientation was not new to India, which, as we have seen, had had long experience of commerce and trade – cash crops, agricultural processing and specialized artisans. The state's taxation, its military and courtly expenditure, and the demands of religious, urban and rural elites had long ensured vigorous markets. Trade also flourished over long distances (to varying degrees), employing *hundis* (bills of exchange) and *arhat*s (commission agencies). Commercial production was supported in the rural communities by local chiefs (*maliks*), zamindars, headmen and surplus householders (*grihastha*), and by local moneylenders (*banias, shahukars*) and *mahajans* (bankers) in markets (*hats*) and principal bazaars. Though they were often most successful when organized as family, clan or caste-based firms, these commercial interests often had the skills and experience to benefit from the modern explosion in trade. This aspect, it will be shown, directs us to focus on the impact of British rule in seeking explanations for India's economic performance.

Hereditary business castes and communities were able to develop large-scale enterprises during the nineteenth and twentieth centuries, sometimes because they had financed long-distance trade from the seventeenth and eighteenth centuries or even earlier. Major examples are the Marwaris, originally from central India, who became import-ant in banking and in the export trades of Calcutta and elsewhere; the south Indian Nattukottai Chettiars who moved into Burma and Malaya from the later nineteenth century; the Gujarati Bhatias, Khojas and Memons who developed opportunities in East Africa; and the western Indian Parsis whose early fortunes in shipping and local trade led them into large-scale industrial and commercial ventures across India and the world. Such groups took advantage of the conditions of colonial rule and world trade, and expanded their influence, often driving out or subordinating more local interests. At the end of the twentieth century, most of the twenty largest Indian industrial houses derived from Marwari and Parsi commu-nities.

On the other hand many of the *companies* could be traced back directly only to the 1920s. Despite the apparent continuities, Indian participation in the higher levels of the economy had been quite limited during the preceding hundred years. The first point about the indigenous economy, in the high colonial period, is that it was subject to European dominance. In the eighteenth century, Indian merchants allied themselves with individual and official European traders, attracted by their economic and military power – expressed for example in the *dastak*, the privilege of toll-free internal trade (1717–73) – and by the lucrative possibilities of Company-sponsored trade with Europe and east Asia. In their turn the Europeans commonly relied on Indian capital and know-how. Some Indian merchants made huge fortunes through their involvement with European trade and enterprise. Some of them operated similarly to European firms and in competition or partnership with them. Most notably Carr, Tagore & Co. brought together new money from Bengal and Europe, and flourished in steam navigation, salt, tea and coal. It was caught up in the crash of the Union Bank in 1848 which followed a collapse in the indigo price and in foreign exchange dealings. The subsequent rise of companies such as Andrew Yule or Jardine Mathieson marked the pre-eminence of enterprises in exclusively European hands.

Even in the eighteenth century, however, European interests had remained fairly distinct from those of their Indian allies and clients. The private European merchant houses were organized as partnerships and agencies (combining people from many Western nations). They raised and advanced capital, helping ensure a flow of credit for European enterprises, and they organized production, processing and shipping. Many were also auctioneers, importers, insurers and general merchants, and were directly or indirectly involved in ship-building, in printing, in house construction and letting, and in indigo and other agricultural ventures. They were deeply implicated with the East India Company, as individuals and for services, contracts and patronage, and they benefited from its rise to power. Also they were fundamentally oriented towards European consumers in India or to the export trade (in cotton, indigo, opium, and so on). With their international agents or partners, they had a growing advantage over local enterprise as exports expanded.

From the eighteenth century such Europeans were setting up in competition with Indian merchants and manufacturers, to meet international and also local demand. Timber was exploited early on, and other building materials – bricks, iron and brass-ware, paints, bricks, and lime – were produced by Europeans as well as Indians. Both Indians and Europeans were spinning cotton, and making chintz and rope, exhausting supplies of raw materials, in Calcutta in the late eighteenth and early nineteenth centuries. The Europeans were often initially unable to compete on price, but frequently managed to overwhelm Indian producers and traders – by using state power (as with opium), or by developing new products and processes. The first tea plantation in Assam was developed, in 1839, after the East India Company had helped bring in plants and Chinese expertise. Coal production began in Bengal from 1820, undertaken by Alexander & Co. at Raniganj, with some Company encouragement (though the industry would long be hampered by the lower costs and higher quality of European imports). James Landon founded an industrial cotton mill in 1854 in Broach (at about the same time as a Parsi, Cowasjee Nanabhoy Davar, in Bombay). The first jute mill was set up near Calcutta by George Acland in 1855.

In the nineteenth century, India's economy was transformed, on the basis of imports of European manufactures, and exports of Indian, largely unprocessed agricultural produce. Nevertheless, there was also a second and secondary revolution, with the development of Indian factories, based on indigenous as well as European enterprise. As early as 1828/9, annual imports of cotton yarn into India were valued at over Rs4 million (nearly 8 per cent of the total) and of cotton piecegoods at just under Rs12 million (22 per cent). From 1867/8 to 1886/7 textile imports rose from 958 million yards to 2156 million yards; they reached a peak at 47 per cent of all imports in 1870/1, and of 2309 million yards in 1910/11. But, about the same time, Indian cotton mills expanded their capacity from just over a million spindles (47 mills, 9000 looms) in 1875/6 to over 6.75 million spindles (271 mills, 104 000 looms) in 1913/14. Indian exports ranged between 156 million yards in 1882/3 and 390 million yards in 1940/1. The factories are also thought to have supplied about 80 per cent of the yarn used in Indian handicraft production. It has been estimated that at the end of the nineteenth century net imports accounted for nearly 63 per cent of the cloth consumed in India, Indian mills for 12 per cent, and handicraft production for about 25 per cent. Between 1909/10 and 1913/14 the corresponding figures were 56 per cent, 23 per cent, and 20 per cent.

Indian capital played an important role in this industrial development. Financiers of western India – and some large landlords and princes – had large profits from other activities which they were able to invest in cotton manufacture. Local banks too were vital for such new enterprises, as also for shipping, minor railways and irrigation, indigo factories, and so on. The Indian role was none the less secondary, considered overall. Locals were much slower in becoming involved in Calcutta than in Bombay, though profit rates were potentially high. In the jute mills, for example, the dividend on the face value of shares was around 20 or 25 per cent in the boom years of 1904 to 1907 and 1911 to 1913. In some instances where Indians did invest, as in Bombay or Ahmedabad cotton mills, they had

had some advantages through their knowledge of local markets; by contrast, jute was mainly exported. Also Indians were actively discouraged from investing, in order to minimize local competition. Something similar happened in some other industries too, including tea, until at least the 1920s. Indian entrepreneurs were to be found in the production and distribution of almost all commodities, but often in smaller numbers or on a smaller scale than Europeans.

Gradually the terms of international trade, the conditions of production in India, and the regulations imposed by its European government had all turned against Indian entrepreneurs and merchants. As international commodity prices began to encourage (or disrupt) local production, so international intelligence was vital to investment decisions. Indian financial resources became sidelined, locked up in precious stones and metals to insure against risk, or deployed as credit for agricultural production and processing, as an auxiliary to European trade (often very profitable but limited and vulnerable). In the long term a greater return might have been obtained from investment in exports and large-scale manufacturing, but there were barriers to Indian participation, including a lack of access to modern credit arrangements. In the 1900s, J. N. Tata, after large expenditure, long surveys, lashings of expert advice, and government guarantees, sought to raise capital in London for a proposed steel-works at Jamshedpur, 150 miles from Calcutta. He found London financiers unwilling to lend to a speculation under Indian management, and succeeded in launching the company only because Indians in (then-flourishing) Bombay invested heavily and quickly. By contrast, the secure, profitable, expensive state-backed loans for major railways and canals were raised internationally.

We have already noted that nineteenth-century colonial policy was notorious for refusing protection to most India-based enterprise, though there was some competition with European commerce, and though officials often claimed to be espousing India's interests, in some cases favouring local producers for the government's own supplies. (This often meant supporting Indian businesses that were already European-owned.) On the whole, official policies probably discouraged Indian investment. Even in the eighteenth century the East India Company had closed local mints, and, especially after the formal institution of the silver rupee in 1835, it imposed a standard currency and tried to standardize measures – all on the claim of freeing-up trade – so that Indian bankers no longer had to operate as money-changers or discounters, and letters of credit were no

longer so frequently used to facilitate transactions in various currencies. Insurance too, originally allied with such exchanges, and with
the provision of transport, became a more specialized and less
expensive service, and increasingly European-dominated, as land
and seaways became safer. Later the British came to treat professional moneylenders as dangerous interlopers in the countryside,
and tried to restrict interest rates, mortgages and land transfer. By
contrast European-style banks, which had existed with mixed
fortunes since the eighteenth century, benefited from Company
and European as well as indigenous business. Presidency banks
came to dominate the financing of Indian export trade, and many
of them moved their headquarters to London after 1850. From the
1840s the Indian banks had been forbidden to deal in foreign
exchange. In India the banks favoured Europeans in their lending
policies.

Ultimately European business success in India, though it followed a commercial rationale, was achieved by monopoly, cartels
and somewhat loose state support, at the expense of Indian interests.
The key was the predominance of Europeans in the major export
trades, in large-scale factory production, in capital markets and in
long-distance transportation, especially for some commodities –
opium through the government monopoly, and exported indigo,
tea and coffee, for example. Other examples of cartels and quasi-
monopolies included the Conference shipping lines, especially
P&O; the state-backed railway companies which enforced standard
rates, timetables and packing; and the All-India Jute Manufacturers'
Association which, especially in the 1920s and 1930s, tried to
control output, keep down raw jute prices, and keep out Indian
factory-owners. European wholesalers and shippers were the
dominant purchasers of export crops and products, even when
they were wholly produced by Indians, financed by Indian capital,
and gathered for export by Indian middlemen. The Europeans
could benefit even where Indian business and capital remained
pre-eminent – in Bombay for example where European companies
became managers of Indian-owned cotton mills. The outcome was
simple enough, at one level. Between about 1880 and 1920, India's
surplus balances of trade with countries other than Britain made
up for Britain's deficits with the other industrialized nations. Meanwhile, in the European imagination, 'India' gradually changed
from being a metaphor for untold riches, and became a byword for
poverty.

VALUES, DE-INDUSTRIALIZATION, DUALISM, ECONOMIC DECLINE

Three common interpretations may be briefly noted, following on from the discussion of rival economies in Chapter 4. The first is the suggestion that Indians lacked a 'spirit of enterprise' – from alleged fatalism, the impact of caste and religion, and so on. Ethics, belief systems and social institutions certainly do influence economic efficiency, but it is plain both that Indians *had* developed sophisticated and 'maximizing' economic strategies, and that the institutional conditions which inhibited further development were mostly produced by colonialism and European industrialization. The question is not why India was 'backward' in the eighteenth century – it was not, on international comparisons – but why its share of world trade and the comparative wealth of its people declined so dramatically during the nineteenth and twentieth centuries.

A second suggestion is that India's relative decline may be attributed to 'de-industrialization' or at least to 'arrested development'. As implied in Chapter 4, this supposes that pre-conditions for an industrial revolution existed in India from the eighteenth century, ideas that seem outdated in the light of recent studies of British and comparative industrialization. Measurements of a fall in artisanal production during the nineteenth century have been made, but for one area of India only, and based on estimates of occupational distribution which probably do not bear the weight that has been placed upon them. (The original claim, by Amiya Bagchi, was a reduction in the 'industrial workforce' from 18.6 to 8.5 per cent of the population. Some deny significant changes in occupational distribution. Others have no difficulty in believing data errors could explain the variation. One reaction – odd, since comparing statistics is the issue – is that accuracy and comparability are not worth debating because no better figures are obtainable. Agreed is the large decline in professional weavers, and especially spinners, in some areas.) What matters in this debate is not the counterfactuals, the 'might-have-beens', but the actual outcome. As said, India experienced *industrialization* at this time, sometimes in competition with English manufacturers. During the first half of the twentieth century, factory production continued to increase rapidly, from a low base – one estimate puts the rate at 14.5 per cent per annum from 1900 to 1946. From the 1870s, if not before, there was a striking increase in the consumption of manufactured and industrially processed goods, even in rural areas, from home production as well as imports – examples are cotton cloth and, somewhat later, sugar. Towns also grew. Whether or not there was a matching decline in small-scale and artisanal processing and manufacture differs from case to case and area to area.

A third argument suggests that the 'modern' colonial economy was a mere enclave and therefore did not pull up India as a whole. Supporting this, many local 'bazaar' economies did continue to flourish – merchants such as the Chettiars with their south-east Asian connections, some hand-producers of cloth for 'niche' markets, specialist jewellers, sweet-makers, and so on – and existing modes (credit networks, agricultural methods, labour recruitment and management) continued to be the backbone of production, even for most export commodities and, for a long time, in factories as well as farms. Secondly, multiplier effects were lacking from certain developments, most notably the railways. Though forests were sacrificed for sleepers, and railway workshops became important sources of employment and training, yet the first few generations of engines and rolling stock were all imported, the lines mostly had an export (or otherwise a strategic) orientation, and rates for freight were cheapest for long-haul bulk commodities directed to the main ports (Calcutta and Bombay). Similarly some important European-dominated production, especially tea, had weak linkages into local economies, and some major exported commodities had only limited internal markets (including opium, indigo and jute, for different reasons).

Yet it is misleading to suggest that there were distinct economies in modern India that did not connect with each other, almost as if colonial rule and world trade were not the main economic influences. Obviously factories were important to the growth of cities, and connected with world markets. Many of those employed in the cotton factories (260 000 in 1913/14) long retained close ties with the countryside, and remittances from urban dwellers and migrants formed an important part of rural incomes in many areas. Landlords and rural wholesale buyers sold crops for export, and borrowed from regular banks as well as from local *banias* (moneylenders). Though evidence is hard to come by, it may be assumed that they would also reuse such loans when they lent to cultivators and share-croppers, because of the generally higher returns of agricultural lending. European planters' and government loans connected these credit systems even more plainly. The cultivators themselves often survived hand-to-mouth, at a basic level of subsistence, in perpetual debt, or even as debt-bonded labourers. But they paid rents and taxes, and, by spending part of their loans on agricultural production, produced surpluses which their creditors obtained at favourable rates, and then sold.

The de-industrialization thesis focused on textiles, and that is a good example also to test the idea that the modern sector was an economic enclave. Certain developments seem clear. Firstly, over the nineteenth century, textile imports rose very considerably: by 116 per cent over the period from 1860 to the end of the 1880s, for example. Secondly, total consumption of cloth probably rose in the six decades after 1860 to an extent roughly proportionate to the increase in imports – that is, by 116 per cent to the end of the 1880s, and by a further 9 per cent to the outbreak of the First World War. This reversed the sharp drop in the demand for Indian cloth which had occurred with the collapse of exports and the decline of agricultural incomes in the first three decades of the nineteenth century. Thirdly, by the end of the nineteenth century, India possessed a vigorously growing factory sector. As said earlier, the capacity of Indian cotton mills expanded sevenfold between 1875/6 and 1913/14.

Fourthly, village-level hand-producers of textiles were not destroyed. There are many examples of apparently viable handloom production in parts of India throughout colonial rule. Competition from factory-produced cloth began after about 1835, but the worst effects had been felt by hand-spinners rather than weavers; the latter were able to lower costs or compete with imports on the basis of imported yarn. Again after 1870, cheaper yarn enabled handicraft weavers to reduce costs; they provided coarser cloth for local consumption. We have already noted the estimate that hand-production still accounted for a quarter of the internal Indian market in cloth in the late nineteenth century. In the twentieth century political considerations probably improved the market for hand-produced cloth; small-scale production remained important. Finally, Indian producers failed to maintain their share of a generally increasing market, even within India. The modern industrial sector was relatively small. Handloom and small-scale production mostly experienced a much lower rate of growth, which depressed the overall performance in manufacturing (perhaps to a growth of 3.5 per cent per annum from 1900 to 1946).

These findings are open to varied interpretations. An increase in the imports of textiles per head might be interpreted as evidence of a marked increase in domestic consumption, and hence an improvement in material welfare. Equally it might be interpreted as evidence of a collapse of domestic textile production in the face of cheap manufactured imports; and that collapse might imply a *fall* in total textile consumption, if the contraction in domestic output was greater than the rise in imports, or when textile imports were replacing local exports, as in early nineteenth-century India. Even if total consumption rose, there could still be local producers who were displaced by foreign competition, and yet others who suffered as former artisans were driven into new occupations – as was the case between 1860 and 1920 when they helped increase the area of cultivated and irrigated land. Connections are always evident.

There was undoubtedly displacement in the early nineteenth century of those whose handloom production had been geared to export. But it is hard to sum up the overall effects on craft communities in general. Perhaps the major consequence of factory competition was the increasing specialization of employment. This affected agriculturists as well as specialist cloth-workers: many cultivators or members of their households had been able to spend time in the off-seasons spinning and weaving. They continued to be able to do so for their own consumption, even if the economic benefits were dubious; but it became less easy to sell such output, and thus to supplement family incomes, profit from surplus labour, and allow for flexibility where incomes were uncertain. Secondly, though the professional spinners and weavers could often still sell their product, if only at depressed prices, yet they were more vulnerable, having ceased to be essential to those collective village arrangements whereby services were supplied and harvests shared.

These last points may alert us to the relationship between national economic performance and the incidence of individual poverty. In an age of international companies, it has become commonplace to play down the importance of the indigenous ownership of assets. India's ranking as a trading nation did not necessarily decline because of European dominance, nor would Indian ownership have guaranteed national success. There were 'national' gains as well as losses from foreign investment. Europeanization was important not so much because it restricted industrialization (if it did) or because it ignored the bulk of Indian economic activities, but because it impoverished India in terms of the invisibles: interest on capital;

insurance premiums; transport profits; dividends and other income from foreign properties and equities; and high-level skills in production, management and finance. One might cite the use of European managing agencies to provide management even for Indian-owned mills, or of European managers for coffee, tea, sugar and indigo production. Though there was increasing employment of educated Indians in landed estates and factories, especially after the First World War, it is telling that in 1895 only 57 per cent of Bombay factory managers and technicians were Indian – telling not only because they tended to be concentrated at lower levels of responsibility, but also because (as part of the much-vaunted rise of the middle classes) a far higher proportion of developed countries' nationals were thus employed, in their own industries and services, or abroad. Such limits on skilled employment in India, and the repeated failure of governments to invest adequately in either human capital or economic redistribution, led to large sections of the population remaining poor in terms of income, purchasing power, security and knowledge.

AGRICULTURE

For the next part of the explanation of India's decline, we need to turn from industry to agriculture, for there the overwhelming majority (70 to 80 per cent) earned their livelihood and the greatest deprivation was to be found, despite appalling conditions in many factories and towns. Poverty remains *the* most pressing issue in India. Therefore, rather than narrating economic events, the following sections will make an extended attempt to explain agrarian distress. They start with famine but then concentrate on structural problems.

In many ways, in the modern era as in the past, Indian agriculture appears a success. It continues to the present day to feed a vast and growing population, through scientific improvements, investment and unyielding effort. Between 1800 and the early twentieth century, the cultivated area expanded greatly, with the incorporation of 'waste' or forest, the reclamation and embankment of flood-plains, the commercial exploitation of under-utilized holdings, and the development of irrigation schemes, large and small. In most regions cultivated and irrigated areas rose markedly as real tax levels fell and agricultural prices rose. In eastern India, for example, there was reclamation of river basins and hilly or outlying districts. In the eastern districts around Dhaka this had started in the sixteenth century, and latterly was focused on expanding the acreage under jute. In the north, from Champaran to Assam, the expansion occurred during the nineteenth century. In central and western India a great expansion of cultivation was encouraged by the cotton boom after the 1860s. In the dry Punjab and Sind, and in previously irrigated tracts in north India and in the southern river valleys, new lands or double-cropping added to the total cultivated area. In the dry (unirrigated) tracts of the south new commercial crops were increasingly grown. Even in heavily populated and already product-ive regions, 'common', fallow and 'waste' lands were absorbed by zamindars for share-cropping, and cultivable but under-utilized village lands were taken up, often by non-resident 'agricultural' castes. At the same time the commercial value of all crops rose markedly until the great crash of 1929–30, and communications were vastly expanded and improved. Most of this expansion of cultivation was due to Indian enterprise, though some occurred through the state-backed irrigation of arid areas, or in hilly tracts where mainly European-owned plantations started growing tea and coffee.

In some parts of the world, economic growth was based on the supply of agricultural produce to industrialized countries or regions – including sheep from Australia and New Zealand, sugar from Mau-ritius, cocoa from Ghana, or cotton and wheat in North America. In India, by contrast, though there were some benefits from trade, many areas suffered from periodic famines throughout the nineteenth century. These were followed during the twentieth century by the chronic malnutrition of a majority of the rural population. Why was this so?

Climate – mainly unseasonal and repeated shortfalls or excesses of rainfall – produced famines by destroying crops, disrupting agricultural production and raising prices. Epidemic disease exacer-bated death rates. Starting in the nineteenth century, however, as famine became legally defined and politicized, more instrumental explanations have also been sought. One claims that the colonial government took too much in revenue (though the land revenue declined in relation to the value of ouput over the nineteenth century), or that land revenue was demanded too inflexibly and at intervals which forced payers into debt. Others assert that, when large-scale irrigation was applied to already productive areas, it

extended problems with weeds, salt deposits and malaria, and
added new burdens of petty oppression and tax, which disadvantages outweighed the benefits of a secure water-supply (if such it
was) and a more efficient distribution of work between seasons. Yet
others argue that there was a shortfall in food, either absolutely or
for the poor, because of a colonially enforced commercialization of
production. Food crops were exported (wheat certainly was) and
cash crops such as cotton, opium and indigo (though probably
not jute which alternated with rice) drove subsistence crops on
to poorer lands, with the result that yield dropped and food
prices rose.

Each of these explanations has its critics, and India's experience
was too varied, and its regional disparities are still too great, to
encourage simple explanations. Moreover the data, though very
valuable where related to specialist revenue surveys and cropping
patterns, are not so useful when aggregated, or (for example) in
regard to yields. Some argue that average yields for cash crops
increased during the nineteenth century, and that average yields
for food crops were markedly higher for most of the nineteenth
century than in the twentieth century before independence – thus
ruling out a direct connection with the nineteenth-century famines.
Some attribute the relative lack of famines after 1901 to improvements
in income and more efficient distribution, as well as more effective
emergency relief by government. Others relate nineteenth-century
famines to a decline in output per acre and per capita, and long-term
endemic poverty to major shortfalls in food-grain supply as well as
in access to employment.

There is little argument about two points. Firstly, famines and
malnutrition were problems of economic differentiation. Explaining
the terrible Bengal famine of 1943, the economist, Amartya Sen, has
attributed hunger and poverty not to an overall shortage of food or
resources, but to the widespread inadequacy of 'exchange entitlement' – people's inability to secure their own subsistence through
paid work, or by retaining the products of their own labour, or
from 'entitlement protection' (welfare provision). Secondly, there were
failures on the part of the colonial government. For decades (as
discussed in Chapter 6) they provided only piecemeal famine-
management, in which local calls for active intervention were
hampered by lack of money and *laissez faire* arguments against
interference in the market. When they began to act, their policies
were always underfunded and sometimes counterproductive. They

finally began to promote protective public works only from the 1870s, and developed codes for famine relief only after the formative Famine Commission of 1880–1 (refined in 1901). After 1880, as discussed, they embarked more seriously on direct measures to benefit agriculture: collecting information, making practical experiments, improving crops and methods, establishing research, training and publicity, setting standards on marketable quality, and co-ordinating markets. Some better seeds, improved implements, methods and fertilizers were found to increase yields. These were probably balanced out by the malign effects of ill-conceived experiments and imported remedies (for example, the failed acclimatization or hybridization of crops).

At the same time, or as an alternative, the government tried to improve security of tenure for landlords and surplus cultivators, and to control the supply of credit, by modifying the law and establishing a co-operative movement. On the whole these measures seem to have increased the power of local elites without concentrating and increasing the scale of commercial production. Nor did government intervention prevent further fragmentation of the majority of landholdings. There is some evidence of greater output per acre from small holdings than large, but such fragmentation implies an efficiency ceiling that would be rapidly reached.

Famine and failures of relief policy certainly created poverty, but neither is a complete explanation. Famines by definition are exceptional; relief could only have had indirect impact. In seeking deeper explanations, one faces two main problems with the data. The first is over-generalization. Data on textile imports, tax revenues, numbers of work animals and modern dwellings, provide only aggregate figures, or average figures if we choose to divide by the size of the population. It is far from certain, for example, that the average quality and quantity of food available per capita declined during colonial rule. It is merely possible that any decline in average yields was greater in common food-grains than in cash crops (which would have affected the average ability to meet subsistence needs alongside market production). Staple-food production also may have been less responsive to price than non-food and export crops. In the 1860s, in parts of the Indian Deccan, cotton cultivation almost doubled in response to soaring prices, but the total cereal acreage rose by only 16 per cent despite a price rise of, for example, 47 per cent for the staple millet (*jowar*). Some even of that relatively modest increase in acreage was attributable to wheat, a crop grown in this area mainly for the market; the price of wheat had risen by 97 per cent. Such statistics give plausibility to the arguments about commercialization taking food from the mouths of the growers – but at the expense of rendering them irrelevant: they return us to what we already knew, that it was the poor (those who were not selling wheat or cotton profitably) who had insufficient food.

The second problem is that the data relate largely to consumption through the market. But it was rare for the major part of cultivable land in a district to be devoted to market production. Cereals and pulses occupied the majority of the cultivated area in all but insubstantial tracts. For example, in the Indian Deccan, it was only in a few years in one or two districts that cotton and other cash crops occupied anything approaching half the cultivated area. Often, too, much of the commercial crop was produced by petty tenants and share-croppers, so that even populations heavily committed to export production might have to rely on household production, barter and casual gathering of work or food to meet their needs for food, clothing and shelter. In considering agriculture in modern India, therefore, we need to consider differences of experience, and varieties of means of survival.

The complexities imply that we should consider production in some detail. The market and government were penetrating ever more deeply into the lives of Indians. Rural producers were relying more on purchases to meet basic subsistence needs. The market also brought them a wider range of articles of consumption which, in time, became essentials. Examining such changes, we will see why the material condition of rural communities became more vulnerable to external collapse, and how the subsistence economy became less effective as a safety net. When we look in detail at villages and fields, one point is plain: the benefits of agricultural expansion became distributed in new ways, and they were unevenly enjoyed. (However, in most cases, basic production methods were relatively little changed until after independence.) Explanations for poverty will be sought first by focusing on labour, land and economic differentiation.

RURAL LABOUR REGIMES

The period of colonial rule saw considerable changes for labour. There were new factory workers. Additional employees were

sought for public and urban works, and for packaging, processing
and transport. There were policemen and supervisors, bricklayers,
canal-diggers, road-builders, cartmen (with the increase in passable
roads), railway- and port-workers, and later truck-drivers. Employment was given to particular groups, such as professional diggers
or *beldars*, Eurasians on the railways, or the caste of Karkanis in the
Punjab carrying trades. We have already noticed a considerable
demilitarization (a ban on private armies and less need for zamindari
strongmen), but also a large recruitment of professional soldiers
from supposedly 'martial' castes and communities, supported by
the bulk of Indian central revenues. There was curtailment of some
itinerants, including 'tribals' and criminal gangs, but increased
demand for migrant labour. There was a decline of courtly occupations, and of some educational and religious foundations – but also
new professions, new sponsorship of public and private institutions,
and a vast expansion of the official bureaucracy.

All of this was numerically insignificant in comparison with the
huge labour force involved in agriculture. In this sector as in others,
caste usually mattered most in determining a household's fortunes.
But leaving that issue aside for the moment, it is possible to identify
four types of worker involved in the nineteenth-century expansion
of commercial agriculture: owner-occupiers, share-croppers, field-
workers, and contract (plantation) labourers. These workers differed in motive – they sought profit or subsistence, and to meet
household or collective needs such as irrigation or religion. Their
work also differed according to the demands of different kinds of
crop. The workers differed thirdly because of ways they obtained
income. They might depend on their own surplus or on cash wages;
in addition they might receive food, shares of produce, housing,
livestock, social returns and protection.

Workers differed in two other main ways. These defined the
terms on which agriculture was conducted – that is, the labour
regimes. The first difference related to access to resources, especially land, which determined the manner in which production was
organized. Owner-occupiers and share-croppers had some access
to land. Field-workers and contract labourers were effectively
landless, though even plantation workers sometimes had small plots.
Secondly, workers differed in independence, in freedom from
coercion. All who worked in agriculture, including land-owners and
tenants, could be controlled, albeit to different degrees. Sanctions
included 'customary' obligations, social prestige, physical force and

debt. Control could be either by superiors directly, or indirectly through gang-masters and agents. Labour might also be managed through bureaucratic structures and laws (job specification, time- and record-keeping, and so on). The forms of control influenced the ways in which labour worked.

Production for the market did not necessarily imply that one type of labour management would be replaced by another, or even that only one type would be used. It certainly did not require competitive wage labour. The distinctions were not absolute. Share-cropping, for example, could have some of the characteristics of tenant-farming or, on the other hand, some of those of forced labour. Some common features kept appearing, even where labour demands were very different – as they were, for example, for plan-tations, and for landlords' and tenants' own lands. Elements of most or all of these mechanisms of labour subordination and control are likely to have been found in any particular locality at any particular time.

THE 'LANDLESS'

In India, the proportion of work undertaken by effectively landless labour (rather than by land-controlling households) varied from place to place, and time to time; the differences have fuelled historical controversy. Despite the many regional variations, it can be said that agricultural labour generally was recruited in one of two main ways.

The first was through customary occupations. Such workers were often 'recruited' by birth, and grew up into their roles – from ploughing to shoe-making to astrology. They provided services to particular landed households, or to a community, as their fathers and uncles had before them. (Such relationships often extended to women's work, but usually according to the status of male rela-tives.) Workers were paid by shares of the harvest, or by wages in cash and kind, and often by small grants of land. Those who were artisans commonly also had to join in agricultural work at times of peak labour demand (harvesting, irrigation, and so on). These arrangements (under such names as *jajmani*, *sepidari*, and so on) are sometimes treated as supportive, harmonious and unchanging. But it is plain that they produced many conflicts and allowed much oppression.

The second category were regular or casual farm-workers, recruited by land grants (as share-croppers), by advances and loans, or by wages in cash or kind. These were people without customary or inherited connections with their employers, and without any substantive tenant rights. Often these workers were employed by quite poor land-owners and tenants of high caste (Brahmans and Rajputs for example) for whom manual labour was demeaning. But all rich peasants and landlords would employ such labour. Some share-croppers provided their own capital and livestock and thus received higher returns; others depended upon the land-owner for all resources.

Demand for labour, however, was seasonal, and also varied from year to year, so that much of the work, especially at peak times, was carried out by temporary migrants and casual workers, often organized in gangs led by contractors who would seek out employers. Casual workers might be paid at higher rates, but they were employed for shorter periods than farm servants. Even in normal seasons, day-labourers were taken on only when farming activity was greatest. At harvest and other periods of peak demand, and in certain places, labourers were able to seek better conditions, but they relied at other times of the year on begging, borrowing, stealing and prostitution, on the produce of forests and common land, and on non-agricultural work. The luckier ones had their own crops from tiny plots of land; much of the casual workforce was made up of those who held too little land for subsistence. For the landless, bondage might be the only way of securing a tiny plot.

As a result, poor workers were often ready to commit themselves and their families to work for others for very small rewards. There is a little evidence to suggest that patrons supported their workers in times of distress. Bonds were agreed by the poor labourers in return for loans needed for survival or for special expenditure (such as a marriage), and in hope of guaranteeing at least minimal employment in the future. Field-labourers given advances worked out their bond, repaying it through shares of the crop or through wages. Most of these bonded workers could not escape the cycle of debt, and many preferred to accept it because it offered some prospect of securing enough work to survive.

Because of problems of definition it is impossible to be precise about the proportions of the population in these two categories. They were not very clearly distinguishable in practice, and the differences were probably diminishing during the colonial period.

Customary workers continued to be common in many areas; but artisans lost out to factory manufactures, or sought opportunities in towns, in processing or in transport, so that the traditional ties tended to become weaker. Customary relations were bolstered up by common or collective rights (for example, to pasturage, fisheries, or forests), and these tended to be withdrawn or to become more disputed from the nineteenth-century onwards, just as some agricultural by-products (such as skins, for leather-workers) became items of commerce where once they had been made available as a customary right. Because there was a trend towards individual property and contracts of employment, there was a corresponding erosion of collective arrangements whereby the state, priests, artisans, village servants and labourers were all entitled to access to land or to shares in village harvests to which they had notionally or actually contributed. This tended to reduce the circumstances of artisans and other customary workers.

All these relationships depended upon force and violence as well as upon legal, social and economic sanctions. However, casual and seasonal labour relations, and cash wages, tended to become more prevalent during the twentieth century. In the Punjab, for example, despite the persistence of grain payments, pure cash wages were common in about 60 per cent of villages by the 1940s. Generally, this detachment of labour from customary roles, from land rights, and from locations, meant that its security and bargaining power were reduced, even though there were more varied demands for labour as production, trade and processing increased.

In addition, many workers experienced sharper changes in their work experiences. New employment patterns affected hunters-and-gatherers who migrated to plantations, peasant smallholders transformed into share-croppers, children employed for longer hours and at younger ages, women working outside the household in plantations and peasant agriculture, and men moving away from the villages to factories and mines. The tea plantations of Assam, for example, employed a new type of landless worker. Plantations were established in areas where there was supposedly little suitable local labour. Men, women and children were brought in by 'free' emigration and by a system of indentures. In both cases most were recruited and managed by various types of intermediary contractor or *sardar*, who recruited workers from long distances and then, usually, acted as their foreman and paymaster. The planters used force and special and general laws of contract to discourage their workers from absconding, and often provided certain services to them, including plots of land. This was intended both to help retain workers, and to reduce the level of money wages which they had to be paid.

Many historians regard the tea workers as particularly oppressed by racialist employers and by law. The plantations seem clearly distinctive, in their recruitment of workers, their alliance with capital and colonial power, their management of time and work, and the distribution of tasks between men and women. They did often mark a dramatic change in the experience of workers, especially those recruited from among swidden agriculturists (shifting cultivators). On the other hand, it may also be noted that even tea planters competed for labour and had to make concessions to keep workers. Despite the difference of plantations' work regimes, in some respects conditions still had to approximate to those of Indian employment generally – the Europeans imitated or fitted in with Indian conditions, and prevailing conditions produced general effects. There were resemblances between the plantation arrangements in Assam, and those made nearby in north Bengal, for example, by village magnates (*jotedars*) who gathered around them households of workers and dependants, sometimes from the same 'tribal' background as the tea-plantation workers, and provided them with services, including plots of land, while paying them very little in cash.

Different kinds of labourers on peasant farms thus shared some experiences not only among themselves, but with plantation-workers. One study of workers in Surat in Gujarat enables us to gauge some of the changes experienced by such workers over time.[1] This is a region whose hinterland, a 'forest' area, had been populated by shifting cultivators. In the nineteenth century, surveys, taxation, forest laws and the incursion of plainsmen produced a pattern of scattered and extensive but settled agriculture. Many of the inhabitants of this hinterland, and its surplus population, were forced to become labourers in the lowlands. In the plains and valleys, peasants and landed proprietors had long conducted an intensive cultivation producing cotton and sugar for distant markets. Output expanded, with some serious fluctuations, throughout the colonial period, and the proportion under cotton increased markedly. After Indian independence, in the 1960s, the area was provided with canal irrigation, and in many villages crops of rice and sugarcane became overwhelmingly important.

The *adivasis* (so-called aboriginals) were landless labourers, their numbers swollen by migrant hillsmen and other immigrants. They formed three-quarters of Gujarat's agrarian population by the 1970s. Such workers had been *halipratha*, debt-bonded workers whose whole families were obliged, over generations, to work for a master (one of the larger landholders) in return for a bare subsistence – food, a tiny plot of land, a little money – some of it provided in advance in order to maintain the relationship of debt. The expansion of cash cropping extended this system, as more farmers could afford to employ labour on these terms.

In the twentieth century the system had begun to change. There were outside schemes to improve the conditions of labour, by the state or social workers who were followers of Mahatma Gandhi. Some bonded labourers absconded to seek their living in towns, and a few gained land. For the majority, however, conditions did not improve. There were still many farm servants, but a preponderance of agricultural workers became casual, seasonal or migrant. Some were indebted to and employed by contractors (*mukadam*) who provided workers for the larger cultivators, just as the *sardar* had for tea planters. All workers were more often paid in cash, and certain agricultural tasks, such as cotton-picking, were paid as piecework. The casual workers were no longer bonded to the landholders, but they were thereby, if anything, poorer and more vulnerable. In these respects, we can trace a considerable continuity, in the conditions experienced, even between plantation workers of nineteenth-century Assam and the casual labourers of modern Gujarat.

A recurrent feature is of impediments to a free labour market. Even when labourers moved to towns or became 'casualized', there were systems to keep them under the command of agents or principal employers. Those in power struggled to maintain such control. Paid workers in eighteenth-century Calcutta were subject to master-and-servant regulations which, while offering some protection against exploitation, allowed employers and labour contractors the use of criminal-law sanctions to force employees to keep to their contracts. This mattered less for household servants who were often paid in arrears, being provided with subsistence, but it was crucial for contractors, skilled workers and ordinary labourers who commonly were paid in advance, largely because of their extreme poverty. The European employers were here applying their idea of contract to employment practices which were ubiquitous in Bengal.

Those land-controllers lording it over bonded workers or employing agricultural gangs, and those jobbers, *sardars* and others who controlled the gangs, were operating with systems that were the direct descendants of these arrangements.

THE 'LANDED'

Seemingly quite different was the experience of those who had access to land. Entrepreneurial peasant groups made successful forays into commercial agriculture, using family or hired labour. They represent a different work-regime certainly, but the crucial point about them was that they enjoyed independent resources. Though this independence was only relative in face of the power of external industrial capital, it was significant in terms of access to local power. The crucial resources included land, seed, water, labour, livestock, implements and information; possession of the technical means of processing and marketing was also important. Many of these 'rich peasant' groups strengthened their position. Marked regional differences continued, and certain depressed groups even enjoyed an improvement in conditions. But, on the whole, the differentiation in landholding was increasing and becoming more entrenched. Trade, population and output were growing, so that differences in land-ownership had a greater impact upon incomes.

At the lower end of the scale, however, this meant that there was a continuum, in terms of dependence, between landless labourers and some of the peasantry. Many of those who appeared to have sufficient land provided some labour to others. Most other small-holding peasants had insufficient land for subsistence. The poor tenants forced to work for others, or as share-croppers, were often very similarly placed to debt-bonded labourers. They were recruited by land grants or through debt, notably to richer tenants, or to landlords, or to traders. They too might have inherited obligations to a social superior or landlord. The difference between these poor tenants and the customary labourers was often more one of status than of well-being or conditions of work. Being regarded as a tenant or agriculturist rather than a labourer was of great social importance, but for our purposes many tenants can be regarded as providing labour for others.

At one extreme, in north Bihar in north-east India, European indigo producers (so-called planters) became the renters of villages, and required the tenants to grow indigo on parts of their holdings and to provide labour to the factories, using local agents and headmen to pay out loans and supervise the cultivation. Again, the tenants' other lands produced subsistence crops which reduced the prices which the planters had to pay for the indigo. As on the tea plantations, payments for work or produce were calculated in cash according to precise measurements of time and task or quantity. But none of the planters paid a 'market' price and all used a mixture of social, political and economic controls in order to attract and retain labour.

This example typifies the methods whereby peasants were tapped for labour. In short, it was not very different from the control over landless workers. Some tenants enjoyed special privileges, by virtue of high social status, or concessions where land needed to be reclaimed for agriculture. These people were often kin or caste-fellows of the landlords, and worked as their agents and allies. But all but the greatest and most independent of tenants would often be working at others' behest. Larger landlords extracted surplus either through semi-permanent intermediaries (such as the indigo planters, or many other levels of Indian rent-farmers), or through direct management, using employees or village officers paid in cash or by land grants. Whatever system was in vogue, landlords and rich peasants mostly controlled the records and other information. They refused to give receipts, and kept tenants' accounts in arrears, regardless of their actual payments.

In north-eastern India, as in most of colonial South Asia, there was little competition in rents, but also, until the early twentieth century or later, little certainty about them either. The assessed area was usually uncertain too, for want of measurement. Such conditions provided opportunities for oppression and privilege (as well as for peasant resistance). The dominant classes also had ready access to markets, many of which were owned by landlords. The rich usually had privileged use of law and favourable terms for obtaining credit. Rent, records, measurement, courts, markets and loans were all used as methods of control and to extract produce. The landlords also had frequent recourse to direct force – many of them employed bodies of armed retainers, more numerous than their rent-collectors and record-keepers, and so extracted rent by violence or intimidation.

Produce was obtained not only as rent but through other demands (the distinction between the two was a modern idea). On the whole rents increased over the first seven decades of the nineteenth century, though not uniformly or invariably. From mid-century, it became harder to increase rents, and very difficult to do so in line with agricultural prices. This was so, on the whole, even in areas with produce-sharing rents, because their commutation to cash rents became more frequent, and legal interference generally increased the likelihood of popular resistance. In the later nineteenth century, recorded cash rents probably declined in real terms. One estimate for eastern Bengal, for example, suggests they fell from 15 to 10 per cent of gross produce between 1870 and 1910.

But such rents often represented only a small part of the enforced payments. Dues were collected also for any number of additional purposes – for community activities, but also to add to the landlord's income or to cover his costs. Fees were charged for presentation of accounts, for transfers of tenancies, for agents' commissions, for funerals and marriages in the landlord's family, for religious ceremonies and village rituals. Moreover, in the first few decades of the twentieth century, there was a decline in the numbers permitted to pay such cash rents, and a refusal to commute into cash rent the various produce rents, which could be levied at 50 per cent of gross produce or more. Many more tenants also became share-croppers at this time.

In many parts of India, extensive lands, and especially part-holdings, were transferred to other cultivators in one way or another (for example, by mortgage) without a transfer of ownership. In Gujarat, the pattern of land distribution does not seem to have altered very much – 60 per cent of the farmers were small landholders occupying about a quarter of the land. But detailed investigation at the end of the 1960s suggested that the smallest owners were tending to work less of their own land and were letting out portions of it to the larger farmers.

These developments, which were repeated in different ways in other areas, produced wealthier cultivators, who retained a large degree of independence and were able to benefit from the market. The middle and larger landholders were able to take advantage of the opportunities of a more expensive but more profitable agricul-ture. The trend was for their land to be farmed either by wage labour or by unregulated tenants and share-croppers, usually on very unfavourable terms. Many of the smallholders had to work for these larger cultivators.

Most of these changes were not absolute. For example, although a worsening man:land ratio now restricted access to land, it had been restricted in the past by states and powerful people, despite a land surplus. Pre-existing differentiation makes it difficult to be sure of the impact of modern influences. However, the effect of colonial law, commercial opportunity, rising land values and population growth together worsened the existing disparities of wealth and power. The disabilities of the 'landless' were extended to some who were technically tenants, and still held small plots of their own land. Larger numbers than in the past became share-croppers, or were forced to provide labour services to others. Effectively, legal changes, in a context of commercialization, enlarged the pool of labour at the expense of peasant cultivators. The process has been called 'depeasantization'. Higher population, fuller occupancy of land, extension of property rights in exclusive possession, and the increasing specialization of production (including imports in competition with local part-time production), all contributed to the change. The tendency was for poor cultivators to be obliged to produce commercial crops for inadequate returns, and for wage labour to be casualized.

Three key factors, working together, underlay the increasing exploitation of peasant labour. They were the control of land, the command of credit, and the restrictions on competitive access to the market. We will consider them in turn.

LAND CONTROL

Land is a convenient, though not necessarily an unambiguous indicator of wealth and opportunity. In mainly agricultural economies and states depending on income from agriculture, most other resources derive from control over land (for example, independence in decision-making, agricultural capital, control of labour, surplus income, credit, social and political power). Secure possession of land, as colonial administrators never tired of saying, was the key to independence for many peasant proprietors and tenants. More secure landholding was the aim of colonial policy. Why then did it produce large numbers of less secure agricultural workers?

The explanation starts with the fact that the basis of land control was being changed. It was a major revolution in the legal nature of landed property, when Indian rights (tenancy and cultivating rights, for example) were recorded and defined under English law. British land policy comprised an immensely detailed mapping of land boundaries and land rights. Even in permanently settled areas, estate boundaries were surveyed for private and public purposes, categories of landholder were progressively defined by law, and (as said) detailed cadastral surveys and records of rights were eventually instituted. From the start, in temporarily settled areas, periodic (roughly thirty-year) surveys and annual reviews of land use formed the basis of land rights and revenue demands.

Surveying and maps familiarized Europeans with the land. They did so as descriptive narratives and picturesque representations (such as route maps), and through in-depth topographies. As noted above, a host of other revenue, historical, social and demographic surveys followed. But colonial rule also imposed Western forms on Indian land. Laws and external scrutiny reduced flexibility, and greater security of title and contract increased land values. As the idea of individual property rights took hold, land was increasingly mortgaged and sold. In Bengal the settlement had been made with those regarded (often erroneously) as an old aristocracy; but in many instances it set the revenue demand at a high level, so that at first, when there was an agricultural recession, it produced a high turnover in land-ownership. In one year, 1788/9, the Bengal estates which were compulsorily sold for arrears were valued at more than 14 per cent of the total (calculated in terms of the revenue demand); and on average the buyers paid less than one year's revenue. As a result of these convulsions, all but one of the very large landed estates of Bengal was broken up; though smaller land-owners were less affected, and some families amassed huge fortunes and new estates.

Then quite quickly it became unusual for landed estates to be compulsorily sold, and they began to increase in value. A market in land developed. At the same time, especially from the middle of the nineteenth century, there was an enormous increase in the number of recognized land-owners, because of the partition of estates between co-sharers – by agreement, by sale or through inheritance. In one large district of north Bihar, for example, there were 1351 estates in 1790, 3018 in 1850, and 31 893 in 1895. Also growing of course were the numbers of intermediary landholders and under-tenants.

These legal and administrative changes had significant effects in the countryside. In pre-colonial India, stable peasant farming had existed, especially in fertile, irrigated and densely populated regions. But it was far from universal. Many people were not fixed on the land, but were peripatetic – ranging from swidden cultivators and migrant farm-workers to traders and soldiers. Even settled villagers, especially the poor, often cultivated 'waste', tracts associated with a village but not in regular ownership or used for paddy cultivation. Such lands provided basic support to cultivators in dry and marginal areas, and acted as an extra resource and safety net where there was artificial irrigation. The importance of such flexibility was not noticed or was underestimated by the colonial observers, and it was severely disrupted by land law and forest regulations. Where rights in land had therefore been varied and overlapping, colonial rule extended settled cultivation, and gradually standardized land rights. It increased the security of property for absentee landlords, and decreased the security for many tenants.

There was a marked reduction in common or 'unclaimed' land. In law, and increasingly in practice, settled agricultural land was more clearly and formally distributed, and access to 'waste' and rent-free lands became more regulated and restricted. In the permanently settled regions, large areas which had paid no state revenue were 'resumed' on to the revenue roll during the first half of the nineteenth century. In temporarily settled western India, too, some 10 per cent of the cultivated area had been revenue-free; and most of this was turned into taxable private property under British rule. All lands were supposed to have owners, and virtually all were taxable, and thus had to produce marketable crops.

One consequence was a restriction on access to land, and often also a reduction in the availability of fodder, fuel and manure, and in the incidence of fallows. Additional dues extracted by landlords for community purposes came to be regarded as private property. All rents were treated as a payment for land use, implying no mutual obligation. They were no longer part of a complex social and ritual system which expressed dominance but also expected an exchange of services – for example free labour given by the cultivators to the landlords, but also irrigation or capital provided by landlords to the cultivators. (Some share-cropping and some debt-bondage later continued this interdependence, but on terms less advantageous to the cultivators.)

Parallel changes were effected by colonial regulations which sought to protect forests by outlawing the traditional gathering of forest products and the slash-and-burn cultivation of 'tribal' inhabitants. Both occupations were considered inferior to settled cultivation, wasteful of 'valuable' resources, economically inefficient and environmentally damaging. Many people who had depended on forests or waste were forced to work in 'regular' agriculture or as migrant labour. Others from settled areas also lost access to forest products.

As a result, though with some significant exceptions, it seems that poorer people lost land to richer people. It had always been possible for land to be transferred in India, but the transfer had been subject to various social and political restrictions. Under British rule, land rather than the person of the holder came to be at risk for debt or arrears of revenue. In Bengal and Bihar some of the further consequences may be traced in the aftermath of the Bengal Tenancy Act of 1885, which extended transferability to tenancies. It instituted detailed surveys of land rights, and records which made sales or mortgages more straightforward and secure.

It also provided that settled tenancies could be sold, without the consent of the landlord, where 'custom' allowed. The last may sound like a measure to prevent change, but in practice custom was defined by the courts. It was in the nature of the system and the evidence heard that powerful people or those with influential backers found it easy to secure judgments in their favour. Most such persons were not in favour of an independent tenantry. Thus the law helped landlords, often those who wanted to seize tenant lands. On the other hand, government officials tended to encourage transferability under the Act, even to the extent of issuing warnings of criminal prosecution to landlords who tried to obstruct it. The officials believed that such full property rights were necessary to encourage tenants to improve their lands and increase productivity. But here again it was mainly the substantial people who could benefit, often at the expense of poorer neighbours.

While population increase and land partition made some landowners too poor to be independent, the more wealthy or successful cultivators were able to accumulate land in their own or neighbouring villages. Often they also had access to the means to develop them. Between 1885 and 1913 the recorded number of private sales of landholdings in Bengal increased by about 500 per cent. The law was increasingly involved in the regulation of propertyholding. Because of earlier under-reporting, the figures undoubtedly overstate the rate of increase, but large proportions of sales continued not to be registered, especially for smaller and partholdings, so that many more transfers occurred than were recorded. The upward trend was unmistakable.

These land rights existed on a new basis, recognized and protected by colonial law. They were commonly enjoyed by inter-mediaries and local elites who played crucial economic, social and political roles – the rent-farmers, lease-holders, headmen and agents who were flourishing in the countryside. Non-agriculturists could also acquire land, though various steps were taken by government to reduce such transfers to 'outsiders', and in any case moneylenders, for example, usually could gain higher returns by lending out capital than by sinking it in land. Landlords too could manipulate the system. Though the law made it more difficult to evict tenants, it permitted landlords to claim lands as their own demesne or to sell holdings to recover rent. Both would enable land to be trans-ferred away from some tenants who had legal rights of occupancy. Share-cropping and produce rents increased partly in order to reduce the chances of outside or legal interference.

This is not to say that modern legal possession of land as private property was the only factor to be considered. On the contrary, in nineteenth-century India, though there were many wealthy rentiers, widening disparities of income were seldom to be traced to land-ownership and rental demands pure and simple. A broader and closer control over production was usually necessary to increase wealth, and a range of related activities – entrepreneurship, bank-ing, trade, government service – were commonly exploited to achieve upward mobility. What happened was that the advantages of modern land-ownership, and indeed of modern trade, were grafted on to an existing system which already offered large priv-ileges to certain classes of people. Changes in land-ownership thus illustrate more general changes in economic power.

THE USE OF CREDIT

If many people became relatively poorer and more vulnerable, it was also because of a second factor, debt – or, rather, of the different ways in which the necessary and perennial demand for credit came to impinge on the cultivators. The case of Bengal jute cultivation (mostly in what is now Bangladesh) will help explain how such debt helped impoverish large sections of the popula-tion. It is a good example because this crop was not one which necessarily damaged the cultivators through the manner of its production.

Most of the jute, like all cash crops, was produced using borrowed capital, in seed, grain or cash. The circumstances of this debt meant that it contributed to disparities of wealth and opportunity, even when (as was often the case) it was the wealthier peasants who were the heaviest borrowers. In east Bengal, the cultivators were not known for being particularly heavily indebted, but they had to have credit all the same, in order to meet outgoings between the harvests. It has been shown (as was also true elsewhere) that the rates of interest which they paid were closely related to their status. On the whole much higher charges were paid by poorer tenants, under-tenants and persons of low social standing. This alone implies sharper stratification whenever borrowing increased in order to meet higher costs or to produce for the market.

Secondly, the interest rates varied according to the calendar of agricultural operations which they supported and of rent-days and festivals for which cash was needed. Official inquiries in eastern Bengal in the 1920s found that a typical interest rate was for 2 or 3 per cent per month after the winter-rice harvest, for 5 to 6 per cent when labour had to be hired for weeding, and for as much as 16 per cent during the jute harvest and the work of fibre separation. These variations offered a further advantage to those in a position to choose the times at which they borrowed.

Thirdly, the local rates of interest were all very high. Compounded monthly charges could top 300 per cent per annum, enormously higher than in the formal banking sector. Thus, again, high charges could be avoided by the wealthiest, who were most likely to be able to choose a different source of credit. The system also increased the likelihood that the poorer peasants would not be able to borrow long-term in order to invest in agricultural improvements.

As if this were not enough, the local interest rates also represented a temptation even to those creditors who had to borrow their own capital, and a means whereby poorer cultivators could be controlled or ruined. Therefore, where there *was* some local choice of creditor for all but the least creditworthy, still none was without its dangers. These problems too had greatest effect on the poorer cultivator, who was of course already more likely than his richer fellows to be at risk, when he borrowed, from natural disasters, age, illness, dependants and so on. Loans might be obtained from village moneylenders. In east Bengal these men were usually not involved in cultivation and were not primarily interested in acquiring land. But their profits and the need to secure their capital gave them an incentive to try to control their clients and the output of their fields. Usually this meant that poor cultivators would be prevented from seeking other employment, from taking up profitable but possibly risky crops, and from delaying the sale of their output until prices were at their highest. Alternatively, loans, especially over longer terms, might be obtained from rich peasants, usually on the basis of a mortgage on the debtor's holding. Such lenders were liable to foreclose on the mortgage if they had a use for extra land, and frequently they were in a position to squeeze the cultivator with a combination of rental and credit demands. Finally, advances could be obtained from traders, concerned to secure a particular crop at a favourable price. They gave harvest loans, stipulating that they would be repaid from the forthcoming crop at a set price. Such arrangements would reduce or remove the cultivator's profit, as well as raise the cost of credit, because the stipulated price could easily be more than 50 per cent below that which could have been obtained on an open market.

In east Bengal, none of these predators made great inroads until after the First World War, when jute profits dropped. But the potential of such credit systems was obvious. They were primarily devices to secure the produce of poorer cultivators – that is, a way of exploiting their labour. They were particularly important in poorer areas as long as trade was increasing and there was no sharp decline in its profitability. Extreme economic downturns tended to hurt the lenders as well as the borrowers, just as large and steady improvements offered some protection to a broader band of debtors.

Debt, however, was often heritable from one generation to another, and tended to become endemic and to rise out of all proportion to the ability to keep up repayments. A long-term relative decline in the returns to Indian agriculture after the nineteenth century, the rising population and pressure on the land, and the cumulative effect of natural and human disasters, all tended to mean that debt exaggerated the effect we have already seen from property laws. Some people became greater controllers of land and labour, and more people became dependent upon them. Increasing disparities meant a loss of some (not all) independent 'peasant' production in favour of various forms of coerced and managed labour. Conversely it also meant an increasing use of casual non-family labour by some 'peasant' households.

ACCESS TO THE MARKET

Another major aspect of rural power was reflected in access to the market. As production increased, some cultivators were able to market their produce competitively. The general expansion of cultivated area through reclamation and irrigation, the rise of a Muslim middle class in Dhaka, the educational advance among Punjabi Jats, the large increase in permanent housing in most parts of India, the consumption of new goods such as manufactured cotton or kerosene or printed matter – all these and more indicate that some areas and classes benefited from the trade revolution. But, as emphasized throughout this chapter, the great majority of Indians became poorer, less well-fed, and more vulnerable to famine and disease.

In the countryside many increased their production, but received low prices because of the power of middlemen: rich neighbours, landlords and moneylenders. Advance payments, as said, led to enforced sales at the point of harvest when prices were lowest. This situation was compounded by the producers' need for cash (or loans) for rent and necessary purchases, often at seasons when their income was depressed, and when their labour was still paid for largely in kind or through minute land grants. Often the gap between producer and wholesaler also reflected an asymmetry in access to information. The prices paid to producers were depressed, in short, through concentrations and distortions of purchasing power, when production, by contrast, was dispersed or fragmented.

Landlords often owned local market-places, and controlled them through their contractors or agents. Most producers gave up their surplus to landlords, village heads or moneylenders, and did not take it to market themselves. Landlords, rich peasants, travelling merchants and rural moneylenders commonly collected produce in repayment for loans they had previously advanced. Having secured crops below market price, they then managed its transportation from producer to consumer. Carts became much more numerous as roads and trade expanded, but generally the rise was somewhat less than proportionate, even to the population increase. There was no improvement in the independent access of many cultivators to the market. Moreover, the profits of cartmen were small, and, though even poor cultivators needed carts, they could not afford them unless they hired them out to traders after the harvests.

Europeans in particular had sought to depress prices from the days of the East India Company by monopoly buying, and by acting in collusion with the locally powerful. International buyers commonly used local agents, benefiting from their broad social and economic control over the producers. Throughout the nineteenth century opium prices, for example, continued to be fixed in advance by the state. Indigo planters controlled villagers in order to prevent their selling to competitors, or growing more profitable crops. Jute producers faced the purchasing power of the jute manufacturers' cartel. Of course the cartels did not work absolutely, and some cultivators (including some of those increasing the acreage under jute and cotton) were directly responding to price incentives. But large proportions, especially in the most depressed areas, were left with very little choice. Then production rose not to benefit producers but because those who controlled the market willed it.

PURCHASING POWER

New demand by Indians was one of the important reasons why commercial production and the export trade increased. That new demand, however, helps confirm the disparities of wealth, and the differential access to markets, as also to processing and the resources of production. It is true that even in quite remote areas high proportions of the population became buyers of some of the new commodities. Sometimes this was because they were cheaper, as with some manufactured clothing, but in most cases it was for want of, rather than extra, choice. Manufactured imports challenged much artisanal production, forcing even (sometimes particularly) the poor to buy products which could only be obtained by money. This increased the vulnerability of the cash-poor.

In the Indian countryside under colonial rule there were clearly large increases in purchasing power for commodities and precious metals. (India remained the world's greatest importer of gold.) But the purchasing capacity was unevenly enjoyed. There was, for example, a considerable increase in brick and masonry houses in many rural areas, suggesting an increase or diversion of disposable income, as well as a readier supply of bricks and other materials. But estimates from 1900 in one Indian district (Gaya in Bihar) give an indication of who would have been able to build such dwellings.

A substantial brick or stone house was thought to cost about Rs25 per 100 cubic feet – say, Rs2250 for a modest bungalow. This was at least six times as much as a house of similar size with mud walls and straw thatching. Brick housing therefore represented a substantial increase in expenditure. Most people still lived in huts and not substantial houses. We see why when we find that the net profit retained by the cultivator in this same tract was thought to average about Rs3.5 per acre per annum, counting two harvests. Similar estimates were given for neighbouring districts. Another indicator of relative economic resources in Gaya is that land was being valued at around twenty times the land revenue, which then represented about 30 per cent of gross rents; Rs160 an acre was the average paid for land acquired for railway construction in this area.

These statistics were disputed at the time and are certainly not wholly reliable; yet they *were* based on actual enquiry. They allow a plausible guess at the available income of ordinary cultivators, those with holdings below 5 acres. Such people might be forced to buy manufactured cloth, or able to acquire utensils and implements produced beyond their villages; but they did not benefit from or understand the market in the manner of the owner of a brick house. In some areas, such as the cotton-rich tracts of western and central India, for example Satara district, a broad band of cultivators *was* able to acquire brick houses. But even these places were not free from economic stratification. In much poorer areas the spread of more substantial buildings must be interpreted as an indication not of general prosperity but of growing disparities of wealth, and probably of a diversion of investment from people (followers and workers) towards property and commodities. Different degrees and terms of access to markets help explain these disparities.

This same argument may be applied to other aspects of consumption and investment. For example, improved sugar mills, an expensive item, were taken up with startling rapidity in north India from the 1870s, but were mainly acquired by substantial cultivators or sugar factors. They decreased the likelihood of ordinary cultivators being able to compete in sugar processing, and increased their dependence on intermediaries. These arguments also imply changes in the livelihood of local artisans and workers. Increased numbers of carts, bullocks, wells, improved ploughs, and items of processing equipment, thus reveal very varied access to the market in the context of widening disparities of wealth. Given existing differences of opportunity, it seems that greater political security, growing trade and advanced technology tended to exaggerate rather than even-out the gaps between the haves and the have-nots. Whether the total economy was expanding or contracting (and therefore in relatively poorer as well as richer areas), those with greater resources captured new opportunities, and often were better able to resist new disadvantages.

DIFFERENTIATION

How do we know socio-economic inequalities increased markedly under colonial rule and beyond it? Indian society was already strongly differentiated at the start of British rule, though to greater or lesser degrees in different regions. In many places 'Untouchables', usually lowly workers, occupied separate settlements in primitive conditions, and were denied access to common resources and services. Landlessness, poverty and disadvantage were not invented by colonialism. And some evidence suggests that occupational distribution did not change very greatly over the two hundred years before Indian independence in 1947.

To provide indicators that inequalities increased, we will return to landholding and to two case studies, one in western India and one in Punjab. Here we can see in more detail the availability of land, which of course, as already discussed, was vital to well-being, along with other factors such as health, family size and age; the political conditions of labour and marketing; and access to capital, work animals, agricultural implements and water.

Two villages in western India were surveyed about the time of the First World War and again after the Second World War. The data showed the landholding patterns and estimated changes which occurred between 1771 and 1947. The figures in Table 1 suggest that, in the first village, the number of holdings had greatly increased, but their average area had declined sharply over the nineteenth century, though there were only minor changes in landholding in the first half of the twentieth. The second village followed a similar pattern, except for the larger holdings, which helps explain this village's apparently smaller drop in the average size of holding. Another reason is that the first village was close to a city – we know that by 1952 more than half its population had non-agricultural incomes. It is often claimed that the proportion of landless labourers in the Indian population remained fairly constant; but the evidence

Table 1 Landholdings in two Indian villages

Area (acres)	Pimple Saudagar village				Jategaon Budruk village		
Year:	1771	1817	1914/15	1947/8	1790	1817	1917
More than 100	–	–	–	–	1	6	2
20 to 100	23	–	11	12	30	22	31
10 to 20	–	–	18	18	3		43
5 to 10	1	–	34	33	–	8	34
1 to 5	–	–	71	78	–		25
below 1	–	–	22	35	–	–	11
Average in acres	43	21	7	6	43	56	16
Number (holdings)	24	48	156	176	34	36	146

Source: Adapted from Dharma Kumar, ed., *Cambridge Economic History of India*, vol. II (Cambridge 1983), p. 201.

from these villages suggests that many more families, having tiny pockets of land, were becoming effectively landless. These data are not conclusive, especially for the earlier period, but they do reinforce what was impressionistically observed in many parts of India: that the majority of holdings multiplied and became smaller on average – too small to sustain a family in many cases – but that certain, larger holdings were less susceptible to fragmentation. We should note for further consideration the particular expansion in the number of holdings of *middling* size.

Similar evidence may be found for areas which apparently benefited from commercial agriculture and for those which were least dynamic. We therefore have to show that both benefits and losses were unevenly shared in the Indian villages. Profits from cash cropping were substantial, but in some areas returns to the cultivators were kept artifically low. This was the case with much opium and indigo production in north India, where local agents and intermediaries gained wealth while cultivators remained poor. But in parts of western and central India, for example, where the cotton acreage grew by just under 100 per cent in the 1860s, much of the increase was apparently voluntary, a response to the fact that the cotton price had leapt by 132 per cent. Moreover, by the 1920s if not before, there were organized markets in raw cotton which, in several districts, were apparently capable of delivering profits to the producers. Benefits seem to have been quite widely enjoyed, and yet, in these same areas, increasing land sales affected some 10 per cent of the cultivated area, and, with informal transfers, swelled the holdings of larger cultivators.

To take another example, it has been shown that jute cultivation produced healthy surpluses for the countryside in east and north Bengal, as well as profits for jute manufacturers, at least until the 1920s. In and around Calcutta, the industry grew from 1854 when there was one mill and a handful of employees, until, in 1914, there were 64 mills employing nearly a quarter of a million people. The jute was grown in conjunction with rice: the two produced estimated annual profits of between Rs20 and Rs40 per acre between 1900 and 1914. It was generally thought that this was an area without very marked disparities of wealth among the cultivators, one with some 80 per cent of the land in the hands of 'occupancy' tenants with security of tenure. Yet by the 1930s, in this area as elsewhere in Bengal, detailed surveys found that as much as 30 per cent of the land was being worked by share-croppers (a scale previously unsuspected by the government). Share-croppers paid rents at rates on average some 90 per cent above those for occupancy tenants; 40 per cent of them were drawn from the lower castes. And below them of course were to be found landless labourers and the poorer artisans.

A study of a village in the Punjab between 1848 and 1968 provides some further statistics which can help to identify the changes in stratification over the colonial period. The village was a compact settlement dominated and inhabited mainly by a clan of Jats, an important social and political group, within which land and other rights were not entirely egalitarian but allocated according to an accepted pattern of shares. The village also contained tenants and agricultural labourers representing a little under 20 per cent of the population, while in a somewhat detached quarter nearby lived lowly artisans and workers, many of whom had a client–patron relationship with cultivating families. Most normal agricultural tasks were none the less carried out by family labour. In the pattern of landholding in this case we are able to distinguish between *owner's holdings* (the legal properties) and *cultivating units* or farms (Table 2). This is important because the two were seldom identical; indeed units of legal ownership commonly differed from units of both management and production. In other words, many families managed or farmed, as one operation, both lands they owned and lands belonging to others. They might also let out some of their own lands at the same time as renting a neighbour's fields, in order to produce consolidated areas for cultivation.

Table 2   Landholding in a Punjab village, I

			1848			
	Own holdings			Cultivating units		
Area*	A	B	C	A	B	C
20+	6	15	36	4	7	20
10–20	21	51	54	25	41	61
5–10	4	10	5	12	20	14
2–5	7	17	4	8	13	5
0–2	3	7	0	12	20	1

			1934			
	Own holdings			Cultivating units		
Area*	A	B	C	A	B	C
20+	2	2	13	1	1	6
10–20	7	6	17	12	10	30
5–10	32	29	41	30	24	42
2–5	36	33	23	23	19	15
0–2	33	30	6	60	47	6

			1968			
	Own holdings			Cultivating units		
Area*	A	B	C	A	B	C
20+	0	0	0	1	1	5
10–20	4	2	13	14	14	38
5–10	27	20	40	22	17	33
2–5	51	34	36	21	17	15
0–2	64	44	12	69	54	9

Note: The table shows owners' holdings and cultivating units:
A = number;
B = percentage of the total;
C = percentage, cultivated area.
*Areas are in acres.
Source: Adapted from T. G. Kessinger, *Vilyatpur 1848–1968*
(Berkeley, 1974), pp. 63, 114–16.

The figures show a marked decline over the nineteenth century in the number, proportion and area covered, for the larger owners' holdings, and also for the larger cultivating units (though to a somewhat lesser degree). The very smallest holdings of both owner-ship and cultivation increased greatly in number and percentage of the total, especially in the first hundred years, though they continued to occupy an insignificant proportion of the area. The small to middle-sized owners' holdings (between 2 and 10 acres) increased most remarkably, their number keeping pace with the proportion of the area they occupied – from 11 taking up 9 per cent of the area, rising to 68 with 64 per cent, and then to 78 with 76 per cent. Cultivating units of this order performed similarly, though appar-ently they fell away from their highest level in the last years – 20 with 19 per cent, rising to 53 with 67 per cent, and then falling to 43 with 48 per cent. Within this group the holdings between 5 and 10 acres were most important in the colonial period, and a propor-tion of them appeared to consolidate their position after 1934, when weaker and smaller holdings continued to fragment.

We can present the data in different ways to show quite clearly what was happening in the village (Table 3). In 1968 there were many fewer owners' holdings larger than 10 acres than there had been in 1848. There had also been a decrease in the number of large cultivation units, but it was much less sharp. The largest proportionate increase was in the number of very small units, but again the change was smaller in cultivation units than in owners' holdings. All kinds and sizes of units of land were not becoming subdivided at similar rates. Rather, middle-sized owners' holdings and, particularly, surplus cultivating units were gaining in number and in the proportion of the cultivated area that they occupied.

In this Punjab village, some measures would seem to imply a gen-eral increase in prosperity, while others suggest that there had been a progressive impoverishment. The population grew in the nine-teenth century, and then declined for forty years until 1931, before climbing again more rapidly than before. The cultivated land per capita declined from 0.95 acres in 1848 to 0.75 acres in 1931 and 0.36 acres in 1968. As a result a majority of the cultivating units were very small (below 5 acres) from the late nineteenth century. On the other hand, the village, like many parts of this region, benefited from public investment in roads, railways and canals, and from military expenditure. It took up new higher-yielding strains of local staples, and of export crops such as cotton and wheat. It gained information

Table 3 Landholding in a Punjab village, II

A. Owners' holdings

Area in acres	Number				% of cult. area			% area per holding		
	1848	1934	1968	% change	1848	1934	1968	1848	1934	1968
10–20	25	39	31	+ 25	59	58	53	2.36	1.48	1.71
5–10	4	32	27	+ 575	5	41	40	1.25	1.28	1.48
2–5	10	69	75	+ 650	4	29	48	0.40	0.42	0.64

B. Cultivating units

Area in acres	Number				% of cult. area			% area per holding		
	1848	1934	1968	% change	1848	1934	1968	1848	1934	1968
10–20	37	42	31	– 16	75	72	71	2.03	1.71	2.29
5–10	12	30	22	+ 83	14	42	33	1.14	1.40	1.50
2–5	20	83	90	+ 350	6	21	24	0.30	0.25	0.26

Source: See Table 2 above.

through participation in travel, migration, marketing and education. Price rises improved returns to its agriculture for much of the nineteenth and early twentieth centuries, and marked improvements in its productivity were apparent from the 1930s and especially the 1960s.

The contradictions unravel if we abandon broad generalizations. Even in 1968 more than 75 per cent of the land was cultivated in units above 5 acres, the smallest area likely to produce a surplus. It was those cultivating such units who had new opportunities for profit. Their hand can be discerned too in the evidence of considerable investment. The village had 54 wells by 1968 (13 of them mechanized tube-wells), 73 carts and 62 sugarcane presses. It had had 30 wells, 7 carts and 3 presses in 1848. Only 31 per cent of the land had been double-cropped in 1848, but 49 per cent was double-cropped in 1935–9, and 71 per cent in 1965–8. The conclusion must be that a section of the population was able to hold on to the lion's share of the land in units of a viable size, and to invest in agriculture. Another large section, however, either had never had land, or ended up with far too little land to farm profitably. The disparities of wealth in the village had increased.

The pattern is similar to those we have seen elsewhere. The weakest sections of the community lost land or were confined to microholdings which were too small to support a family, and might well be let out to larger cultivators to add to their lands. The very largest owners' holdings and cultivating units either maintained their position or lost ground (as here), depending on the conditions of agriculture and social and legal status. The story is not repeated in *exactly* the same way everywhere. In India there is a variety year on year, and from place to place. In this case the group that was prospering relative to others was quite large. In some other places it was quite small. In the Punjab the village elite depended mainly on agricultural skills; in other regions the beneficiaries were those who relied on non-agricultural incomes or on an ability to manage and corner the production of others. But in each locality the people best equipped to take advantage of opportunities in agriculture gained at the expense of the remainder.

FOOD AND HEALTH

Life expectancy rose in India under colonial rule. But patterns of morbidity and mortality in these periods of demographic growth imply that many people suffered undue malnutrition and disease. In colonial India (excluding Burma), the total population according to the census (fairly reliable between 1881 and 1921 at least) was, in millions, 250.2 in 1881; 279.6 in 1891; 283.9 in 1901; 303 in 1911 and 305.7 in 1921. Earlier totals are speculative, but all estimates assume that there was an increase between the early and late nineteenth century. The implied average rate of increase was 0.6 per cent per annum over the period from 1871 to 1941. The earlier part of this period was severely affected by famine and epidemics, which caused large temporary drops in numbers, perhaps especially in women of childbearing age – though in fact population and birth rates seem to have recovered remarkably quickly. The bulk of the increase was concentrated after 1921. There are significant variations between decades and also between regions, producing average annual rates of change varying from minus 1.04 (central zone, 1891–1901) to plus 1.68 (east zone, 1931–41). Not all of these are statistical anomalies. The age and sex distributions have also changed over time. The dependency ratio (persons 0–14 and over 60) was highest (83.6) in the east zone in 1881 and lowest (70.4) in the central zone in 1901, but declined somewhat unevenly on average from 79.1 in 1881 to 75.1 in 1941. There were 5.3 per cent of persons over 60 in 1881, and 4.4 per cent in 1941.

The death-rate and infant mortality figures are rendered problematic by inadequacies of registration. But those data also show marked changes. The indications for the early nineteenth century suggest the possibility of infant mortality rates above 25 per cent, and rates above 50 per cent for children under ten. From records kept by the East India Company it has been deduced that at age 20 life expectancy for males may have averaged a further 24.5 years, and that average life expectancy at birth may have been only 18 years. The infant mortality rate was 204.2 per thousand in 1911, and 161 in 1941; the corresponding death rates were 30.2 and 22.5. Life expectancy at birth increased from 25.1 years in 1881 to 32.1 in 1941. Some estimates reduce the steepness of these changes but all agree as to their trend.

The increase of Indian population was delayed by epidemics and famines which may reflect the failures of government, communications and production, in a period of transition. At an early and at later stages the population increase was mainly urban. It may none the less have been related to increased security of property and person, and to increased rural investment and output, under conditions which deliberately favoured settled and market-oriented rural production. In the majority of cases across the world, population grew in the wake of significant increases in agricultural production. But if population was steady or growing, despite famine and epidemics and consequentially high death rates, it must imply that birth rates were exceptionally high.

India's population was seen as a problem – and in itself a cause of ill-health and death – from at least the later nineteenth century. In India, as in Western countries, as we have noted, the British also recognized that the health and nutrition of the poorer classes were important issues, and a test of good government. Famine commissions and other inquiries investigated these problems. There were debates about whether or not the food supply of India was sufficient overall. In the twentieth century, experiments sought to measure the food value of the different diets prevailing in India. They concluded that perceived differences in physique derived largely from difference in food intake. It was found too that the prevalence and severity of many diseases in India could be attributed in part to deficiencies of nourishment, especially in rural areas. In the early 1930s an inquiry was conducted into health and diet in 571 villages across India, representing a population of nearly three-quarters of a million. The survey concluded that only 39 per cent of the population were well nourished, and that 20 per cent were very poorly nourished. Significant proportions were affected by diet-related diseases (rickets, 6.6 per cent; night-blindness, 10.4; tuberculosis, 4.4; and so on). The infant mortality rate was 232 per 1000 live births against a national estimate of 160, and maternal mortality 24.5 per 1000 births.

The argument is not necessarily that on average people ate poorer grains than before – in successful irrigated or cash-cropping areas, the evidence is that many were able to change to foods of higher status. The argument is about different outcomes for rich and poor. Poverty and famine conditions often forced the poorest sections to eat fodder crops and wild products, and even in extreme cases to consume what was thought to be poisonous if taken in quantity. In 'normal' times too very many farmers and labourers ate coarser grains – millets, Indian maize or poorer strains of rice – while selling their wheat or superior paddy.

Similar discrimination was shown by disease. The best example is malaria. In most parts of the country 'fever', including malaria, was the largest single cause of mortality, except during epidemics of other diseases. In British India, it was the cause, for example, of nearly 60 per cent of deaths in the period 1929–35. It was seasonal, peaking in the autumn after the hot-weather monsoon rains. It was particularly high during and after famine periods, whenever heavy rains ended a period of drought. Medical opinion at the time was that both diagnoses and record-keeping were very defective, and that less than half of the 'fever' deaths were actually from malaria.

Even so, the consensus is that the incidence of malaria increased from the eighteenth to the twentieth centuries. Regions of India (for example the moister areas of western and central India, and parts of the Bengal delta) had long been malarious, and some such tracts had been abandoned by cultivators before the start of colonial rule. Population increase, land-revenue demands, the constriction of waste and revenue-free lands, and pressure from commercial cropping, all forced cultivation increasingly back on to these marginal and malarious tracts. Also, during the nineteenth century, several areas once thought healthy became subject to endemic malaria. As was recognized as early as the 1840s (long before the identification of the vector, the anopheline mosquito, at the end of the nineteenth century), the building of road and railway embankments, and the spread of canal irrigation, greatly increased the incidence of malaria. Finally, paradoxically, the disease was associated with population growth, even though it affected pregnant women and young children disproportionately. One reason may have been that as population grew and migrated, the numbers of infected humans increased and spread. Thus endemic malaria, which debilitated whole populations, probably had a more serious long-term effect than epidemics, in which large numbers died at one time.

The poor were always more vulnerable but shortcomings of official policy made the discrepancy worse. The colonial government took measures to improve drainage and reduce waterlogging, but could not prevent the spread of the disease. For malaria, as more generally, measures to improve the health of the Indian population started early but were thinly and unevenly spread. To try to deal with malaria in the late nineteenth century, the government sought to encourage the people to use quinine, recognized for its prophylactic qualities by the British in India for over a hundred years. However, an experiment to distribute quinine through the post offices was a failure and was not pursued. In the 1930s a government malaria institute was set up, with a budget of £15 000 per annum.

More generally, public health policies offered too little too late. The first public hospital had been operating in Calcutta by the 1790s, and even as early as 1664 medical treatment, particularly for 'fever', had been available to East India Company servants (mainly but not exclusively for Europeans). Vaccination for smallpox was introduced energetically in the early nineteenth century, and sanitation was a concern in towns much earlier. But by 1840, in addition to what was provided in Calcutta, Bombay and Madras, there were hospitals for Indians in only about a dozen towns. Not until 1880 was public health given much official recognition as an important function of government. Public health provision remained concentrated in the towns; and only 128 of the 247 districts of British India and Burma had appointed medical officers of health in the early twentieth century. In 1935 only a million in-patients and 65 million out-patients were treated in the 6700 hospitals and dispensaries of British India, as against a total population recorded at 338 million in the 1931 census.

The Calcutta Medical College was founded in 1835, and by the early twentieth century there were ten medical colleges and 28 medical schools, with about 12 000 students in 1935. Much important medical research was done in nineteenth-century India, including Sir Ronald Ross's identification of the malaria vector in 1898. But the government did not organize research centrally until 1911; and even in the 1930s state medical services employed somewhat under 10 000 qualified people. In general terms the prevailing view was that little could be achieved by the unaided efforts of the state: 'The first step', wrote Sir John Megaw, one-time Director-General of the Indian Medical Service, 'must be to arouse in the minds of the people a desire for better conditions of life'.[2] In other words the Indians were somehow to blame for their own illnesses.

COLONIAL LEGACIES

In general terms, during the colonial era, there was a move towards more demanding crops, greater competition for land, and the cultivation of more marginal areas. There was an increase in settled as opposed to occasional cultivation, and, initially, in settled as opposed to casual or part-time cultivators. There was an increase in irrigation, both collective (public and private canal schemes) and individual (simple or artesian wells). There was some increase in the range or cost of other inputs of production. There were more roads, more selling of produce, and hence more carts, and, later, motor vehicles. There was more intervention by external forces of law and government to regulate the ownership of property (land and other means of production, and produce) by individuals. There was a decline in collective modes of production. There was greater consumption of imported goods, both manufactures and food. Money became the main measure of wealth.

These technological and other advances improved agricultural profitability but their costs widened the gap between those who did and those who did not have access to capital and information. There were medium-term consequences for economic development. Cultivators were likely to wish to improve the productivity of land or labour only if they were able to keep the profits. Once subjected by intermediaries, they lost control of their surplus, and also became less likely to have access to capital, or to be knowledgeable about markets, new crops or improved technologies. Such conditions diminished choice, as did environmental degradation or a declining man:land ratio. In turn, the controlling landlord, merchant or moneylender often found it easier to increase production not by intensification (increasing output per capita and per acre) but by extension, involving more cultivators or increasing acreages at the same level of output. Capital invested in improving productivity would probably not have produced such a good return. Except at times of peak demand, such as harvests, when more competitive pay sometimes prevailed, labour was provided by family members who had to be supported whether or not they worked, or by share-croppers and farm labourers paid at low rates, in kind, or in land. Overall too, the rise of population from the early nineteenth century necessitated additional production, but also reduced the extent to which per capita output mattered to employers. Had competition from industrial and other wages produced labour shortages (and wealthier local markets for agricultural produce), then it might have been worthwhile to invest in labour saving. As it was, there was no significant competition, and (on the whole) neither intolerable popular protest nor effective state intervention. Low social status and relative lack of political clout denied agricultural labour a voice over much of the colonial period. Either it was household-based, under patriarchal control, or it was kept under tight socio-political command. This involved unavoidable costs of recruitment, supervision and coercion, but often in other ways labour was 'cheap', having little or no direct cost in money terms. Thus, a rising population merely reduced the importance of labour's well-being to employers and managers, and productivity increased less than it otherwise might have done, considering the worldwide expansion of demand.

The demand for labour increased in the colonial era, with the expansion of agriculture, the development of the infrastructure, and the growth of cities. But the choices and bargaining power of labour were reduced, and labour's dependence upon employers was increased. It is a paradox that slavery was formally abolished in colonial territories, but that the dependence and oppression of labour often intensified. Agricultural production expanded because of profits and new consumption, but also because of harsh conditions for labour. Some workers undoubtedly benefited from greater and wider mobility, increasing demand, higher profits for employers, remittances from family members in towns and factories, labour organization, state regulation, and so on. But many of the changes were negative, and made workers more vulnerable.

Alternative jobs were relatively few in the industrial and service sectors, at the same time as demand for agricultural produce increased. Labour was attracted into agriculture (as later into bondage) for want of alternatives. There was a general movement towards regular and specialized work, individual contracts, casual employment, and money wages at competitive rates. New disciplines of labour and coercive law permitted an increasing workload, alongside restrictions of rates of pay according to task, and under-payment especially through control exercised by intermediaries. Population grew and some opportunities were lost in the countryside for work and subsistence. A lack of education, land and other resources became ever more serious. Wage labour tended to imply casualization and seasonal employment – and there were often reductions in the proportion of each year during which employment was available, and reductions too caused by famine, drought and economic depression. Some workers were at greater risk because of disease, isolation from family support systems, or gender imbalance.

Indian famine conditions showed up the vulnerability of such labourers, and illustrate the problems which arose for them to some degree in any agrarian distress or downturn. When drought struck, there might be a limited increase in the demand for labour to assist irrigation. But, as hope died because the crops had shrivelled or the ground was too hard to plough, and as employers tried to rely

entirely on family labour, there would be less and less work for
more and more available workers. It has been shown that this tendency did not apply in the canal-irrigated areas of north India, which
attracted labour from surrounding districts in times of drought.
But even irrigated areas were at risk from a depression of agricultural
prices. It is interesting too that an impoverished and dependent
labour force continued to be characteristic of Indian canal-irrigated
areas, such as in Gujarat, or even in the Punjab canal colonies
where a planned pattern of new settlement had been designed to
favour peasant proprietors.

The relationship between the rate of population increase and the
rate of economic growth holds the key to improving or declining
standards of living. How this relationship was structured depended
upon – still depends on – the policies of governments and the terms
of economic exchanges. In so far as the profits of increased production stayed within the local community, then local people would
benefit. In so far as profits reached the farmers and workers
involved in the production, processing and marketing, then they
too would gain. But if the wealth was extracted from producers, or
altogether from the local economy, then local people would see
little material improvement.

The first economic plans of independent India – devised by the
Planning Commission, vital to Nehru's development strategy – built
on the assumptions of colonial policy and on then-current economic dogma. The emphasis was placed upon 'basic' industry –
meaning coal and steel, machine-making, electricity and chemicals.
The priority was defined by theory, prestige and military strategy
rather than an empirical analysis of what was best suited to India's
immediate needs and opportunities. Such industry was generally
capital- rather than labour-intensive. It was supported by a high
degree of regulation, and by bureaucratic and fiscal protection.
Output increased markedly, but employment did not keep pace
with needs; labour-intensive secondary industries did not grow
sufficiently, as hoped, in tandem with the state-backed enterprises.
Agriculture was cited in the plans (but not really treated) as an
equal priority. Land reforms were halfhearted; and rural underemployment increased. Some regions benefited more than others from
technological innovations such as tube-wells, tractors, chemical
fertilizers, and high-yielding crops. India achieved agricultural
growth, and a somewhat fragile self-sufficiency in food, subject to
a very high incidence of undernourishment. Agricultural exports

continued, especially in plantation crops such as tea, but food exports came under suspicion (as in anti-colonial rhetoric) in a context of general poverty. Little was done to build the all-important internal market for manufactured or agricultural produce, for example by providing secure incomes to ordinary farm-workers rather than intermediaries, or by achieving adequately paid and efficient employment for the masses flocking into the towns.

10

Epilogue: After Modernity?

CASTE, COMMUNITY AND NATION

This book has examined the evolution of caste, community and nation in India. Societies evolve by interactions between ideas, economy and power, and in particular (as Habermas would have it)[1] by transformations in the nature of and relations between state and society, public and private. But social relations existed in particular forms in India. It follows that there were Indian norms of civil society – meaning organized public association which could be distinguished from the institutions of the state or those of private life, production and exchange. 'Public sphere' (if the term is to be of general use) may be defined *variously* with regard to the character of the location between households or localities and the state. It may express ascribed (inherited) and actual connections between individuals rather than elective and notional ones. It may be subjective, personal and direct rather than objective and bureaucratic. Its means may be ritualistic and mythological, rather than material and technological (printing, records, formal meetings, and so on). In short, the private and the public, and indeed state and society, may all mean different things.

Similarly, in general, we distinguish firstly between compulsory and elective communities: the former those determined by birth, location or authority, and the latter those which people join. Secondly we distinguish between mixed and homogeneous communities: those made up of varied people who, say, visit a shrine, inhabit a place or depend on a lord or official, and those whose members are defined by their sharing a faith, political aim or economic role. However, actual allegiances often operate in between these four categories. For example, a festival may serve adherents of one or of several religions, and a village or an army contain either one or several cultural and political identities. Degrees of heterogeneity will also differ according to the point from which groups are observed.

On the other hand, the dichotomies are all variants on the familiar distinctions between societies based around status and societies based around contract, or between micro- and macro-politics and economics, or between *Gemeinschaft* and *Gesellschaft*. India moved, erratically, along that line from a very early period. In colonial times, aspects of the bourgeois European transformations were exported to India on the assumption that they were universal (both before and during the later nineteeenth-century rise of racist, evolutionary and relativist thinking). Ideas of subjectivity and individuality entered the law codes and ethical calculus; social criticism, forms of rationality and empiricism provided a basis of vigorous literary and intellectual debates among Indians as well as Europeans. These erupted in print, public associations and educational institutions, in regard to history, tradition, language, science, politics and economics. In Indian towns a new public of letters and association developed, distinct from the intelligentsia and service elites of Mughal times, though (like them) made possible by the development of markets in labour and commodities, and the emergence of knowledge-based professions. This public was dominated by the yardsticks established in the West, even while it mounted a defence of the East. So Vedic texts were authoritative and even monotheistic; *jati* became 'nation'; India became spiritual, vegetarian and abstaining; ayurvedic medicine was re-established as 'scientific'; yoga gained popularity as health therapy rather than spiritual exercise; and so on.

The usual assumption is that secular nationalism similarly grew (on the model set in the West) within the orbit of 'modern' economic and political institutions, and so as to supersede other forms of identity that related to other 'older' forms of institution, chiefly cultures centred upon religion, or hierarchical societies focused on hereditary dynasties. In India there was a secular (and sometime Protestant) ideology of the nation which matched the development of interest- and even class-based political parties and representative government, and before that of individual legal rights, private property, capitalist enterprise, printing and state-regulated education. The particular recent forms of these ideologies and technologies were undoubtedly imported, in the main because of British colonial rule.

Westernization in these senses was hegemonic, in the century after about 1870, in that it shaped public institutions and practices, from caste to Constitution, from media to medicine. Indians experienced many of the influences identified by scholars (such as Ernest Gellner or Benedict Anderson) as leading towards 'modern' views of identity, and to demands, by *citizens*, for representative institutions and legal rights. Where ideas took new forms, as with the 'nation' or self-determination or rights for women and children, many Indians were quickly converted. Most people were willing to make adjustments, once they could see an advantage – as when Hindus, having at first complained they would lose caste if they had to swear an oath in a court of law, soon became leading exponents and ready if selective clients of a 'foreign' legal system. In certain senses at least, India *is*, as commentators delight in saying, the world's largest democracy.

Still, the story does not altogether fit in the Indian case. We cannot lump together each and every kind of Indian intermediary body, or every organization from *sadhus* and *pirs* (Hindu and Muslim holy men) to dacoits (armed bandits). A new political sphere certainly interpreted and mediated between the 'Western' colonial state and the 'Eastern' subject population; but it was also curiously detached from both. In practice, all societies contain ambiguities and contradictions. India's institutions are especially mixed. It experienced the generalizing tendencies in its own versions.

The 'caste association', for example, became a characteristic institution of the later nineteenth century, combining attributes of sect, friendly society and pressure group. A caste association was a closed and ascriptive body organized for both public and private purposes. It was based around a category ('caste') that seemed to be a given. In fact, it had to be created or redefined, implying choices and leadership, and the use of rules, bureaucracy, publicity and technology to produce cohesion. A caste association might be considered part of a new Indian civil society, as it organized social groups to battle for their economic and political interests. The same must be said for religious societies, or temple and mosque committees, though they were ostensibly based on largely inherited religious affiliation. The Indian Muslims represent another example of people combining on the basis of religion but in a 'modern' way. Most groups aspiring to political recognition employed a quasi-'secular' vocabulary with its supposedly objective categories and universal goals, but their claims were often based upon religious or sectarian differences.

Equally, Indian political parties, peasant movements, trade unions, professional associations and clubs, which are part of civil society on any Eurocentric definition, were often to some degree also communities of caste or faith. Superficially modern, they had religious or caste affiliations at their core. Certainly there were very substantial developments in the number and type of public associations over the last two hundred years. But the secular nationalist ideal was never the only or even the main mode of identity in India. The most important point here may be the dissonance between the growth of colonial and national *political* institutions and expectations (the state), and the development of countervailing *social and representative* associations, or civil society.

One reason for the persistence of an 'Indian way' was the vigour of ideas and practices that contested the Western hegemony. Obviously, a major part was played by indignant rejections of racist stereotypes and the political, economic and intellectual domineering of the West. Self-assertion – a revaluation and revitalizing of 'India' – was essential for self-respect. But, also, it is important to note the long vitality of Indian forms of civil organization that had a public as well as a caste-like face, from ancient or mediaeval times, such as scribal, scholarly and merchant communities, or socio-religious and devotional sects (*bhakti*, Sufism, Sikhism and so on). Many 'modern' practices had long existed in India, and did not suddenly appear under colonial rule while nationalist claims were being promoted. Indian peoples had had long experience too of some ideas which form part of the secular ideal, for example notions of the responsibilities of rulers, of charity to the oppressed, and of freedom of conscience – for India's history does not really match the dichotomy proposed by the political philosopher, Michael Oakeshott, between states of 'civil' or of 'enterprise association'. Indian states were 'civil' in upholding ancient law for its own sake, even in colonial times, but they also had 'enterprise', with agenda of improvement and protection, embedded in some degree of market economy. Ashoka's boast that his moderate policies had *created* better conduct among his people was merely the first of many such state aspirations. State-sponsored economic development too was not invented in modern times. Though of course states did diverge in energy and influence, their more fundamental differences were rather in the area of means and technologies than of objectives.

These points refer yet again to the persistence of civilizational unities, but taken as a whole they also reinforce the caution expressed at the start of this book about ahistorical essentializing. Secular values were reinvented for conditions outside those in which they were first applied, and modern institutions were often modified to meet Indian expectations. All those defining their identities chose appropriate aspects of their inheritance at different times. What this implies is not a free choice of labels and customs, but one constrained by 'tradition' on the one hand, and by self-interest or present utility on the other.

A HINDU INDIA?

India was strongly affected by religious or quasi-theological allegiances, to caste and community. Does that make India 'Hindu'? Faced with a recent growth in the political importance of religion, some recent scholars have argued that religious identities are an *alternative* to secular nationalism. Hence what developed in European conditions was inappropriate to India. They claim that Western-dominated historiography has exaggerated the universality of Western experience. The latter is true, but two main problems about applying the substantive conclusion to India today have already been set out in the preceding discussion, and in this book as a whole.

Firstly, as said, where the state has promoted institutions and laws which depend on secular values, these built on long experience of the secular ideal and of social and political ethics. Even in 'Islamic' Pakistan and Bangladesh, these have been internalized by important sections of the people (especially lawyers and liberal intellectuals). Indians have had particular reason to endorse certain of the secular values – especially those relating to the rule of law and individual rights – because they were and still are vital in a plural society, and would be, even if they *were* 'inappropriate'. Secondly, as also remarked, many foes of 'colonial' and 'foreign' impositions continue unwittingly to employ indigenized versions of what they profess to reject. Even the opponents of plurality apply the notions which define it, of categorization, identity, nation and rights.

One reason for the present situation is the state's past ambivalence. After all, despite what has just been said, secular values were quite weakly advanced both by the colonial state and in independent India. In practice the state offered religious neutrality and mutual toleration. The British, for all the heated rhetoric of some missionaries, soldiers and officials, mostly took great care to avoid attacking religious sentiment. Often they gave succour to religion, respecting Brahman dietary arrangements, or giving semi-clandestine support to mosques and temples, or promoting the political identities and interests of castes and religions. The 'secular' political parties of India themselves used religious symbols and categories to garner support, in colonial times and still more since independence – not only Gandhi as Congress supremo and Jinnah as Muslim separatist leader, but even that patrician social democrat, Jawaharlal Nehru. In his *Discovery of India* (1946), despite his English education and his modernist and internationalist sympathies, Nehru struggled with sentimental images of blood-line, landscape and nurture to express his feelings for India, its history and people. In other words, the religious emphasis of modern Indian politics has proximate not primordial causes.

We see all this as a problem only if we are using false analogies and dichotomies, between Western-modern-secular and Indian-traditional-religious, in order to construct a false history in which the modern ousts the traditional, the secular supersedes the religious, and the Western is incompatible with the Indian. The burden of this discussion has been to show that there are historical tendencies, but that they do not go from one essentialized condition to another. No society is wholly defined by values of one 'type' or another, any more than history is an inevitable progress from one kind of identity to another. As we notice the great centralizations and standardizations, due to changes in politics, technology and economy, we should not equate them with, say, *becoming* Western rather than Indian, or secular rather than religious. We may label some practices and ideas as 'modern', for convenience since similarities and distinctions do exist, but should not suppose that 'modernity' wholly permeates any society, or that it has exactly the same meaning in every case. There are differences of scale and of means and of category, but in India as elsewhere this cannot mean, for example, that the religious is not political, or the political never religious.

Some political developments since the 1970s – in particular the politics of the Hindu right, and a certain coalescence of view even among its opponents – were thus premised on a division that is largely artificial and ahistorical. It obscures the responsive, adaptive nature of the substantive changes this book examined – the coming of modern forms of society and government, the impact of capitalism and international trade, the rise of the middle classes, and the oppression of paupers. At the same time, it is misleading about the character of Indian opposition to these trends.

TRANSITIONS AND PROSPECTS

Among many remarkable, touching and inspiring books that chronicle the experiences of Indians in the modern era, is Prafulla Mohanti's *Changing Village, Changing Life* (London, 1990). It begins with a lecture reflecting on Mohanti's life and on an earlier memoir. He came, he says, from a Hindu village in Orissa, where days began and ended with the sun, and the year (determined by harvests and the monsoon) was punctuated by festivals and visiting hawkers and players. A river gave the village its identity; its houses were of mud and thatch; art was a part of its daily life. A local deity was worshipped for protection against epidemic diseases. Astrologers made horoscopes; priests gave blessings. But Prafulla went to school. He learnt 'Bande Mataram', and remembered the first hoisting of the Indian flag on Independence Day, 15 August 1947. He did not then understand what the headmaster meant by 'freedom' from British rule – the village had no radio; he had never seen an Englishman. However, later he would go to university and to live in London, where he realized 'for the first time' that he was an Indian.

His book tells of his revisiting his village. Much seemed unchanged. It was still 'difficult for a woman to survive alone'; the *dalits* (weavers and fishermen) still lived apart; the household gods merely seemed more numerous. But the outside world, to which Mohanti had had to travel, now reached further into the village, with its concepts and its appetites. Electricity, television and movies had arrived. People travelled by bus and lorry. They sought government aid, and followed politics – and cricket.

This is one story of India's 'modernization'. It is not about integration. The villages, as has been explained, were never really insulated, and they are not now sharing in the goods and aspirations of the urban middle classes. This story is about a reformulation of everyday Indian life under conditions of rapid communications and more powerful governments, technologies and markets. Such changing infrastructures have been outlined in this book too.

The political thread also continues, and ultimately it will determine the fate of these millions of villagers. A brief resumé will suffice to highlight the successes and difficulties. When Jawarharlal Nehru died in 1964, and was succeeded by Lal Bahadur Shastri, India had been integrated, from its provinces, territories and princely states, and it remained so. Its parliamentary and governmental system had bedded down, and already, as we have seen, had survived several major crises. Nevertheless, when Shastri died suddenly in 1966, the ruling Congress party turned to Jawaharlal's daughter, Indira Gandhi. Arguably, the 1971 general elections, at the mid-point of her first period as Prime Minister (1966–77), marked an end to the immediately post-colonial era, as also for Pakistan with the secession of Bangladesh. It seems (subject to the caveats above) that a new period began, with the retreat of the old certainties established during colonial rule. It was a watershed parallel to (though different from) those in the world generally.

Firstly, the Congress – the split in 1969 having been a quarrel of policy as well as personality – re-embarked on a populist quest with promises to end poverty, and dangerous appeals to atavistic and regional sentiment. We noted that it then lost its way in a new authoritarianism, culminating in the Emergency of 1975–7, when laws were suspended or sharpened to confront an alleged crisis of public order. Civil liberties and secularism were threatened. Congress hegemony eroded, never to be recovered – the party's vote falling overall from 46 per cent before 1967 to under 30 per cent in 1997. Having first been ousted from the central government by the Janata Party coalition (1977), it again succumbed to defeats by non-Congress governments under Morarji Desai (1977–9) and Charan Singh (1979–80).

Secondly, government became less and less stable. Regional conflicts flared, most savagely in the Punjab where Sikh activists sought autonomy or independence. Two prime ministers were assassinated – Indira Gandhi in 1984 at the hands of her Sikh bodyguards, and her son, Rajiv, in 1989, allegedly by the Tamil Tigers of Sri Lanka. Democracy worked to remove corrupt governments, but equally to elect them. Then the pro-*dalit* anti-corruption policies of Janata Dal under V. P. Singh (Prime Minister, 1989–90) seemed, improbably, about to usher in a new populism of 'social justice'. Instead, thirdly, local or Hindu chauvinist parties rose to power, after what came to seem a Congress/regional-party interregnum under P. V. Narasimha Rao (1991–6). The well-organized Bharatiya Janata Party of L. K. Advani and A. B. Vajpayee (Prime Minister from 1996) edged its way to office in several states and at the centre, amidst growing militancy over Hindu (and largely

high-caste) 'rights', focused on a campaign to demolish the Babri
Masjid, a disused mosque in Ayodhya, the alleged birthplace of
Ram. Rioting and murder punctuated the advance of communal
sentiment.

Over the same timespan, the population, prosperity and pollution
of the larger Indian cities increased markedly. Much technological
and industrial development took place, pushing the agricultural
sector back to about 30 per cent of gross domestic product, though
it too grew, under the stimulus of investment, new crops and fertil-
isers, after a disastrous slump in the early 1960s. The middle and
technological classes have gained skills and wealth. The poor have
become poorer. From the 1970s, but particularly during the 1990s,
the economy began gradually to be liberalized and opened, in
a partial retreat from centralized planning and bureaucratic controls.

In different ways these everyday, political, communal and economic
developments all represented an unravelling of the Nehruvian
project, and the beginnings of new directions. India had maintained
a continuity of institutions and public ethos, in parliament, political
party, army, the courts and the civil service. Increasingly, however,
this is thought to have concealed a different trajectory. New uses
were being found for Nehru's legacies and those of the colonial
era – that is, those features of government, society and economy
which in this book have been labelled 'modern'. Alternatively, institutions declined. The experiences and compromises of the colonial
and post-colonial era were rejected or abandoned, and older, informal or subterranean practices and attitudes resurfaced. Either
way, India was redefining itself again, so that the last quarter of
the twentieth century may well come to be regarded, in future,
as another period of transition.

A major cause is probably that, at material levels, the history of
independent India has continued to be depressing, on international comparisons. As said, there has been impressive economic
growth in some sectors, and a vast increase in the size and wealth of
the richer sections of the population, which at last (with the relaxation of regulations) are becoming a force in international markets.
The world is also increasingly recognising India's vast pool of
talent, especially in electronics and computing. But environmental,
social and political problems have also grown, and, on the whole,
economic progress has been slow in relation to population. Efforts
to promote social justice and redistribution have been feeble, even
though many depressed groups, encouragingly, are organizing

themselves to voice their protests. Indicators of public welfare such as literacy and child mortality remain poor. In 1992 only 49.9 per cent of adults were technically literate. In 1993 Indians aged under five died at a rate of 122 per thousand. Pakistan's figures were even worse, at 35.7 per cent and 137 per thousand; but India's post-independence history was strikingly different from that of Pakistan at the level of politics. The margins therefore offer little comfort, and suggest no very great dividend for democracy and relative stability.

Above all, India continued to show startling disparities between rich and poor, with at least one-third of the population estimated to be clinically malnourished, a total representing a significant proportion of world poverty. In such circumstances, with more articulate and organized protest but no evidence that the disparities are being reduced, it is hardly surprising that dominant groups sought new weapons to contain the lower classes: ranging from Indira Gandhi's Emergency and other special measures to suppress dissent, through many examples of regional separatism and communal violence, to *Hindutva* (Hindu-ness) and the demonizing of Muslims, Christians and foreigners.

Once again we confront our themes of empire and region, general and local, powerful and oppressed. Despite all the strong modern forces of integration, from television to factory production to state planning – and despite the mobility of all the Prafulla Mohantis, across the world – India's prosperous English-knowing 'imperial' elites are still kept distinct from the people as a whole, just as in the old empires of realm and thought. Many gross economic disparities, and differences of culture, language, knowledge, access and power, have persisted or been exaggerated in India since independence. Violence remains too often the main means of 'solving' problems. Judicial impartiality and a free press are held up, rightly, as major achievements, but the poor have little access to justice in the face of official or private oppression, and mostly they cannot read.

There seem to be only three routes on offer towards a more inclusive nationhood. One would build upon the regional and linguistic identities that have been developing in India, with difficulty, over more than a thousand years. Sharp and growing gaps of comfort and potential between Indian states suggest that this is a plausible option; but there are political and institutional obstacles to it, and worldwide tendencies seem to favour larger rather than smaller units. A second possibility is one which occupies much of the political ground in India at the start of the twenty-first century: the attempt to generate solidarity in terms of *Hindutva*. This is bound not to include everyone in India, but it has already altered the parameters of intellectual and political debate, even for many of its opponents. The third possibility is the political inclusivity that would flow from more successful policies of economic and social integration under a rule of law. This was the choice of Jawaharlal Nehru. Often today, it is glibly held to have failed. It remains the only scenario for anyone wanting to be optimistic about India, or indeed about the chances for more equitable societies in general.

Notes

Chapter 1   Introduction: Region and Civilization

1. *Brindaranyaka Upanishad*, first Adhyaya, fourth Brahmana, 7; tr. Max Müller, in Nicol Macnicol, ed., *Hindu Scriptures* (London, 1938).
2. In the translation of Robert Ernest Hume, *The Thirteen Principal Upanishads* (1921; reprinted Delhi, 1995).

Chapter 2   Early India

1. *Chandogya Upanishad* 6, 1–3, translation in Wm Theodore de Bary, ed., *Sources of Indian Tradition* (New York, 1969), vol. I, pp. 31–2.
2. Daud Ali, private communication. (His comments have helped modify my discussion of early religion and polity, here and in Chapter 1.)
3. *Dígha Nikáya*, 3, 80 ff., in de Bary, *Sources*, vol. I, pp. 128–33.
4. *Uttarádhyayana Sútra*, 19, 61–7 in de Bary, *Sources*, vol. I, pp. 56–7.
5. De Bary, *Sources*, vol. I, p.41.
6. *Bhagavad Gita*, I. 24, tr. L. D. Barnett, in Macnicol, *Hindu Scriptures*.
7. *Kama Sutra*, II and IV, in the translation by Sir Richard Burton and F. F. Arbuthnot.
8. Seventh Pillar Edict; tr. in de Bary, *Sources*, vol. I, p. 149.
9. See de Bary, *Sources*, vol. I, pp. 236–52.
10. *Nárada-smrti, Epigraphica Indica* XXX, tr. adapted from Md. Aquique, *Economic History of Mithila (c.600 B.C.–1097 A.D.)* (New Delhi, 1974), p. 130.

Chapter 3   Mediaeval India

1. Somadeva, *Nectar of Aphorisms on Polity* (tenth century); tr. in Wm Theodore de Bary, ed., *Sources of Indian Tradition* (New York, 1969), vol. I, p. 86.

Chapter 4   Early Modern India I: Mughals and Marathas

1. Shah Wali Ullah, *The Muslim World*, vol. XLV, 4, cited in Wm T. de Bary, ed., *Sources of Indian Tradition* (New York, 1969), vol. I, p. 453.

2. Francisco Pelseart, 'Remonstrantie', tr. by W. Moreland and P. Geyl as *Jahangir's Empire* (Cambridge, 1926), quoted by P. Hardy, *The Muslims of British India* (Cambridge, 1972), p. 13.

Chapter 5   Early Modern India II: Company Raj

1. Minute by Hastings, 17 April 1781, in Lynn Zastoupil and Martin Moir, eds, *The Great Education Debate: Documents relating to the Orientalist-Anglicist controversy, 1781–1843* (Richmond, Surrey, 1999), p. 74.
2. Radhakanta Deb to H. H. Wilson, 1835, quoted Zastoupil and Moir, *Education Debate*, p. 40.
3. Diary of Richard Blechynden, 31 December 1799, Add. Mss.45611, British Library.
4. *Reformer*, 14 November 1837, quoted in *Asiatic Journal*, March 1838, and in S. R. Mehrotra, *The Emergence of the Indian National Congress* (Delhi, 1971), p. 8.

Chapter 6   Modern India I: Government

1. George Couper, 'General questions of famine', Add. Mss. 43615, British Library.

Chapter 7   Modern India II: Politics

1. Ernest Gellner, *Thought and Change* (London, 1964); Anthony Smith, *Theories of Nationalism* (London, 1971); Karl Deutsch, *Nationalism and Social Communication* (Cambridge, Mass., 1966); and Benedict Anderson, *Imagined Communities* (1983; rev. ed., London, 1991).
2. Indian Statutory Commission Report, vol. 2, App.VII, Cmd.3569 (1930).
3. *Hindu Rashtra Darshan*, pp.72–6, quoted in C. H. Philips, ed., *The Evolution of India and Pakistan, 1858–1947. Select Documents* (London, 1962).
4. Proceedings of the Indian Round Table Conference (Second Session), Cmd. 3997 (1932).
5. V. P. Menon, *The Transfer of Power in India* (Calcutta, 1957), p. 105.
6. Indian Round Table Conference, Sub-Committees, pt. II (1931).
7. Secretary of State to Viceroy, 8 February 1942, quoted in Sekhar Bandyopadhyay, 'Transfer of power and the crisis of dalit politics in India, 1945–47', *Modern Asian Studies*, 34, 4 (2000), p. 904.
8. See Ranajit Guha, ed., *Subaltern Studies*, vols. I–VI (New Delhi, 1982–9), *et al.*, vols. VII–IX, continuing.
9. Partha Chatterjee, *The Nation and its Fragments* (Delhi, 1994), ch. 1.

Chapter 9   Modern India IV: Economy

1. Jan Bremen, *Of Peasants, Migrants and Paupers* (Delhi, 1985).
2. Sir Edward Blunt, ed., *Social Service in India* (London, 1939), p. 199.

Chapter 10   Epilogue: After Modernity?

1. Jurgen Habermas, *The Structural Transformation of the Public Sphere*, tr. Thomas Burger (Cambridge, 1989).

References and Readings

After a list of general studies (included for information, not as sources for this book), the entries below fall into two categories. Part 1 follows the book's chapterization, and gives works particularly drawn on for major sections. Part 2, with subject headings, cites works also used or relevant. Both parts may be consulted for further reading on particular topics. The order of each list is roughly thematic and chronological. Though the lists are quite long, they are not exhaustive. Works identified with an asterisk have particularly useful and often annotated bibliographies.

Only one entry is made per title, even though many may be relevant under several headings. Subtitles are included only so far as necessary to indicate subject-matter. Works cited in the notes are *not* repeated here. However, it should be noted that some attributed but unsourced quotations in Chapters 6 and 7 may be found in the Philips' *Documents* (see Ch.7, note 4), and that, although references are made to the two-volume *Sources of Indian Tradition* under the general editorship of de Bary, revised versions have also appeared, edited by Ainslie Embree and Stephen Hay (1988).

GENERAL STUDIES

Francis Robinson, ed., *The Cambridge Encyclopedia of India, Pakistan, Bangladesh* . . . (1989).

J. E. Schwartzberg, *A Historical Atlas of South Asia* (1978; 1992).

For a narrative giving weight to the earlier periods, John Keay, *India: A History* (2000).

For a study also including much earlier history, Hermann Kulke and Dietmar Rothermund, *A History of India* (1986).

For an overview, from a mediaeval and early modern historian, Burton Stein, *A History of India* (1998).

For a narrative of the colonial era, Anthony Read and David Fisher, *The Proudest Day: India's Long Road to Independence* (1998).

For a more thematic approach, Claude Markovits, dir., *Histoire de l'Inde moderne, 1480–1950* (1994).

For a 'broadly Marxist' view, Bipan Chandra *et al.*, *India's Struggle for Independence* (1989).

For an unusual dramatized approach, Mushirul Hasan, *John Company to the Republic* (2001).

For invaluable illustrations and short commentaries, C. A. Bayly, ed., *The Raj: India and the British, 1600–1947* (1990).
For modern history, but including antecedents, Sugata Bose and Ayesha Jalal, *Modern South Asia* (1997).*

PART I

Chapters 1 and 10

See related sections in other chapters. The quotations from *Rig Veda* are from *Hindu Scriptures*, ed. Nicol Macnicol, 1938, from the E. J. Lazarus edition, Banaras, 1896; the translation, unacknowledged in Macnicol, is by Ralph T. H. Griffith.
For discussions of 'modern' and problems of the term, as in Ch. 1 and elsewhere, for example: *Journal of the Economic and Social History of the Orient* 40, 4 (November 1997); Michael Adas, *Machines as the Measure of Men* (1990); and Sugata Bose, ed., *South Asia and World Capitalism* (1990).
On environment, territory and regions, David Ludden, *An Agrarian History of South Asia* (1999)* and *Peasant History in South India* (1985); Sumit Guha, *Environment, Ethnicity and Politics in Western India, 1350–1991* (1999); W. C. Neale, 'Land is to rule' in R. E. Frykenberg, ed., *Land Control and Social Structure in Indian History* (1969); and A. T. Embree, 'Frontiers into boundaries: from the traditional to the modern state' in R. G. Fox, ed., *Realm and Region in Traditional India* (1977).
On the impact of war on the state, see Thomas Ertman, *Birth of the Leviathan: Medieval and Early Modern Europe* (Cambridge, 1997). He emphasizes that the elements of state-building need not develop together, and that pre-existing conditions and timing influence the state's form.

Chapters 2 and 3

A. L. Basham, *The Wonder that was India* (1956).
Romila Thapar, *A History of India*, vol. I (1957).
Hermann Kulke, ed., *The State in India, 1000–1700* (1997).*
Burton Stein, *Peasant, State and Society in Medieval South India* (1980) and *Vijayanagara* (1989).*
Irfan Habib and Tapan Raychaudhuri, eds, *Cambridge Economic History of India*, vol. I (1982).

Chapters 4 and 5

J. F. Richards, *The Mughal Empire* (1993).*
Muzaffar Alam and Sanjay Subrahmanyam, eds, *The Mughal State, 1526–1750* (1998).*

Stewart Gordon, *The Marathas, 1600–1818* (1993).*
P. J. Marshall, *Bengal, the British Bridgehead* (1989).*
C. A. Bayly, *Imperial Meridian: The British Empire and the World, 1780–1830* (1989) and *Indian Society and the Making of the British Empire* (1988).*
Sanjay Subrahmanyam, ed., *Merchants, Markets and the State in Early Modern India* (1990); especially, for Jaipur, the essay by Madhavi Bajekal.
Figures on Bengal rice prices were calculated from Rajat Datta, *Society, Economy and the Market: Commercialization in Rural Bengal, c. 1760–1800* (New Delhi, 2000), pp. 199 and 221–7.
Some reference was made to Percival Spear, *The Oxford History of Modern India* (1965) which is reliable on chronology and events, though dated, as is the same author's Penguin history.

Chapters 6 and 7

Peter Robb, *Ancient Rights and Future Comfort: Bihar, the Bengal Tenancy Act of 1855 and British Rule in India* (1997).
Sumit Sarkar, *Modern India, 1885–1947* (1983).*
S. R. Mehrotra, *The Emergence of the Indian National Congress* (1971).
G. Krishna, 'The development of...Congress as a mass organisation', *Journal of Asian Studies*, 25, 3 (1966).
Francis Robinson, *Separatism Among Indian Muslims: The Politics of the United Provinces' Muslims, 1860–1923* (1974).
Mushirul Hasan, ed., *India's Partition: Process, Strategy and Mobilization* (1993).*
David Hardiman, ed., *Peasant Resistance in India, 1858–1914* (1992).*
Dilip Menon, 'Intimations of equality' in Peter Robb, ed., *Dalit Movements and the Meanings of Labour in India* (1993).
Paul R. Brass, *The Politics of India since Independence* (1990).*
For Bhils in Surat, see David Hardiman, *The Coming of the Devi* (New Delhi, 1987).
Reference was also made to an unpublished paper by Majid Siddiqi.

Chapter 8

Peter Hardy, *The Muslims of British India* (1972).*
Kenneth W. Jones, *Socio-Religious Movements in British India* (1989).*
Susan Bayly, *Caste, Society and Politics in India from the Eighteenth Century to the Modern Age* (1999).*
S. N. Mukherjee, 'Class, caste and politics in Calcutta, 1815–38' in E. Leach, ed., *Elites in South Asia* (1970).
Rosalind O'Hanlon, *Caste, Conflict and Ideology: Mahatma Jotirao Phule and Low Caste Protest in Nineteenth-Century Western India* (1985) – for the discussion of 'Maratha'.
Geraldine Forbes, *Women in Modern India* (1987).*

Chapter 9

Rajat K. Ray, ed., *Entrepreneurship and Industry in India, 1880–1947* (1992).*
Dharma Kumar, ed., *Cambridge Economic History of India*, vol. II (1983).*
B. R. Tomlinson, *The Economy of Modern India, 1860–1970* (1993).*
Tirthanka Roy, ed., *Cloth and Commerce: Textiles in Colonial India* (1996).
Sumit Guha, *The Agrarian Economy of the Bombay Deccan, 1818–1941* (1983)
    and, ed., *Agriculture and Productivity in British India* (1992).*
Neil Charlesworth, *Peasants and Imperial Rule: . . . Bombay Presidency, 1850–1935*
    (1985).
Omkar Goswami, *Industry, Trade and Peasant Society: The Jute Economy of
    Eastern India, 1900–1947* (1991).
Peter Robb, 'Peasants' choices? Indian agriculture and the limits of
    commercialization in nineteenth-century Bihar', *Economic History Review*,
    45, 1 (1992).
On intensification, L. G. Reynolds, *Economic Growth in the Third World*
    (1986).

PART II

Early and Mediaeval History

Niharranjan Ray, B. Chattopadhyay *et al*., *A Sourcebook of Indian Civilization*
    (2000).
Vincent Smith, *The Early History of India from 600 BC to the Muhammadan
    Conquest* (1924).
R. C. Majumdar, ed., *The History and Culture of the Indian People*, vols. I–V (1956).
D. D. Kosambi, *An Introduction to the Study of Indian History* (1956).
R. T. M. Wheeler, *The Indus Valley Civilization and Beyond* (1966).
F. R. Allchin, *The Archaeology of Early Historical South Asia* (1995) and, with
    Bridget Allchin, *The Rise of Civilization in India and Pakistan* (1982).
M. Deshpande and P. Hook, eds, *Aryan and non-Aryan in South Asia* (1979).
Louis Renou (tr. Philip Spratt), *Vedic India* (1971).
S. N. Mukherjee, ed., *India: History and Thought* (1982).
D. K. Chakrabarti, *Ancient Indian Cities* (1995).
Romila Thapar, *From Lineage to State: Social Formations in the Mid-First
    Millennium B.C. in the Ganga Valley* (1984); *Asoka and the Decline of the Mauryas*
    (1973); *Interpreting Early India* (1993); and *Communalism and the Writing of
    Indian History* (1969).
J. C. Heesterman, *The Ancient Indian Royal Consecration* (1957).
Kumkum Roy, *The Emergence of Monarchy in North India* (1994) and, ed.,
    Women in Early Indian Societies (1999).
R. S. Sharma, *Perspectives in Social and Economic History of Early India* (1983);
    Looking for the Aryans (1995); *Material Culture and Social Formations in
    Ancient India* (1983); *The Origin of the State in India* (1957); and *Indian
    Feudalism c.300–1300* (1965).
Uma Chakravarti, *The Social Dimension of Early Buddhism* (1987).

R. G. Bhandarkar, *Vaisnavism, Saivism and Minor Religious Systems* (1913).
Jan Gonda, *Visnuism and Saivism* (1970).
Paul Dundas, *The Jains* (1992).
P. V. Kane, *History of Dharmasastra* (1968).
J. K. Brockington, *Righteous Rama* (1985).
J. Duncan Derrett, ed., *Religion, Law and the State in India* (1999).
H. Scharfe, *The State in Indian Tradition* (1989).
D. C. Sircar, *Political and Administrative Systems of Ancient and Medieval India* (1974).
Charles Drekmeir, *Kingship and Community in Early India* (1962).
D. N. Jha, ed., *Feudal Social Formations in Early India* (1987) and, ed., *Society and Ideology in India* (1996).
B. D. Chattopadhyaya, *Aspects of Rural Settlements and Rural Society in Early Medieval India* (1990), and *The Making of Early Medieval India* (1994).
Ronald Inden, ed., *Querying the Medieval* (2000).
D. C. Sircar, *Indian Epigraphy* (1965).
Richard Saloman, *Indian Epigraphy* (1998).
B. M. Morrison, *Political Centers and Culture Regions in Early Bengal* (1970).
Sushil Kumar De, *Early History of the Vaishnava Faith and Movement in Bengal* (1961).
A. Escheman, H. Kulke and G. C. Tripathi, eds, *The Cult of Jagannatha and the Regional Tradition of Orissa* (1986).
George Michell, *The Hindu Temple* (1977).
Burton Stein, *South Indian Temples* (1978).
Paula Richman, ed., *Many Ramayanas* (1991).
Mahammad Habib and K. A. Nizami, *A Comprehensive History of India*, vol. V *The Delhi Sultanate* (1970).
K. A. Nizami, *Some Aspects of Religion and Politics in India during the Thirteenth Century* (1961).
A. B. M. Habibullah, *The Foundation of Muslim Rule in India* (1961).
A. S. Tripathi, *Some Aspects of Muslim Rule in India* (1956).
I. H. Qureshi, *The Administration of the Sultanate of Delhi* (1945).
Simon Digby, *Warhorse and Elephant in the Delhi Sultanate* (1961).
H. K. Sherwani, *The Bahmanis of the Deccan* (1953).
Peter Hardy, *Historians of Medieval India* (1960).

Early Modern History, Before c.1800

S. A. A. Rizvi, *The Wonder that was India*, vol. II (1987).
M. S. Hodgson, *The Venture of Islam*, vol. III, bk 4 (1974).
Irfan Habib, *The Agrarian System of Mughal India, 1556–1707* (1963); *An Atlas of Mughal India* (1982); and *Essays in Indian History* (1995).
A. Ali, *The Mughal Nobility under Aurangzeb* (1986).
S. P. Blake, *Shahjanabad . . . 1639–1739* (1990).
H. Q. Naqvi, *Urbanization and Urban Centres under the Great Mughals* (1972).
K. A. Nizami, *Akbar and Religion* (1989).
W. H. McLeod, *The Evolution of the Sikh Community* (1976).

S. H. Moosvi, *The Economic History of the Mughal Empire, c.1595* (1987).

Richard Eaton, *The Rise of Islam and the Bengal Frontier, 1204–1760* (1993).

A. J. Qaisar, *The Indian Response to European Technology and Culture, 1498–1717* (1982).

D. H. S. Kolff, *Naukar, Rajput and Sepoy:... 1450–1850* (1990).

M. Alam, *The Crisis of Empire in Mughal North India* (1986).

S. Chandra, *Mughal Policies: The Rajputs and the Deccan* (1993).

J. F. Richards, *Mughal Administration in Golconda* (1975); ed., *The Imperial Monetary System of Mughal India* (1989); and, ed., *Kingship and Authority in South Asia* (1978).

G. Bhadra, 'Two frontier uprisings in Mughal India', in R. Guha, ed., *Subaltern Studies*, vol. II (1983).

'Symposium: decline of the Mughal empire', *Journal of Asian Studies*, 35, 2 (1976).

M. Athar Ali, 'The passing of empire: the Mughal case', *Modern Asian Studies*, 9, 3 (1985).

Stewart Gordon, *Marathas, Marauders and State Formation in Eighteenth Century India* (1994).

Andre Wink, *Land and Sovereignty in India: Agrarian Society and Politics under the Eighteenth-Century Maratha Svaraja* (1986).

J. S. Grewal, *The Sikhs in the Punjab* (1990).

Richard Barnett, *North India between Empires* (1980).

Kate Brittelbank, *Tipu Sultan's Search for Legitimacy* (1997).

Ashin Das Gupta and M. N. Pearson, eds, *India and the Indian Ocean, 1500–1800* (1987).

Sanjay Subrahmanyam, *The Political Economy of Commerce: Southern India, 1500–1650* (1990); 'The Mughal state – structure or process?', *Indian Economic and Social History Review*, 28, 3 (1992); *Improvising Empire: Portuguese Trade and Settlement in the Bay of Bengal, 1500–1700* (1990); and, ed., *Money and the Market in India, 1100–1700* (1994).

Holden Furber, *John Company at Work* (1948) and *Rival Empires of Trade in the Orient, 1600–1800* (1976).

S. Asaratnam, *Merchants, Companies and Commerce on the Coromandel Coast (1650–1740)* (1986).

O. Prakash, *The Dutch East India Company and the Economy of Bengal, 1630–1720* (1985).

K. N. Chaudhuri, *The East India Company* (1965).

Peter Marshall, *East Indian Fortunes: The British in Bengal in the Eighteenth Century* (1976).

Kumkum Chatterjee, *Merchants, Politics and Society in Early Modern India: Bihar, 1733–1820* (1996).

John McLane, *Land and Local Kingship in Eighteenth Century Bengal* (1993).

C. A. Bayly, *Rulers, Townsmen and Bazaars: North Indian Society..., 1770–1870* (1983).

I. G. Khan, 'Changing patterns of authority and control in post-Mughal North India, c.1740–1830' in J. P. Neelson, ed., *Gender, Caste and Power in South Asia* (1991).

Indrani Chatterjee, *Gender, Slavery and Law in Colonial India* (1999).

Company and Colonial Government

P. J. Marshall, 'British expansion in India in the eighteenth century', *History*, 60 (1975).

Sushil Chaudhury, *The Prelude to Empire* (2000).

A. M. Khan, *The Transition in Bengal, 1756–1775* (1969).

Michael Fisher, *Indirect Rule in India....1764–1857* (1991); *A Clash of Cultures: Awadh, the British and the Mughals* (1987); and, ed., *The Politics of the British Annexation of India 1757–1857* (1993).

B. N. Pandey, *The Introduction of English Law into India* (1967).

M. Anderson, 'Work construed', in Peter Robb, ed., *Dalit Movements and the Meanings of Labour in India* (1993).

M. H. Edney, *Mapping and Empire: ...1765–1843* (1997).

Bernard S. Cohn, *An Anthropologist among the Historians* (1987) and *Colonialism and its Forms of Knowledge: The British in India* (1997).

Ainslie Embree, *Charles Grant and British Rule in India* (1962).

John Rosselli, *Lord William Bentinck* (1974).

Raymond Callahan, *The East India Company and Army Reform, 1783–98* (1972).

Seema Alavi, *The Sepoys and the Company* (1995).

R. E. Frykenberg, *Guntur District, 1788–1848* (1965).

W. J. Barber, *British Economic Thought and India, 1600–1858* (1975).

Burton Stein, ed., *The Making of Agrarian Policy in British India, 1770–1900* (1992).

Ranjit Guha, *A Rule of Property for Bengal* (1963).

Ratnalekha Ray, *Change in Bengal Agrarian Society, 1760–1830* (1980).

Sirajul Islam, *The Permanent Settlement in Bengal* (1979).

Eric Stokes, *The English Utilitarians and India* (1959); *The Peasant and the Raj* (1978); and *The Peasant Armed: The Indian Rebellion of 1857* (ed. C. A. Bayly, 1986).

Neeladri Bhattacharya, 'Colonial state and agrarian society' in S. Bhattacharya *et al.*, *Situating Indian History* (1986).

Javed Majeed, *Ungoverned Imaginings: James Mill's* The History of British India *and Orientalism* (1992).

Norbert Peabody, 'Tod's *Rajast'han* and the boundaries of imperial rule in nineteenth-century India', *Modern Asian Studies*, 30, 1 (1996).

Peter Penner, *The Patronage Bureaucracy in North India: ...1820–70* (1986).

Eugene Irshick, *Dialogue and History: Constructing South India, 1795–1815* (1994).

T. H. Beaglehole, *Thomas Munro* (1966).

Burton Stein, *Thomas Munro* (1989).

Dharma Kumar, *Land and Caste in South India* (1965) and *Colonialism, Property and the State* (1998).

D. A. Washbrook, 'Law, state and agrarian society in colonial India', *Modern Asian Studies*, 13, 1 (1981) and *The Emergence of Provincial Politics: The Madras Presidency 1870–1920* (1976).

John Pemble, *The Raj, the Indian Mutiny and the Kingdom of Oudh, 1801–1859* (1977).

M. N. Pearson, ed., *Legitimacy and Symbols: The South Asian Writings of F. W. Buckler* (1985).

R. Mukherjee, *Awadh in Revolt* (1984).

Thomas R. Metcalf, *Ideologies of the Raj* (1994); *Land, Landlords and the British Raj* (1979); and *The Aftermath of Revolt: India, 1857–1870* (1964).

Dietmar Rothermund, *Government, Landlord and Peasant in India* (1978).

Richard Saumarez Smith, *Rule by Records: Land Registration and Village Custom in Early British Punjab* (1996).

C. J. Dewey, *Anglo-Indian Attitudes* (1994).

Kenneth Ballhatchet, *Race, Sex and Class under the Raj* (1980).

G. Studdert-Kennedy, *Providence and the Raj* (1998).

R. J. Moore, *Liberalism and Indian Politics, 1872–22* (1966).

S. Gopal, *The Viceroyalty of Lord Ripon, 1880–4* (1953).

Briton Martin, *New India 1885* (1969).

Ranajit Guha, *Dominance without Hegemony* (1997).

David Arnold, *Police Power and Colonial Rule: Madras, 1859–1947* (1986).

David Omissi, *The Sepoy and the Raj: The Indian Army, 1860–1940* (1994).

P. G. Robb, *The Government of India and Reform: . . . 1916–21* (1976) and *The Evolution of British Political Policy* (1992).

R. J. Moore, *The Crisis of Indian Unity* (1974) and *Churchill, Cripps and India, 1939–45* (1979).

B. R. Tomlinson, *The Political Economy of the Raj, 1914–47* (1979).

G. Balachandran, *John Bullion's Empire* (1996).

V. P. Menon, *The Transfer of Power in India* (1968).

H. V. Hodson, *The Great Divide* (1969).

R. J. Moore, *Escape from Empire* (1983).

Lord Wavell, *A Viceroy's Journal* (1973).

Ian Copland, *The Princes of India and the Endgame of Empire, 1917–47* (1997).

D. Potter, *India's Political Administrators, 1919–83* (1986).

Modern Political History Before 1950

Judith Brown, *Modern India: The Origins of a Modern Democracy* (1985).

Jim Masselos, *Indian Nationalism: An History* (1985) and *Towards Nationalism . . . Urban Politics* (1974).

Partha Chatterjee, *The Nation and its Fragments* (1994).

Ravinder Kumar, *Western India in the Nineteenth Century* (1968); *Essays in the Social History of Modern India* (1983); and ed., *Essays in Gandhian Politics: The Rowlatt Satyagraha* (1971).

John R. McLane, *Indian Nationalism and the Early Congress* (1977).

Anil Seal, *The Emergence of Indian Nationalism* (1968).

C. A. Bayly, *The Local Roots of Indian Politics: Allahabad, 1880–1920* (1975) and *The Origins of Nationality in South Asia* (1998).

Rajat Ray, 'Political change in British India', *Indian Economic and Social History Review*, 14 (1982) and *Social Conflict and Political Unrest in Bengal, 1875–1927* (1984).

N. G. Barrier, ed., *The Census in British India* (1981).

M. Torri , '"Westernized middle class": intellectuals and society in late colonial India' in John L. Hill, ed., *The Congress and Indian Nationalism: Historical Perspectives* (1991).

Gordon Johnson, *Provincial Politics and Elite Nationalism* (1973), and ed., *et al.*, *Locality, Province and Nation*, and *Power, Profit and Politics* (1973 and 1981; both also special issues of *Modern Asian Studies*).

J. H. Broomfield, *Elite Conflict in a Plural Society: Twentieth-Century Bengal* (1968).

Sumit Sarkar, *The Swadeshi Movement in Bengal* (1973).

S. R. Mehrotra, *India and the Commonwealth, 1885–1929* (1965).

DeWitt Ellinwood and S. D. Pradhan, eds, *India and World War I* (1978).

Shashi Joshi and Bhagwan Josh, *Struggle for Hegemony in India*, 3 vols. (1992; 1994).

Tanika Sarkar, *Bengal, 1928–1934* (1987).

D. E. U. Baker, *Colonialism in an Indian Hinterland: The Central Provinces, 1820–1920* (1993).

Ian Talbot, *The Punjab and the Raj, 1849–1947* (1988).

A. D. Gordon, *Businessmen and Politics: Rising Nationalism and a Modernising Economy in Bombay, 1918–1939* (1978).

Claude Markovits, *Indian Business and Nationalist Politics, 1931–39* (1985).

D. A. Low, ed., *Congress and the Raj* (1977).

B. R. Tomlinson, *Indian National Congress and the Raj, 1929–42* (1976).

G. Pandey, ed., *The Indian Nation in 1942* (1988).

Modern Indian Leaders, and Memoirs

Stanley Wolpert, *Tilak and Gokhale* (1952).

Richard Cashman, *The Myth of the Lokamanya: Tilak and Mass Politics in Maharashtra* (1975).

Nirad Chaudhuri, *Autobiography of an Unknown Indian* (1975).

M. K. Gandhi, *An Autobiography or The Story of my Experiments with Truth* (1927–9; 1940).

Shahid Amin, 'Gandhi as Mahatma: Gorakhpur district, eastern UP, 1921–2' in Ranajit Guha, ed., *Subaltern Studies* vol. III (1984).

Judith Brown, *Gandhi's Rise to Power* (1972); *Gandhi and Civil Disobedience* (1977); and *Gandhi, Prisoner of Hope* (1990).

David Arnold, *Gandhi* (2001).

Bhikhu Parekh, *Colonialism, Tradition and Reform: An Analysis of Gandhi's Political Discourse* (1999).

B. R. Nanda, *Gokhale* (1977) and *The Nehrus: Motilal and Jawaharlal* (1962).

S. Gopal, *Jawaharlal Nehru*, vols. I, II and III (1975, 1979, 1980).

Jawaharlal Nehru, *An Autobiography* (1958).

Sonia Gandhi, ed., *Freedom's Daughter: Letters Between Indira Gandhi and Jawaharlal Nehru 1922–39* (1989).

Leonard Gordon, *Brothers against the Raj: A Biography of Sarat and Subhas Chandra Bose* (1990).

Rani Dhavan Shankardass, *Vallabhbhai Patel* (1988).

Rajmohan Gandhi, *Understanding the Muslim Mind* (1988).

Ayesha Jalal, *The Sole Spokesman: Jinnah, the Muslim League and the Demand for Pakistan* (1985).

Akbar S. Ahmed, *Jinnah, Pakistan and Islamic Identity: The Search for Saladin* (1997).

Prakash Tandon, *Punjabi Century, 1857–1947* (1961) and *Beyond Punjab* (1971).

Cities, Education, Middle Classes and Social Reform

Nigel Crook, ed., *The Transmission of Knowledge in South Asia: Essays on Education, Religion, History and Politics* (1996).

C. H. Philips and M. D. Wainwright, eds., *Indian Society and the Beginnings of Modernisation, 1830–50* (1978).

Pradip Sinha, *Calcutta in Urban History* (1978) and, ed., *The Urban Experience: Calcutta...* (1987).

P. Chatterjee, ed., *Texts of Power* (1995).

Sumanta Banerjee, *The Parlour and the Streets: Elite and Popular Culture in Nineteenth Century Calcutta* (1989).

D. Kopf, *British Orientalism and the Bengal Renaissance* (1969).

M. M. Ali, *The Bengali Reaction to Christian Missionary Activities, 1833–57* (1965).

John McGuire, *The Making of a Colonial Mind:... Calcutta, 1857–85* (1983).

Veena Talwar Oldenburg, *The Making of Colonial Lucknow, 1856–77* (1984).

Nita Kumar, *The Artisans of Banaras:... 1880–1986* (1988).

Sandria Freitag, ed., *Culture and Power in Banaras* (1989).

Anand Yang, *Bazaar India: Markets, Society and the Colonial State in Bihar* (1998).

Rajat Ray, 'Evolution of the professional structure in modern India: older and new professions in a changing society', *Indian Historical Review*, 9, 1–2 (1982–3).

B. B. Misra, *The Indian Middle Classes* (1961).

K. N. Panikkar, 'The intellectual history of colonial India' in Sabyasachi Bhattacharya and Romila Thapar, eds, *Situating Indian History* (1986).

Tapan Raychaudhuri, *Europe Reconsidered* (1988).

Narayani Gupta, *Delhi between Two Empires, 1803–1931* (1981).

Christine Dobbin, *Urban Leadership in Western India* (1972).

Miriam Dossal, *Imperial Designs and Indian Realities: The Planning of Bombay City, 1845–75* (1991).

C. Heimsath, *Indian Nationalism and Hindu Social Reform* (1964).

D. D. Karve, ed., *The New Brahmans* (1963).

Michael Anderson and Sumit Guha, eds, *Changing Concepts of Rights and Justice in South Asia* (2000).

Emma Tarlo, *Clothing Matters: Clothing and Identity in India* (1996).

M. Hasan, ed., *Knowledge, Power and Politics: Educational Institutions in India* (1998).

Sanjay Srivastava, *Constructing Post-Colonial India: National Character and the Doon School* (1998).

Popular and Peasant Movements

William R. Pinch, *Peasants and Monks in British India* (1996).
Douglas Haynes and Gyan Prakash, eds, *Contesting Power: Resistance and Everyday Social Relations in South Asia* (1991).
Ranajit Guha, *Elementary Aspects of Peasant Insurgency in India* (1983).
B. B. Kling, *The Blue Mutiny* (1966).
Peter Heehs, *The Bomb in Bengal: The Rise of Revolutionary Terrorism in India, 1900–10* (1994).
L. I. and S. H. Rudolph, *The Modernity of Tradition* (1967).
Sekhar Bandyopadhyay, *Caste, Politics and the Raj: Bengal, 1872–1937* (1990).
Rajat Ray, 'Masses in politics:...Bengal, 1920–2', *Indian Economic and Social History Review*, 11, 4 (1974).
Sumit Sarkar, 'The conditions and nature of subaltern militancy: Bengal from swadeshi to non-cooperation, c.1905–22', in Ranajit Guha, ed., *Subaltern Studies*, vol. III (1984).
Christopher Baker, 'Non-cooperation in South India' in Baker and D. A. Washbrook, *South India* (1975).
Mridula Mukherjee, 'Peasant resistance and peasant consciousness in colonial India: "Subalterns" and beyond', *Economic and Political Weekly* (8 & 15 October 1988).
Jacques Pouchepadass, *Champaran and Gandhi: Planters, Peasants and Gandhian Politics* (1999) and 'Local leaders and the intelligentsia in the Champaran satyagraha', *Contributions to Indian Sociology*, 8 (1978).
S. Henningham, 'The social setting of the Champaran satyagraha', *Indian Economic and Social History Review*, 13, 1 (1976).
Shahid Amin, *Event, Metaphor, Memory: Chauri Chaura, 1922–92* (1995).
D. N. Dhanagare, *Peasant Movements in India 1920–1950* (1983).
Kapil Kumar, *Peasants in Revolt:...Oudh, 1886–1922* (1984) and, ed., *Congress and Classes* (1988).
Majid Siddiqi, *Agrarian Unrest in North India:...1918–22* (1978).
G. Pandey, *The Ascendancy of the Congress in Uttar Pradesh, 1926–34* (1978).
S. Mukherji, *Peasants, Politics and the British Government, 1930–40* (1984).
K. N. Panikkar, *Against Lord and State: Religion and Peasant Uprisings in Malabar, 1836–1921* (1989).
Dilip Menon, *Caste, Nationalism and Communism in South India: Malabar 1900–48* (1994).
David Hardiman, *Peasant Nationalists of Gujarat* (1981).
Harald Tambs-Lyche, *Power, Profit and Poetry: Traditional Society in Kathiawar, Western India* (1997).
Hira Singh, *Colonial Hegemony and Popular Resistance* (1998).

Castes and *Dalits*: Socio-political Change among Hindus and Sikhs

Ronald Inden, 'Orientalist construction of India', *Modern Asian Studies*, 20, 3 (1986) and *Imagining India* (1990).

P. J. Marshall, ed., *The British Discovery of Hinduism in the Eighteenth Century* (1970).

A. M. Hocart, *Caste: A Comparative Study* (1950).

Declan Quigley, *The Interpretation of Caste* (1993).

D. G. Mandelbaum, *Society in India*, 2 vols (1970).

C. J. Fuller, ed., *Caste Today* (1996).

Robin Jeffrey, *The Decline of Nayar Dominance: Society and Politics in Travancore, 1847–1930* (1976).

Karen Leonard, *The Social History of an Indian Caste: The Kayasths of Hyderabad* (1978).

Frank Conlon, *A Caste in a Changing World: The Chitrapur Saraswat Brahmans, 1700–1935* (1977).

Gail Omvedt, *Cultural Revolt in a Colonial Society: The Non-Brahman Movement in Western India, 1873–1930* (1976).

Eleanor Zelliot, 'Learning the use of political means: the Mahars of Maharashtra', in R. Kothari, ed., *Caste in Indian Politics* (1970) and 'Religion and legitimation in the Mahar movement' in Bardwell Smith, ed., *Religion and Legitimation in South Asia* (1978).

Kenneth W. Jones, *Arya Dharm: Hindu Consciousness in Nineteenth-Century Punjab* (1976).

Richard G. Fox, *Lions of the Punjab: Culture in the Making* (1990).

Harjot Oberoi, *The Construction of Religious Boundaries: Culture, Identity and Diversity in the Sikh Tradition* (1994).

Christophe Jaffrelot, *The Hindu Nationalist Movement and Indian Politics, 1925–94* (1996).

James M. Freeman, *Untouchable: An Indian Life History* (1979).

Mark Juergensmeyer, *Religion and Social Vision: The Movement Against Untouchability in 20th-Century Punjab* (1982).

S. Bandyopadhyay, *Caste, Protest and Identity in Colonial India: The Namasudras of Bengal, 1872–1947* (1997) and, ed. with Suranjan Das, *Caste and Communal Politics in South Asia* (1993).

Women

Julia Leslie, 'Suttee or *sati*: victim or victor', in D. Arnold and P. Robb, eds, *Institutions and Ideologies: A SOAS South Asia Reader* (1993) and, ed. with Mary McGee, *Invented Identities* (2000).

Rosalind O'Hanlon, *A Comparison Between Women and Men: Tarabai Shinde and the Critique of Gender Relations in Colonial India* (1994) and 'Issues of widowhood: gender and resistance in colonial Western India' in Douglas Haynes and Gyan Prakash, eds, *Contesting Power: Resistance and Everyday Social Relations in South Asia* (1991).

Kumkum Sangari and Sudesh Vaid, eds, *Recasting Women: Essays in Colonial History* (1989).

Sudhir Chandra, *Enslaved Daughters: Colonialism, Law and Women's Rights* (1998).

Tanika Sarkar, 'Rhetoric against the age of consent: resisting colonial reason and the death of a childwife', *Economic and Political Weekly*

(4 September 1993), and 'The Hindu wife and the Hindu nation: domesticity and nationalism in nineteenth century Bengal', *Studies in History*, 8, 2 (1992).

Gail Minault, *Secluded Scholars: Women's Education and Muslim Social Reform in Colonial India* (1998).

Lucy Carroll, 'Law, custom and statutory social reform: the Hindu Widows' Remarriage Act of 1856', *Indian Economic and Social History Review*, 20, 4 (1983).

Meredith Borthwick, *The Changing Role of Women in Bengal, 1849–1905* (1984) and 'The Bhadramahila and changing conjugal relations in Bengal' in M. Allen and S. N. Mukherjee, eds, *Women in India and Nepal* (1982).

Ghulam Murshid, *Reluctant Debutant: Responses of Bengali Women to Modernization* (1983).

Sonia Nishat Amin, *The World of Muslim Women in Colonial Bengal, 1876–1939* (1996).

Prem Chowdhry, *The Veiled Woman: Shifting Gender Equations in Rural Haryana, 1880–1990* (1994).

Charu Gupta, *Sexuality, Obscenity, Community* (2001).

Ritu Menon and Kamla Bhasin, 'Recovery, rupture, resistance: Indian state and abduction of women during partition', *Economic and Political Weekly*, 28 (24 April 1993).

Bina Agarwal, *A Field of One's Own* (1994).

Amrita Basu, *Two Faces of Protest: Contrasting Modes of Women's Activism in India* (1995).

History, Language and Region

S. N. Mukherjee, *Sir William Jones* (1968).

O. P. Kejariwal, *The Asiatic Society of Bengal and the Discovery of India's Past* (1988).

Thomas Trautmann, *Aryans and British India* (1997).

Daud Ali, ed., *Invoking the Past* (2000).

Nicholas Dirks, *The Hollow Crown* (1987).

Pamela Price, *Kingship and Political Practice in Colonial India* (1996).

Carol A. Breckenridge and Peter van der Veer, eds, *Orientalism and the Postcolonial Predicament* (1994).

Sumit Sarkar, *Writing Social History* (1998).

Christopher R. King, *One Language, Two Scripts: The Hindi Movement in Nineteenth Century North India* (1994).

Sudhir Chandra, *The Oppressive Present: Literature and Social Consciousness in Colonial India* (1992).

Eugene Irshick, *Politics and Social Conflict in South India: The Non-Brahman Movement and Tamil Separatism, 1916–29* (1969, 1978).

R. L. Hardgrave, *The Dravidian Movement* (1965) and *The Nadars of Tamilnad* (1969).

C. J. Baker, *The Politics of South India 1920–1937* (1976) and 'Leading up to Periyar' in B. N. Pandey, ed., *Leadership in South Asia* (1977).
D. A. Washbrook, 'The development of caste organization in south India, 1880–1925' in C. J. Baker and Washbrook, *South India* (1975) and 'Ethnicity and racism in colonial Indian society' in Robert Ross, ed., *Racism and Colonialism* (1982).
Marguerite Ross Barnett, *The Politics of Cultural Nationalism in South India* (1976).
Sumathi Ramaswamy, *Passions of the Tongue: Language Devotion in Tamil India 1891–1970* (1997).

Muslim Socio-political Movements

Susan Bayly, *Saints, Goddesses and Kings: Muslims and Christians in South Indian Society, 1700–1900* (1989).
Kenneth W. Jones, ed., *Religious Controversy in British India: Dialogues in South Asian Languages* (1992).
Avril Powell, *Muslims and Missionaries in Pre-Mutiny India* (1993).
Usha Sanyal, *Devotional Islam and Politics in British India: Ahmad Riza Khan Barelwi and his Movement, 1870–1920* (1996).
G. Kozlowski, *Muslim Endowments and Society in British India* (1985).
M. M. Ali, 'Hunter's *Indian Musulmans*: a re-examination of its background', *Journal of the Royal Asiatic Society*, 1 (1980).
B. Metcalf, *Islamic Revival in British India: Deoband, 1860–1900* (1982).
Francis Robinson, 'The ulama of the firangi mahal and their adab' in B. Metcalf, ed., *Moral Conduct and Authority in South Asia* (1984).
W. Cantwell Smith, *Modern Islam in India* (1946).
Aziz Ahmed, *Islamic Modernism in India and Pakistan, 1857–1964* (1967).
D. Lelyveld, *Aligarh's First Generation* (1978).
C. Troll, *Sir Saiyyid Ahmed Khan* (1978).
M. S. Jain, *The Aligarh Movement* (1965).
G. Minault, *The Khilafat Movement: Religious Symbolism and Political Mobilization in India* (1982).
Rafiuddin Ahmed, *Bengal Muslims, 1871–1906* (1981).
Mohammad Shah, *In Search of an Identity: Bengal Muslims 1880–1940* (1996).
Tazeen Murshid, *The Sacred and the Secular: Bengal Muslim Discourses 1871–1977* (1995).

Communal Conflict and Partition

Peter van der Veer, *Religious Nationalism: Hindus and Muslims in India* (1994).
M. Hasan, ed., *Communal and Pan-Islamic Trends in Colonial India* (2nd ed. 1985).*
Sandria Freitag, *Collective Action and Community: Public Arenas and the Emergence of Communalism in North India* (1989).

Gyanendra Pandey, *The Construction of Communalism in Colonial North India* (1990) and 'The prose of otherness', in D. Arnold and D. Hardiman, eds, *Subaltern Studies* vol. VIII (1994).

David Page, *Prelude to Partition: The Indian Muslims and the Imperial System of Control, 1920–32* (1982; 1999).

Anita Singh, *The Origins of the Partition of India, 1936–47* (1987).

Joya Chatterji, *Bengal Divided: Hindu Communalism and Partition 1932–47* (1994).

Ian Talbot, *Freedom's Cry: The Popular Dimension in the Pakistan Movement*... (1996); 'Muslim political mobilisation in rural Punjab' in Peter Robb, ed., *Rural India* (1983; 1992).

J. A. Gallagher, 'The Congress in Bengal... 1930–9', *Modern Asian Studies* 7, 7 (1973).

Deepak Pandey, 'Congress–Muslim League relations, 1937–9', *Modern Asian Studies*, 13, 3 (1978).

Francis Robinson, 'The Congress and the Muslims' in P. R. Brass and Robinson, eds, *Indian National Congress and Indian Society, 1885–1985* (1987).

Mushirul Hasan, *Nationalism and Communal Politics in India* (1991).

D. Gilmartin, *Empire and Islam: Punjab and the Making of Pakistan* (1988).

Farzana Shaikh, *Community and Consensus in Islam: Muslim Representation in Colonial India, 1860–1947* (1989).

James Chiriyankandath, '"Democracy" under the Raj: elections and separate representation...', *Journal of Commonwealth and Comparative Politics*, 30, 1 (1992).

Colonial Economy

Asiya Siddiqi, ed., *Trade and Finance in Colonial India, 1750–1860* (1995).

Neil Charlesworth, *British Rule and the Indian Economy, 1800–1914* (1982).

W. J. Macpherson, 'Economic development in India:... 1858–1947', in A. J. Youngson, ed., *Economic Development in the Long Run* (1976).

C. Simmons, '"De-industrialization", industrialization and the Indian economy 1850–1947', *Modern Asian Studies*, 19, 3 (1985), reprinted in R. Jeffrey *et al.* eds, *India: Rebellion to Republic* (1990).

Clive Dewey, ed., *Arrested Development in India* (1988) and, with A. G. Hopkins, *The Imperial Impact* (1978).

K. N. Chaudhuri and C. J. Dewey, eds, *Economy and Society* (1979).

J. Krishnamurti, 'Deindustrialisation in Gangetic Bihar during the nineteenth century: another look at the evidence', *Indian Economic and Social History Review*, 22 (1986).

A. K. Bagchi, 'Deindustrialisation in Gangetic Bihar, 1809–1901' in Barun De, ed., *Essays in Honour of Prof. S. C. Sarkar* (1976); 'De-industrialisation in India and some of its theoretical implications', *Journal of Development Studies*, 12, 2 (1976); *The Evolution of the State Bank of India:... 1806–76*, pts.1 and 2 (1987); and *The Presidency Banks and the Indian Economy, 1876–1914* (1981).

G. Pandey, 'Economic dislocation in nineteenth-century Uttar Pradesh', in Peter Robb, ed., *Rural South Asia* (1983).

Marika Vicziany, 'The deindustrialisation of India in the nineteenth century', *Indian Economic and Social History Review*, 16 (1979).

Burton Stein and Sanjay Subrahmanyam, eds, *Institutions and Economic Change in South Asia* (1996).

Famine, Health and Ecology

Michael Mann (tr. Benedict Bacon), *British Rule on Indian Soil: North India in the First Half of the Nineteenth Century* (1999).

Christopher Hill, *River of Sorrow: Environment and Social Control in Riparian North India 1770–1994* (1997).

Mark Harrison, *Climates and Constitutions: Health, Race, Environment and British Imperialism 1600–1850* (1999) and *Public Health in British India* (1994).

David Arnold, *Colonizing the Body: State Medicine and Epidemic Disease in Nineteenth-Century India* (1993) and 'Famine in peasant consciousness and peasant action: Madras 1876–8' in Ranajit Guha, ed., *Subaltern Studies*, vol. III. *Writings on South Asian Society and History* (1984).

Sanjay Sharma, *Famine, Philanthropy and the Colonial State: North India in the Early Nineteenth Century* (2000).

B. H. Bhatia, *Famines in India* (1967).

Ira Klein, 'Death in India', *Journal of Asian Studies*, 32 (1973).

Elizabeth Whitcombe, 'Famine mortality', *Economic and Political Weekly*, 26 (5 June 1993).

S. Ambirajan, 'Malthusian population theory and Indian famine policy in the nineteenth century', *Population Studies*, 30 (1976) and 'Political economy of Indian famines', *South Asia*, 1 (1976).

A. K. Sen, 'Famine mortality: a study of the Bengal famine of 1943', in E. J. Hobsbawm *et al.*, eds, *Peasants in History* (1980).

Lance Brennan, 'The development of the Indian famine codes', in Bruce Currey and Graeme Hugo, eds, *Famine as a Geographical Phenomenon* (1984).

M. B. McAlpin, *Subject to Famine: Food Crises and Economic Change in Western India, 1860–1920* (1983).

Mahesh Rangarajan, *Fencing the Forest: Conservation and Ecological Change in India's Central Provinces, 1860–1914* (1996).

Ajay Skaria, *Hybrid Histories: Forests, Frontiers and Oral Traditions in Western India* (1999).

V. Elwin, *Leaves from the Jungle: Life in a Gond Village* (1936).

Agrarian Conditions

David Ludden, ed., *Agricultural Production and Indian History* (1994).

Daniel Thorner, *The Agrarian Prospect in India* (2nd ed. 1973).

Clive Dewey, 'Images of the village community: a study in Anglo-Indian ideology', *Modern Asian Studies*, 6, 3 (1975).

R. E. Frykenberg, ed., *Land Tenure and Peasant in South Asia* (1977).

Elizabeth Whitcombe, *Agrarian Conditions in Northern India: The United Provinces under British Rule, 1860–1900* (1972).

Ian Stone, *Canal Irrigation in British India* (1984).

Malcolm Darling, *The Punjab Peasant in Prosperity and Debt* (modern edition with intro. by C. J. Dewey, 1977).

Himadri Banerjee, *Agrarian Society of the Punjab* (1982).

Imran Ali, *The Punjab under Imperialism* (1988).

M. Mufakharul Islam, *Irrigation, Agriculture and the Raj: Punjab, 1887–1947* (1997).

Neeladri Bhattacharya, 'Lenders and debtors: Punjab countryside, 1880–1940', *Studies in History* n.s. 1 (1985).

Arun Bandopadhyay, *The Agrarian Economy of Tamilnadu, 1820–55* (1992).

C. J. Baker, *An Indian Rural Economy: The Tamilnad Countryside* (1984).

Haruka Yanagisawa, *A Century of Change: Caste and Irrigated Lands in Tamilnadu 1860s-1970s* (1996).

M. S. S. Pandian, *The Political Economy of Agrarian Change: Nanchilnadu, 1880–1939* (1990).

R. Ray, 'The crisis of Bengal agriculture, 1870–1927: dynamics of immobility', *Indian Economic and Social History Review*, 10, 3 (1973).

Dharm Narain, *The Impact of Price Movements in Areas under Selected Crops in India, 1900–39* (1965).

Chitta Panda, *The Decline of the Bengal Zamindars: Midnapore . . .* (1997).

Nariaki Nakazato, *Agrarian System in Eastern India, c.1870–1910* (1994).

Sugata Bose, ed., *Credit, Markets, and the Agrarian Economy of Colonial India* (1994)* and *Peasant Labour and Colonial Capital: Rural Bengal Since 1770* (1993).

Jacques Pouchepadass, *Paysans de la plaine du Gange* (1989) or *Land, Power and Market: A Bihar District under Colonial Rule, 1860–1947* (2000).

Anand Yang, *The Limited Raj: Agrarian Relations, . . . Saran District, 1793–1920* (1989).

Gyan Prakash, *Bonded Histories* (1990) and, ed., *The World of the Rural Labourer in Colonial India* (1992).*

Shahid Amin, *Sugarcane and Sugar in Gorakhpur* (1984).

Premchand (Dhanpat Rai Srivastava), *Godan* (Gift of a cow; various translations).

Meghnad Desai, *et al.*, *Agrarian Power and Agricultural Productivity in India* (1984).*

K. N. Raj, ed., *Essays on the Commercialization of Indian Agriculture* (1985).

Trade, Industries and Urban Labour

S. B. Singh, *European Agency Houses in Bengal, 1783–1833* (1966).

A. Tripathi, *Trade and Finance in the Bengal Presidency* (1956).

B. B. Kling, *Partner in Empire: Dwarkanath Tagore . . .* (1976).

R. S. Rungta, *The Rise of Business Corporations in India, 1851–1900* (1970).

D. R. Gadgil, *The Industrial Evolution of India . . . , 1860–1939* (1924; 1971).

Rajat Ray, *Industrialization in India, 1914–47* (1979).

Rajnarayan Chandavarkar, *The Origins of Industrial Capitalism in India: ...Bombay, 1900–40* (1994).

D. Kooiman, *Bombay Textile Labour* (1989).

Dipesh Chakravarty, *Rethinking Working Class History: Bengal, 1890–1914* (1989).

Subho Basu, 'Strikes and "communal" riots in Calcutta in the 1890s', *Modern Asian Studies*, 32, 4 (1998).

Arjan de Haan, *Unsettled Settlers* (1994).

T. A. Timberg, *The Marwaris* (1978).

D. Tripathi, *Business Communities of India* (1984) and *Business Houses in Western India: ...1850–1956* (1990).

Ian J. Kerr, *Building the Railways of the Raj, 1850–1900* (1995).

Ian Derbyshire, 'Economic change and the railways in north India, 1860–1914', *Modern Asian Studies*, 21, 3 (1987).

M. B. McAlpin, 'Railroads, prices and peasant rationality: India, 1880–1900', *Journal of Economic History* (1974) and 'Railroads, cultivation patterns and foodgrains availability', *Indian Economic and Social History Review*, 12 (1975).

Government and Politics in Independent India

V. P. Menon, *The Story of the Integration of the Indian States* (1956).

W. H. Morris-Jones, *The Government and Politics of India* (1987).

Stanley A. Kochanek, *The Congress Party of India* (1968).

M. Brecher, *Succession in India* (1966).

Sunil Khilnani, *The Idea of India* (1997).

Atul Kohli, ed., *India's Democracy* (1988).

P. Brass, *Factional Politics in an Indian State: The Congress Party in Uttar Pradesh* (1975).

S. Kochanek, *The Congress Party of India* (1968).

Anthony Carter, *Elite Politics in Rural India* (1974).

H. L. Erdman, *The Swatantra Party and Indian Conservatism* (1967).

Mushirul Hasan, *Legacy of a Divided Nation: India's Muslims Since Independence* (1997).

M. J. Akbar, *The Seige Within: Challenges to a Nation's Unity* (1985).

S. Bose and A. Jalal, eds, *Nationalism, Democracy and Development: State and Politics in India* (1997).

Rajni Kothari, *State against Democracy* (1988).

Richard Hardgrave, *India: Government and Politics in a Developing Nation* (5th ed., 1993).

F. Frankel, *India's Political Economy, 1947–77* (1978).

Lloyd and Suzanne Hoeber Rudolph, *In Pursuit of Lakshmi* (1987).

T. Byres, ed., *The State and Development Planning in India* (1993).

Indian Economic and Social Development

Pramit Chaudhuri, *The Indian Economy: Poverty and Development* (1978).

R. Cassen, *India: Population, Economy, Society* (1978).

Partha Chatterjee, ed., *Wages of Freedom: Fifty Years of the Indian Nation-State* (1997).

Myron Weiner, *The Child and the State in India: Child Labor and Education Policy...* (1991).

W. van Schendel, *Three Deltas: Accumulation and Poverty in Rural Burma, Bengal and South India* (1991).

Jan Breman, *Of Peasants, Migrants and Paupers: Rural Labour Circulation ... in West India* (1985).

William and Charlotte Wiser, *Behind Mud Walls, 1930–60* (with a sequel, 1971).

Susan Wadley, *Struggling with Destiny in Karimpur, 1925–84* (1994).

Ramachandra Guha, *The Unquiet Woods: Ecological Change and Peasant Resistance...* (1989) and, with Madhav Gadgil, *Ecology and Equity* (1995).

Roger Jeffrey, *The Politics of Health in India* (1988).

Ashis Nandy *et al.*, *Creating a Nationality* (1995).

David Ludden, ed., *Contesting the Nation: Religion, Community and the Politics of Democracy in India* (1996); also called *Making India Hindu* (1996).

Mushirul Islam and Nariaki Nakazato, eds, *The Unfinished Agenda: Nation-Building in South Asia* (2001).

Index

Entries are listed in letter-by-letter order.

Indians and especially Muslims are listed by first names, except (somewhat arbitrarily) for Hindus and Parsis from the nineteenth century, or where last names are more usually employed in English – for example 'Jinnah'. Page-numbers in italics refer to maps (1 to 6 only) or boxes (1 to 6).